Pere Marquette

A Michigan Railroad System before 1900

Graydon M. Meints

Michigan State University Press | *East Lansing*

♾ The paper used in this publication meets the minimum requirements
of ANSI/NISO Z39.48-1992 (R 1997) (Permanence of Paper).

Michigan State University Press
East Lansing, Michigan 48823-5245

LIBRARY OF CONGRESS CATALOGING-IN-PUBLICATION DATA
Names: Meints, Graydon M., author. Title: Pere Marquette : a Michigan railroad system before 1900 / Graydon M. Meints. Description: East Lansing : Michigan State University Press, [2020] | Includes bibliographical references and index.
Identifiers: LCCN 2019037089 | ISBN 9781611863659 (cloth) | ISBN 9781609176402
Subjects: LCSH: Pere Marquette Railway. | Railroads—Michigan—History. Classification: LCC HE2791.P4695 M45 2020 | DDC 385.09774/09034--dc23
LC record available at https://lccn.loc.gov/2019037089

Book and cover design by Charlie Sharp, Sharp Des!gns, East Lansing, MI
Cover art: Pentwater, terminus of the Chicago & Michigan Lake Shore.
Author's collection.

Michigan State University Press is a member of the Green Press Initiative and is committed to developing and encouraging ecologically responsible publishing practices. For more information about the Green Press Initiative and the use of recycled paper in book publishing, please visit www.greenpressinitiative.org.

Visit Michigan State University Press at *www.msupress.org*

I dedicate this book to my wife
Gerlinde

From my first book to this one, for forty years,
she has supported and encouraged me in my railroad travels
and helped to make all of this possible.

Contents

Preface

As my eighty-fourth birthday was approaching, I thought I might have one more book in me about a Michigan railroad. The Pere Marquette Railroad was a subject I had never explored thoroughly and it has not one but two histories—one for the twentieth century and one for the nineteenth. The twentieth-century record of the PM has been studied and preserved, in text and in photographs, by scholars, historians, and enthusiasts, and it is to their credit that we have so much documentation. Their efforts have produced a number of books and publications, including those of the Pere Marquette Historical Society and the Chesapeake and Ohio Historical Society. Regrettably, the nineteenth century has not been so well served. For a variety of reasons that I came upon as I went into the project, there has been little study of this part of the corporate history and not a great deal of interest in it. It certainly was not for a lack of controversial actions or of interesting personalities who formed and led those roads—there were many of them. This work will focus on the nineteenth-century part of the company's past, the men who formed and directed these early roads, and the development of the system.

The railroad's name came from Father Jacques Marquette, a Jesuit priest, missionary, and explorer. He founded the first permanent settlement in Michigan in about 1668. He was the first explorer of the Mississippi River, but died unexpectedly and was buried in 1675 near the mouth of the Michigan river bearing his name, not far from Ludington, Michigan.

The Pere Marquette Railroad was born 1 January 1900 by a merger of three roads and disappeared on 6 June 1947 by merger into the maw of the Chesapeake & Ohio Railroad—a life span of forty-seven years, five months, and five days. In the twentieth century the PM became a Midwest carrier serving as a bridge line between Chicago and the Niagara River. It was known for its extensive Lake Michigan car ferry service, the Berkshire-type (2–8-4 wheel arrangement) steam locomotives that moved fast freight trains, and the post–World War II streamlined *Pere Marquettes* that ran between Detroit and Grand Rapids. Most of its operations were within one state, and it became known as "Michigan's railroad."

Before the 1900 merger the PM's predecessors made up a motley collection of disconnected and unaffiliated short, local rail lines. Nearly ninety companies were in this mix, and through construction, purchases, foreclosures, and mergers, covering more than a thirty-year period, most of them coalesced into three roads: Flint & Pere Marquette, Chicago & West Michigan, and Detroit, Lansing & Northern (which was renamed Detroit, Grand Rapids & Western not long before 1900). Each of these three main constituents, and many of their predecessors, were built to make profits moving lumber and other forest products from the woods. But by the mid-1880s this traffic was beginning to fall off, and by the 1890s lumber and forest products were no longer the most important revenue source. The changing mix of freight traffic and the increasing passenger traffic affected profits, and the responses varied between building to new markets, expense retrenchments, and some foreclosure sales. There always was a need for money to operate, to pay interest on debt, and to build more lines, but particularly those with declining profits found it difficult to pay interest on the funds borrowed to build the road. Companies responded differently to this problem, some hoping it might be possible to borrow more money to increase operations, some by curtailing operating expenses, or at the last resort the bondholders forced some into receivership. By the mid-1870s New England money interests began to secure financial control of these Michigan roads, and over time merged them into the three major companies. Once involved with a company, New England control never disappeared. A few companies were wild speculations and some others probably imprudent ventures. But once the New Englanders gained control, their influence was generally beneficial, if for no other reason than theirs was a more conservative and fiscally responsible approach.

Three chapters of this work treat the three major constituent companies that made up the 1900 Pere Marquette. Each describes the lines that its predecessors built and those it acquired to assemble the system. A fourth chapter treats the lines that were controlled by subsidiaries built before 1900 that were merged after 1900, and a number of lines bought by the PM after 1900 that were built before 1900. This work attempts to illuminate what was dark, to put into a sequence a multiplicity of random acts, and to present the reader with the careers of railroad men whom history has seen fit to overlook.

The corporate history of the pre-1900 years of the PM's predecessors has received only indifferent coverage. Part of this can be attributed to a paucity of company records, but there also appears to be some disinterest by historians about the development of such small and local railroads. The lack of corporate records presents problems for any historian. The Interstate Commerce Commission commented on this in 1917 in its study of the financial problems of the Pere Marquette, and again in 1928 in its valuation docket. In Michigan, for the years treated in this study, the commissioner of railroads' annual reports provide considerable financial data, but these lack the informative explanations and discussions of future plans that might have been disclosed in the company's annual reports. After the late 1880s, when the three major lines had developed, their annual reports are available and these supplement the commissioner of railroads reports. In some cases other sources may shed light on corporate acts, but in other cases the historian is forced to put forward his own reasonable insight.

The 1927 valuation study of the Pere Marquette has a wealth of material about the road both before and after the 1900 merger.[1] Its one hundred pages are heavily weighted toward the financial dealings of the company and their impact on the value of the company as a determinate for setting rates and profitability. As to the construction and abandonment record, the study is vague in the extreme; it has only years instead of full dates, and only full miles rather than precise measurement.

The Michigan Railroad Commission's study, *Aids, Gifts, Grants, and Donations to Railroads, including Outlines of Development and Successions in Titles to Railroads in Michigan*, has better detail of construction dates and mileage built or abandoned.[2] It appears that the study takes the mileage of the Pere Marquette as it existed in 1919 and does not always treat earlier abandonments. Much of its data appears to be compiled from the *Annual Reports* of the commissioner of railroads, and the commissioner had to rely heavily on information furnished by the railroad company.

The Interstate Commerce Commission's study is a 263-page investigation that concentrates on the financial dealings of the two companies, particularly after the Prince syndicate came to control the roads in 1902.[3] The document adds little to the subject of this work that is not readily available in other documents.

Paul Wesley Ivey's study *The Pere Marquette Railroad Company* was prepared as a doctoral thesis at the University of Michigan.[4] In 259 pages Ivey reviews the testimony taken in hearings that resulted in Document 137, mentioned earlier. Ivey's study is valuable for its coverage of a wide range of material, including incorporations, mergers, construction, financing, and profitability. His study is readily available in reprint form.

In 1916, three company-appointed committees studied the affairs of the railroad to recommend ways to preserve it and provide for the soundness of its capital and debt structure. The reorganization of 1917 put their recommendations in place. The document, however, is related entirely to capital and debt and does not address construction, abandonment, reorganizations, or mergers.

The *C&O Historical Newsletter* of November 1975 has an extensive record of construction and abandonment of the company's lines compiled by Thomas L. Underwood Jr. It updates the data found in *Aids, Gifts, Grants.*

Incorporation dates present a problem for any historical study. Most Michigan county and state histories use the date on which the papers were filed with Michigan's secretary of state as the incorporation date. That date is the most widely accessible public record. The Michigan Railroad Commission's study, *Aids, Gifts, Grants*, uses these filing dates as the incorporation dates. For my study, *Michigan Railroads and Railroad Companies*, I read the articles of incorporation, kept in boxed files of Michigan's Department of Commerce, Corporations and Securities Division (since renamed), for the corporate legal name, the date signed, the corporate purpose or franchise, and the names of organizers signing the document. The corporate names, at the first use in my text, were from this source. Corporate names, in the nineteenth century, were surprisingly inconsistent. Some corporate articles preceded the company name with a capitalized "The" but many did not. Some used "Railroad," some used "Rail Road, and a few used "Railway." Most included the word "company" at the end, but a few did not. The "and" and ampersand use is inconsistent. In this text when a corporate name is first used, it is the full legal name as given in the articles of incorporation. This first use is accompanied by the company's initials using an ampersand enclosed in parentheses. Any subsequent use of the name most often is by initials or a shorter form of the name.

In several of the endnotes that document the incorporations, I have added the names of the original founding directors of the company—information I believe is of interest. To me, knowing the men who deliberated, decided, and acted is as important as the record of the details of their companies' actions. In appendix 1 of this work I attempt to flesh out the life and career of some of the more important figures in the Pere Marquette's predecessors. In addition to the sources previously mentioned, I have reviewed many of the Michigan county histories of the period and national biographical dictionaries. For basic information I consulted a number of online genealogy sites: Findagrave, Rootsweb, Ancestry, Family Search, and The Political Graveyard. I wish that I had been able to give fuller justice to these men.

Equally frustrating, to illustrate this work, has been the attempt to find portraits of these men. A few of them have literally disappeared, while some others were found only with considerable difficulty. So too images of early railroad structures, particularly depots, are exceedingly scarce. These may be hidden in local libraries and museums, but a reasonable search found very few to use in this work.

It may appear that, in assembling the material for this study, I have rambled rather far afield. As the bibliography will attest, information is where you find it. My only regret is that I have not been able to study more corporate annual reports or newspaper reports. Outside of the two railroad historical societies mentioned earlier, these may still exist in local libraries and archives or as articles in local newspapers. But this is a part of the effort that I bestow to future students of the Pere Marquette.

CHAPTER 1

The Flint & Pere Marquette

> In a few years these impenetrable forests will have fallen; the sons of civilization and industry will break the silence of the Saginaw; its echoes will cease; the banks will be imprisoned by quays; its current, which now flows on unnoticed and tranquil through a nameless waste, will be stemmed by the prows of vessels. More than a hundred miles sever the solitude from the great European settlements, and we are perhaps, the last travelers allowed to see its primitive grandeur.

So wrote Alexis de Tocqueville in response to his July 1831 visit to Saginaw, Michigan. Within the decade Tocqueville's view of the future came true. Sawmills were devouring the forests of northern Michigan that were being felled with abandon. Thirty years later the railroads discussed herein were snaking through the trees to complete his somber view of the future.[1]

Saginaw to Flint

The oldest and largest component of the Pere Marquette system was the Flint & Pere Marquette Railway Company (F&PM), which was incorporated on 21 January 1857 to own a 170-mile rail line from Flint to the town of Pere Marquette at the mouth of the Pere Marquette River in Mason County. The river, the town, and the railroad all came to be named for the missionary and explorer Jacques Marquette. Father Marquette died unexpectedly in 1675 near the mouth of the river bearing his name. Cities, counties, rivers, schools, and universities honor his name today.

The town later was renamed in honor of Wisconsin lumberman James Ludington. In 1859

Ludington foreclosed on a loan made to sawmill owner and became involved with the village of Pere Marquette. In 1867 he platted his land into a community and in 1873 had it chartered, using his own name, as Ludington. He continued to support the town until his death in 1891.[2]

Two conditions helped the fledgling rail line. Earlier, in 1850, U.S. senator Stephen A. Douglas finally persuaded Congress to make a grant of federal land to support a pet project of his, the Illinois Central Railroad, north and south across the state to Chicago. When completed the IC was such a success it encouraged a host of other states to lobby for similar land grants. In the Thirty-Fourth Congress Senators Lewis Cass and Charles E. Stuart lobbied for Michigan, with the support of its four members in the House of Representatives and Alabama senator Clement C. Clay. In July 1856 President Franklin Pierce signed a grant act giving Michigan 3,775,000 acres to help in building several Upper Peninsula railroads and four in the Lower Peninsula. One of these four was a railroad that extended across the state from "Pere Marquette to Flint, and thence to Port Huron." This was a part of the route of the Lake Superior Railroad that it hoped to build as far as several mining districts in the Upper Peninsula. Just what influenced this particular grant is not clear; it may be due in part to memorials written by Pontiac lawyer Morgan L. Drake to the state legislature in 1855 and 1857, or to an 1862 letter written by Drake to Lewis Cass. Drake, as secretary of the Lake Superior Railroad, stated that the purpose of his company was to connect Pontiac with Upper Peninsula iron mines on a line through Wisconsin. He urged Cass to solicit Congress for a land grant "from Pontiac . . . by way of Flint, to Marquette Bay in the County of Mason." Charles T. Harvey, who claimed considerable importance in building the canal on the St. Marys River at Sault Ste. Marie, also maneuvered for support the land grant legislation, as he describes it in "Great Railway Connections between Lake Superior and the Gulf of Mexico."[3] The extent of Harvey's influence has been questioned by several historians.[4]

The federal land grant law designated the routes to be subsidized, then gave the states all of the administration of their programs and allowed them to decide which companies would receive a grant. When Michigan's legislature met in January 1857 it had its hands full. Several of the routes had more than one company eager to get the grant. The line between Flint and Pere Marquette had two bidders: the Lake Superior Railroad and the Flint & Pere Marquette. There is no record of the political maneuvering that went on in Lansing, but apparently the F&PM men from Flint won the grant, apparently with more political muscle than the Lake Superior men from Pontiac. Michigan's grant legislation required that the railroad build 20 miles of railroad each year until the entire route was complete. When built the railroad was entitled to each odd-numbered mile-square section of land for 6 miles on either side of line. If some of the land had been sold to occupants, the distance could be extended. When each required twenty miles of rail line was certified complete by the governor, the railroad would receive title to one-half of the grant lands, with the other half held by the state until the entre line was finished.

William B. Sears, who later became the F&PM chief engineer, led the survey party. The F&PM filed its location map with the state and the federal General Land Office in August 1857. The onset of the financial panic of 1857 made money to start construction hard to find. The company had to go back to the legislature several times for extensions of time to build

LEFT: George M. Dewey. He was the first president of the Flint & Pere Marquette.
FROM FRANKLIN ELLIS, *HISTORY OF GENESEE COUNTY, MICHIGAN* (PHILADELPHIA: EVERTS & ABBOTT, 1879).

RIGHT: Henry C. Potter. In 1859 he came to Saginaw as a contractor on the Flint & Pere Marquette. He remained with the railroad for most of his career.
FROM CHARLES E. POTTER, *GENEALOGIES OF THE POTTER FAMILIES* (BOSTON: A. MUDGE & SON, 1888).

the required sections. When it finally settled up with the state, the F&PM received 511,502.2 acres. With 640 acres equaling 1 square mile, the road received 799 square miles of land, or the equivalent of about one and one-half counties.[5]

Saginaw was not named specifically on the land grant route, but the Flint-based F&PM founders found it convenient to start building there to reach Lake Michigan. In the 1850s there were two towns named Saginaw: Saginaw City and East Saginaw. Saginaw City was the older, founded in 1836 by Norman Little on the west side of the Saginaw River. The 1837 financial panic had forced Little to sell out. He returned to his townsite in 1848, but was unable to buy it back. With financing from James Hoyt and his son Jesse Hoyt, both of New York City, Little bought twenty-four thousand acres of land along the east bank of the river and began to lay out a new town he called East Saginaw. Since the Flint plank road ended in East Saginaw, and steamships landed there, Little's new town grew faster and larger than Saginaw City. By 1860 East Saginaw was a thriving sawmill city with about three thousand residents; Saginaw City had fewer than two thousand.[6]

The dense forest found around Flint and throughout Genesee County was a valuable natural resource that would become still more profitable if it could be shipped to other markets. Saginaw, located on the Saginaw River, was then developing into a sawmill city and was an excellent port city. The river emptied into Saginaw Bay and Lake Huron, which gave access to the Great Lakes and, with the Erie Canal, to markets as far away as New York State. The Flint River was used to raft logs from the western part of the county as early as the 1830s to sawmills that developed in the interior of the county to serve mostly local buyers. But a means to ship sawed lumber to Saginaw would benefit the entire county, and a railroad to connect Flint to Saginaw would be very desirable.[7]

George M. Dewey was named the first president of the Flint & Pere Marquette in 1857. He was a major landowner and dealer in lands in the Flint area, and provided substantial financial support for the new railroad. The first rail route considered was to skirt south of East Saginaw and Brady Hill, then cross the Saginaw River into Saginaw City in the vicinity of Mackinaw Street. Aghast at being bypassed, businessmen in East Saginaw persuaded Dewey to build instead through their town. He put its depot on the site of the present Potter Street station. When the extension toward Ludington was built, the route lay well north of the Saginaw City business district, but what persuaded Dewey to make this change in route cannot be determined. The financial panic of 1857 slowed building, but some grading of the line did begin at East Saginaw by Francis W. Paul, a railroad contractor from Canandaigua, New York. During 1859 new money came into the undertaking, apparently from Samuel Farwell, who replaced Paul as the principal contractor. Farwell brought his son-in-law Henry C. Potter, then in his mid-thirties, with him from Utica, New York. Farwell, after working on the Erie Canal and several other waterworks projects, had turned to railroads, building parts of the Erie Railroad, the Great Western of Canada, and the Utica & Black River. It appears that by 1859 Farwell and Potter replaced Paul in building the F&PM.[8]

The first 8 miles of rail was laid at East Saginaw on 19 August 1859, but work stopped on 1 November for a lack of money. In September the company bought a secondhand locomotive named *Pollywog*. One observer remarked, "That is no Pollywog, but a damned old frog." Sanford Keeler, then a young mechanic fresh from his apprenticeship, repaired the engine, renamed it *Pioneer*, ran it on its first trips, and stayed with the railroad the rest of his working career. By late summer 1860 the company was able to finish the first 20 miles from East Saginaw to north of Clio. Governor Moses Wisner certified it complete, and the company was entitled to the first part of its land grant on 5 September 1860. During 1861 the road was extended to Mount Morris, 26.1 miles from East Saginaw. The line was opened formally on 20 January 1862, when a locomotive hauled the road's baggage car and one coach, all of the passenger equipment it owned. Heavy snows slowed the train trip to Mount Morris to four hours long, but the riders all agreed the trip was a success. Despite the violence of the Civil War the F&PM was completed into Flint in December 1862 and formally opened for business on Monday, 8 December. Flint's sawmills now could ship finished lumber to Saginaw and then move it over the Great Lakes to Chicago and eastern markets. Lumbermen benefited because logs moving by rail was far better than driving them down the difficult Flint River to Saginaw sawmills. The line brought service to the sawmill of Flint's most important lumberman, Henry H. Crapo, who shipped some lumber over the F&PM.[9]

Henry Howland Crapo moved from New Bedford, Massachusetts, and began sawing in Flint in 1857. He preferred using the Detroit market and port to move his lumber. The Detroit & Milwaukee rail line had been built from Detroit to Fentonville (now Fenton) in 1856, and a plank road had been built between Flint and Fentonville. Crapo believed that a Port Huron–Flint rail line would be good for his business, but despite his hope, it was not built during his lifetime. He built lumberyards at Fentonville and Holly to ship over the D&M line, and began

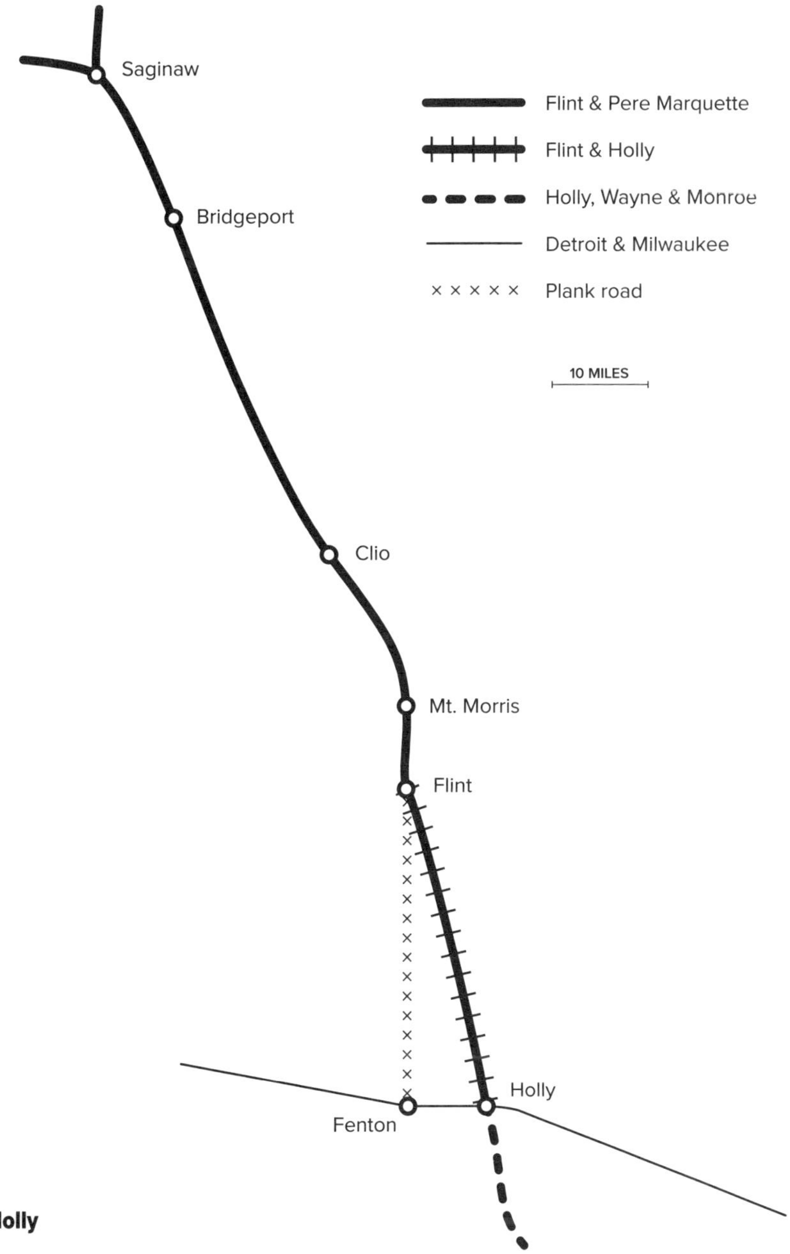

Saginaw–Holly

hauling his lumber over the plank road to Fentonville. Using the plank road was a temporary expedient, and rail service from Flint would have served Crapo far better.[10]

Despite the constraints of the Civil War, Crapo decided he needed a rail outlet from Flint that was under his control. He believed that if Dewey's F&PM built the line, it might not treat him fairly. In 1861 Crapo wrote his son William that if the F&PM would "let my lumber go over

Henry H. Crapo. He was a major lumberman from Flint and governor of Michigan from 1865 to 1869. He built the Flint & Holly road to serve his lumbering interests.
FROM UNIVERSITY OF MICHIGAN BENTLEY HISTORICAL LIBRARY.

your road in summer to be shipped in Saginaw for Chicago, or to any of the Lake ports, for Cincinnati or the 'East,' at fair rates, and we will take your salt and lumber in the winter over our road to Fentonville, and then to Detroit, etc. at fair rates." Crapo wanted to hold the strongest hand by being able to use the F&PM when he wanted and his own rails when it suited him better. Crapo formed the Flint and Fentonville Railroad Company (F&F) on 3 January 1863. The road was to build a 16-mile line between its namesake points. Crapo insisted that the $200,000 authorized capitalization be raised entirely by the sale of stock that would keep the road free from debt. Thanks to son William's efforts back in New England, the stock was oversubscribed, with a large share of the money coming from New Bedford investors.[11]

Fentonville was Crapo's preference as the line's southern rail terminus, but apparently some businessmen from Holly gained the ear of his directors to urge a change. Crapo finally agreed to build his rail line to Holly, and on 8 August 1863 renamed his road as The Flint and Holly Rail Road Company (F&H). The revised articles of incorporation called for a 17-mile railroad capitalized at $300,000. In September construction was underway, and the road began operations on 1 November 1864. In September 1865 Crapo hired George C. Kimball as his road's superintendent and delegated some work to him.[12]

Crapo's lumbering operations and building a railroad filled his day, but he let his name be put forward as a candidate for the Michigan State Senate in 1862. As a Republican he won handily. The next year Crapo was talked about for appointment as a U.S. senator, but before his term in the state senate was over he was put forward as a candidate for governor of Michigan. Crapo won the November election, took office on 4 January 1865, and was reelected two years

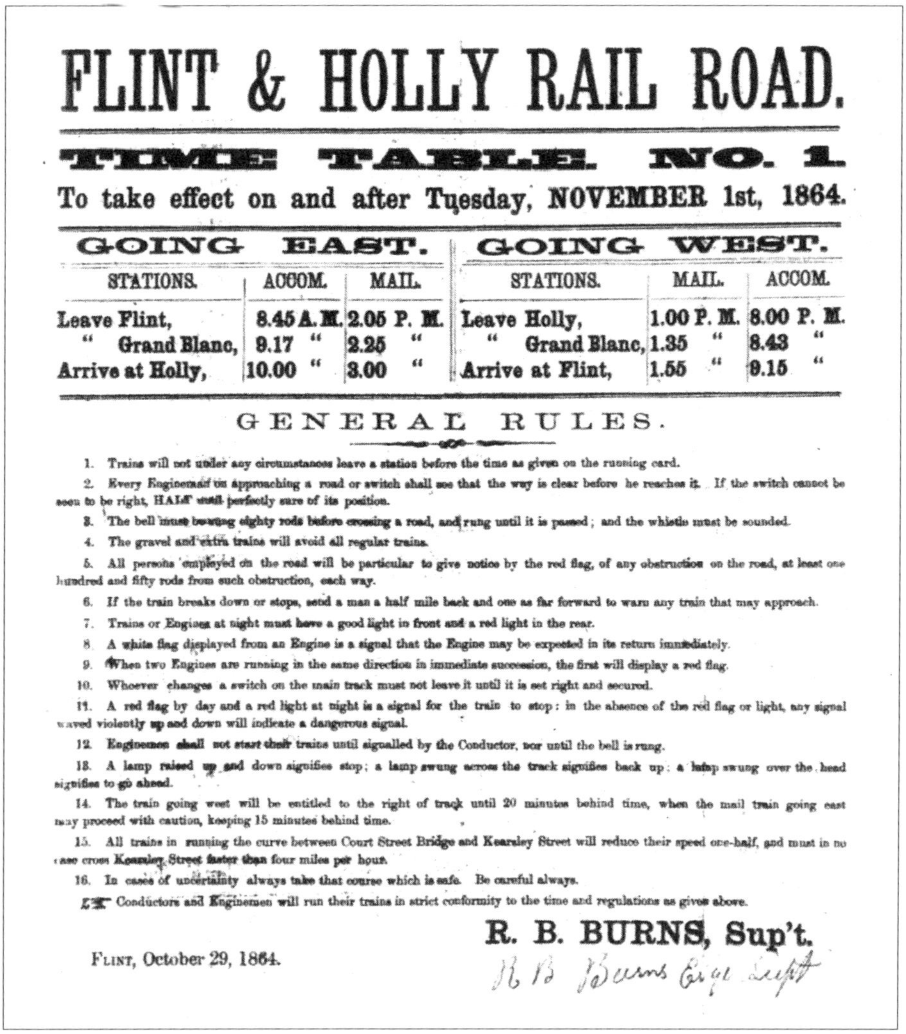

FLINT & HOLLY RAIL ROAD.

TIME TABLE. NO. 1.

To take effect on and after Tuesday, NOVEMBER 1st, 1864.

GOING EAST.

STATIONS.	ACCOM.	MAIL.
Leave Flint,	8.45 A. M.	2.05 P. M.
" Grand Blanc,	9.17 "	2.25 "
Arrive at Holly,	10.00 "	3.00 "

GOING WEST.

STATIONS.	MAIL.	ACCOM.
Leave Holly,	1.00 P. M.	8.00 P. M.
" Grand Blanc,	1.35 "	8.43 "
Arrive at Flint,	1.55 "	9.15 "

GENERAL RULES.

1. Trains will not under any circumstances leave a station before the time as given on the running card.
2. Every Engineman on approaching a road or switch shall see that the way is clear before he reaches it. If the switch cannot be seen to be right, HALT until perfectly sure of its position.
3. The bell must be rung eighty rods before crossing a road, and rung until it is passed; and the whistle must be sounded.
4. The gravel and extra trains will avoid all regular trains.
5. All persons employed on the road will be particular to give notice by the red flag, of any obstruction on the road, at least one hundred and fifty rods from such obstruction, each way.
6. If the train breaks down or stops, send a man a half mile back and one as far forward to warn any train that may approach.
7. Trains or Engines at night must have a good light in front and a red light in the rear.
8. A white flag displayed from an Engine is a signal that the Engine may be expected in its return immediately.
9. When two Engines are running in the same direction in immediate succession, the first will display a red flag.
10. Whoever changes a switch on the main track must not leave it until it is set right and secured.
11. A red flag by day and a red light at night is a signal for the train to stop: in the absence of the red flag or light, any signal waved violently up and down will indicate a dangerous signal.
12. Enginemen shall not start their trains until signalled by the Conductor, nor until the bell is rung.
13. A lamp raised up and down signifies stop; a lamp swung across the track signifies back up; a lamp swung over the head signifies to go ahead.
14. The train going west will be entitled to the right of track until 20 minutes behind time, when the mail train going east may proceed with caution, keeping 15 minutes behind time.
15. All trains in running the curve between Court Street Bridge and Kearsley Street will reduce their speed one-half, and must in no case cross Kearsley Street faster than four miles per hour.
16. In cases of uncertainty always take that course which is safe. Be careful always.

☞ Conductors and Enginemen will run their trains in strict conformity to the time and regulations as given above.

FLINT, October 29, 1864.

R. B. BURNS, Sup't.

R B Burns Engr Supt

Flint and Holly 1864 schedule.

FROM ARCHIVES OF MICHIGAN.

later.[13] In January 1867, with his health not the best, Crapo had a second attack of a bladder ailment. He finished his second term as governor and returned to Flint to resume his hectic pace in lumbering. But as his medical problems worsened, Crapo was forced to reconsider his ability to continue at his accustomed pace. A further complication arose with the announcement that the long-proposed Port Huron–Flint railroad would soon be built. If this line was built and connected to the Flint & Pere Marquette, Crapo's Flint & Holly road might be adversely affected. Late in 1867 Crapo accepted an offer from the Flint & Pere Marquette to buy the Flint & Holly for $500,000, payable in a new F&PM 10 percent bond issue. The final price appears to have been $550,000 in the bonds. The sequence of events is not completely clear, but the annual report for 1868 reports that on 24 April 1868 the F&PM executed a lease of the F&H

LEFT: George C. Kimball. Henry H. Crapo brought him to Michigan in 1865, and he was readily promoted here and with several non-Michigan railroads.

FROM WILLIAM RICHARD CUTTER, *GENEALOGICAL AND PERSONAL MEMOIRS RELATING TO THE FAMILIES OF THE STATE OF MASSACHUSETTS* (NEW YORK: LEWIS HISTORICAL PUBLISHING CO., 1910).

RIGHT: Eber Brock Ward. He was the second president of the Flint & Pere Marquette. At his death in 1875, he was the richest man in Michigan and one of the richest in the Midwest.

FROM *HISTORY OF MANISTEE, MASON, AND OCEANA COUNTIES, MICHIGAN* (CHICAGO: H. R. PAGE, 1882).

to be effective 1 May, and issued bonds to pay for the property. The F&PM absorbed Crapo's company in early September 1868.[14]

At the July 1860 annual F&PM meeting Eber Brock Ward replaced George M. Dewey as president. Ward was a Detroit industrial magnate and very likely Michigan's wealthiest citizen. The record is silent, but it is likely that Ward's arrival may have improved the F&PM's financial situation, and that in turn allowed Farwell to restart construction. When a young man Ward bought an interest in one of his uncle's Great Lakes sailing ships. By the late 1840s he had his own fleet of ships on the Great Lakes. In 1853 he founded the Eureka Iron and Steel Company in Wyandotte, the first U.S. company to use the Bessemer process to manufacture steel. The F&PM's rails came from Ward's works at Wyandotte. He also started a steel mill in Chicago that was the first manufacturer of railroad rails. With that money Ward put his hand to anything that could make a profit. He invested in newspapers, iron mines, and a shipyard and beginning in 1852 he bought large tracts of timberlands along the Pere Marquette River. In 1871 he built a large sawmill in Ludington and a few years later a second mill. At his death in 1875 he was the richest man in Michigan and one of the richest in the Midwest.[15]

Saginaw to Ludington

At the end of 1867 the F&PM main line extended 53.3 miles from Flint, through East Saginaw, to Midland. On 26 October 1868 it completed another 5.9 miles from Midland west to Averill. Reaching Averill was important to the F&PM for two reasons. First, it marked the completion of 60 miles of line, and this allowed the F&PM to receive more of its land grant—another

76,300 acres of land. Also, the tracks lay next to the Tittabawassee River, and in future years substantial tons of logs were hauled to Averill and put into the river to be floated to Saginaw and Bay City sawmills.[16]

As the F&PM prepared to build west from Saginaw, Chief Engineer Sears returned to the field to review the survey used for the line for the 1856 land grant. The original survey had placed the line farther north, through Gladwin and Clare Counties. Sears reported to the board that the line had good location as far as the Tobacco River at Clare. Sears then ran a number of surveys south of the original land grant survey, between Clare and the Muskegon River crossing at Evart, and was able to locate a route with better grades and fewer curves.[17]

By 29 December 1870 the F&PM built another 36.6 miles to reach Lake in western Clare County. In September 1871 the line finished 13.4 miles into Evart and by November another 13.3 miles into Reed City. At Reed City it crossed the line of the Grand Rapids & Indiana, a road that had been built only months earlier. The Panic of 1873 somewhat slowed the pace of building into Ludington; it was not until 1 December 1874 that the final 48.4 miles was put in service between Reed City and the docks at Ludington. President Ward had pushed for the completion of the line to Lake Michigan since he owned a considerable amount of timberland

166. **FLINT AND PERE MARQUETTE RAILWAY.**

GEORGE C. KIMBALL, Gen. Superintendent.

Trains Leave. May 11, 1868. Trains Arrive.

Mail	Mxd.	Mxd.	Exps	Mail	Acc.	Mls.	STATIONS.	Mls.	Mxd.	Exps	Acc.	Mail	Exps	Mail
P. M.	A. M.	P. M	P. M.	A. M.	A. M				A. M.	P. M	P. M.	P. M.	P. M.	A. M.
		3 00			5 50		..... **Midland**		10 45		6 05			
		3 15			6 00		.......Bluffs..		10 30		5 50			
		3 40			6 25		......Freelands......		10 10		5 30			
		4 15			7 00		J. L. & S. R.R. Crossing		9 35		4 55			
6 00	10 45		1 20	6 30			....**Bay City** [1]....		10 25			9 05	12 40	8 05
6 05	10 50		1 25	6 35			..... Portsmouth.....		10 1[illegible]			9 00	12 35	8 00
6 35	11 30		1 50	7 00			.... East Saginaw		9 40			8 30	12 10	7 30
		4 20			7 05		arr } **East** { lve		9 30		4 50			
		4 30	2 05	7 15			lve } **Saginaw** [2] { arr		9 15	12 20		8 20		
		4 50	2 2[illegible]	7 30			.... Bridgeport. . ..		8 55	12 05		8 05		
		5 20	2 38	7 50			......Birch Run......		8 25	11 47		7 42		
		5 30	2 43	— —			....County Line.....		8 15	11 42		7 35		
		5 40	2 53	8 05			.. Pine Run and Clio..		8 05	11 35		7 28		
		6 00	3 05	8 18			...Mount Morris....		7 40	11 23		7 15		
		6 25	3 23	8 35			} ...**Flint**... { lve		7 15	11 05		6 55		
		6 55	3 30	8 40			.. } { arr		7 10	11 00		6 50		
		7 30	3 45	9 00			..Grand Blanc [2] ...		6 50	10 45		6 35		
		8 05	4 05	9 25			arr } **Holly** [3] { lve		6 20	10 25		6 15		
		8 15	4 10	9 30			lve } { arr		6 05	10 20		6 05		
		9 45	5 05	10 30			.......Pontiac.......		4 15	9 30		5 10		
		11 45	6 15	11 45			......**Detroit** [4]....		2 05	8 20		4 00		
P. M.	A. M.	P. M	P. M.	A. M.	A. M.		ARRIVE] [LEAVE		A. M.	A. M.	P. M.	P. M.	P. M.	A. M.

1 Connects with steamers for various ports on Lake Huron.
2 Connects with Bay City Branch.
3 Connects with Detroit and Milwaukee Railway.
4 Connects with Michigan Southern and Northern Indiana Railway.
4 Connects with Grand Trunk Railway.
4 Connects with Michigan Central Railway.

The Clock in East Saginaw office is Standard Time for all Trains on this Road.

Flint & Pere Marquette 1868 schedule. An 1868 timetable showing service between Holly and Midland, before the line had been completed to Ludington.

FROM AUTHOR'S COLLECTION.

James G. Birney. He moved to Bay City in 1856 and, like his father, played a critical role in the development of the city. He was an important force in building the Bay City & East Saginaw Railroad, the first railroad into Bay City.
FROM AUTHOR'S COLLECTION.

near Ludington and in Mason and Lake Counties to the east. In 1870 he had built a sawmill to produce lumber and in 1871 built a second larger mill. He thought the port would be an ideal site for a steelmaking mill; hardwoods were available to make charcoal for smelting, iron ore could be easily shipped in from the Upper Peninsula, and the projected rail line and Great Lakes ships could move the finished product. Ward already owned two steel mills, and he never built a mill at Ludington.[18]

Bay City & East Saginaw

During his fifteen years as president, Eber Brock Ward added valuable lines to the Flint & Pere Marquette. The Flint & Holly acquisition in 1868 was the first of these. The construction record of the F&PM became complicated by the construction of branch lines to meet additional markets and to serve the needs of lumbermen involved in the line. Ward's next addition was the Bay City and East Saginaw Rail Road Company (BC&ES), which was formed on 8 April 1864 to build a 14-mile line from Bay City to East Saginaw. The road's first president, James Fraser, a Bay City founder and pioneer, retired to Connecticut after just a few months in office. James G. Birney Sr. came to Bay City in 1841 and worked with Fraser to develop his new hometown. As his health failed, his son James G. Birney Jr. came to Bay City in 1857 to take charge of his father's businesses. The younger Birney replaced Fraser as president of the BC&ES in 1857. The son was as much involved with politics as was his father; he served as a state senator and one year as Michigan's lieutenant governor. In 1864 Bay County, very likely at Birney's urging, authorized $75,000 in bonds to assist in building the line. The road itself issued another $100,000 in bonds.[19]

At the end of the Civil War Birney turned his attention to the railroad. In January 1866 he hired Algernon S. Munger to build the rail line. From a few miles north of Saginaw the line had to be built through swamps, an undertaking then considered impossible. Munger found that the soil at the bottom of the swamp was a heavy clay that could provide a base for the tracks. He dredged a canal along the line, brought up the clay soil, and used it to make the grade for the tracks. Munger started work in August 1866, and the first excursion train ran over the line on Saturday, 23 November 1867—the first rail line into Bay City. Birney finished his line only a month and a half before the Jackson, Lansing & Saginaw was built along the west side of the Saginaw River to an area called Wenona. Birney's road connected with the F&PM main track at Washington Street in Saginaw and came into Bay City with its tracks in the center of Jefferson Street north from Lafayette Street. The Bay City station was located just north of 5th Street, about at the site of the present depot, 12.5 miles from East Saginaw. During 1868 the line was extended another half mile to the north to reach piers in the Saginaw River. The BC&ES had cost $215,000 to build when the F&PM bought control of the road in December 1868.[20]

Holly, Wayne & Monroe

The Detroit & Milwaukee Railway provided the southern outlet for Henry Crapo's F&H and for the F&PM after it bought Crapo's road in 1868. The sequence of events is not clear, but the D&M's service was severely affected by an April 1866 fire in Detroit that destroyed buildings, freight, eighty railcars, and its Detroit River ferry in a loss that totaled more $1 million and took eighteen lives. At some time about 1868 F&PM superintendent George Kimball, dissatisfied with the D&M's service, began to look for an alternative. By then a group of men from Oakland, Wayne, and Monroe Counties had decided that an alternate rail route from Holly could be profitable and formed the Holly, Wayne & Monroe Railway Company (HW&M). It was incorporated on 15 November 1865 and proposed to build a 65-mile road south to Monroe from a connection with the Detroit & Milwaukee at Holly. After the end of the Civil War the company started grading near Holly and "at various places along the line." One Oakland County historian credits Henderson Crawford, a Milford teacher and politician, as the most important supporter of the road. It appears he was aided in this effort by Jared S. Lapham, a merchant and banker in Northville. By December 1868 the company had graded some 26 miles of its line, but it was out of money, and several contractors could not be paid. During 1869 and 1870 some more grading was done, but "it became evident to the projectors and promoters of the scheme that even if they succeeded in completing their roadbed, it would be difficult to put on equipment, and the line would remain weak."[21]

Investors in Monroe apparently brought new life to the company and made David A. Noble, a local attorney and politician, the new president of the HW&M. Kimball struck a deal with the HW&M promoters to complete the grading, lay rails, and provide equipment, and he agreed to finish the line into Monroe by 1 January 1872. With Eber Brock Ward's money available, building moved readily. The section between Wayne and Northville was finished on 30 May 1871, but a celebratory excursion was run on 17 May. Northville to Holly was completed on 6 November 1871, and the section from Wayne to Monroe on 1 January 1872.[22]

While Kimball pushed construction toward Monroe, he took no steps to build a bridge across the River Raisin to make the expected connection with a Lake Shore & Michigan Southern subsidiary, the Detroit, Monroe & Toledo (DM&T), in downtown Monroe. By December

1871 Kimball had decided on a different and more economical route into Monroe. Rather than build on a direct line that required a bridge over the River Raisin in downtown, he swung his road sharply to the east a mile north of the city and made a connection with the DM&T line about a mile and one-half north of the river. If the historian's description is to be believed, Kimball put his tracks on the DM&T's roadbed and installed a connecting switch downtown near Front Street by 24 December 1871. Kimball kept to the letter of his agreement with Monroe financiers, but in the minds of the latter he had not kept its spirit. The first HW&M train ran into Monroe on 8 November 1871. The F&PM set up arrangements for the Lake Shore road to move F&PM cars between Monroe and Toledo. The HW&M line also hauled timber from the Saginaw Valley to Monroe, put it into the River Raisin, then rafted through the St. Lawrence River to European buyers. The F&PM continued to use the Detroit & Milwaukee to reach Detroit until 28 June 1875, when it began using the tracks of the Michigan Central from Wayne into Detroit.[23]

Flint River and Cass River

The next addition to the F&PM was The Flint River Railroad Company. Formed on 3 November 1871, it was a creation of the Flint & Pere Marquette. It was to build a 16-mile line from the F&PM in Genesee County to Otter Lake. The line tapped timber northeast of Flint, and touched a tract of timberland that Henry H. Crapo had invested in. When finished from its F&PM connection at Horton, 0.4 miles north of Carpenter Road in Flint, into Otter Lake in 8 October 1872, the line was 14.4 miles long. At Otter Lake it connected with the Detroit & Bay City Railroad, newly built and supported by the Michigan Central Railroad.[24]

The Cass River Railroad Company was formed on 3 November 1871—the same day as the Flint River Railroad. It too was created by and controlled by the Flint & Pere Marquette. It was authorized to build a 35-mile line from East Saginaw to Caro, and it was planned to tap the timberlands in Tuscola County along the Cass River. Although a part of the route may have been graded, it appears that none of its rail line was ever built.[25] On 30 May 1868 the Flint & Pere Marquette acquired the Flint & Holly, and on 1 February 1872 it bought the lines of the Bay City & East Saginaw, the Flint River, and the Holly, Wayne & Monroe, routes that totaled 108.4 miles. It also bought the rights of the Cass River Railroad.

The F&PM strengthened its place in Saginaw by forming the East Saginaw and St. Clair Railroad Company on 9 October 1872. The company was organized by F&PM officers, and proposed to build a 95-mile line from South Saginaw, through Vassar, to the St. Clair River. By 1874 it had built about 4 miles of road from the southeast side of Saginaw, where it connected with the F&PM south of Holland Avenue, west to the shore of the Saginaw River to sawmills in the area of Rust Park. The construction made the road more of an industrial track than an intercity undertaking. Although the company had rights to build to the St. Clair River, probably in the vicinity of Port Huron, it never built more than a few miles of line in Saginaw.[26]

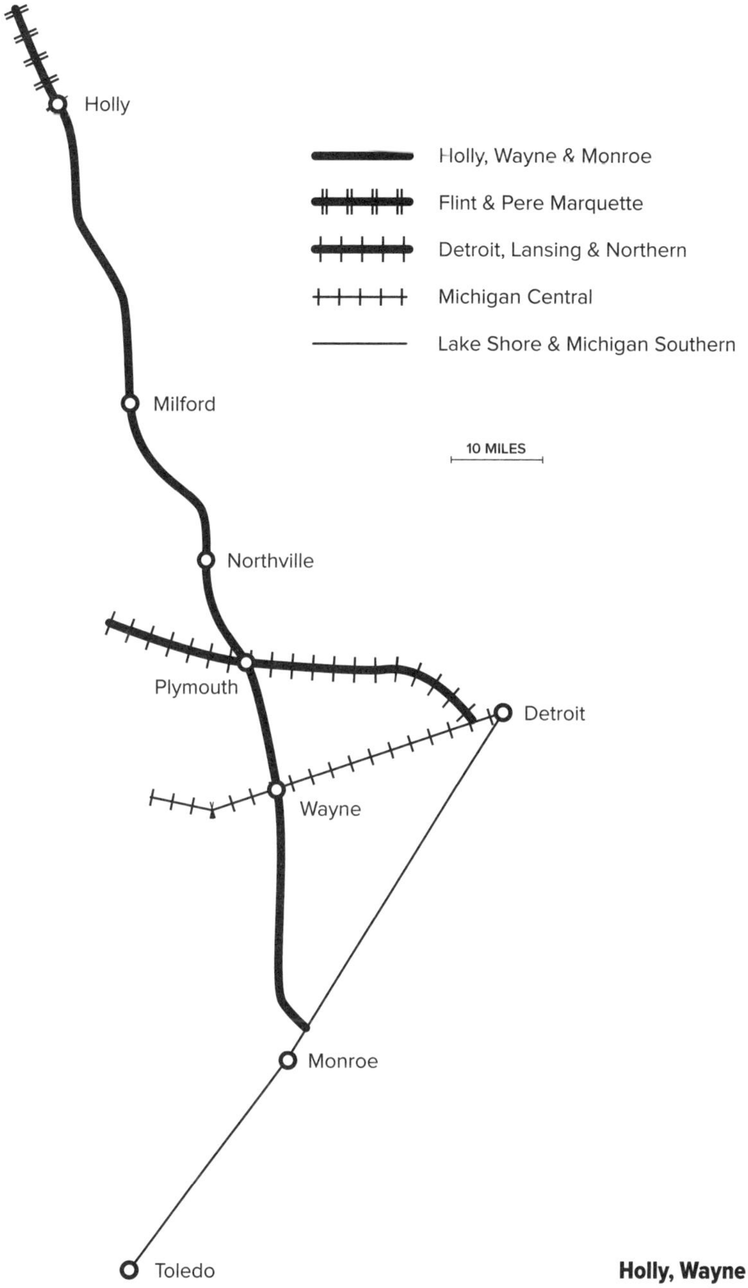

Holly, Wayne & Monroe

LEFT: William L. Webber. In 1857 he became an attorney for the Flint & Pere Marquette. He was the executor of Jesse Hoyt's estate and first president of the Saginaw Tuscola & Huron Railroad into the Thumb of Michigan.

FROM FINDAGRAVE.

RIGHT: Jesse Hoyt. An important promoter of and investor in the city of Saginaw, his generosity was essential to the community's development. He served as the second president of the Flint & Pere Marquette.

FROM THE PUBLIC LIBRARIES OF SAGINAW.

Clare County and Mt. Pleasant Branches

When the F&PM was completed into Ludington in 1874, it leased the side-wheel steamer *John Sherman* to move freight and passengers to Sheboygan, Wisconsin. Apparently the vessel was too small for the traffic demands, and it was replaced in 1876, when President Hoyt began chartering steamships from the Goodrich Transit Company. That line had started business in 1856, sailing principally from Muskegon and Grand Haven to Wisconsin ports. For the F&PM the principal route sailed was that between Ludington and Milwaukee.[27]

When the F&PM rail line was finished into Ludington, the company qualified for all of its land grant, and the state released it. By 1877 the company had received 511,502.2 acres of land, but had sold barely half of it. The land sales provided $2.3 million toward building the railroad, and allowed the road to be built more quickly than it would have been otherwise. In 1870 William L. Webber, the road's attorney, had been named land commissioner to manage grant land sales. He aggressively advertised the railroad land throughout the Midwest. He offered land to farmers with a one-quarter down payment and the balance due in three to five years at 7 percent interest. For timberlands, lumber companies paid Webber cash up front.[28]

On Saturday, 2 January 1875, F&PM president Eber Brock Ward dropped dead from a heart attack while walking on Griswold Street in Detroit. In his fifteen years as president Ward had made the F&PM into an important Michigan rail line. Under his guidance the company now reached Toledo, Ohio, and extended 270 miles across the state to Ludington. From Ludington

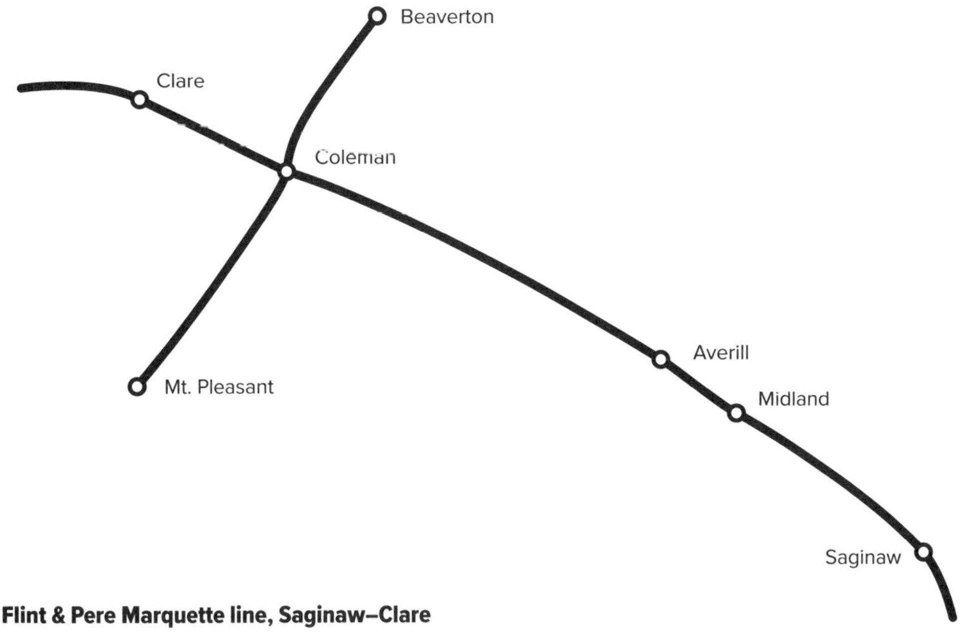

Flint & Pere Marquette line, Saginaw–Clare

F&PM freight moved across Lake Michigan to Wisconsin by ship. Also he added an important branch that reached the shipping port of Bay City. His investments in a wide variety of businesses made the F&PM a success and himself a very rich man. His own investment in the F&PM was extensive, and he put the company's net income back into the railroad rather than paying dividends to himself. For all that he contributed to the territory served by his road, Ward's name is rarely mentioned and little known.[29]

New Yorker Jesse Hoyt replaced Ward as president. Now sixty years old, Hoyt was an early investor in the F&PM and a strong promoter of businesses and development in East Saginaw. Hoyt maintained his home in New York City and relied heavily on general manager Henry C. Potter. Hoyt visited Saginaw often and encouraged and supported the town's growth. His many benefactions to his second home are well known for his name appearing on them. In November 1875 Vice President Samuel Farwell died, placing more of a burden on general manager Potter as the local representative of the company.[30]

With the line completed into Ludington in 1874 and money coming in from land grant sales, Hoyt wanted to increase the quantity of logs coming to the Saginaw mills. His first step was to incorporate the Saginaw and Clare County Railroad Company (S&CC) on 4 September 1877, a branch that penetrated the forests of Clare County. The F&PM controlled the company from its start. The S&CC was authorized to build a 20-mile line from Clare, via Farwell, northwest to Lake George, with a branch of unstated length to a lake in section 17, Town 19 North, Range 4 West, now identified as Budd Lake in Harrison. The construction details of this branch are unclear, and state and corporate records seem incomplete. During 1879 the S&CC completed 8.9 miles of line north from Harrison Junction and in 1880 another 6.6 miles for a total of 15.5

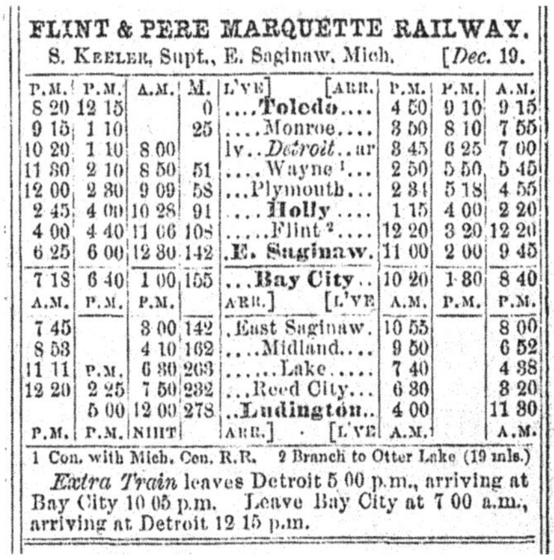

FLINT & PERE MARQUETTE RAILWAY.

S. KEELER, Supt., E. Saginaw, Mich. [*Dec.* 19.

P.M.	P.M.	A.M.	M.	L'VE] [ARR.	P.M.	P.M.	A.M.
8 20	12 15		0	....**Toledo**....	4 50	9 10	9 15
9 15	1 10		25	....Monroe....	3 50	8 10	7 55
10 20	1 10	8 00		lv..*Detroit*..ar	3 45	6 25	7 00
11 30	2 10	8 50	51	....Wayne ¹...	2 50	5 50	5 45
12 00	2 30	9 09	58	...Plymouth...	2 34	5 18	4 55
2 45	4 00	10 28	91	...**Holly**....	1 15	4 00	2 20
4 00	4 40	11 06	108	.....Flint ²....	12 20	3 20	12 20
6 25	6 00	12 30	142	.**E. Saginaw.**	11 00	2 00	9 45
7 13	6 40	1 00	155	...**Bay City**..	10 20	1 30	8 40
A.M.	P.M.	P.M.		ARR.] [L'VE	A.M.	P.M.	P.M.
7 45		3 00	142	.East Saginaw.	10 55		8 00
8 53		4 10	162	....Midland....	9 50		6 52
11 11	P.M.	6 30	203	......Lake.....	7 40		4 38
12 20	2 25	7 50	232	...Reed City...	6 30		3 20
	5 00	12 00	278	..**Ludington**..	4 00		11 30
P.M.	P.M.	NIHT		ARR.] [L'VE	A.M.		A.M.

1 Con. with Mich. Cen. R.R. 2 Branch to Otter Lake (19 mls.)

Extra Train leaves Detroit 5 00 p.m., arriving at Bay City 10 05 p.m. Leave Bay City at 7 00 a.m., arriving at Detroit 12 15 p.m.

Flint & Pere Marquette 1875 schedule. This schedule of service was issued less than a year after the road was built into Ludington. Several trains through Monroe into Toledo and trains into Detroit ran via Wayne and the Michigan Central.

FROM AUTHOR'S COLLECTION.

miles. Harrison Junction was located 1.7 miles west of Clare and branched off the Ludington main line just west of Washington Road. The distance from Harrison Junction to Harrison is 12 miles. The north end of the 1879 construction was in the vicinity of Monroe Road; of the 1880 work the end was about 3 miles north of Harrison. The most reasonable reconciliation of this data is that the 1879 building extended from Harrison Junction to the vicinity of Hatton and included about 3 miles of logging spurs. The 1880 work completed the line from Hatton to the Beech Street station in Harrison. The 1880 commissioner of railroads annual report indicates the road had 15.5 miles of main line and 15.2 miles of sidings and other tracks, most likely logging spurs. Regular train service started to Harrison on 30 September 1880. On 22 November 1883 the company completed another 14.4 miles by extending its line from Harrison to Meredith, for a total of 29.9 main-track miles. In 1887 the Toledo, Ann Arbor & North Michigan (later Ann Arbor Railroad) built its line from Mount Pleasant, through Clare, north into Clare County, and parallel to the F&PM line from Clare to Farwell, and crossed the Harrison Branch at Harrison Junction. Rather than maintain another rail crossing, the F&PM opted to build a new line between Clare and Harrison Junction that lay on the north side of the Ann Arbor line. This added about 2.5 miles to the branch and lengthened the line to Meredith to 32.4 miles. In the years after 1883 the S&CC built nearly 40 miles of branches off the S&CC although the commissioner of railroads reported that 55 miles were built by 1891.[31]

Hoyt formed a second new subsidiary, the Saginaw and Mount Pleasant Railroad Company (S&MP) on 11 February 1879. Capitalized at $100,000, it was to build a 14-mile line to Mount Pleasant from a connection with the F&PM at Coleman. The 14.4-mile line was put in service on 15 December 1879. The line was built as narrow-gauge road—three feet between the rails. Apparently the road was conceived during the national enthusiasm for narrow-gauge lines of the 1870s and 1880s. The logic may have been that the substantially lower cost of building and equipping the road offset the cost of transferring freight between cars at the ends of the line. With only two locomotives and fifteen freight cars, it is likely that the road handled conventional freight and was unlikely to have carried logs. It cost $96,600 to build the road and $13,500 to provide engines and cars, a total of $110,100.[32] Citizens put up $15,000 in cash

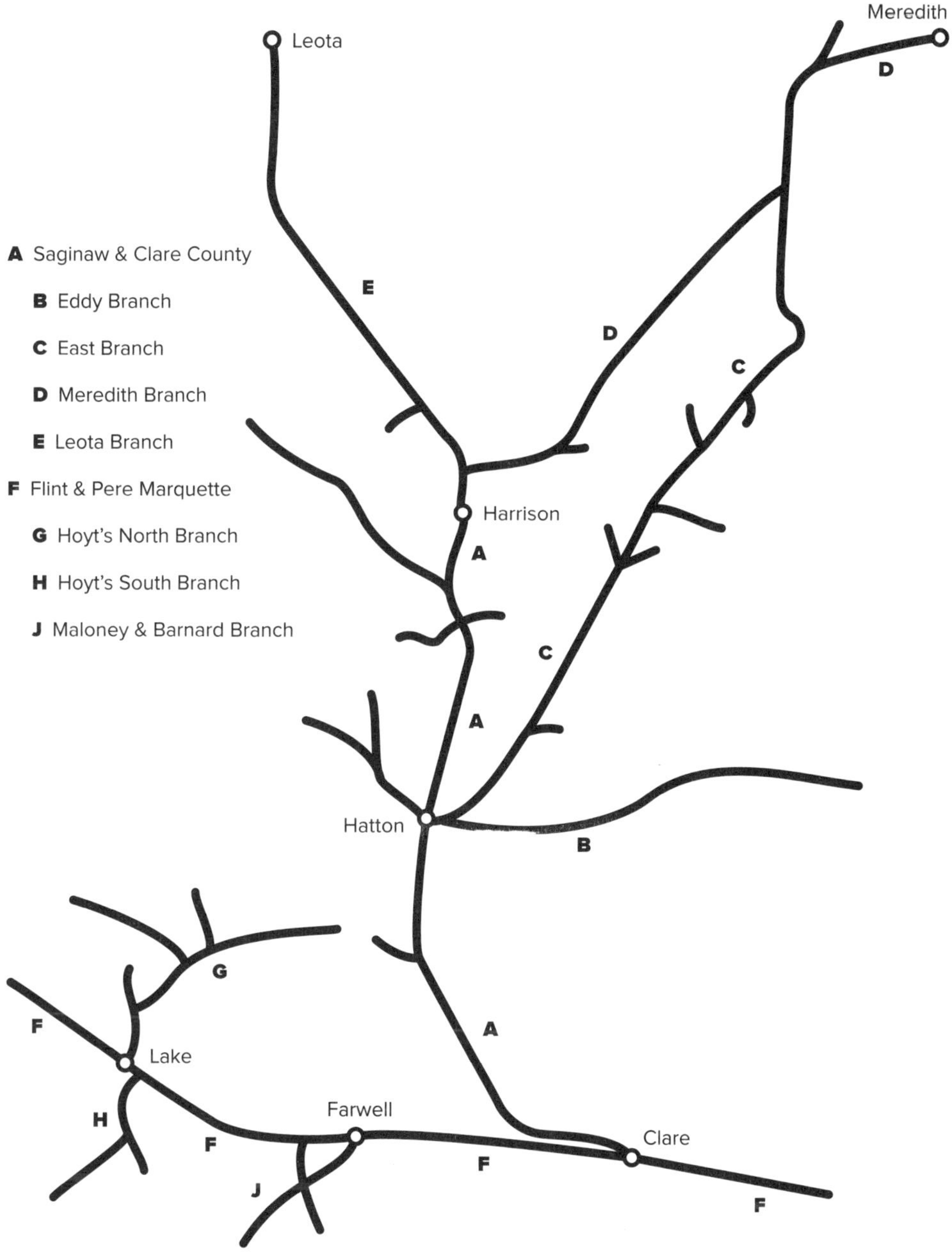

Clare Co. (Saginaw & Clare County main line and branches)

and also provided the right-of-way and depot grounds in Mt. Pleasant. Local historian Isaac A. Fancher wrote, "It was a happy day for the people of Mt. Pleasant and vicinity when they felt that they were in touch again with the outside world by the bands of steel." Businesses closed the day the first train arrived. It was met with the obligatory address by the village president, and followed by a parade to the county courthouse. The historian commented that the "coming of the railroad was the dawn of a new era for Mt. Pleasant." In 1884, after five years of operations, the line was rebuilt to standard gauge and the narrow-gauge anomaly eliminated. The 1885 annual report shows a charge of $3,220 for the changeover in gauge. When first built the line extended from Coleman to the east side of the river in Mt. Pleasant in the vicinity of Chippewa Street, a total of 14.5 miles. About 1887 the road was extended another half mile to make a connection with the Toledo, Ann Arbor & North Michigan, which was built into Mount Pleasant in 1886.[33]

On 2 November 1888 the F&PM consolidated both the Saginaw & Clare County and the Saginaw & Mt. Pleasant. Also in 1888 the F&PM began building a branch northeast from Coleman toward Beaverton. It completed 7.8 miles in 1888 and another 3.3 miles in 1889. About 1891 it finished the last major extension of the S&CC line, a 10-mile branch from Harrison to Leota. The F&PM did not report S&CC and S&MP traffic and revenue data separately, but included those numbers in its own reports.[34]

It appears that both Presidents Ward and Hoyt urged a rapid expansion of the F&PM and then used the increased revenues that followed to pay for the construction costs incurred. Money from the sales of grant lands also supported building new lines. Had the Panic of 1873 not caused a business depression, their plan might have succeeded. But lumber traffic dropped dramatically after 1873 and did not recover until 1879. In that period company debt rose from $5.3 million to $9.1 million. With an interest rate averaging 7.5 percent, the annual interest charge was $680,000—an amount that was double the average net income of the company. To protect the road Hoyt had no choice but to put the company in the hands of a receiver to reorganize it. On 1 July 1879 the court named general manager Henry C. Potter as receiver. His reorganization eliminated nearly $4 million of debt and replaced it with $6.5 million of preferred stock. The advantage to the company was that the interest on the preferred stock was payable only when earned. Fortune began to smile on Potter and Hoyt. When the reorganization was completed on 24 August 1880, the road was renamed the Flint and Pere Marquette Railroad, and freight traffic and revenue began a strong recovery in 1879 and 1880 as the effects of the financial panic of 1879 waned and the demand for lumber began to grow.[35]

Manistee Branch

Lumber traffic began to grow and Potter decided to build a branch to Manistee to gather freight traffic from its sawmills. On 31 May 1880 the F&PM incorporated a new subsidiary, the Manistee Railroad Company, to tap this traffic. The company's line was to be 22 miles from Mason County's Branch Township to the Manistee River. The road was wholly owned by the F&PM

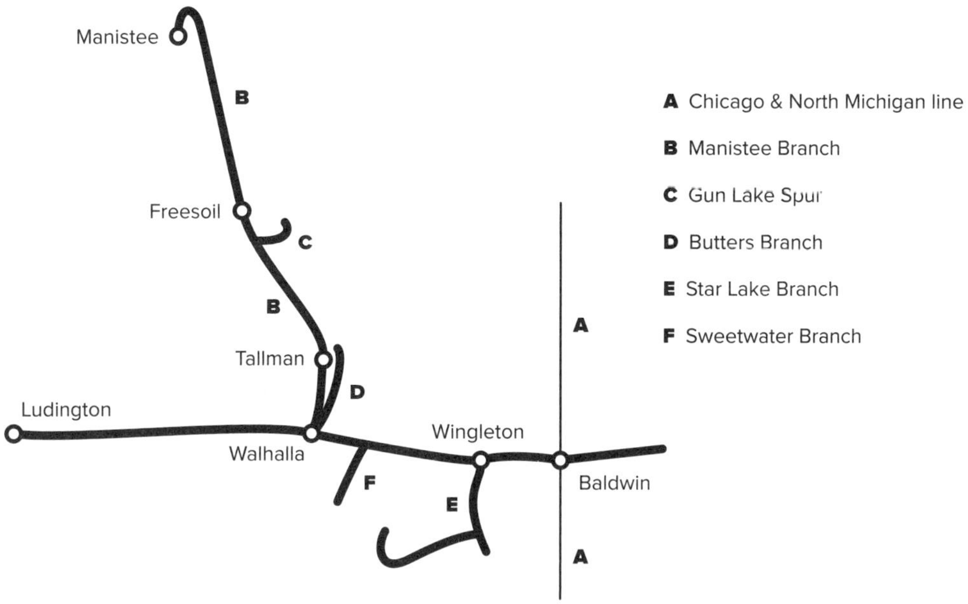

Baldwin–Ludington line plus branches

and all of its officers and directors were F&PM men. The commissioner of railroads reported 23.96 miles completed by 31 December 1881 between Tallman and Manistee.[36]

Before work started on the Manistee Branch in 1880, the F&PM completed a Butters Branch that was started in 1879 and finished in 1880. The commissioner of railroads reports its length as 3.18 miles, the distance from a connection just east of Walhalla north to the Butters Mill located on the west shore of Tallman Lake near the end of Decker Road. This line was located a short distance east of and parallel to the present line to Manistee. The record is unclear, but it appears that the Butters Branch, between Walhalla and Tallman, at first connected to the Manistee Railroad at Tallman. By the end of 1882 the 26.8-mile length of the branch between Walhalla and Manistee was in service, indicating that a new line was built between Walhalla and Tallman, and the Butters Branch remained in service. The F&PM depot in Manistee was located just north of Harrison Street. The new line gave access to the sawmills around Manistee that could provide new year-round freight revenue.[37] About 1882 the F&PM built a short spur from the Manistee line to the sawmill at Tallman Lake, and that year also built a short logging spur to Gun Lake. The Gun Lake Spur may have been about 3 miles in length, left the Manistee Branch 2.3 miles north of Fountain, at Mile Post 10.4, and curved around the east side of Gun Lake to its north end. Some of the spur's grade appears to be on Town Line Road. The record is unclear or missing about the abandonment of the Butters Branch, the Gun Lake Spur, and the Tallman Lake Spur. The Butters Branch apparently was abandoned by 1884, since Tackaberry's 1884 *Atlas of Michigan* does not show it. The commissioner of railroads reports imply that the Manistee Railroad was completed between Walhalla and Tallman in 1883.[38] On 19 December 1881 the F&PM extended its Flint River Branch by building 5.1 miles from Otter Lake to Fostoria.[39]

William W. Crapo. The son of Michigan governor and Flint lumberman Henry H. Crapo, he was involved with railroads most of his adult life.

FROM WIKIPEDIA.

Jesse Hoyt, the F&PM's president since 1875, died on 14 August 1882, in New York City. His younger brother, Alfred M. Hoyt, joined the F&PM board in 1880, and another brother, Samuel N. Hoyt, came on in 1883. After Hoyt's death William W. Crapo was named the new president of the F&PM. Crapo was the only son of Henry H. Crapo of Flint, a former governor of Michigan. William Crapo had been named an F&PM vice president in 1876. He owned successful businesses in Massachusetts, visited Michigan periodically, but continued his permanent residence in New Bedford.[40]

Crapo continued to expand the F&PM. The roster of logging branches includes Hoyt's North Branch, Hoyt's South Branch, Maloney & Barnard Branch, Joiner Spur, Star Lake Branch, Sweetwater Branch, Coleman Branch, Stearns Branch, and numerous named and unnamed branches and spurs off the Saginaw & Clare County. For this study, it is unfortunate that the construction and abandonment records are scant, unclear, or missing. A somewhat more complete record begins with the year 1891 in the annual reports of Michigan's railroad commissioner.[41]

The Hoyts' North Branch and South Branch ran out of Lake, 7.3 miles west of Farwell. An account of their construction is not of record, but it appears that serious building did not start until the years 1883 and 1884. By 1891 the railroad commissioner reported the line as 20.58 miles in length. The longest part of the North Branch was about 10 miles and the South Branch, from Lake to Sherman City, also about 10 miles. A spur of about 3 miles extended from the South Branch to Brinton. A number of unnamed spurs ran off the North Branch, totaling possibly 10 to 12 miles of road. Most of the two branches were still in use in 1900.

Work started on the Maloney & Barnard Spur in 1882 and continued through 1884. This 5.62-mile line extended from Farwell southwest into Gilmore Township's section 4. A separate spur left the main line about 2.5 miles west of Farwell, and extended south 1.5 miles to the south line of Clare County. The Joiner Spur was started in 1883 and completed in 1884. It extended from the station at Chase west and south 1.8 miles to Richard M. Joiner's sawmill on the Little Pere Marquette River in section 7 of Chase Township. The Dorr Spur also was built about 1883. Only 0.33 miles in length, it curved around the west shore of Perch Lake from the station at

Saginaw. The Potter Street station was the Flint & Pere Marquette's largest station. Built in 1887, the two-story red brick building housed passenger waiting rooms and on the second floor the management and operating offices of the railroad. Trains ran on six different F&PM lines from this station.

FROM MICHIGAN RAILROAD HISTORY MUSEUM.

Lake to reach the log-loading operation of Temple E. Dorr. Farthest west was the Star Lake Branch. It left the Ludington line at the original site of Wingleton, 2 miles west of Baldwin. Apparently, line construction started in 1882. During the 1890s the line's length varied between 17.39 and 23.80 miles.[42]

In 1882 president Crapo ended chartering ships from Goodrich Transit, but the reason for the change is not available in the records. It may have been that the month-to-month fluctuations in the freight handled did not provide consistent revenues, while the lease did demand regular payments. Another possibility is that F&PM was enjoying good profits, and Crapo may have believed company ownership would be more profitable than chartering. At a cost of $130,000 Crapo bought two new freighters, *F&PM No. 1* and *F&PM No. 2*. The business depression during 1883 did not provide enough revenue to sail the ships, and they were laid up for almost all of 1884. Within two years the business recovery that followed caused a new need for shipping across Lake Michigan, this time from Ludington to Manitowoc, Wisconsin. In 1886 the road ordered *F&PM No. 3*. It took delivery in 1887 and that year ordered *F&PM No. 4*. Apparently *F&PM No. 5* was received in 1890. All five of these ships, as was the earlier *John Sherman*, were break-bulk freighters, and except for *F&PM No. 5*, all were designed to carry both freight and passengers. As break-bulk carriers, the freight had to be moved from railcars into the ship at one port, and at the destination unloaded from the ship and reloaded in railcars. Although the F&PM owned the freighters sailing from Ludington, Goodrich continued operating into Manistee and handled some F&PM freight from that port.[43]

When William L. Webber gave up the land commissioner's office in 1885 after fifteen years, he had sold 329,308 acres of land at an average of $11.53 per acre. The sales brought a total of $4,041,839 to the F&PM treasury, and included $553,691 in interest payments from the buyers. Webber reported that as of 1 January 1885 101,009 acres remained unsold, about 20 percent of the original 1857 grant of 511,502 acres. Alfred W. Newton, his associate in office, succeeded him as land commissioner.[44]

In 1887 the F&PM began building a branch from the main line at Coleman northeasterly to Beaverton. The Tobacco River was an important water route for logs to Saginaw. Three branches of the river came together at Beaverton; the town's sawmills gave the railroad new traffic. In 1888 and 1889 it built the 11-mile line into Beaverton. By 1895 the company had built another 10.8 miles of extensions off this branch. Of this total about 5 miles was for a branch to Curtis; the remaining mileage has not been located.[45]

Bay City Belt Line

In 1889 a separate company, the Bay City Belt Line Railroad (BCBL), was formed, and in 1890 it built 5.4 miles of its road, extending from the F&PM line at about 27th Street East and then north to the Saginaw River in Essexville. The record is unclear, but it appears that the F&PM leased the BCBL in 1891. Sometime between 1891 and 1895 the road was extended west toward the Saginaw River, and that 1.9 miles was leased to the Michigan Central Railroad when built. About 1890 a 1.9-mile line was built on the east side of the F&PM yard in Saginaw to connect the Toledo-Saginaw main line to the Bay City Branch. This line was sometimes called the Bay City Loop Line and should not be confused with any trackage in Bay City.[46]

Port Huron & Northwestern

After the F&PM completed its line west from Saginaw to Lake Michigan in 1874, the company began building several longer branches and a number of spur lines to reach fresh timberlands east of Saginaw, in what is called the Thumb of Michigan, the point of land in the eastern part of the Michigan's Lower Peninsula that extends north into Lake Huron, embracing the three counties of Huron, Sanilac, and Tuscola, as well as the northern parts of Lapeer and St. Clair. The largest cities on the fringes of the Thumb are Saginaw on the west and Port Huron at the southeastern corner. Some logging started in the 1850s, but the entire area remained sparsely populated and until 1871 forested with hardwoods and some white pine. The great Chicago fire jumped across Lake Michigan and on Sunday night 8 October 1871 burned its way across much of the Thumb. The next year some of the burned-over land was put to agricultural use, but it developed slowly for a lack of transportation to reach markets.[47]

Table 1. Revenue and operating statistics for Flint & Pere Marquette, 1868–1899

YEAR	MILES OF ROAD OWNED	PASSENGER REVENUE	NUMBER OF PASSENGERS	PASSENGER MILES (THOUS.)	FREIGHT REVENUE	FREIGHT TONS	TON MILES (THOUS.)	OPERATING EXPENSE & TAXES	NET INCOME*
1868	77.0	$191,735			$184,523				
1869									
1870									
1871	218.0	$270,407	311,240	6,224				$402,811	
1872	231.7	452,648			$600,116			$677,013	$96,683
1873	231.7	426,767	492,365	14,181	635,772	370,800		735,050	355,743
1874	279.8	381,852	465,518	12,831	600,359	346,946	n.a.	692,439	328,123
1875	279.8	404,260	498,384	13,827	581,175	346,115	27,382	717,633	304,514
1876	279.8	366,129	466,439	13,529	573,748	339,767	26,628	654,772	320,870
1877	279.8	386,003	489,579	14,144	552,838	334,823	27,149	600,832	369,866
1878	280.1	431,078	540,556	15,900	592,874	408,053	34,691	667,231	388,786
1879	303.4	452,008	552,753	16,838	653,636	495,817	42,044	745,982	405,219
1–9/1880		403,846	515,012	15,135	704,010	603,396	48,046	884,622	252,806
10–12/1880		161,443	197,197	5,816	290,360	265,420	20,369	261,514	200.683
Year 1880	317.7	565,289	712,209	20,951	994,370	868,816	68,415	1,146,136	453,489
1881	317.7	655,478	813,131	24,449	1,157,367	1,013,965	80,894	1,315,322	549,204
1882	346.9	792,714	993,076	29,438	1,299,010	1,113,355	89,352	1,412,703	730,047
1883	346.9	860,167	1,048,496	32,214	1,552,327	1,393,150	114,515	1,684,256	782,452
1884	361.6	703,849	872,970	13,081	1,402,695	1.220,679	97,972	1,458,093	737,527
1885	361.6	613,674	749,577	22,665	1,185,786	1,118,621	88,239	1,269,416	595,130
1886	369.3	667,356	852,676	24,913	1,307,920	1,382,747	107,936	1,415,545	661,700
1887	363.6	788,676	906,462	25,396	1,607,477	1,779,546	125,911	1,671,019	762,518
1888	379.6	667,729	986,351	25,120	1,395,144	1,574,002	125,798	1,468,683	682,269
1889†	624.9	775,819	1,161.879	31,132	1.449,242	1,596,888	133,049	1,552,164	780,115
1890	627.1	798,582	1,257,129	32,447	1,708.689	1,809,366	173,795	1,813,309	801,039
1891	772.2	778,809	1,239,279	32,819	1,652,169	1,187,998	168,848	1,789,022	755,737
1892	772.1	768,421	1,307,737	33,312	1,704,026	1,945,226	175,823	1,827,025	751,989
1893	773.6	748,192	1,221,927	31,892	1,479,918	1,633,494	148,439	1,786,221	553,953
1894	782.7	670,792	1,107,477	29,131	1,293,499	1,359,710	129,793	1,511,052	566,124
1895	776.4	650,629	1,070,197	30,010	1,362,312	1,528,694	162,843	1,607,877	527,559
1896	783.7	593,860	977,308	28,086	1,388,234	1,605,878	188,005	1,589,198	529,600
1897	789.1	642,137	1,010,236	29,550	1,614,643	1,898,179	231,351	1,732,986	647,572
1898	723.4	695,016	1,048,536	31,643	1,845,294	2,334,120	272,283	1,980,236	688,635
1899	712.4	777,635	1,137,709	34,980	2,033,488	2,724,369	328,110	2,252,238	694,656

Source: 1868–1871 data from Michigan Auditor General, *Annual Reports*; 1872–1899 data from Michigan Railroad Commission, *Annual Reports*. The data in the reports of the auditor general and in the very early reports by the Railroad Commission is incomplete.

* Net income is passenger revenue, freight revenue, and miscellaneous revenue, less operating expense.

† Consolidated data from Saginaw & Clare County, Saginaw & Mt. Pleasant, Manistee, and Port Huron & North Western.

Table 2. Costs, equipment, capitalization for Flint & Pere Marquette, 1868–1899

YEAR	MILES OF ROAD OWNED	COST OF ROAD (THOUS.)	COST OF EQUIPMENT (THOUS.)	NUMBER ENGINES	NUMBER FREIGHT CARS	NUMBER PASSENGER CARS	NUMBER EMPLOYEES	COMMON STOCK (THOUS.)	TOTAL DEBT (THOUS.)	DIVIDEND PAID (THOUS.)
1868	77.0	$1,860	$359	13	163	18	n.a.	$1,099	$1,520	$157.4
1869								1,099	n.a.	
1870								1,099	3,066	0
1871	218.0				562	32	n.a.	1,099	3,066	0
1872	231.7	10,249	1,135	33	619	48	n.a.	3,298	5,266	0
1873	231.7	9,770	1,371	42	739	40	n.a.	3,297	7,370	0
1874	279.8	10,365	1,373	42	717	41	c.1,000	3,298	8,059	0
1875	279.8	7,310	1,383	42	717	42	1,022	3,298	8,193	0
1876	279.8	7,319	1,381	43	714	43	835	3,298	7,921	0
1877	279.8	7,326	1,382	43	715	43	905	3,298	8,656	0
1878	280.1	7,361	1,468	43	871	43	988	3,298	9,079	0
1879*	303.4	7,416	1,494	46	883	43	1,008	3,298	9,706	0
1–9/1880		9,463	c. 1,500	51	1,129	44	1,215	3,298	7,665	0
10–12/1880		8,172	c. 1,500	51	1,229	54	1,215	6,305	3,367	0
Year 1880	317.7	8,172	c. 1,500	51	1,229	54	1,215	6,305	3,367	0
1881	317.7	8,662	c. 1,700	62	1,729	68	1,726	6,500	4,822	357.5
1882	346.9	8,954	c. 1,900	68	1,682	69	1,846	6,500	5,028	422.5
1883	336.9	c. 8,800	c. 2,000	70	1,959	80	2,000	6,500	5,197	455.0
1884	361.6	c. 8,850	c. 2,200	78	2,152	82	2,000	6,500	5,299	455.0
1885	361.6	c. 9,058	c. 2,200	77	2,136	82	1,700	6,500	5,299	260.0
1886	369.3	c. 9,156	c. 2,200	78	2,086	83	1,700	6,500	5,299	325.0
1887	363.6	c. 9,078	c. 2,200	80	2,839	83	1,950	6,500	5,509	422.5
1888	379.6	c.13,677	c. 2,300	86	2,886	83	2,186	10,000	5,359	449.5
1889†	624.9	c.17,518	c. 2,400	103	2,952	118	2,263	10,000	9,119	380.5
1890	627.1	c.18,083	c. 2,400	104	3,307	118	2,098	10,000	9,579	317.1
1891	772.2	c.18,489	c. 2,400	104	3,322	118	2,013	10,000	9,889	253.7
1892	772.1	c.18,837	c. 2,400	104	c.3,400	118	2,150	10,000	10,249	353.7
1893	773.6	c.18,655	c. 2,400	103	c.3,400	117	2,268	10,000	10,219	0
1894	782.7	c.18,950	c. 2,400	103	3,385	117	1,930	10,000	10,179	0
1895	776.4	c.18,979	c. 2,400	103	3,359	117	2,045	10,000	10,429	0
1896	783.7	c.19,006	c. 2,400	103	3,295	117	2,077	10,000	10,389	0
1897	769.1	c.19,406	c. 2,400	107	c.3,300	117	2.069	10,000	11,819	0
1898	723.4	c.19,467	c. 2,400	108	c.3,300	117	2,088	10,000	11,897	63.4
1899	712.4	c.19,630	c. 2,400	110	c.3,300	115	2,224	10,000	12,547	0

Source: 1868–1871 data from Michigan Auditor General, *Annual Reports*; 1872–1899 data from Michigan Railroad Commission, *Annual Reports*. The data in the reports of the auditor general and in the very early reports by the Railroad Commission is incomplete.

* After 1879 the F&PM did not separate cost of road from cost of equipment. The cost of equipment amount is an estimate and with the cost of road sums to the total of the two costs.

† Consolidated data from Saginaw & Clare County, Saginaw & Mt. Pleasant, Manistee, and Port Huron & North Western.

Table 3. Freight and lumber traffic statistics for Flint & Pere Marquette, 1868–1899

YEAR	REVENUE	YTY % CHANGE	REVENUE TRAIN MILES (THOUS.)	REVENUE TONS (THOUS.)	YTY % CHANGE	REVENUE PER TON	REVENUE TON MILES (THOUS.)	TONS LUMBER (THOUS.)	YTY % CHANGE	% OF ALL TONS
1868	$184,523	70.1		119.2				88.5		74.2
1869										
1870										
1871	369,892	183.6		232.1		$1.59		156.7		67.5
1872	600,116	62.2		344.5	48.4	1.74		196.9	25.7	69.2
1873	635,772	5.9	356.1	370.8	7.6	1.71		215.7	9.5	62.6
1874	600,359	-5.6	325.3	347.6	-6.3	1.72	n.a.	212.2	-1.6	61.2
1875	581,175	-3.2	366.0	346.1	-0.4	1.68	27,382	226.8	6.9	65.5
1876	573,748	-1.3	366.9	339.7	-1.8	1.69	26,628	207.1	-8.7	61.0
1877	552,838	-3.6	365.0	334.8	-1.4	1.32	27,149	204.8	-1.1	58.9
1878	592,874	7.2	501.2	408.1	21.9	1.43	34,691	190.0	-7.2	46.6
1879	653,636	10.2	457.3	495.8	21.5	1.31	42,044	243.5	28.2	49.1
1–9/1880	704,010		537.8	603.4		1.17	48,046	367.0		68.8
10–12/1880	290,360		200.0	265.4		1.09	20,369	151.9		57.2
Year 1880	994,370	52.1	737.8	868.8	75.2	1.14	68,415	518.9	113.1	59.7
1881	1,157,367	16.4	719.4	1,014.0	16.7	1.14	80,894	651.8	25.6	64.3
1882	1,299,010	12.2	754.7	1,113.4	9.8	1.16	89,352	681.5	4.6	60.2
1883	1,552,327	19.5	1,045.9	1,393.2	25.1	1.11	114,514	862.0	26.5	61.9
1884	1,402,695	-3.8	871.5	1.220.7	-12.0	1.14	97,972	751.5	-12.8	61.1
1885	1,185,786	-15.5	789.5	1,118.6	-8.4	1.06	86,239	691.1	-8.0	61.7
1886	1,307,920	10.3	914.4	1,382.7	23.6	0.95	107,936	882.9	27.8	63.9
1887	1,607,477	22.9	1,221.6	1,779.5	28.7	0.90	125,911	1,256.4	42.3	66.8
1888	1,395,144	-13.2	1,113.4	1,574.0	-11.5	0.88	125,798	1,122.2	-10.7	71.3
1889*	1.449,242	3.9	1,101.7	1,596.9	1.5	0.91	133,049	1,048.8	-6.5	65.7
1890	1,708,689	17.9	1,286.5	1,809.4	13.3	0.94	173,795	1,051.7	0.3	58.1
1891	1,652,169	-3.3	1,273.1	1,818.0	0.5	0.91	166,848	1,100.7	4.7	60.5
1892	1,704,026	3.1	1,291.3	1,945.2	7.0	0.88	175,823	1,170.7	6.4	60.2
1893	1,479,918	-13.2	1,249.4	1,633.5	-16.0	0.90	143,439	886.9	-24.2	54.3
1894	1,293,499	-12.6	1,014.2	1,359.7	-16.8	0.95	129,793	632.1	-26.7	48.5
1895	1,362,312	5.3	1,142.3	1,528.7	12.4	0.89	162,843	664.5	5.1	43.5
1896	1,388,234	1.9	1,210.6	1,605.9	5.1	0.86	188,005	418.5	-37.0	30.1
1897	1,614,643	16.3	1,276.9	1,898.2	18.2	0.85	231,351	372.8	-10.9	19.6
1898	1,845,294	14.3	1,254.9	2,334.1	23.0	0.79	272,283	491.5	31.8	21.1
1899	2,033,488	10.2	1,329.3	2,724.4	16.7	0.75	328,110	653.4	32.9	24.0

Source: 1868–1871 data from Michigan Auditor General, *Annual Reports*; 1872–1899 data from Michigan Railroad Commission, *Annual Reports*. The data in the reports of the auditor general and in the very early reports by the Railroad Commission is incomplete.

* Consolidated data from Saginaw & Clare County, Saginaw & Mt. Pleasant, Manistee, and Port Huron & North Western.

Table 4. Freight traffic statistics for Flint & Pere Marquette, 1868–1899

YEAR	REVENUE TONS (THOUS.)	LUMBER TONS (THOUS.)	% OF ALL TONS	AG. PRODS. TONS (THOUS.)	% OF ALL TONS	MANUFACTURES TONS (THOUS.)	% OF ALL	MERCHANDISE TONS (THOUS.)	% OF ALL TONS
1868	119.2	88.5	74.2	8.9	7.5	n.a.	n.a.	15.7	13.2
1869									
1870									
1871	232.1	156.7	67.5	24.7	10.6	n.a.	n.a.	43.9	18.9
1872	344.5	196.9	69.2	41.6	12.1	n.a.	n.a.	104.1	30.2
1873	370.8	215.7	62.6	30.9	9.0	39.3	11.4	80.7	23.4
1874	347.6	212.2	61.2	21.1	6.1	18.3	5.3	84.8	24.4
1875	346.1	226.8	65.5	33.4	9.7	6.1	1.8	59.2	17.1
1876	339.7	207.1	61.0	33.6	9.9	6.6	1.9	76.0	22.4
1877	334.8	204.8	58.9	51.6	15.4	5.1	1.5	66.1	19.3
1878	408.1	190.0	46.6	96.3	23.6	5.2	1.3	84.5	20.7
1879	495.8	243.5	49.1	86.2	17.4	8.1	1.6	103.3	20.8
1–9/1880	603.4	367.0	68.8	68.9	11.4	6.9	1.1	111.0	18.4
10–12/1880	265.4	151.9	57.2	40.7	9.3	2.1	0.8	49.0	18.5
Year 1880	868.8	518.9	59.7	109.6	12.6	9.0	1.0	160.0	18.4
1881	1,014.0	651.8	64.3	84.5	8.3	11.8	1.2	157.8	15.6
1882	1,113.4	681.5	60.2	89.0	7.9	16.7	1.5	141.5	12.8
1883	1,393.2	862.0	61.9	119.7	8.6	14.7	1.1	185.2	13.3
1884	1,220.7	751.5	61.1	93.5	7.7	14.7	1.2	160.0	13.1
1885	1,118.6	691.1	61.7	112.1	10.0	17.0	1.8	131.0	11.7
1886	1,307.9	882.9	63.9	153.9	11.8	22.2	1.6	146.9	10.6
1887	1,607.5	1,256.4	66.8	141.2	8.8	20.1	1.1	186.8	9.9
1888	1,395.1	1,122.2	71.3	155.7	11.2	24.0	1.5	162.3	10.3
1889*	1,449.2	1,048.8	65.7	200.3	13.8	35.7	2.2	171.5	10.7
1890	1,708.7	1,051.7	58.1	289.6	16.9	38.8	2.1	279.5	15.5
1891	1,651.2	1,100.7	60.5	344.6	20.9	54.5	3.0	149.0	9.2
1892	1,945.2	1,170.7	60.2	323.1	16.6	68.1	3.5	183.3	9.4
1893	1,633.5	886.9	54.3	327.6	20.1	58.8	3.6	159.0	9.7
1894	1,359.7	632.1	48.5	303.3	22.3	62.8	4.6	134.9	9.9
1895	1,528.7	664.5	43.5	361.9	23.7	69.7	4.6	167.3	10.9
1896	1,605.9	418.5	30.1	495.6	30.9	127.1	7.9	162.4	10.1
1897	1,898.2	372.8	19.6	472.4	24.9	198.2	10.4	185.9	9.8
1898	2,334.1	491.5	21.1	507.7	21.8	268.1	11.5	206.4	8.8
1899	2,724.4	653.4	24.0	542.1	19.9	301.1	11.1	324.9	11.9

Source: 1868–1871 data from Michigan Auditor General, *Annual Reports*; 1872–1899 data from Michigan Railroad Commission, *Annual Reports*. The data in the reports of the auditor general and in the very early reports by the Railroad Commission is incomplete.

* Consolidated data from Saginaw & Clare County, Saginaw & Mt. Pleasant, Manistee, and Port Huron & North Western.

Daniel B. Harrington. This Port Huron lumberman and civic spirit was a founder and the first president of the Port Huron & Northwestern Railroad in 1878.
FROM ST. CLAIR COUNTY LIBRARY.

Early in 1878 a group of Port Huron businessmen believed a railroad running north from their city to tap the new farming region would be a success. With $400,000 in capital, they proposed to build a 100-mile line reaching to the tip of the Thumb at Port Austin and were certain it would bring business to Port Huron. On 21 March 1878 they formed the Port Huron and Northwestern Railway Company (PH&NW). Daniel B. Harrington was named the road's president, and Charles Richards Brown as secretary and company attorney. Brown was a long-standing believer in the practicality of narrow-gauge railroads and very possibly may have influenced the company's decision to build a narrow-gauge road, three feet between the rails, instead of standard gauge. Narrow-gauge railroads reflected a newly developed enthusiasm for that type of railroad, as we saw earlier with Hoyt's Saginaw and Mount Pleasant Railroad Company. This is a subject far too broad to be considered adequately here. Dr. George W. Hilton's admirable study *American Narrow Gauge Railroads* covers the subject thoroughly. Enthusiasts held conventions across the nation to promote the narrow-gauge idea, and several roads were built. The reasoning appears to have been that narrow-gauge roads would be less expensive to build and to operate than conventional ones, and that they would be operated as a local, not intercity, carrier that would bring freight to the terminal city. The goal of the PH&NW's founders was a road that would support Port Huron businesses and bring traffic from throughout the Thumb area.[48]

Building started in 1878 on the bank of the river at Port Huron's Pine Grove Park, went west along Thomas Street, then north along 12th Avenue. By May 1879 the company completed 25.3 miles to Croswell. The next year it extended north, through Palms, to the Lake Huron port of Harbor Beach (then called Sand Beach). It also built south, through Pine Grove Park, toward the Black River, for a total of 71 miles. But, having built this part of its line, the officers seemed unsure what to do next. In January 1880 they amended the corporate articles to build a branch from Kingsley, a point apparently near Atkins, northwest through Brockway Center (now renamed Yale) and Cass City to Caseville. In November 1880 they added to this by authorizing a branch from Marlette, on the proposed Caseville branch, 45 miles to Bay City and also a 55-mile branch from Port Huron to Detroit. In March 1881 the directors authorized building a 46-mile branch from Marlette to East Saginaw, and later that month also reaffirmed their decision to build to Port Austin. To improve its entry into Port Huron, the railroad gained city permission in early 1881 to build a drawbridge across the Black River. This bridge allowed the road much better access to a downtown site for a new station at Court Street. At Court Street the PH&NW made a connection with the Port Huron & Lake Michigan. That road, after a decade of changes in ownership and construction, and with support from the Grand Trunk Railway of Canada, eventually assembled a line from Port Huron to Chicago, and was renamed the Chicago & Grand Trunk.[49]

The PH&NW directors sorted through their choices and then decided to continue extending the line north, building from Palms, through Ubly, Bad Axe and Kinde, to Port Austin. Also, they opted to build the line that would connect Port Huron and Saginaw that had been authorized in pieces in 1880 and 1881. Work started on both lines during 1880. The company spent more than $600,000 on the extension to Port Austin and on the branch to Marlette during the year, and raised most of the money by a bond issue. By January 1881 the rails were laid into Marlette. The branch to Marlette joined the main line at a now-forgotten point first named Saginaw Junction, and later called Zion, 1 mile north of Atkins, at Metcalf Road. Going northwest this line crossed the Black River by a 798-foot wooden trestle bridge; the approach required a steep grade on both sides of the river. By September the line was completed from Marlette 13 miles to west Mayville, and on 1 December another 12 miles into Vassar. By year's end the tracks were laid into East Saginaw, but the line was not put in service until 21 February 1882. In Saginaw the road used Flint & Pere Marquette tracks to reach that road's East Saginaw station. Most likely it put in a third rail on the F&PM tracks for narrow-gauge trains to use.[50]

On 27 January 1882 the PH&NW directors decided to make yet another expansion. They formed the Port Huron and Southwestern Railway Company (PH&SW) to build a 32-mile line from Port Huron southwest to the farm community of Almont. All of its founding directors were directors of the PH&NW, with one exception. The company built south from the PH&NW Court Street station, skirted along the south side of the Grand Trunk line west as far as Tappan, then headed southwest to Almont. It was completed in short order—on 3 October 1882. On 13 September, before the road was put in service, the company was merged into the PH&NW.[51]

The 35-mile extension from Palms, through Bad Axe, into Port Austin was put in service on 11 December 1882. The company owned 215 miles of line, but reported an additional 3 miles to reach the F&PM station in East Saginaw. The company had spent $3,210,000 to build its line and another $300,000 for engines and cars. This amount exceeded what the local owners could raise and forced the company to issue $1,387,000 in bonds, half of them at 6 percent interest and half at 7 percent. The interest cost was $119,000 annually, an amount that exceeded net income every year except 1882. The money had been easy to borrow, but the profits needed to pay the interest were lacking.[52]

In early September 1881 another damaging forest fire raged across the northern part of the Thumb. It burned out after three days, but 125 people lost their lives and thousands were

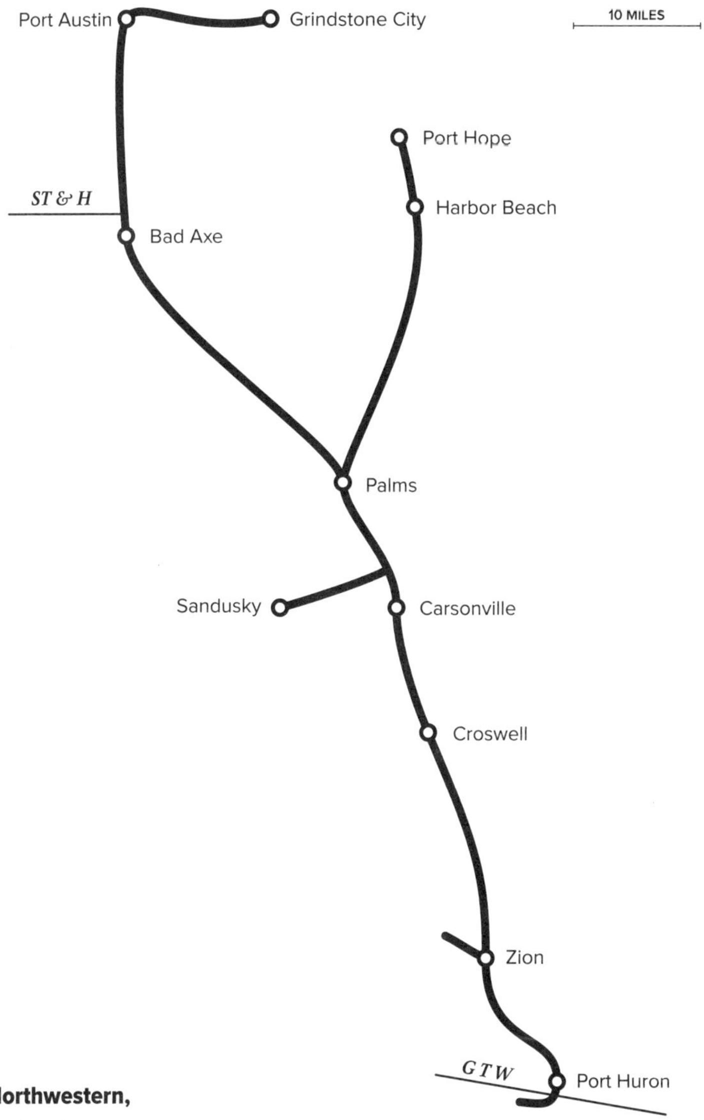

Port Huron & Northwestern, line Port Huron–North

made homeless. New settlers did move in, drawn to the new farmland created on burned forestlands. For the railroad, its freight cars now moved more agricultural products than forest products. In 1886 50 percent of its freight business came from the farm with just 18 percent from the forest. The neighboring Flint & Pere Marquette believed that the PH&NW's Port Huron–Saginaw branch had value as an extension of its own road. Port Huron could provide the Saginaw sawmills with better access to eastbound Great Lakes shipping and make a good connection to the Great Western and Grand Trunk Railways of Canada in Ontario. The Port Huron–Saginaw line had several drawbacks. The narrow-gauge tracks would have to be changed

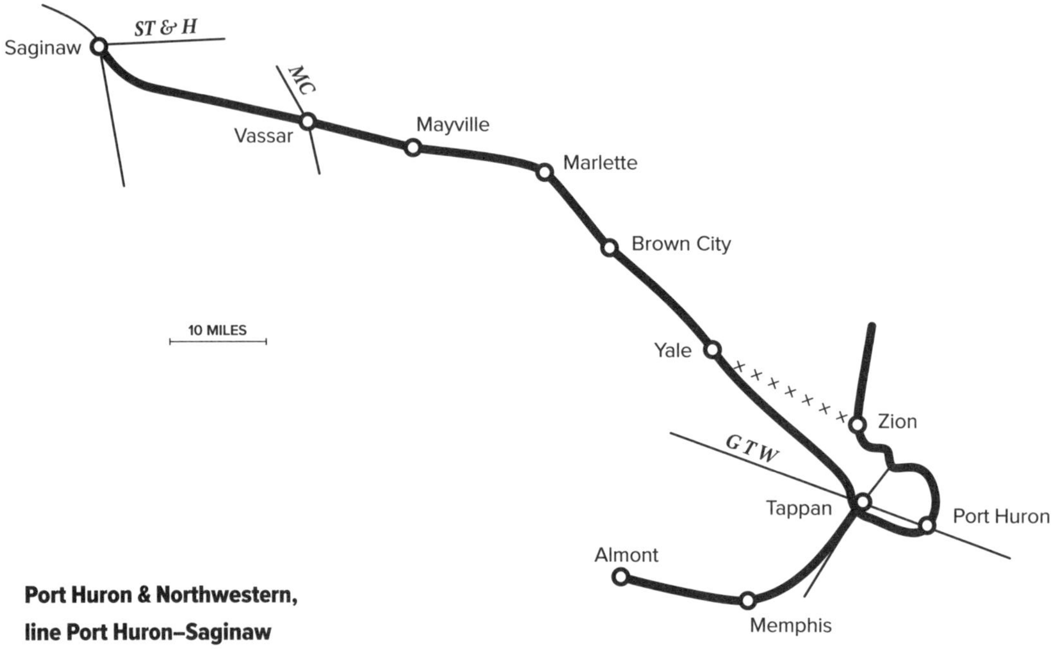

Port Huron & Northwestern, line Port Huron–Saginaw

Harbor Beach. The first Port Huron & Northwestern station at Harbor Beach was built about 1881. The village's name was changed from Sand Beach to Harbor Beach in 1899. The train is headed for Port Hope.

FROM MICHIGAN RAILROAD HISTORY MUSEUM.

Table 5. Revenue and operating statistics for Port Huron & Northwestern, 1879–1888

YEAR	MILES OF ROAD OWNED	PASSENGER REVENUE	NUMBER OF PASSENGERS	PASSENGER MILES (THOUS.)	FREIGHT REVENUE	FREIGHT TONS (THOUS.)	TON MILES	OPERATING EXPENSE	NET INCOME*
1879	25.3	$7,559	11,880	270	$4,128	3,220	80	$7,344	$5,043
1880	71.0	29,340	47,703	1,140	19,388	14,272	585s	23,451	28,251
1881	151.0	66,774	80,938	2,240	63,287	40,625	2,234	65,585	68,910
1882	218.0	129,021	158,377	5,269	99,999	65,365	2,870	112,935	132,282
1883	218.0	170,612	197,940	6,910	120,494	81,427	3,914	198,530	116,250
1884	218.0	148,970	190,624	5,855	112,768	79,399	3,623	211,368	77,596
1885	218.0	138,359	207,201	5,339	132,732	100,333	5,114	213,479	84,283
1886	218.0	159,279	222,139	6,341	127,393	96,079	4,630	214,323	101,662
1887	218.0	169,179	219,206	6,961	127,987	98,458	5,317	213,754	114,308
1888	218.0	169,958	224,875	6,635	128,796	90,299	5,247	224,858	105,440

Source: Data from Michigan Railroad Commission, *Annual Reports*.
* Net income is passenger revenue, freight revenue, and miscellaneous revenue, less operating expense.

Table 6. Costs, equipment, capitalization for Port Huron & Northwestern, 1879–1888

YEAR	MILES OF ROAD OWNED	COST OF ROAD (THOUS.)	COST OF EQUIPMENT (THOUS.)	NUMBER ENGINES	NUMBER FREIGHT CARS	NUMBER PASSENGER CARS	NUMBER EMPLOYEES	COMMON STOCK (THOUS.)	TOTAL DEBT (THOUS.)	DIVIDEND PAID (THOUS.)
1879	25.3	$230	$20	2	33	3	29	$133	$125	0
1880	71.0	620	55	4	59	6	83	278	612	0
1881	151.0	1,722	261	11	261	22	202	604	755	0
1882	218.0	3,210	303	14	259	24	365	1,090	1,942	$65
1883	218.0	3,232	306	13	258	25	365	1,090	2,430	0
1884	218.0	3,258	308	13	257	25	300	1,090	2,586	0
1885	218.0	3,262	307	13	257	25	312	1,090	2,646	0
1886	218.0	3,267	308	13	268	28	326	1,090	2,680	0
1887	218.0	3,271	308	13	268	28	391	1,090	2,745	0
1888	218.0	3,273	308	13	268	28	396	1,090	2,642	0

Source: Data from Michigan Railroad Commission, *Annual Reports*.

to standard-gauge operations. F&PM engineers did not like running through Pine Grove Park and on several Port Huron city streets, and believed that the Black River bridge northwest of Zion should be avoided.[53]

In 1883 Henry Howard, the PH&NW's second president, resigned. He was replaced by Port Huron businessman John P. Sanborn, who had been collector of customs from 1866 to 1883. He conducted the sale negotiations with the Flint & Pere Marquette that started in 1888. The F&PM lawyers were unsure if Michigan law allowed one railroad company to buy another. Up to that time nearly all acquisitions were not purchases but foreclosure sales, corporate reorganizations, or leases. A one-page act by the legislature, Public Act No. 10 of 1889, put the matter to rest.[54] Also during 1888 the Grand Trunk Railway of Canada was preparing to build a tunnel under the St. Clair River from Port Huron to Sarnia, Ontario. The F&PM bought land near the tunnel mouth to gain access to the tunnel. Also it decided it would use some of this land as part of a 20.15-mile new line from Tappan, west of Port Huron on the Port Huron & South Western line, northwest to Yale, where it would join the present Port Huron–Saginaw line. This new line would allow abandoning the 12-mile Zion-Yale section, the unsatisfactory Black River bridge, and reduce some of the on-street operations in Port Huron. On 20 February 1889 PH&NW stockholders approved the sale of their company to F&PM for $2.3 million. The F&PM issued $3.5 million in bonds, of which $2.3 million was used to buy the PH&NW and $1.2 million was to change the route of the Port Huron–Saginaw line and convert it to standard gauge. Included in the project was a 4.85-mile spur from Brown City to a gravel pit, probably to furnish ballast. The relocation of the Saginaw Branch and its change to standard gauge was completed 15 November 1889; the other Port Huron road's lines remained as narrow gauge. PH&NW ownership was transferred to the F&PM on 1 April 1889.[55]

President Crapo was in no hurry to convert the rest of the PH&NW tracks to standard gauge. He did complete an extension on 10 July 1892 with a 5.3-mile branch from Port Austin east to Grindstone City. There the road tapped several quarries and started moving grindstones and whetstones. Crapo remarked that in its first months of operations "the gross earnings from that extension have already exceeded [the construction cost of $11,404]." He expected earnings would "undoubtedly be increased largely in the future."[56]

Saginaw, Tuscola & Huron

Three years after the Port Huron & North Western was conceived and its construction begun, another line was proposed to build into the Thumb. The Saginaw, Tuscola and Huron Railroad Company (ST&H) was incorporated 14 February 1881. With a capital of $600,000 it proposed to build a 60-mile line from East Saginaw to Bad Axe and Caseville. Historians credit the idea for the road to Flint & Pere Marquette's president, Jesse Hoyt, and his attorney, William L. Webber, who became the road's president after Hoyt's death in August 1882. Hoyt and Webber opted to build the ST&H as a narrow-gauge line with three feet between the rails, possibly under the assumption that the road would bring freight to Saginaw, but not much of it would need interchange to the standard-gauge F&PM. Hoyt built the road from East Saginaw as far as Sebewaing, 37 miles, and began service on 4 April 1882. The road got an immediate bonus when coal was discovered in several areas along the route: Uncle Henry Mine near Saginaw and other mines at Akron, Unionville, and Sebewaing. On 15 June 1884 Webber completed another 9 miles to reach Bay Port. There he built the Bay Port Hotel, a sumptuous hostelry on Wild Fowl Bay that featured 117 rooms, electric lights, hot and cold baths, a bowling alley, and a casino. Travelers rode to the hotel by train; many of them on one-day excursions.[57]

From Bay Port Webber proposed to build either to Caseville, 9 miles northeast on Saginaw Bay, or east to Bad Axe, where his road would connect with the Port Huron & North Western

Bay Port. The Saginaw, Tuscola & Huron rails were laid into Bay Port in 1884. To boost business the railroad built the very impressive Bay Port Hotel and ran special trains to bring in the tourists. The second story of the depot provided the agent's living quarters.

FROM MICHIGAN RAILROAD HISTORY MUSEUM.

Bay Port Hotel. Built in 1886 by the Saginaw, Tuscola & Huron's owners, this luxurious hotel boasted 117 rooms with electric lights, hot and cold baths, a bowling alley, pool tables, a casino, and barbershop. Guests came by train from Saginaw for a night's or a week's stay. The hotel developed some reputation as being haunted, but it remained a success for two decades. The hotel was torn down in 1907. Its front steps remain at the intersection of Second and Cedar Streets.

FROM MICHIGAN RAILROAD HISTORY MUSEUM.

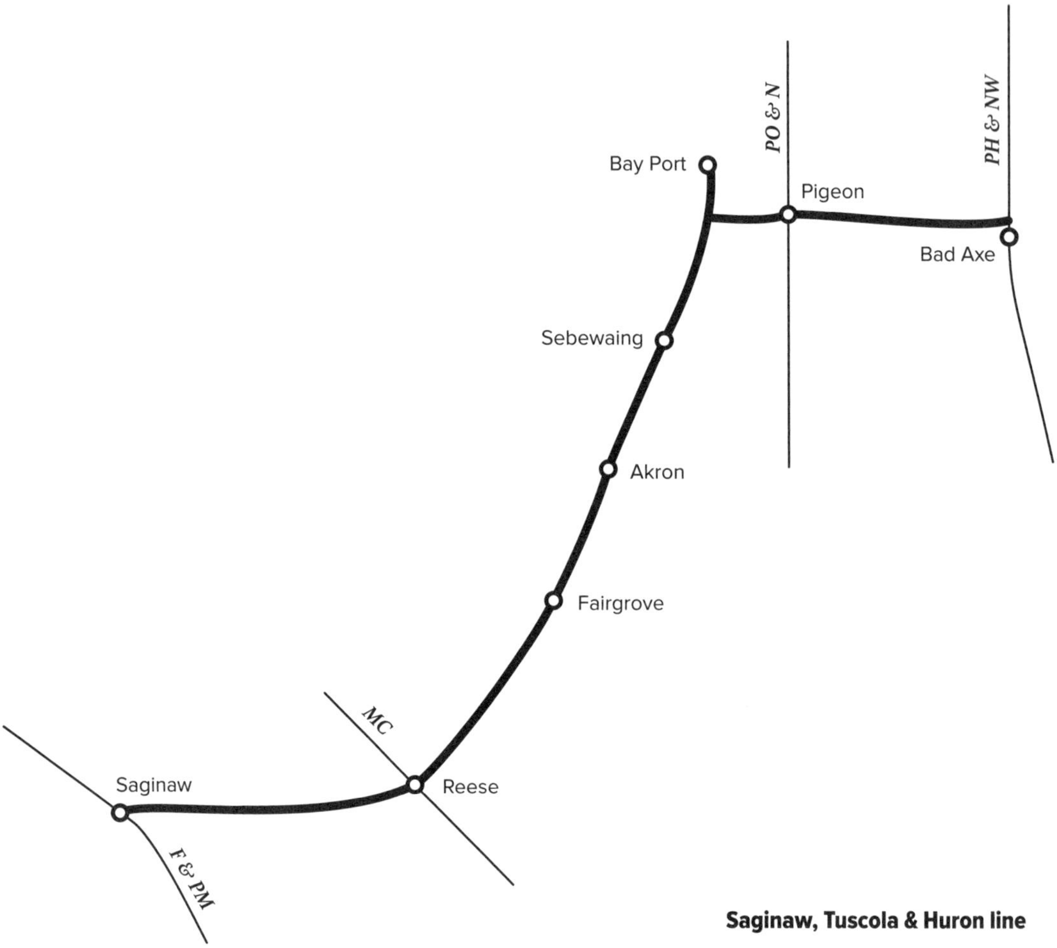

Saginaw, Tuscola & Huron line

(PH&NW). The route to Bad Axe also passed near a large limestone bed, and Webber worked to develop the quarry. The ST&H invested some money in both the hotel and the quarry and completed the line into Bad Axe on 1 July 1886. The connection with the PH&NW in Bad Axe was a half-mile north of that road's station. By 1896 limestone shipments from the Bay Port quarry and coal from the mines along the line made up nearly half of the freight tonnage of the road.[58]

Webber remained the road's president until the January 1900 merger of the controlling Flint & Pere Marquette into the new Pere Marquette Railroad. He was replaced by the Pere Marquette's general manager, Stanford T. Crapo, as the new S&TH president.[59] The road remained profitable through the 1900 merger.

The F&PM's forest products traffic dropped sharply in 1894 and 1895. Its freight revenues dropped 25 percent, and did not begin to recover until 1897, as shown in table 7. But President Crapo found one good prospect. In October 1893 Russell Alger's Detroit, Bay City & Alpena Railroad went into receivership. Alger decided he liked politics better than railroading and cut his ties to the company he had formed a decade earlier. Receiver Don M. Dickinson and New

Table 7. Revenue and operating statistics for Saginaw, Tuscola & Huron, 1882–1899

YEAR	MILES OF ROAD OWNED	PASSENGER REVENUE	NUMBER OF PASSENGERS	PASSENGER MILES (THOUS.)	FREIGHT REVENUE	FREIGHT TONS (THOUS.)	TONS MILES	OPERATING EXPENSE & TAXES	NET INCOME*
1882	37.1	$14,569	30,432	657	8,447	$9,981	226	$14,013	$10,145
1883	47.7	20,949	42,940	802	20,077	19,958	479	29,137	13,952
1884	49.2	17,334	34,123	666	23,067	24,944	759	34,707	7,690
1885	49.2	16,912	34,802	720	27,479	30,924	912	40,016	8,164
1886	66.6	24,843	47,339	1,026	32,087	34,653	1,207	46,980	13,362
1887	66.6	34,963	62,771	1,574	43,046	51,556	2,001	61,113	20,777
1888	66.6	37,600	69,697	1,744	51,148	66,984	2,331	79,538	12,878
1889	66.6	39,070	72,773	1,775	64,191	85,990	3,628	77,029	29,955
1890	66.6	40,998	70,376	1,511	57,469	72,002	2,742	75,825	26,759
1891	66.6	44,117	81,898	1,879	58,618	79,171	2,800	78,945	27,836
1892	66.6	50,129	111,493	2,792	68,387	103,883	3,447	87,229	36,545
1893	66.6	51,066	117,241	3,215	68,459	107,126	3,625	87,255	38,474
1894	66.6	41,102	63,602	2,048	71,216	131,977	4,528	84,806	33,793
1895	66.6	37,771	54,575	1,516	70,204	114,642	3,646	89,247	24,924
1896	66.6	35,828	61,884	1,653	68,351	95,266	3,542	91,566	19,137
1897	66.6	38,070	73,191	1,882	68,391	98,308	3,860	90,485	23,267
1898	66.6	43,326	84,077	2,128	88,116	134,474	5,192	105,805	33,424
1899	66.6	51,281	102,535	2,733	83,981	132,563	4,573	107,108	35,916

Source: Data from Michigan Railroad Commission, *Annual Reports*.
* Net income is passenger revenue, freight revenue, and miscellaneous revenue, less operating expense.

York railroad reorganizer Charles H. Coster formed the Detroit & Mackinac (D&M) late in 1894 to buy Alger's road, and decided to extend the road south along the Lake Huron shore into Bay City. About 1896 Coster brought in James D. Hawks from the Michigan Central to manage the road, and on 20 September 1896 Hawks completed the new line into Bay City. It appears that Coster or Hawks had contacted President Crapo, who saw potential benefits for his road. During 1896 the F&PM and the D&M jointly built a new bridge across the Saginaw River in Bay City. Sometime between 1890 and 1895 the F&PM line that touched the Saginaw River north of the F&PM Bay City station was extended to reach the new bridge at a point named Foss.[60]

On 17 December 1891 Crapo stopped running his passenger trains from Saginaw through to Toledo over Lake Shore & Michigan Southern (LS&MS) tracks. Freight cars continued to be interchanged to LS&MS for movement to Toledo, but passengers now had to change to LS&MS trains at Monroe or Michigan Central trains at Detroit. Having lost his access to Toledo, Crapo organized the Monroe & Toledo Railway on 28 March 1893 to build a line from his tracks on the north side of Monroe into Toledo. The 15.2-mile line was completed from Monroe to Alexis, on the north side of Toledo, on 15 November 1896. He announced that he had made arrangements with the Ann Arbor Railroad to use its tracks from Alexis to its Toledo station on Cherry Street. The new line allowed Crapo to move both passengers and freight directly to connecting railroads in Toledo and to bypass the LS&MS. President Crapo said the new connection with the D&M

Table 8. Costs, equipment, capitalization for Saginaw, Tuscola & Huron, 1882–1899

YEAR	MILES	COST OF ROAD	COST OF EQUIPMENT	NUMBER ENGINES CARS	NUMBER FREIGHT CARS	NUMBER PASSENGERS (THOUS.)	NUMBER EMPLOYEES	COMMON STOCK (THOUS.)	TOTAL DEBT (THOUS.)
1882	37.1	$295,981	$65,679	3	59	9	45	105	$261
1883	47.7	342,495	65,890	3	59	8	45	109	316
1884	49.2	383,591	79,477	5	84	13	49	109	371
1885	49.2	394,029	85,641	5	127	10	48	109	512
1886	66.6	511,295	85,945	5	127	10	67	122	532
1887	66.6	519,460	104,120	8	194	10	73	123	576
1888	66.6	518,114	108,541	8	215	9	79	123	604
1889	66.6	523,544	110,069	8	235	12	81	123	642
1890	66.6	524,355	109,784	7	220	15	96	123	671
1891	66.6	702,299	202,030	10	252	16	86	124	947
1892	66.6	703,913	193,643	9	196	11	74	124	983
1893	66.6	725,757	208,763	9	173	16	104	124	1,105
1894	66.6	730,533	209,832	9	173	15	111	124	1,136
1895	66.6	746,191	212,639	9	170	16	157	124	1,187
1896	66.6	760,574	219,889	10	173	16	97	124	1,263
1897	66.6	763,395	219,889	10	172	16	112	124	1,319
1898	66.6	773,565	219,889	10	172	16	127	124	1,396
1899	66.6	776,397	219,889	10	208	16	122	124	1,446

Source: Data from Michigan Railroad Commission, *Annual Reports*.
Note: No dividends were paid.

"is now bringing to us a substantial addition of traffic." Of the Toledo extension he wrote that the "increase of traffic which thus far has come to this company by means of this construction has been exceedingly gratifying and is demonstrating the wisdom of the expenditure."[61]

The need to add still more revenue forced Crapo to find a way to increase the traffic crossing Lake Michigan from Wisconsin. The F&PM had moved passengers and freight in steamships from Ludington since 1875, and Crapo watched the success of the railroad car ferry at the Straits of Mackinac. In 1895 he ordered his road's first car ferry, *Pere Marquette*, with a capacity to move thirty railcars. It went into revenue service in February 1897, sailing between Ludington and Manitowoc, Wisconsin. Crapo expected the ferry to make two round trips a day. In the 1896 annual report Crapo wrote that he anticipated no further extensions of the line. Between the terminals in Wisconsin and those in Detroit, Port Huron, and Toledo, "The Flint & Pere Marquette is advantageously situated for local and through traffic." All that was needed was for business activity to improve.[62]

During 1897 President Crapo prepared to widen the narrow-gauge lines between Port Huron and Grindstone City and the branch from Palms to Harbor Beach. The actual widening was completed on 17 July 1898. Only the line between Tappan and Almont remained narrow gauge. Crapo remarked that "it is believed the character of the business along the line warrants the proposed improvement, and that economies of operation and increase of traffic will abundantly meet the outlay involved in the change.[63]

Early in 1899 William Crapo and Nathaniel Thayer began serious discussions about a merger of their three railroads: Flint & Pere Marquette, Chicago & West Michigan, and Detroit, Grand Rapids & Western. A merger plan was put forward on 20 May 1899 and a final agreement was signed in December 1899. The new Pere Marquette Railroad Company was incorporated on 1 November 1899, combining the three roads, and began operations effective 1 January 1900.

CHAPTER 2

The Detroit, Lansing & Northern and Its Predecessors

The Detroit, Lansing & Northern Rail Road was one of the three railroad companies that came together to form the Pere Marquette system. By building and securing control of a number of shorter lines, the DL&N assembled a system that began near Detroit and extended westward toward Lansing, then northwesterly to Ionia, Greenville, and Howard City. Through a confusing sequence of fits and starts, by dreamers and schemers, the system to haul lumber was brought together.

Ionia & Lansing

The Ionia and Lansing Railroad Company (I&L) was the first of the companies that made up the Detroit, Lansing & Northern. The Detroit & Milwaukee Railway (later the Grand Trunk Western) had been built into Ionia from Detroit in 1857 and was completed to Lake Michigan at Grand Haven in 1858. A group of businessmen, most of them from Ionia and joined by a few from Portland and Eagle, wanted to link their town with the new state capital at Lansing. A new rail line had been built from Owosso to Lansing in 1863, and an extension from Jackson to Lansing was completed in December 1865. The new I&L line would break the D&M's monopoly on Ionia traffic and its ability to charge freight rates that many considered too high. The Ionia & Lansing was formed on 13 November 1865 to build the 34-mile line from Lansing to Ionia. Hampton Rich, a successful Ionia merchant for nearly thirty years, was named the road's first president. He persuaded the state legislature to pass a bill that allowed townships along the line to issue bonds to raise money to build the railroad. The bonds raised about $100,000. But

Hampton Rich. He served as the first and only president of the Ionia & Lansing.

FROM FINDAGRAVE.

Rich's name and local enthusiasm failed to raise enough money, and two more years passed before serious construction could start. An 1869 bond issue raised $770,000, only 42 percent of its face value. The road issued a second bond issue of $300,000, and that netted only 50 percent of its face value. The interest rate on both bonds was 8 percent, but considering the discount made, the interest yield to the buyer was at least 16 percent.[1]

One county historian records that James Turner, an affluent Lansing entrepreneur, was at some time a director and treasurer of the I&L after its organization. Turner is reported to have been associated earlier with a Howell-to-Lansing plank road and with the builders of the Lansing & Jackson and the Jackson, Lansing & Saginaw Railroads that built the line between Jackson and Bay City. Turner is given credit for persuading James F. Joy and the Michigan Central Railroad to assist in building the I&L in 1868. Turner was the contractor that built the first part of the I&L.[2]

The I&L used the tracks of the Jackson, Lansing & Saginaw Railroad in Lansing from Michigan Avenue to North Lansing at Grand River Avenue. With a ready-made line to downtown

196 **IONIA AND LANSING RAILROAD.**

HAMPTON RICH, President and Treasurer. | E. H. LEAMING, Supt. and Chief Engineer.
CHARLES BORLAND, Vice-President. | R. J. BRISCOE, Asst. Supt.
A. F. BELL, Sec'y and Attorney. | J. M. Turner, Cashier.

Leave. May, 1870. **Arrive.**

Exs.	Mix	Mls	STATIONS.	Mls	Exs.	Mix
P. M.	A. M.				A. M.	P. M.
4 25	8 10	0	lve. **Lansing** .ar	37	10 15	6 20
4 30	8 15	1	...N. Lansing...	36	10 10	6 15
4 52	9 53	8	..... Delta......	29	9 48	5 40
4 59	9 07	10	...Daniells....	27	9 40	5 27
5 10	9 27	13	..Grand Ledge..	24	9 27	5 10
5 27	9 50	17	.....Eagle......	20	9 10	4 45
5 45	10 15	21	.....Danby.....	16	8 53	4 20
5 58	10 35	24	....Portland....	13	8 40	4 00
6 15	11 05	28	.....Orange	9	8 23	3 30
6 33	11 35	32	.....Lyons.....	5	8 05	3 00
7 00	12 10	37	.....**Ionia**[2]....	0	7 40	2 20
P. M.	P. M.		ARRIVE] [LEAVE		A. M.	P. M.

CONNECTIONS.
[1] At Lansing, with trains on the Jackson' Lansing and Saginaw Railroad for the North, South, East and West.
[2] At Ionia with Detroit and Milwaukee Railroad for Grand Rapids, Grand Haven, Muskegon, &c.; also, with stages for the Northwest.

N. B. Standard of time, Jackson time 15 minutes faster than Chicago.

Ionia and Lansing 1870 schedule. This 1870 schedule shows service just months after the road was completed.

FROM AUTHOR'S COLLECTION.

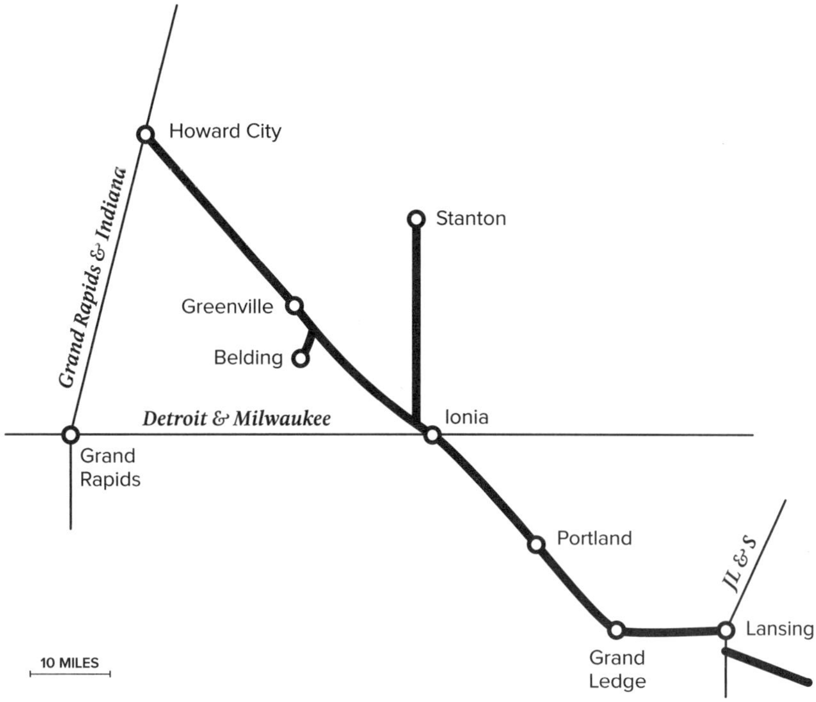

The Detroit, Lansing & Lake Michigan lines from Lansing to Howard City in between 1869 and 1871 with two branches and major connecting roads

Lansing, Rich began building from the connection at Grand River Avenue. He completed the first 23 miles from Lansing to Portland on 18 November 1869, and another 14 miles to Ionia in December. Soon after, the company decided to extend its line and completed new articles of incorporation on 13 January 1869 that authorized the road to own a 125-mile line between Lansing and the mouth of the Pentwater River. Within a year grading was underway from Ionia toward Greenville, and officials predicted it would be complete by midwinter 1869–1870. One historian stated that the road was going to be built to Muskegon, with Lake Michigan ships sailing to Wisconsin. The extension to Greenville was put in service in September 1870, a distance of 55.7 miles from North Lansing.[3]

Detroit, Howell & Lansing

Although the line between Detroit and Lansing was formed before the I&L, it was the second part to be built. In 1832, when Michigan was still a territory, the federal government had ordered that a road be established between Detroit and the mouth of the Grand River on Lake Michigan, the future site of Grand Haven. The road followed an Indian trail. Some improvement

Theodatus T. Lyon. He was the president of the Detroit, Howell & Lansing and its predecessors, the Detroit & Howell and the Howell & Lansing.
FROM FINDAGRAVE.

was made out of Detroit, but west of Brighton, 30 miles out, little work was done. By the 1840s a new type of roadway—the plank road—was promoted as the much better way to connect cities. The Michigan legislature passed a general plank road law in 1848 to encourage building them and allowed the owners to charge users a toll. Wood planks laid on a log and timber bed allowed faster smoother travel than dirt roads. Mark Twain once wrote about his trip on the Kalamazoo–Grand Rapids plank road, "It would have been good if some unconscionable scoundrel had not now and then dropped a plank across it." In 1848 a company was formed to build a plank road from Detroit to Howell, which it completed in 1850, and by 1852 another company extended it from Howell to Lansing. Stagecoaches could move easily between Detroit and the new state capital at Lansing. But the wooden planks decayed rapidly and eventually the best replacement was solid earth grading.[4]

The oldest part of the Detroit, Lansing & Northern was formed at a meeting held at New Hudson, a hamlet a few miles north of Brighton. The Detroit and Howell Railroad Company (D&H) was formed on 17 June 1864, the night of the meeting. Capitalized at $400,000, it planned to build a 48-mile rail line between Detroit and Howell. Theodatus T. Lyon of Plymouth was named president of the new company, but the spark plug behind the venture appears to have been the company's treasurer, William F. McPherson of Howell. Lyon was a successful nurseryman and served as president of the Michigan State Horticultural Society and vice president of the American Horticultural Society. At age twenty-one in 1850 McPherson had emigrated from Scotland to Howell and set up in business as a merchant. As the railroad's treasurer he had the hardest work—to collect money from reluctant stock subscribers.[5]

Within two years the company stock subscriptions and pledges brought in $200,000, enough that President Lyon decided to start building. Surveying for the route started in 1866 and grading started the next year. By 1868 the money ran out. The railroad, anticipating the difficulty of raising adequate funds, went to Lansing to seek help. In 1864 the state legislature, urged by railroads in need of financial help, obliged with legislation that authorized cities and

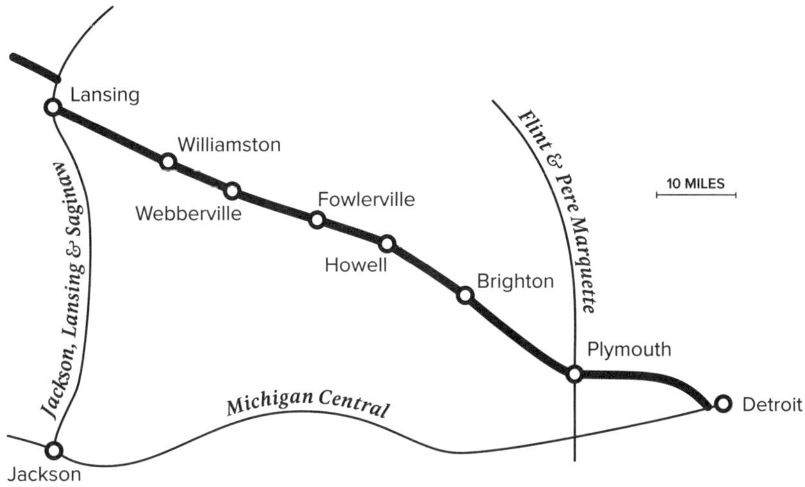

The Detroit, Lansing & Lake Michigan line from Detroit to Lansing as built in 1871, with major connecting roads

townships to provide financial assistance. Most often this was in the form of municipal bonds guaranteed by the taxpayers. Brighton Township responded with $11,097. Salem Township voters approved bonds, but the township board refused to issue them. The railroad then sued the township to force it to issue the bonds, and the case went to the Michigan Supreme Court in 1870. After an eight-day hearing the court ruled that such bonds violated a provision in the state constitution establishing that "the credit of the state shall not be granted to, or in aid of, a person, association, or corporation." The Salem Township decision killed the possibility of any added municipal financing for the Detroit & Howell. The Brighton Township bonds did remain valid since they were issued before the court's decision.[6]

To improve its prospects the promoters of the Detroit & Howell formed an extension railroad, the Howell and Lansing Rail Road Company (H&L). This new company was to build a 33-mile line extending from Howell to Lansing, and was organized on 23 June 1868. Theodatus Lyon was made president of this road as well. It appears that the company did very little toward building its line before Lyon combined his two railroads, the Detroit & Howell and the Howell & Lansing, into a new company named the Detroit, Howell and Lansing Railroad Company (DH&L) on 29 March 1870.[7]

To strengthen the financing Lyon and William McPherson brought in some new powerful players. These included Alvin N. Hart, a Lansing merchant, real estate dealer, politician, and railroad promoter; William A. Howard of Grand Rapids, an attorney, politician, and land agent for the Grand Rapids & Indiana Railroad; Merrill I. Mills and William H. Tefft, owners of the Detroit Stove Works; Harvey King, a Detroit streetcar line owner; and William B. Wesson, a real estate dealer, bank president, and railroad promoter from Detroit. Later, in September 1870, James F. Joy and "other capitalists" bought the franchise rights of the DH&L. According

James F. Joy. With a degree from Dartmouth College, he moved to Detroit in 1836 as an attorney. He became one of the founders of the Michigan Central Railroad, continued to expand his involvements, and eventually became president of the MC as well as several predecessors of the Pere Marquette.
FROM CLARENCE M. BURTON, *THE CITY OF DETROIT, MICHIGAN, 1701–1922* (DETROIT: S. J. CLARKE PUBL. CO., 1922.).

to one historian the road was a gift to Joy in repayment for the work he had done, to the value of "nearly a quarter million dollars." While it is unclear what infusion of cash may have come from the new investors, the company accomplished little more than grading of some part of its line during its five-year life.[8]

Joy had become the president of the Michigan Central Railroad (MC) in 1867. As an attorney in Detroit in 1846 he was one of the organizers of the MC, and as a politician he encouraged the state to sell its "Central" railroad line to the MC. During his years as the MC's attorney Joy developed new skills as a railroad builder and then as the manager of the Burlington & Missouri River Railroad. About 1870 Joy began expanding the MC by helping companies that were building lines that connected to the MC and would feed it traffic. Joy bought the new road's bonds, and when the line was built he added it to the MC family by leasing it. Joy's aggressiveness developed his reputation as a "railroad baron."

Detroit, Lansing & Lake Michigan

On 16 March 1871 James F. Joy expanded his involvement by incorporating the Detroit, Lansing and Lake Michigan Railroad Company (DL&LM). A year earlier Joy had invested in the Chicago & Michigan Lake Shore road, another Pere Marquette predecessor discussed later, and became its president. Now the Detroit, Howell & Lansing road presented Joy with another opportunity. Joy had the new DL&LM, capitalized at a robust $2 million, consolidate the Detroit, Howell & Lansing and the Ionia & Lansing, in a move that gave it a franchise for a line that would extend from Detroit, through Lansing, Ionia and Greenville, to Lake Michigan. Joy named Hiram H. Smith of Jackson as president of the DL&LM. Smith had worked with Joy on a number of other MC ventures, most importantly in building new lines. Joy brought Hampton Rich and Robert B. Smith over from the Ionia & Lansing; William H. Tefft and William B. Wesson from the Detroit, Howell & Lansing; the trusted John W. Brooks of the MC; and a group of four Boston investors. This group included Nathaniel Thayer, a vice president of the MC, William F. Weld, an 1846

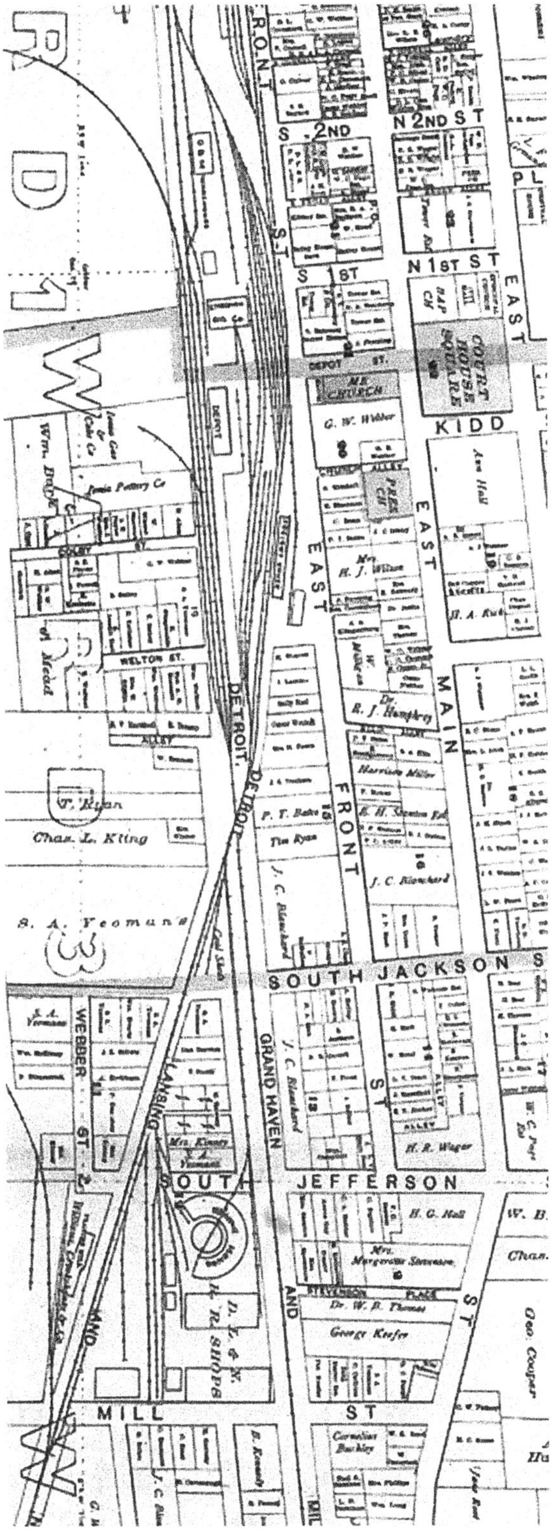

investor in the MC, George O. Shattuck, and John A. Burnham. As local directors left the board, they were replaced: in 1872 by Charles L. Young, Charles Merriam in 1873, and Charles Francis Adams Jr., the great-grandson of President John Adams, in 1874.[9]

On 16 March 1875 the Detroit, Lansing & Lake Michigan acquired the DH&L When the DL&LM was formed, the Ionia road had been completed between Lansing and Greenville; however, the Howell road was only partly graded between Detroit and Lansing. Joy and Smith aggressively pushed track-laying. By 30 June 1871 the road was finished from Plymouth to a connection with the MC at West Detroit. From West Detroit DL&LM trains ran over MC rails into its Third Street depot. This was a change from Theodatus Lyon's original plan to extend the line east to the vicinity of Fullerton and Grand River Roads, then to run southeast on Grand River to a station on Fourth Street. On 31 July the sections between Plymouth and Brighton and from Lansing to Williamston were completed, and on 31 August the two separated parts were linked up at Fowlerville by a line from Williamston to Brighton. The new line was 82.2 miles long. Ionia County historian Elam E. Branch wrote that Fowlerville had a "great gathering" complete with an orator. He added that "the general rejoicing was unbounded."

Ionia. This 1891 map show the two east-west rail lines through Ionia and the Detroit, Lansing & Northern shops facility just east of the two roads crossing.

FROM D. C. CRAWFORD, *ATLAS OF IONIA COUNTY* (NEW YORK: J. B. BEERS & CO., 1891).

Ionia. The Detroit, Lansing & Northern station in Ionia was built in 1874. The second story had offices for railroad officials. Postcard.

FROM AUTHOR'S COLLECTION.

The first excursion train into Howell, before the formal opening, was met with "something of an ovation," according to a *Detroit Post* reporter. "An immense concourse of people" and a cannon salute greeted the train as it moved to the depot. There were cheers "and waving of handkerchiefs" and ladies giving out bouquets. James F. Joy rode the train, and "the people called on Mr. Joy for a speech, but he did not see fit to respond."[10]

Pushing on, Joy finished the DL&LM west into Gowen, then called Kaywoods, on 30 September 1871 and by the end of November into Howard City, 164 miles from Detroit. Here it connected with the newly built Grand Rapids & Indiana Railroad that was then being built from Grand Rapids north to Petoskey, and ultimately to the Straits of Mackinac. The DL&LM gained an important source of traffic from the GR&I: forest products from the north Michigan woods. These accounted for about half of the line's freight revenues—nearly $300,000.[11]

With his line complete, Joy had to face problems of financial weakness. He had issued $6.06 million in mortgage bonds at 8 percent interest—a charge of $484,800 per year. As table 9 shows, net income covered barely half of the interest expense. The results of operations were not promising, and were made worse by the Financial Panic of 1873. Forest products accounted for more than half of the road's freight tonnage, and this traffic was hit hard by the panic. Another more startling statistic came from the annual report: as of 1 April 1873 the road had cost $6,358,500 to build and equip, but the estimated value of the whole property was only $4,137,545.[12]

Table 9. Detroit, Lansing & Lake Michigan revenues, expenses, and net income, 1871–1876

YEAR	MILES OF ROAD	PASSENGER REVENUE	PASSENGERS CARRIED	FREIGHT & OTHER	TONS CARRIED	OPERATING EXPENSE & TAXES	NET INCOME
1871	164	$90,192	87,152	$147,757	42,233*	$200,097	$37,852
1872	189	219,114	–	363,507	166,663	505,321†	
1873	189	183,580	269,523	385,635	212,540	331,183	238,032
1874	187	222,393	281,817	585,304	269,267	425,942	316,290
1875	187	215,595	261,406	524,109	261,535	528,807	210,897
1876	187	220,393	254,434	511,993	264,235	531,755	211,333

Source: Data from railroad annual reports and Michigan Railroad Commission, *Annual Reports*.
* Amount for last four months of 1871.
† Amount for fifteen months to 1 April 1873.

Table 10. Freight traffic statistics for Detroit, Lansing & Lake Michigan, 1872–1876

YEAR	REVENUE TONS (THOUS.)	LUMBER TONS (THOUS.)	% OF ALL TONS	AGRICULTURAL PRODUCTS TONS (THOUS.)	% OF ALL TONS	MANUFACTURES TONS (THOUS.)	% OF ALL TONS	MERCHANDISE TONS (THOUS.)	% OF ALL TONS
1872	166.1	93.1	56.1	40.1	24.1	0.5	0.3	30.5	18.4
1873	212.5	136.5	64.2	36.3	17.1	2.3	1.1	32.3	15.2
1874	269.3	166.7	61.9	64.1	23.8	2.7	1.0	28.8	10.7
1875	261.5	163.0	62.3	59.6	22.8	3.9	1.6	27.2	10.4
1876	264.2	159.8	59.7	57.2	21.7	1.8	0.7	38.9	14.7

Source: Data from Michigan Railroad Commission.

In 1872 Joy added two small roads to his DL&LM. A group of Ionia businessmen had formed the Ionia and Stanton Railroad Company (I&S) on 29 December 1869. It proposed to build a line from Ionia north 22 miles to Stanton; Osmond Tower was its president. Before it was able to lay any tracks it was replaced by a new company, the Ionia, Stanton and Northern Rail Road Company (IS&N), which was incorporated on 16 July 1872.[13] It had the more ambitious goal of a 62-mile line from 3 miles north of Ionia, through Sheridan and Stanton, to Chippewa in Osceola County. Joy and Hiram Smith were behind this company, but they did bring in some of the organizers of the earlier Ionia & Stanton line. Presumably construction was underway when the DL&LM merged the company on 1 October 1872. The 20-mile line between Haynor, 4 miles north of Ionia on the original I&L line, and Stanton was completed in February 1873.[14]

The second road Joy added was the family-owned Patterson Rail Road Company. About 1860 Hiram H. Belding had begun selling silk products house-to-house in his namesake village. One of the family's four factories was built in Belding and eventually became its largest mill. On 21 September 1870 Hiram was among the incorporators of the company that proposed to build a 2-mile line from the Patterson Mill in Belding to a connection with the I&L northeast of the village at Kiddville. The record is unclear, but apparently the Belding family made Joy and Smith a gift of their private railroad and donated it in an unfinished condition on 18 July 1872.[15]

DL&LM president Hiram H. Smith stepped down in 1873 and James F. Joy took his place. To shore up affairs, Joy invited some more New Englanders to the DL&LM board, possibly to strengthen the balance sheet. Of the resulting board, seven of the nine directors lived in Boston, with only James F. Joy and John W. Brooks living in Michigan. A recovery in lumber traffic still did not provide enough revenue to allow the company to pay its interest charges. By 1875 affairs had not improved and the company defaulted on a payment of interest on its bonds. Trustees for the bondholders took over to arrange a reorganization of the DL&LM.[16]

But the DL&LM was among the smaller of Joy's problems. His flagship Michigan Central Railroad paid a stock dividend in 1873 but was not able to pay its cash dividend. The years 1874 and 1875 were even worse financially. The vultures began to circle. The Vanderbilt family began buying MC stock, very likely to keep the MC from regaining its strength as a competitor to their Lake Shore & Michigan Southern. The proverbial handwriting was on the wall. On 31 July 1876 Joy put the DL&LM into receivership. This move preserved the company he had nurtured and also provided for a reorganization on a basis that might be friendly enough put the road on a better financial footing. When the receiver took over, the DL&LM had $1,680,000 in common stock issued, no preferred stock issued, $6,054,000 in bonds outstanding, all of them issued by the Ionia & Lansing as first mortgage bonds totaling $4,695,000, and a second mortgage bond of $1,359,000. The interest cost, at 8 percent, was $488,960 per year. In addition the DL&LM built up a total of $907,180 in unpaid interest on its debt. The receiver sold the DL&LM to a new company, the Detroit, Lansing & Northern, on 11 December 1876.[17]

Detroit, Lansing & Northern—Detroit, Grand Rapids & Western

The receivership began on 31 July 1876, forced in part by the effects of the Panic of 1873 and more so by the weight of the DL&LM's debt. The DL&LM interest about equaled the annual net income from operations—and had no prospects for improving this situation. The receiver had to find a way to reduce the company's annual interest cost and deal with the accumulated unpair interest. To reorganize the road Joy formed The Detroit, Lansing & Northern Rail Road Company (DL&N), incorporated on 21 December 1876, and on 31 December it took ownership of the DL&LM property.[18]

The DL&N's common stock issue was increased from the DL&LM's $1,680,000 to $1,825,617, but what use was made of the increase is not clear. The three smallest bond issues totaled $901,000, at 8 percent interest, and were assumed by the DL&N without change. The remainder of the bonds and the accumulated unpaid interest was refinanced by a new issue of $2,503,380 in preferred stock and a new 7 percent 30-year bond issue of $1,975,000. These changes reduced the annual interest charge to $210,330—a far more manageable amount. The preferred stock also had a noncumulative 7 percent dividend, but it was payable only if the company made a profit. The net loss because of unpaid interest was erased as part of the reorganization, allowing the DL&N to start with a clean financial slate. Also, the franchise rights it inherited from

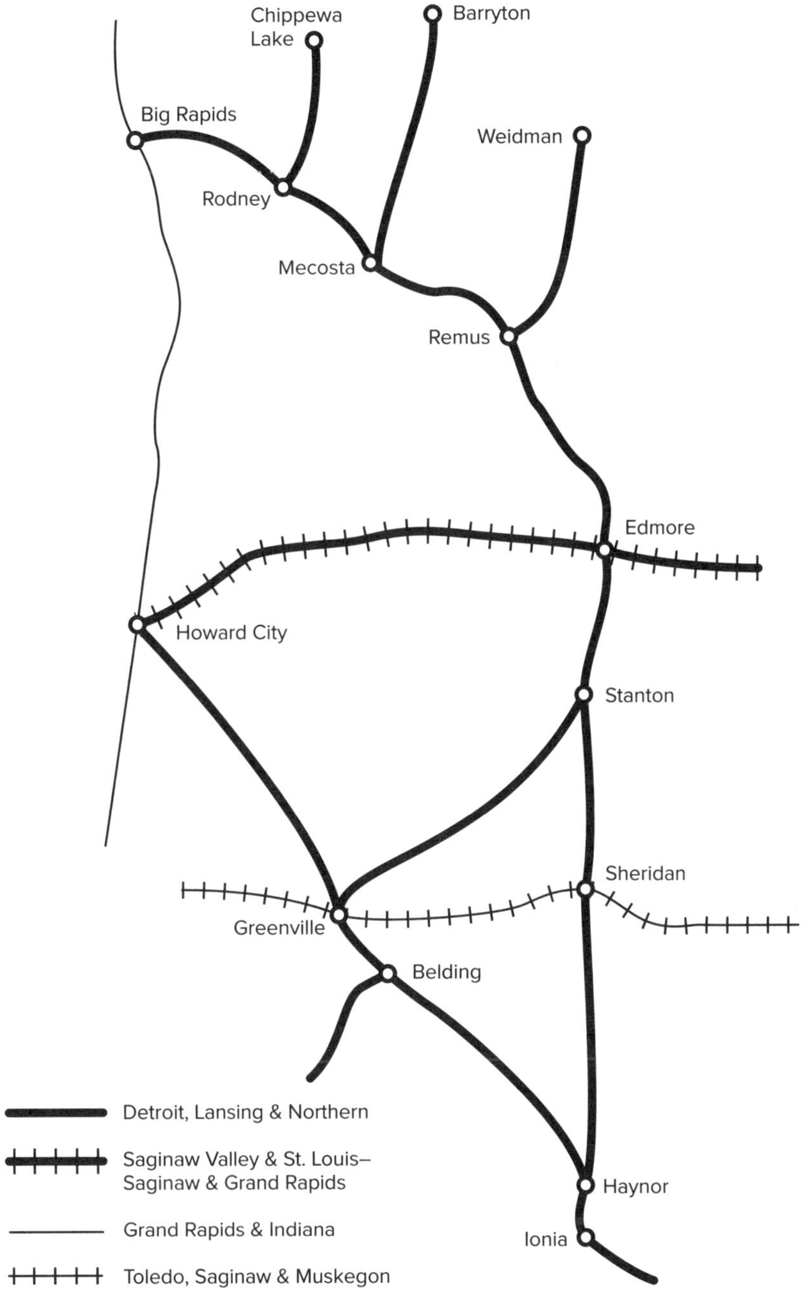

Ionia–Big Rapids. In 1873 the Detroit, Lansing & Northern built from Greenville to Stanton, and between 1878 and 1880 it extended farther north from Stanton to Big Rapids as well as building three branches east of Big Rapids.

Edmore. In 1885 the Detroit, Lansing & Northern built this unusual brick station at the crossing of the Ionia–Big Rapids line (track in foreground) and the DL&N's Saginaw & Western line. The eastbound standing train has come from Howard City. The second story of the station had the official's offices.
FROM MARK WORRALL COLLECTION.

the DL&LM were unchanged: a line from Detroit, through Lansing, Ionia, and Howard City, to Lake Michigan, and a branch from Ionia to Stanton.[19]

In 1877 President Joy decided the DL&N should be extended farther north to tap more forestlands. By January 1878 he built a 4.4-mile extension from Stanton to McBride, by September another 3.6 miles from McBride to Edmore, and in January 1879 another 9.4 miles from Edmore to Blanchard. The extension cost $124,000 to build. At Edmore the new line crossed the Chicago, Saginaw & Canada line. On 30 October 1879 the DL&N corporate articles were then amended to authorize building a branch to Big Rapids. Work toward Big Rapids had already started in May 1879. Sinkholes caused delays, but the tracks were completed into Big Rapids on 4 July 1880. It reached the sawmills on the east side of the Muskegon River and connected with the Grand Rapids & Indiana.[20]

During 1878 Joy resigned as president of the DL&N. A year earlier he had left the presidency of the Michigan Central, a road he had helped establish more than thirty years earlier. The forces at work that caused his departure can only be assumed. Joy had built up the MC to the point it was a serious competitor to the Vanderbilt's Lake Shore & Michigan Southern and as well as an attractive prize for Jay Gould. Both wanted Joy's road. It appears that the MC's Boston owners were selling out and were being replaced by New Yorkers. Three Vanderbilt family members joined the MC board of directors in 1878, a signal that Joy was no longer wanted.[21]

The DL&N's Boston owners replaced Joy with one of their own. Alpheus Hardy had worked with Joy on railroads in Missouri and had served as president of the Burlington & Missouri

LEFT: Alpheus Hardy. A very wealthy New England investor, he was the Detroit, Lansing & Northern's president from 1878 until his death in 1887.
FROM ARTHUR S. HARDY, *LIFE AND LETTERS OF JOSEPH HARDY NEESIMA* (BOSTON: HOUGHTON MIFFLIN & CO., 1892).

RIGHT: John B. Mulliken. He moved to Detroit in 1875 to be general superintendent of the Detroit, Lansing & Northern. In 1884 he was made vice president of the DL&N and Chicago & West Michigan.
FROM TERRI MULLIKEN ALLEN.

River Railroad. With its corporate headquarters in Boston and the board meetings held there, Hardy had little need to come to Michigan. On the ground general manager John B. Mulliken worked out of an office in Detroit; Henry T. Thomas was an assistant superintendent stationed at Ionia. In 1879 the DL&N's owners bought most of the Saginaw Valley & St. Louis stock and took control of that road, as discussed subsequently. With the SV&SL came control of the Saginaw & Grand Rapids line between St. Louis and Alma. In December 1880 Thomas M. Fish joined the DL&N as general superintendent at Ionia, replacing Thomas. Fish came from the Chicago & North Western, where he last served as an assistant superintendent. In 1883 John J. McVean was promoted from division engineer to chief engineer; McVean had joined the DL&N in 1878.

In June 1883 the DL&N completed a 5.7-mile branch from Rodney to Chippewa Lake, off the recently built Big Rapids branch, at a cost of $35,843. This branch reached a supply of some 150 million feet of pine that was to move by rail. The road also completed a new complex of buildings for repair shops at Ionia that replaced an older and much smaller facility in front of the depot at a total cost of $137,862.[22]

Saginaw Valley & St. Louis

The earliest segment of the Detroit, Lansing & Northern was the Ionia & Lansing Railroad that ran along the far west side of a forested area north of Lansing that sprawled out of Gratiot County. The Pine River angled across the county, flowing toward the sawmills at Saginaw. Log

LEFT: Loton H. Eastman. He was the first president of the Saginaw Valley & St. Louis Railroad.
FROM FINDAGRAVE.

RIGHT: Ammi W. Wright. He came to Michigan in 1850 and made his headquarters in Saginaw. He was a large-scale lumberman and later an investor on the Mesabi iron range. He was an important promoter of the Saginaw Valley & St. Louis and several other railroads.
FROM FINDAGRAVE.

drives were an annual event in St. Louis, then the largest community in the county. In the early 1860s Gratiot County businessmen got up their hopes that the Amboy, Lansing & Traverse Bay Railroad, with its land grant, could be persuaded to build from Lansing directly north through St. Johns to Alma or St. Louis. Teamsters at St. Johns, located on the Detroit & Milwaukee Railroad, had a monopoly of the freighting over the muddy roads into Gratiot County and successfully opposed the Amboy road proposal.[23]

Among the construction projects undertaken by Saginaw millwright William F. Glasby was a plank road between Saginaw and St. Louis in 1868. He established several communities along his road, then built a number of sawmills as well as a hotel in Hemlock. Just a few years after he finished his road, local businessmen wanted to replace it with a railroad. To tap the center of Gratiot County the Saginaw Valley and St. Louis Railroad Company (SV&SL) was formed on 16 May 1871. It was to build a 34-mile line from East Saginaw, apparently through Saginaw City at the intersection of Washington and Farley Streets, to St. Louis. At that time East Saginaw was a separate city on the east side of the Saginaw River and Saginaw City was another on the west side of river; its Washington Street has been renamed Michigan Street. The largest sawmills in eastern Michigan were located on the east and west banks of the Saginaw River. A railroad that hauled lumber to the markets located in Saginaw would be an ideal substitute for driving logs down the longer Pine River. Loton H. Eastman, an East Saginaw sawmill owner and lumberman, was named the road's first president; Saginaw merchant George W. Morley its vice president; Saginaw merchant and future state governor David H. Jerome its secretary; and Saginaw lumberman and railroad promoter Ammi W. Wright its treasurer.[24]

David H. Jerome. Another lumberman from Saginaw who also served as president of the Saginaw Valley & St. Louis, he had extensive political interests and served as governor of Michigan in 1881 and 1882.

FROM FINDAGRAVE.

Thanks to Ammi Wright's financial support the rail line was built in short order. Frank Eastman, Loton Eastman's grandson, surveyed the rail route and kept the tracks close to the plank road. The land for the railroad was reasonably level, and no great amount of grading was required. Construction apparently started at St. Louis on 15 September 1872, with the 28.7-mile line put in service on 1 January 1873. Tracks extended from the Pine River in St. Louis east to the line of the Jackson, Lansing & Saginaw (JL&S) at Paines. When the railroad builders arrived at Paines they faced several obstacles. The original plans called for building a bridge over the Tittabawassee River, then buying land through Saginaw City up to the Saginaw River, then another bridge to reach East Saginaw. Practicality and economy very likely dictated that it was more prudent to use running rights over the JL&S road through Saginaw City north to a connection with the Flint & Pere Marquette that would allow it to reach East Saginaw. The company paid $40,000 for "joint and equal use in perpetuity" of the JL&S tracks. This allowed the SV&SL to be built with very little debt; in 1873 it had just a $446,000 first mortgage bond outstanding that was about equal to the cost of building the line. As was often the case with local projects, these bonds had to be discounted about 25 percent to be sold, and needed a further incentive of free shares of stock.[25]

In 1874 David H. Jerome replaced Loton Eastman as president of the company. The road, so conservatively financed, made a profit nearly every year. It came through the Panic of 1873 unscathed hauling little but forest products. On 22 July 1878 the company decided to expand by extending its main line from St. Louis to Grand Rapids, and to build a branch from St. Louis is Mt. Pleasant. Neither of these extensions was built. On 22 October 1878 the SV&SL's owners looked again at building a line from St. Louis to Grand Rapids and this time formed a separate company, the Saginaw and Grand Rapids Railroad Company (S&GR), to build it. That company built only a 3.7-mile line in March 1879, from St. Louis, along the south side of the Pine River into downtown Alma. The SV&SL owned all the stock of the S&GR and, apparently, held a lease of the road.[26]

President Alpheus Hardy and the Boston investors of the Detroit, Lansing & Northern bought most of the stock in the Saginaw Valley & St. Louis Railroad from its early local

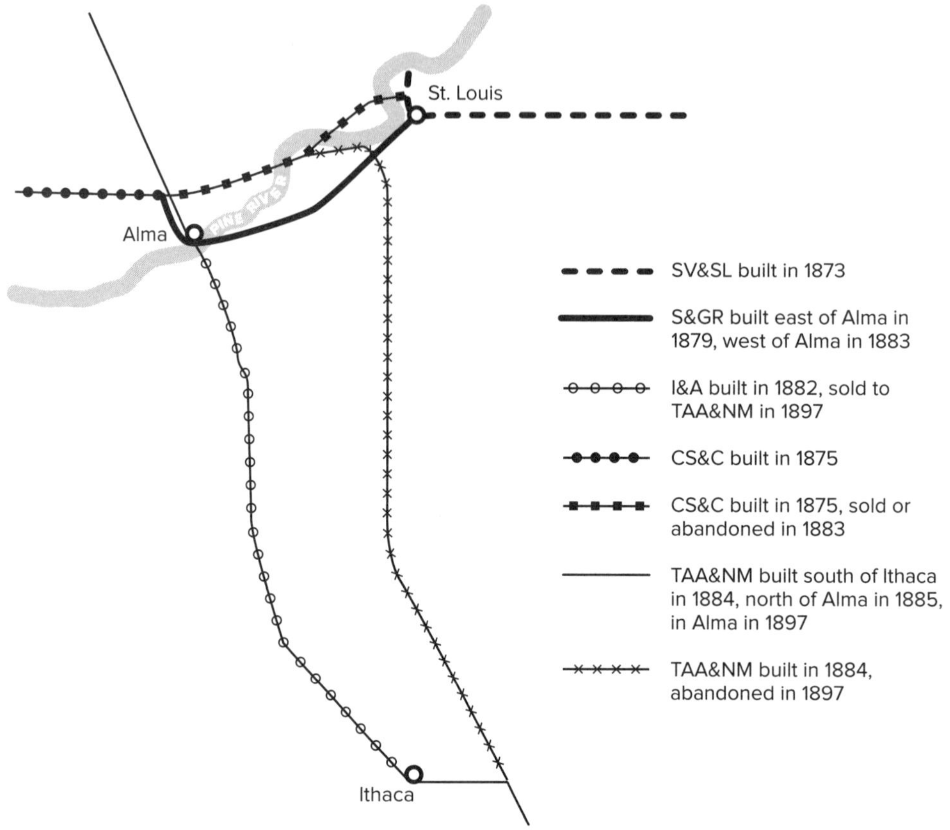

Alma and St. Louis. The Saginaw Valley & St. Louis line runs into St. Louis from the right. The Chicago, Saginaw &Canada/Saginaw & Western line runs from St. Louis to the left and skirts the north side of Alma. The SV&SL–Saginaw & Grand Rapids line from St. Louis to Alma is south of the river. The line of the Ithaca & Alma also is shown.

IMAGE BASED ON E. L. HAYES, *ATLAS OF GRATIOT COUNTY, MICHIGAN* (PHILADELPHIA: LAKE & HAYES, 1889).

investors. The new owners took over in 1879. With the SV&SL came control of the Saginaw & Grand Rapids Railroad that owned a line between St. Louis and Alma. These two lines gave Hardy access to the important sawmill city of Saginaw—an important destination point for hauling logs and timber. Ammi Wright, the last of the local investors, stayed on the board of directors until 1886. John B. Mulliken, general manager of the Detroit, Lansing & Northern, had the SV&SL added to his responsibilities. But the lumber traffic that provided profits in the early years began to shrink. In 1882 revenues and expenses still were favorable, but a drop in freight traffic in 1883 was followed by two more years of declines. Operating expenses increased by 17 percent in 1883, and net income no longer covered interest expense of $35,680. The company also had the added expense of $7,000 in dividends it guaranteed on the S&GR stock. The road's DL&N owners, who owned the majority of the debt, did allow affairs to continue without change.[27]

St. Louis. The early station at St. Louis before the trackside overhang was added to it.
FROM MICHIGAN RAILROAD HISTORY MUSEUM.

Table 11. Saginaw Valley & St. Louis revenues, expenses, and net income, 1872–1883

YEAR	MILES OF ROAD OWNED	PASSENGER REVENUE	NUMBER OF PASSENGERS	PASSENGER MILES	FREIGHT REVENUE	FREIGHT TONS	TON MILES & TAXES	OPERATING EXPENSE	NET INCOME
1872	25.7	$0			$1,885			$1,902	-$17
1873	28.7	29,336			105,257	61,875		54,811	79,810
1874	28.7	32,132	40,431	870,927	80,308	45,327	1,194,013	51,811	61,123
1875	28.7	30,107	38,366	861,933	59,741	37,437	1,029,221	36,166	53,682
1876	28.7	27,245	35,481	775,033	50,476	29,285	792,305	28,858	48,855
1877	28.7	20,855	35,897	908,039	58,610	35,964	1,042,655	30,965	57,519
1878	28.7	31,325	37,074	944,285	53,618	44,170	1,392,476	32,986	51,967
1879	35.6	34,973	48,088	1,076,976	43,282	32,708	969,018	51,997	25,866
1880	35.6	40,355	63,419	1,276,042	45,063	34,666	1,031,496	43,467	41,951
1881	38.6	43,734	67,938	1,389,836	54,749	35,707	1,003,961	54,150	46,189
1882	35.6	49,790	78,291	1,651,124	59,539	39,548	1,138,521	74,104	36,130
1883	35.6	54,138	88,272	1,795,052	54,882	40,783	1,120,297	87,292	22,438
1884	35.5	43,591	82,331	1,518,671	40,538	40,652	971,074	65,979	19,058
1885	35.5	36,441	68,835	1,186,620	38,500	39,341	884,467	52,697	22,909
1886	35.5	45,261	87,427	1,500,270	44,131	46,166	1,025,487	82,283	7,848
1887	35.5	50,360	95,898	1,694,057	48,519	60,247	1,261,090	76,566	23,218

Source: Data from Michigan Railroad Commission, *Annual Reports*.

Chicago, Saginaw & Canada and Saginaw & Western

While the Saginaw Valley & St Louis was being built east from St. Louis to Saginaw, another road started building toward St. Louis from the west. The Chicago, Saginaw and Canada Railroad Company (CS&C) was incorporated on 24 December 1872 to build a line from Grand Haven to the Detroit River at St. Clair. The road was to be capitalized at $4.2 million to reflect "Captain" Edward L. Craw's grand vision as president of the railroad. The compiler of the *Portrait and Biographical Album of Gratiot County, Michigan* considered Craw to be "an impecunious individual, but his zeal and desire to attain notoriety resulted in the building of the road mentioned [CS&C], which he not only undertook but virtually accomplished without having a dollar of money invested." When the road was organized, Craw printed up a bundle of $1,000 first mortgage gold bonds and took to the road to peddle them to investors.[28]

Craw came to St. Louis in about 1873 to meet with the management of the Saginaw Valley & St. Louis. Craw agreed that he would build a railroad west from St. Louis as a connecting line. With some money raised in Alma he began grading in 1874 out of St. Louis through the north side of Alma. Craw then sent a "Professor" McChesney to Europe to sell as many of the gold bonds as possible. McChesney's success lay more in a lifestyle that Craw would have admired rather than his ability to sell bonds. Next Craw was able to sell $100,000 of his bonds to General Daniel E. Sickles, of Civil War fame. In 1875, having gone through Sickle's money, Craw raised another $100,000 from Benjamin Richardson, a wealthy manufacturer of New York City, in a confusing and improbable mélange of bonds, loans, and bonuses. Richardson brought along several Philadelphians in 1875 that brought new vigor to the company.[29]

The money from Sickles and Richardson allowed Craw to start building, apparently in 1874. A historian recounts that the CS&C's first Alma station was of brick and built in part by the ladies of Alma by money raised by "entertainments and dances." In 1880 that station was destroyed by fire, but the bricks were reused in a church in St. Louis.[30] The road began operations in October 1875 from St. Louis as far Riverdale and on 1 December completed the 20 miles into Cedar Lake. During 1876 the revenue taken in did not cover the cost of operating the road, and a new president, William J. Kelly of Philadelphia, who had replaced Craw, decided the road should be put into receivership. David D. Erwin, a Muskegon lawyer, was named receiver on 20 November 1877. In 1877 Benjamin F. Ham replaced Kelly as the road's president. Ham was a New York City banker and stockbroker who had honed his skills while the treasurer of Credit Mobilier—the disgraced company that insiders used to enrich themselves as they built the Union Pacific Railroad. Receiver Erwin promptly leased the CS&C to John A. Elwell, a personal friend of CS&C investor Benjamin Richardson, who insisted on the lease. Elwell and Richardson had visited St. Louis in 1874 at the invitation of Edward Craw to look for investment opportunities. Elwell made St. Louis his home.[31]

Elwell and Receiver Erwin were able to build 3 miles of road from Cedar Lake to Edmore, completed on 1 October 1878, to provide a connection with the Detroit, Lansing & Northern. It completed another 12 miles to Lakeview on 1 August 1879.[32] Ham resigned the presidency in 1878 and General Sickles replaced him. Although he brought no business management experience

LEFT: Daniel E. Sickles. Civil War general Sickles served two years as president of the Chicago, Saginaw & Canada.

FROM WIKIPEDIA.

RIGHT: John A. Elwell. He was the manager of the Chicago, Saginaw & Canada from 1876 until 1883.

FROM *BIOGRAPHICAL MEMOIRS OF GRATIOT COUNTY, MICHIGAN* (CHICAGO: J. B. BEERS & CO., 1906).

Table 12. Chicago, Saginaw & Canada revenues, expenses, and net income, 1872–1883

YEAR	MILES OF ROAD OWNED	PASSENGER REVENUE	NUMBER OF PASSENGERS	PASSENGER MILES	FREIGHT REVENUE	FREIGHT TONS	TON MILES	OPERATING EXPENSE & TAXES	NET INCOME (LOSS)
1875*	20.0	$1,024	2,459	24,590	$1,139	n.a.	n.a.	$1,130	$1,033
1876	20.0	4,805	8,869	97,292	5,557	3,015	39,743	13,269	(2,907)
1877	20.0	7,348	14,310	146,958	10,044	12,746	201,821	15,325	2.067
1878	23.5	12,625	24,467	298,861	37,704	74,821	1,316,556	32,887	18,698
1879	38.0	22,756	47,254	489,786	38,152	59,061	1,154,792	41,383	19,526
1880	38.0	31,526	75,200	1,062,186	74,857	125,068	2,041,157	58,977	48,222
1881	38.0	35,931	83,323	1,047,828	64,638	69,036	1,139,157	49,975	51,490
1882	38.0	42,773	91,558	1,474,856	72,809	116,467	1,497,456	57,397	58,185

Source: Data from Michigan Railroad Commission, *Annual Reports*.
* Three months, October through December 1875.

to his position, his contacts with New York City money and politics very likely were thought to be valuable. Elwell's lease, Erwin's receivership, and Sickles's presidency all came to an end in 1883 when the CS&C was sold at foreclosure on 10 May to the Detroit, Lansing & Northern.[33]

Sickles's father had bought some of Craw's bonds, as had Richardson. Richardson's heirs and Sickles claimed they were due money from the proceeds of the foreclosure sale. The case finally was heard by the U.S. Supreme Court in 1889. Its decision gave Richardson nothing, while Sickles had to be satisfied with twenty-five cents on the dollar.[34]

Craw's thousand-dollar gold bonds had a second life. The Friends of the Grand Rapids

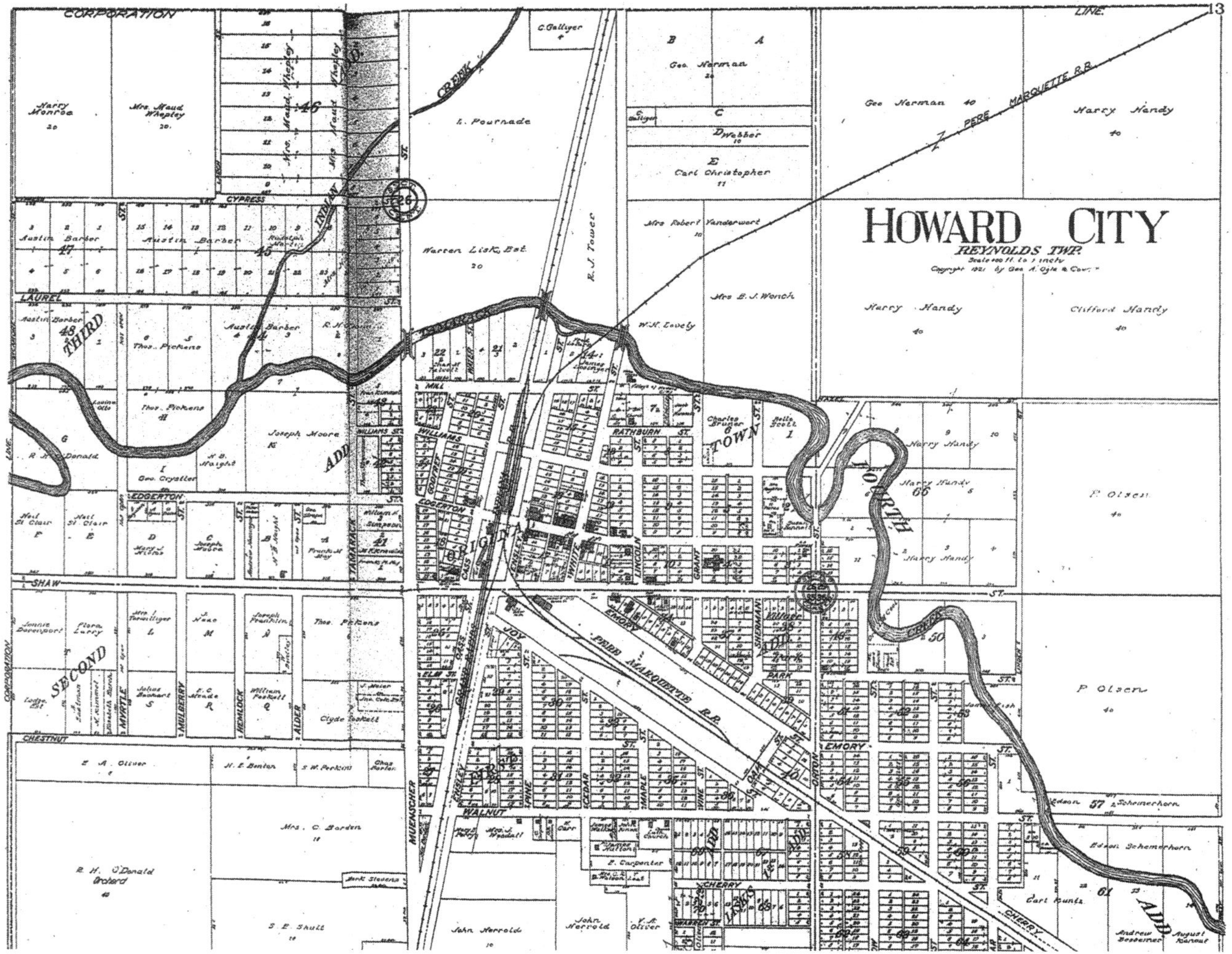

Howard City. The Detroit, Lansing & Lake Michigan line came in from the lower right in 1871, and the Saginaw & Western line came in from the top right in 1886. Both connected with the Grand Rapids & Indiana at its depot on Edgerton Street.

FROM *STANDARD ATLAS OF MONTCALM COUNTY, MICHIGAN* (CHICAGO: GEORGE A. OGLE & CO., 1921).

Museum discovered a cache of the bonds and began selling them as souvenirs in its shop. In 1992 it published a short history of the now-defunct railroad and packaged one of the bonds with the book. In the early 1990s two men saw there was money to be made by selling the bonds to speculators. Their bait was that the uncancelled bonds had a thousand-dollar face value payable in gold, plus the bonus of 7 percent interest compounded for 125 years, and a stake in the mortgaged railroad line that was pledged as security. Acting as a professional curator, one of them represented the bonds as having a value of nearly $100 million. They found holders willing to part with their souvenir bonds and plenty of "investors" to buy them. The investors paid as little as $40,000 and as much as $150,000 for the CS&C bonds. By 1996 CSX Corporation, then the owner of the rail line, began getting calls from buyers wanting to collect their bonanza. In 1998 the Securities and Exchange Commission filed injunctions against two men for fraudulent activities. The FBI and IRS tried to trace what happened to the nearly $12 million that passed through the bank accounts of the two. Through all of this professional curators continued to value the bonds as a historical document and having no other worth. The library put its inventory of bonds back into a city vault. The bond buyers were out their money.[35]

After years of financial improvidence the CS&C was sold at foreclosure and was reorganized as the Saginaw and Western Railroad Company (S&W). The new company was formed on 5 June 1883 and was wholly owned by the Detroit, Lansing & Northern, with Nathaniel Thayer as its president. Its 34.5-mile line extended from St. Louis to Lakeview with franchise rights to build to Howard City. The DL&N leased the Saginaw & Western for thirty years, effective 1 July 1883. The cost of the lease was a guarantee of the principal and 6 percent interest on $445,000 of S&W bonds as well as the 7 percent dividend on its stock, a total cost of $26,980 each year. As part of the lease the S&W line (originally built by the Chicago, Saginaw & Canada) from St. Louis to the north side of Alma was abandoned and the Saginaw & Grand Rapids line through downtown Alma substituted for it. As part of its plans Mulliken urged that the S&W be extended from Lakeview to Howard City. By using the Grand Rapids & Indiana south of that point the DL&N would gain a through route between Saginaw and Grand Rapids. This would allow the DL&N to "control a good share of the valuable traffic between those points, and, at the same time, by giving better facilities for communication, stimulate and increase all kinds of traffic between the eastern and western portions of the state."[36]

With the lease of the Saginaw & Western in Alma the DL&N also gained a connection to another local rail line, the Ithaca and Alma Rail Road Company (I&A). That company was organized on 21 March 1882 to build a 7.5-mile line between its namesake towns. Alma lumberman Ammi W. Wright supported the project, but Ithaca pioneer Nathan Church spent both time and money to get the railroad built to his community. Construction was finished on 28 December 1882; the first passenger trains ran on 25 June 1883. The owners contacted the SV&SL about operating their road. The details of any agreement have not been found, but very likely the SV&SL simply ran trains for the line's owners. This operation continued until February 1897 when the Ithaca line was sold to the Toledo, Ann Arbor & North Michigan and made a part of its main line.[37]

Detroit, Lansing and Northern Railroad.

LOCAL TIME TABLE—In Effect October 5th, 1884.

Trains run Daily, Sunday excepted. | MAIN LINE. | Central Standard Time.

Going West—Read Down. Exp. No. 9.	Exp. No. 5.	Exp. No. 1.	Distance	STATIONS.	Going East—Read Up. Exp. No. 2.	Exp. No. 6.	Exp. No. 10.
5.00 P. M.	9.35 A. M.	6.15 A. M.	0	Lv Detroit Ar	11.50 A. M.	3.30 P. M.	9.00 P. M.
5.10 "	9.45 "	6.25 "	3	" Springwells "	11.40 "	3.20 "	8.50 "
*5.20 "	9.57 "	‡6.35 "	8	" Greenfield "	*11.30 "	3.09 "	‡8.48 "
5.35 "	10.12 "	6.49 "	14	" Beech "	11.18 "	2.56 "	8.25 "
*5.39 "	*10.16 "	....	16	" Elm "	*11.14 "	*2.45 "	....
5.46 "	10.23 "	6.56 "	19	" Stark "	11.58 "	2.40 "	8.15 "
5.55 "	10.31 "	7.04 "	23	" Plymouth "	11.00 "	2.32 "	8.07 "
5.57 "	10.33 "	*7.05 "	....	" F. & P. M. Crossing "	10.58 "	2.30 "	8.05 "
*6.10 "	10.46 "	*7.17 "	29	" Salem "	10.46 "	2.17 "	*7.51 "
6.22 "	11.01 "	7.28 "	34	" South Lyon "	10.34 "	2.07 "	7.40 "
*6.29 "	11.08 "	‡7.34 "	38	" Green Oak "	*10.26 "	1.59 "	*7.32 "
6.42 "	11.20 "	7.45 "	43	" Brighton "	10.15 "	1.49 "	7.20 "
7.01 "	11.39 "	8.02 "	52	" Howell "	9.57 "	1.31 "	7.01 "
[illegible]	[illegible] A. M.	[illegible]	60	" Fowlerville "	9.40 "	1.14 "	6.42 "
7.34 "	12.14 P. M.	8.30 "	65	" Webberville "	9.26 "	1.00 "	6.28 "
7.47 "	12.26 "	8.42 "	71	" Williamston "	9.15 "	12.48 "	6.16 "
*7.56 "	12.38 "	‡8.50 "	75	" Meridian "	9.07 "	12.38 "	*6.06 "
*8.04 "	12.47 "	*8.58 "	79	" Okemos "	8.58 "	12.29 "	*5.58 "
8.11 "	12.55 "	9.05 "	82	" Trowbridge "	8.51 "	12.22 "	5.51 "
8.20 "	1.05 " 1.25 "	9.10 "	85	Ar / Lv Lansing Lv / Ar	8.45 "	12.15 P. M. 11.55 A. M.	5.46 " 5.25 "
8.32 "	1.33 "	9.20 "	86	" North Lansing "	8.35 "	11.50 "	5.20 "
*8.43 "	1.45 "	*9.31 "	92	" Delta "	*8.22 "	*11.38 "	*5.09 "
....	*1.49 "	....	94	" Ingersoll's "	....	*11.34 "	....
8.55 "	1.56 "	9.41 "	97	" Grand Ledge "	8.12 "	11.28 "	4.59 "
*9.04 "	2.05 "	*9.50 "	101	" Eagle "	*8.01 "	11.19 "	*4.50 "
9.20 "	2.21 "	10.04 "	109	" Portland "	7.46 "	11.04 "	4.35 "
*9.31 "	2.32 "	*10.14 "	114	" Collins "	*7.35 "	10.54 "	*4.24 "
9.38 "	2.39 "	10.21 "	117	" Lyons "	7.28 "	10.47 "	4.17 "
9.50 " 9.55 "	2.50 " 3.05 "	10.35 "	123	Ar / Lv Ionia Lv / Ar	7.15 "	10.35 " 10.20 "	4.05 " 4.00 "
10.07 "	3.17 "	10.45 "	137	" Stanton Junction "	7.00 "	10.10 "	3.48 "
*10.16 "	3.27 "	10.55 "	131	" Orleans "	6.52 "	10.00 "	*3.39 "
*10.22 "	3.33 "	*11.01 "	134	" Chadwick's "	*6.46 "	9.54 "	3.33 "
10.28 "	3.38 "	11.05 "	136	" †Kiddville "	‡6.41 "	9.49 "	3.28 "
10.40 P. M.	3.50 "	11.18 "	142	" Greenville "	6.30 A. M.	9.39 "	3.16 "
....	4.03 "	11.30 "	147	" Gowen "	....	9.26 "	3.03 "
....	4.15 "	11.42 "	152	" Trufant's "	....	9.14 "	2.53 "
....	4.20 "	*11.46 "	154	" Maple Valley "	....	9.09 "	*2.49 "
....	4.25 "	*11.51 A. M.	156	" Coral "	....	9.04 "	2.44 "
....	4.35 P. M.	12.00 Noon.	161	Ar Howard City Lv	....	8.55 A. M.	2.35 P. M.
	Exp. No. 7.	**Exp. No. 3.**		**STANTON BRANCH.**		**Exp. No. 4.**	**Exp. No. 8.**
....	3.10 P. M.	7.55 A. M.	123	Lv Ionia Ar	....	10.10 A. M.	3.35 P. M.
....	3.22 "	7.46 "	127	" Stanton Junction "	....	9.57 "	3.17 "
....	3.31 "	*7.56 "	131	" Wood's Corners "	....	9.48 "	*3.06 "
....	3.37 "	*8.02 "	134	" Shiloh "	....	9.42 "	3.00 "
....	3.44 "	*8.09 "	137	" Fenwick "	....	9.34 "	2.53 "
....	3.56 "	8.22 "	141	" Sheridan "	....	9.21 "	2.42 "
....	*3.58 "	*8.24 "	....	" Wagar's "	....	*9.17 "	*2.38 "
....	....	....	....	" Fish Creek Branch "	....	....	....
....	4.05 "	8.32 "	146	" Colby "	....	9.10 "	2.32 "
....	4.12 "	8.39 "	147	" Stanton "	....	9.05 "	2.26 "
....	*4.15 "	*8.43 "	149	" Wood's Mill "	....	*8.57 "	*2.20 "
....	....	....	....	" Slaght's Track "	....	....	....
....	4.22 "	8.51 "	151	" McBride's "	....	8.51 "	2.15 "
....	*4.26 "	....	....	" Nelson "	....	....	*2.10 "
....	....	*8.57 "	155	" Graffville "	....	‡8.43 "	*2.08 "
....	4.35 "	9.04 "	154	" Edmore "	....	8.40 "	2.05 "
....	4.42 "	9.13 "	159	" Wyman "	....	8.29 "	1.53 "
....	....	....	160	" Remick's "	....	....	....
....	4.55 "	9.28 "	165	" Blanchard "	....	8.15 "	1.40 "
....	5.03 "	9.37 "	167	" Millbrook "	....	8.07 "	1.31 "
....	*5.13 "	*9.48 "	171	" Remus "	....	7.56 "	*1.21 "
....	5.25 "	10.01 "	176	" Mecosta "	....	7.43 "	1.09 "
....	5.42 "	10.20 "	182	" Rodney "	....	7.25 "	12.51 "
....	....	....	188	" Marshfield "	....	....	....
....	6.05 P. M.	10.45 A. M.	190	Ar Big Rapids Lv	....	7.00 A. M.	12.30 P. M.
GOING EAST.				**SAGINAW DIVISION.**			**GOING WEST.**
....	3.55 P. M.	9.40 A. M.	0	Lv Lakeview Ar	....	9.20 A. M.	2.45 P. M.
....	4.35 "	10.20 "	12	" Edmore "	....	8.40 "	2.05 "
....	4.44 "	10.29 "	15	" Cedar Lake "	....	8.28 "	1.53 "
....	4.52 "	10.37 "	19	" Vestaburg "	....	8.20 "	1.45 "
....	5.02 "	10.47 "	24	" Riverdale "	....	8.11 "	1.36 "
....	5.25 "	11.10 "	32	" Alma "	....	7.50 "	1.15 "
....	5.35 P. M.	11.20 A. M.	35	Ar St. Louis Lv	....	7.40 A. M.	1.05 P. M.
GOING EAST.				**SAGINAW VALLEY & ST. LOUIS R. R.**			**GOING WEST.**
6.05 A. M.	....	12.20 P. M.	0	Lv Ithaca Ar	6.25 P. M.	....	11.30 A. M.
6.25 "	....	12.40 "	7	" Alma "	6.05 "	....	11.10 "
6.35 "	....	12.50 "	10	" St. Louis "	5.55 "	....	11.00 "
6.51 "	....	1.06 "	17	" Breckenridge "	5.39 "	....	10.44 "
7.22 "	....	1.37 "	29	" Hemlock "	5.09 "	....	10.14 "
7.45 "	....	2.00 "	39	" Paines "	4.45 "	....	9.50 "
8.00 "	....	2.15 "	43	" Saginaw City "	4.30 "	....	9.35 "
8.15 A. M.	....	2.30 P. M.	45	Ar East Saginaw Lv	4.15 P. M.	....	9.20 A. M.
GOING NORTH.				**GRAND RAPIDS & INDIANA R. R.**			**GOING SOUTH.**
8.47 A. M.	10.36 P. M.	12.10 P. M.	161	Lv Howard City Ar	6.08 P. M.	8.47 A. M.	2.29 P. M.
9.04 "	10.52 "	12.26 "	168	" Morley "	5.51 "	8.33 "	2.13 "
9.43 "	11.28 "	1.05 "	183	" Big Rapids "	5.12 "	7.56 "	1.34 "
10.00 "	11.42 "	1.21 "	189	" Paris "	4.56 "	7.43 "	1.21 "
10.17 "	11.59 "	1.40 "	296	" Reed City "	4.39 "	7.26 "	1.05 P. M.
11.25 A. M.	1.05 A. M. 1.20 "	3.10 " 3.20 "	225	Ar / Lv Cadillac Lv / Ar	3.3 P. M.	6.00 " 5.40 "	11.35 A. M. 11.25 "
....	2.11 "	4.12 "	246	" Walton "	....	4.34 A. M.	10.35 A. M.
....	....	5.45 P. M.	272	Ar Traverse City Lv	....	....	9.00 A. M.
....	2.25 A. M.	4.33 "	251	" Fife Lake "	....	4.22 A. M.	10.14 A. M.
....	3.10 "	5.09 "	265	" Kalkaska "	....	3.41 "	9.41 "
....	3.49 "	5.41 "	278	" Mancelona "	....	3.05 "	9.12 "
....	4.48 "	6.41 "	302	" Boyne Falls "	....	2.02 "	8.10 "
....	5.30 "	7.20 "	318	Ar Petoskey "	....	1.20 "	7.30 "
....	5.32 "	7.42 "	319	" Bay View "	....	1.18 A. M.	7.28 "
....	7.00 A. M.	9.10 P. M.	353	Ar Mackinaw City Lv	....	11.50 P. M.	6.00 A. M.
GOING WEST.				**DETROIT, MACKINAC & MARQUETTE R. R.**			**GOING EAST.**
....	10.00 A. M.	....	357	Lv St. Ignace Ar	....	8.50 P. M.	....
....	12.20 P. M.	....	411	" Newberry "	....	6.33 "	....
....	12.45 "	....	419	" McMillan "	....	6.10 "	....
....	1.15 "	....	431	" Seney "	....	5.40 "	....
....	2.55 "	....	464	" Munising "	....	4.06 "	....
....	3.56 "	....	485	" Onota "	....	3.17 "	....
....	4.50 P. M.	....	507	Ar Marquette Lv	....	2.30 P. M.	....

*Flag Stations. ‡Trains do not Stop. †Horse Car to and from Belding. Dining and Refreshment Rooms at Detroit and Lansing.

Detroit, Lansing & Northern 1884 schedule. This 1884 timetable shows the DL&N service from Detroit to Howard City and to Big Rapids, but also service on connecting lines to Mackinaw City and Marquette and on the subsidiary Saginaw Valley & St. Louis road.

FROM JOHN W. ROTHWELL COLLECTION.

For the year 1884 the DL&N experienced a sharp 20 percent drop in freight tonnage, with much of it in reduced forest products movements. About 1885 general manager John B. Mulliken built an extension at Big Rapids that connected the line from Ionia with the Chicago & West Michigan. A bridge across the Muskegon River allowed DL&N trains to reach the C&WM station at Pine and State Streets. In August 1886 the S&W line completed 10.8 miles from Lakeview into Howard City and made the connection with the Grand Rapids & Indiana (GR&I). The S&W issued $90,000 in 6 percent bonds to pay for the work with the interest guaranteed by the DL&N. A deal was made with the GR&I allowing a morning and afternoon through passenger train in each direction between Saginaw and Grand Rapids.[38]

Extension to Grand Rapids

In his 1886 annual report general manager Mulliken announced that he authorized a survey to build a line between Grand Ledge and Grand Rapids. The new line would provide a connection between Michigan's two largest cities, Detroit and Grand Rapids, and would pass through the state capital at Lansing. At Grand Rapids the DL&N would connect with the Chicago & West Michigan—a road that came up the eastern shore of Lake Michigan. The C&WM is dealt with later in greater detail. The C&WM and the DL&N were initially supported by James F. Joy, had a continuing close relationship, and had developed a common ownership. With such a community of interest, the directors supported a connection between the two roads. Mulliken estimated the 53-mile line could be built for about $14,000 per mile; when completed it would add $250,000 in revenue each year. The Grand Rapids, Lansing and Detroit Railroad Company (GRL&D) was authorized by the board on 8 April 1887 and was incorporated on 13 May; it was to build and own a 53-mile railroad from Grand Rapids to Grand Ledge, where it would connect with the DL&N line to Detroit. All of the new road's $450,000 of capital stock was owned by DL&N, which also guaranteed the principal of its bonds and their 5 percent interest rate.[39]

Mulliken and Hardy undertook this major construction project to respond to a fundamental problem the DL&N faced—it served a territory that did not show a potential for growth. Beginning in 1883 freight revenues and freight tonnage had begun to decline. By 1888 revenues had dropped by 50 percent; tonnage was down 40 percent, as shown in table 13. Mulliken considered part of the problem to be reduced traffic in forest products, and another part to crop failures. During the same years the DL&N also faced new competition from new rail lines built into its territory. Between 1884 and 1885 James M. Ashley built his Toledo, Ann Arbor & North Michigan out of Ann Arbor as far as Mount Pleasant. His road intersected the DL&N at Howell and Alma. A more serious invasion was Ashley's Toledo, Saginaw & Muskegon (TS&M) built in 1887 and 1888. Its Lake Michigan terminal was at Muskegon; its route crossed the DL&N at Sheridan and Greenville and the Chicago & West Michigan at Sparta. Ashley leased the TS&M to a formidable competitor—the Grand Trunk Railway of Canada. The Grand Trunk already crossed the DL&N at Ionia and east of Lansing at Trowbridge.[40]

When James Ashley built his north-south line through Howell in 1885 he had to cross the DL&N line. He made his first crossing about one thousand feet east of the present Ann Pere crossing and put tracks in a cut under the DL&N tracks. In his rush to complete the work without disrupting too many DL&N trains, he built a bridge for the DL&N over his own tracks. The DL&N immediately complained that the bridge was twelve inches too high and did not provide a level grade. It threatened to remove the bridge, fill in the cut, and make the crossing at grade level. Ashley immediately went to court claiming he had a legal permission to build. The matter went to circuit court and ended up before the Michigan Supreme Court. In November 1886 the court ordered Ashley to make the DL&N grade level, probably by lowering his own grade, and to do so at his expense. The court strongly criticized Ashley: "The case presents one of the most aggravated wrongs that we have had brought to our notice. It is impossible to hold that this invasion of defendant's [DL&N] premises was made in good faith."[41]

The eastern section of the GRL&D route, the 30 miles from Grand Ledge to just east of Elmdale, was on reasonably level terrain and allowed long, straight tangents of track. More grading and curves were needed west from Elmdale as the line worked downhill into Grand Rapids. In the end the Grand Ledge–Grand Rapids line cost considerably more to build than Mulliken expected: $1,220,466, or just over $22,000 per mile. New passenger cars added another $45,000. Mulliken complained that the company had to spend $159,000 for land and $59,000 for right-of-way near Grand Rapids after construction was underway, costing two or three times what he felt was the value of the property. Rising prices for materials, and particularly for steel rails, made everything more expensive than originally planned. When completed in August 1888 the new line extended 52.1 miles from a connection at West Grand Ledge into Grand Rapids at Wealthy Street. There it connected with the Chicago & West Michigan (C&WM) to reach that road's Grand Rapids station. As a bonus, that same year Mulliken built a 2.4-mile branch from Oakdale Park to Reeds Lake—the site of a popular amusement park that later became known as Ramona Park. The line ended just west of Lake Drive in East Grand Rapids. A city streetcar line already ran to the park, but Mulliken now could move in an entire train.[42]

The new line transformed the DL&N into an east-west carrier. The connection with the C&WM gave the DL&N access to lumber traffic originating in Muskegon and along Lake Michigan's east shoreline. A bonus was that the C&WM reached Chicago over Michigan Central rails and its branch to La Crosse in northern Indiana gave connections to southern lines and coal carriers. Coal, in particular, was growing in importance. As shown later, DL&N revenues improved modestly in 1889, and continued to grow in 1890 and 1891. But the amount of growth in traffic and the added contribution to net income that Mulliken hoped for did not materialize.

President Alpheus Hardy, who served ten years as the DL&N president, died on 7 August 1887. Nathaniel Thayer Jr., also of Boston, replaced him. Thayer's father, also named Nathaniel, had been a director of the DL&N and its predecessor, Detroit, Lansing & Lake Michigan. The son joined the DL&LM board in 1874 and continued with the successor. At age thirty-seven, Thayer apparently brought financial management skills to the road, but very likely left the operational management to Mulliken. About April 1889 Thomas Fish resigned as general superintendent and was replaced by John K. V. Agnew. Agnew was then general superintendent of the Chicago

LEFT: Nathaniel Thayer Jr. (III) succeeded Morrison as president of the C&MLS in 1874. His involvement with Pere Marquette predecessors continued until the Prince takeover in 1902.
FROM ELLIS, *MEMOIR OF NATHANIEL THAYER, A.M.*

RIGHT: Charles M. Heald. He was general manager of the Detroit, Lansing & Northern and the Chicago & West Michigan. He held executive positions until he resigned in 1902 after the Prince takeover.
FROM GEORGE N. FULLER, *HISTORIC MICHIGAN*, 3 VOLS. (CHICAGO: LEWIS PUBLISHING CO., 1939).

& West Michigan, headquartered at Grand Rapids. Agnew moved the Ionia division offices of the DL&N to Grand Rapids.

Throughout 1889 John Mulliken's health began to decline, in part from the stress he placed on himself as vice president and general manager. He was unable to prepare his required annual report for 1889 and resigned from the railroad in March 1890. Charles M. Heald, Mulliken's successor, was given responsibility for both the DL&N and the Chicago & West Michigan. Heald brought nearly twenty years of railroad management experience, most recently a one-year stint as president of the New York, Susquehanna & Western Railroad. In 1892 Heald reported that he had a survey made for a new rail line between Howard City and Sparta. He did not elaborate, but it appears he may have planned that this extension would connect with the Chicago & West Michigan at Sparta and would provide a wholly owned line for Saginaw–Grand Rapids traffic that would avoid using the Grand Rapids & Indiana. The extension was considered for several years, but was never built.[43]

In 1893 the DL&N gained a new Detroit passenger terminal. While under James F. Joy's influence it had used running rights for twenty years over the Michigan Central from a connection at West Detroit to the MC's Third Street depot. Now the DL&N joined with the Flint & Pere Marquette to build a new line between the Oak station, just west of Greenfield Road on Detroit's west side, to Delray. From Delray it used the tracks of the Detroit's Fort Street Union Depot and the 4Union Depot roads. A huge Romanesque Revival building designed by James Stewart, Fort Street Union Depot was opened on 21 January 1893, and both the DL&N and the F&PM began running their trains to it on 22 January. The two roads also built a new jointly owned freight house at Third and Congress Streets.[44]

Signs of another financial depression reappeared early in 1893. Economists and historians assign blame to a wide variety of events: a coup in Argentina, the repeal of the Sherman Silver

Detroit, Fort Street Union Depot. This union station was a monument to railroad transport. Designed by James Stewart in the very popular Richardsonian Romanesque style, building started in 1891 at the southwest corner of Fort and Third Streets and was completed in January 1893. Trains of the Flint & Pere Marquette; Detroit, Lansing & Northern; the Wabash Railroad; and the Canadian Pacific used the station. During the 1920s the Canadian Pacific left and the Pennsylvania Railroad began using the station. Trains stopped using the building in April 1971 with the advent of Amtrak. Despite attempts to save this "ornament to the city," it was demolished in January 1974.

FROM AUTHOR'S COLLECTION.

Purchase Act, a selloff in the U.S. stock market, and a financial panic in the United Kingdom that led investors to sell more U.S. securities. U.S. bank failures began, and bankruptcy overtook the Philadelphia & Reading, Northern Pacific, Union Pacific, and Atchison, Topeka & Santa Fe railroads. The financial collapse led to a business and economic depression that lasted until at least 1897. The unemployment rate in Michigan rose to 43 percent and soup kitchens were started to help the unemployed. Detroit mayor Hazen Pingree started a program of "potato patches" as community gardens to raise food.[45]

The DL&N built two branches in 1894 to tap new timberlands. In September a 13-mile branch was completed from Remus to Weidman and in November an 11-mile line from

Table 13. Detroit, Lansing & Northern revenues, expenses, and net income, 1877–1896, and Detroit, Grand Rapids & Western, 1897–1899

YEAR	MILES OF ROAD OWNED	PASSENGER REVENUE	NUMBER OF PASSENGERS	PASSENGER MILES (THOUS.)	FREIGHT REVENUE	FREIGHT TONS	TON MILES (THOUS.)	OPERATING EXPENSE & TAXES	NET INCOME
1877	181.5	$226,682	288.340	7,047	$537,502	287,628	24,903	$505,615	$282,946
1878	192.1	258,715	372,981	8,890	694,372	364,737	32,263	597,835	372,199
1879	208.4	306,016	434,102	10,921	786,765	417,768	40,427	659,787	432,994
1880	221.6	342,646	499,785	12,204	852,931	508,450	46,392	739,005	464,147
1881	221.6	403,253	555,725	13,741	959,814	567,371	56,069	934,429	428,638
1882	221.6	445,821	635,473	15,858	1,136,868	743,998	65,278	1,136,061	461,082
1883	221.6	492,992	700,834	17,131	1,090,015	646,864	61,752	1,058,570	537,875
1884	221.6	477,304	622,055	14,870	893,444	517,187	51,278	865,270	463,321
1885	221.6	386,323	549,787	13,399	824,938	509,807	47,878	771,271	457,200
1886	221.6	406,850	587,724	14,241	802,008	504,043	48,338	727,819	265,985
1887	221.6	443,546	590,017	15,202	704,336	496,121	44,383	696,115	451,045
1888	221.6	466,283	621,956	16,759	565,210	453,355	36,838	720,630	321,169
1889	221.6	516,527	695,853	18,400	601,881	486,624	39,924	806,924	325,062
1890	221.6	527,796	714,809	19,564	679,979	562,683	50,864	826,866	392,797
1891	221.6	527,983	759,764	22,146	660,270	626,249	48,429	878,653	375,446
1892	221.6	522,140	765,145	22,364	669,720	656,381	53,352	924,071	341,502
1893	221.6	567,752	731,045	22,147	619,130	602,401	49,745	970,787	234,306
1894	221.6	508,246	642,582	19,649	575,737	540,716	45,585	898,554	200,169
1895	221.6	508,841	648,889	20,759	618,603	595,750	43,858	895,352	254,303
1896*	221.6	540,746	665,882	22,162	610,677	584,285	44,402	990,580	175,205
1897	380.0	562,090	679,946	24,634	741,945	695,648	64,354	984,363	322,377
1898	380.0	642,970	839,792	24,514	838,183	871.510	77,933	1,170,585	319,637
1899	380.0	662,528	816,820	27,768	891,766	1,064,137	84,833	1,243,436	322,219

Source: Data from Michigan Railroad Commission, *Annual Reports*.
Note: All amounts include data of Saginaw & Grand Rapids, Saginaw & Western, and Grand Rapids, Lansing & Detroit, but not of Saginaw Valley & St. Louis.
* Total of railroad operations from January to March, and under the receiver from April to December.

Mecosta to Barryton. Despite some added business from these two new lines, freight traffic dropped in 1893 and 1894 and lumber traffic continued to decline, reducing net income to the point it no longer covered interest on the company's debt and the guaranteed dividends on stock. The interest due 1 January 1894 was not paid, and by 6 March the company had assembled a reorganization plan. Some of the parties involved financially would not agree to the March plan, and it took until 1 February 1896 for a new reorganization plan to be finally agreed to. The Interstate Commerce Commission's hearing set the DL&N's operating loss at $103,005. The DL&N went into receivership on 1 April 1896 with President Heald as the court-appointed receiver. On 10 November 1896 the road was sold at foreclosure to the Detroit, Grand Rapids & Western. Included in the sale were all of the companies the DL&N controlled: Grand Rapids, Lansing & Detroit; Saginaw & Grand Rapids; Saginaw & Western; and Saginaw Valley & St. Louis.[46]

Table 14. Detroit, Lansing & Northern, costs, equipment, capitalization, 1877–1896, and Detroit, Grand Rapids & Western, 1897–1899

YEAR	MILES OF ROAD OWNED	COST OF ROAD (THOUS.)	COST OF EQUIPMENT (THOUS.)	NUMBER ENGINES	NUMBER FREIGHT CARS	NUMBER PASSENGER CARS	NUMBER EMPLOYEES	COMMON STOCK (THOUS.)	TOTAL DEBT (THOUS.)	DIVIDEND PAID ON COMMON (THOUS.)
1877	181.5	$6,582	$545	26	732	21	624	$4,280	$2,979	0
1878	197.3	6,673	545	27	800	21	659	4,329	3,199	0
1879	208.4	6,853	545	28	799	24	727	4,329	3,411	0
1880	221.6	6,927	623	30	851	30	833	4,329	3,411	0
1881	221.6	6,927	623	30	950	31	973	4,329	3,485	0
1882	221.6	6,855	623	34	975	32	1,012	4,329	3,522	0
1883	221.6	6,856	623	41	994	35	1,190	4,329	3,257	110
1884	221.6	6,847	623	41	994	40	979	4,335	3,563	110
1885	221.6	6,836	623	41	994	41	862	4,335	3,488	0
1886	221.6	6,826	623	41	994	42	996	4,335	3,579	0
1887	221.6	6,817	623	41	994	42	926	4,335	3,678	55
1888	221.6	6,904	623	41	984	56	927	4,336	3,442	0
1889	221.6	6,901	623	41	991	58	1,076	4,336	3,909	0
1890	221.6	6,872	633	41	1,091	57	1,003	4,336	3,813	0
1891	221.6	6,857	655	40	1,193	63	1,105	4,336	3,924	0
1892	221.6	6,867	655	40	1,184	65	1,325	4,336	3,904	0
1893	221.6	6,859	655	44	1,194	66	1,310	4,336	4,003	0
1894	221.6	7,042	671	44	1,194	66	1,117	4,336	4,245	0
1895	221.6	7,044	716	44	1,194	66	1,176	4,336	4,547	0
1896	–	–	–	47	1,243	69	1,112	–	–	
1897	380.0	9,736	637	42	1,137	67	1,196	5,693	5,119	0
1898	380.0	10,461	686	44	1,452	65	1,255	5,693	5,404	0
1899	380.0	10,725	696	46	1,452	69	1,358	5,693	5,757	0

Source: Data from Michigan Railroad Commission.
Note: All amounts include data of Saginaw & Grand Rapids, Saginaw & Western, and Grand Rapids, Lansing & Detroit, but not of Saginaw Valley & St. Louis.

In its three years of life, from 1 January 1897 to 31 December 1899, the Detroit, Grand Rapids & Western had net profits of $963,000, paid interest on its debt of $570,000, and retained a net profit of $393,000. The Remus and Mecosta branches, built in 1894, provided nearly $100,000 of income in 1897. On 27 December 1897 the DGR&W started up a Muskegon-Milwaukee railcar ferry service from a dock at Port Sherman to the Chicago, Milwaukee & St. Paul road's slip at Maple Street. The Chicago & West Michigan provided running rights from Grand Rapids to Muskegon. Heald rented *Shenango No. 2* from its Lake Erie service, and when the company bought it in December 1898 for $147,000, the ship was renamed *Muskegon.* It had a checkered career. In October 1898 it rammed a grain elevator then being built in Milwaukee. In December 1899, just out of Milwaukee, the steering gear failed in heavy seas, causing freight cars on the deck to derail. Two months later while crossing in a gale, the ship again lost its steering.[47]

Table 15. Detroit, Lansing & Northern, freight and lumber traffic statistics, 1877–1896, and Detroit, Grand Rapids & Western, 1897–1899

YEAR	FREIGHT REVENUE	YTY % CHANGE	REVENUE MILES (THOUS.)	REVENUE TONS (THOUS.)	YTY % CHANGE	REVENUE PER TON	REVENUE TON MILES (THOUS.)	TONS LUMBER (THOUS.)	YTY % CHANGE	% OF ALL TONS
1877	$537,502		282.9	287.6		$2.16	24,903	174.7		60.7
1878	694,372	29.2	325.9	364.7	26.8	1.90	32,263	225.9	29.3	61.9
1879	786,765	13.3	394.2	417.8	14.6	1.88	40,428	269.3	19.2	64.5
1880	852,932	8.4	466.2	508.5	21.7	1.67	46,392	352.0	30.7	69.2
1881	959,814	12.5	602.0	567.4	11.6	1.69	56,070	418.0	18.8	73.7
1882	1,136,868	18.4	717.3	744.0	31.1	1.52	65,278	552.6	32.2	74.3
1883	1,090,015	-4.1	732.9	646.9	-13.2	1.68	61,752	450.7	-18.4	69.7
1884	893,444	-18.0	559.5	517.2	-20.0	1.72	51,278	354.0	-21.5	68.4
1885	824,938	-7.7	411.6	509.8	-1.4	1.61	47,878	318.5	-10.0	62.5
1886	802,008	-2.8	410.7	504.0	-1.1	1.59	48,339	312.8	-1.8	62.1
1887	702,824	-12.4	407.5	496.1	-1.6	1.42	44,383	310.2	-0.8	62.5
1888	562,941	-19.9	392.2	453.4	-8.6	1.24	36,838	284.0	-8.4	62.6
1889	601.881	6.9	448.1	486.6	7.3	1.24	39,924	299.4	5.4	61.5
1890	677,192	12.5	471.7	562.7	15.6	1.33	50,864	294.7	-1.6	52.4
1891	658,731	-2.7	454.1	636.2	13.1	1.15	48,424	259.4	-12.0	41.4
1892	668,748	1.5	497.1	656.4	3.2	1.25	58,352	244.3	-5.8	37.2
1893	619,130	-7.4	516.1	602.4	-8.2	1.21	40.845	228.4	-6.5	37.9
1894	573,251	-7.4	466.4	540.7	-10.2	1.26	45,585	194.2	-15.0	35.9
1895	616,872	7.6	460.2	595.8	10.2	1.19	51,945	250.9	29.2	42.1
1896	610,667	-1.0	490.6	599.7	0.7	1.15	52,721	235.9	-6.0	38.6
1897	741,945	21.5	478.2	695.6	16.0	1.16	64,354	243.8	3.3	32.9
1898	838,183	13.0	572.2	871.5	25.3	1.08	77,934	256.2	5.1	29.4
1899	891,766	6.4	555.2	1,064.1	22.1	1.04	84,838	334.2	30.4	31.4

Source: Data from Michigan Railroad Commission.
Note: All amounts include data of Saginaw & Grand Rapids, Saginaw & Western, and Grand Rapids, Lansing & Detroit, but not of Saginaw Valley & St. Louis.

In the annual report for 1898 Heald wrote that "the entrance into the Northwest, gained through the car ferry, opens up a field from which a considerable traffic in grain, flour, and other products can be drawn, while at the same time a fair share of return tonnage from the East, in the way of structure iron, timber, merchandise, etc., is insured." On the rail line, installing automatic couplers, begun the year before, was completed, and Heald planned to complete the air brakes installation the next year. In 1898 the 1-mile spur line into Lyons was built off the Grand Ledge–Ionia line.[48]

Early in 1899 Nathaniel Thayer and William Crapo began serious discussions about a merger of their three railroads: Detroit, Grand Rapids & Western, Chicago & West Michigan, and Flint & Pere Marquette. A merger plan was put forward on 20 May 1899 and a final agreement was signed in December 1899. The new Pere Marquette Railroad Company was incorporated on 1 November 1899 to combine the three roads. The new company began operations on 1 January 1900.

Table 16. Detroit, Lansing & Northern, freight traffic statistics, 1877–1896, and Detroit, Grand Rapids & Western, 1897–1899

YEAR	REVENUE TONS (THOUS.)	LUMBER TONS (THOUS.)	% OF ALL TONS	AGRICULTURAL PRODUCTS. TONS (THOUS.)	% OF ALL TONS	MANUFACTURES TONS (THOUS.)	% OF ALL TONS	MERCHANDISE TONS (THOUS.)	% OF ALL TONS
1877	287.6	174.7	60.7	59.6	20.7	2.1	0.7	41.1	14.3
1878	364.7	225.9	61.9	94.3	25.9	3.5	1.0	20.8	8.5
1879	417.8	269.3	64.5	94.5	22.6	6.3	1.5	31.1	7.4
1880	508.5	352.0	69.2	88.4	17.4	7.7	1.5	38.7	7.6
1881	602.0	418.0	73.7	79.3	13.2	8.5	1.5	40.7	7.2
1882	744.0	552.6	74.3	86.4	11.6	6.2	0.8	55.1	7.4
1883	646.9	450.7	69.7	94.9	14.7	13.3	2.1	44.6	6.9
1884	517.2	354.0	68.4	93.4	18.1	7.4	1.4	37.3	7.2
1885	509.8	318.5	62.5	108.7	21.3	12.9	2.5	39.4	7.7
1886	504.0	312.8	62.1	113.6	22.5	8.4	1.7	43.8	8.7
1887	496.1	310.2	62.5	92.0	18.5	5.5	1.1	41.1	8.3
1888	453.4	284.0	62.6	83.3	18.4	8.3	1.8	31.9	7.0
1889	486.6	299.4	61.5	86.9	17.9	12.2	2.5	39.4	8.1
1890	562.7	294.7	52.4	100.2	17.8	16.3	2.9	79.8	14.2
1891	636.2	259.4	41.4	127.7	20.1	19.6	3.1	59.8	9.6
1892	656.4	244.3	37.2	154.1	23.5	25.7	3.9	57.1	8.7
1893	602.4	228.4	37.9	148.6	24.7	23.0	3.8	66.4	11.0
1894	540.7	194.2	35.9	141.9	26.2	26.3	4.9	67.3	12.4
1895*	595.8	250.9	42.1	120.3	20.2	60.4	10.1	42.5	7.1
1896	599.7	235.9	39.3	158.6	26.4	65.8	11.0	46.1	7.7
1897	695.6	243.8	35.0	187.2	26.9	41.9	6.0	72.6	10.4
1898	871.5	256.2	29.4	239.0	27.4	90.1	10.3	107.6	12.3
1899	1,064.1	334.2	31.4	252.9	23.8	114.4	10.8	89.1	8.4

Source: Data from Michigan Railroad Commission.

Note: All amounts include data of Saginaw & Grand Rapids, Saginaw & Western, and Grand Rapids, Lansing & Detroit, but not of Saginaw Valley & St. Louis.

* In 1895 apparently the classifications of different kinds of freight were modified.

Central Standard Time—In Effect June 19, 1898.

DETROIT GRAND RAPIDS WESTERN RAILROAD

MAIN LINE GOING WEST.

DETROIT TO LANSING AND GRAND RAPIDS.

Miles	STATIONS	No. 1 Week Days	No. 3 Week Days	No. 7 Week Days	No. 49 Freight Week Days
0	Lv DETROIT	8.00AM	1.10PM	6.10PM	
5	Lv DELREY	8.11AM	* 1.20PM	6.21PM	
6	Lv ROUGEMERE				
13	Lv OAK				
16	Lv BEECH	8 30AM		* 6.39PM	
18	Lv ELM	*		*	
20	Lv STARK	8.38AM		* 6.46PM	
25	Lv PLYMOUTH	8.48AM	1.49PM	6.55PM	
31	Lv SALEM	* 9.01AM		* 7.07PM	
36	Lv SOUTH LYON	9.11AM	2.09PM	7.17PM	
40	Lv GREEN OAK	* 9.16AM			
42	Lv ISLAND LAKE				
45	Lv BRIGHTON	9.26AM	2.23PM	7 31PM	
53	Ar HOWELL JUNC	9.38AM			
	Lv HOWELL JUNC	9.42AM		7.42PM	
54	Lv HOWELL	9.52AM	2.39PM	7.49PM	
63	Lv FOWLERVILLE	10.06AM	2.52PM	8.04PM	
68	Lv WEBBERVILLE	10.15AM		8.13PM	
74	Lv WILLIAMSTON	10.25AM	3.09PM	8.23PM	
78	Lv MERIDIAN	*10.30AM			
82	Lv OKEMOS	*10.36AM		8.34PM	
85	Lv TROWBRIDGE	*10.41AM		* 8.40PM	
88	Lv LANSING	10.50AM	3 34PM	8.48PM	
89	Lv NORTH LANSING	10.55AM		8 53PM	
95	Lv DELTA	*11.04AM		* 9.02PM	
100	Ar GRAND LEDGE	11.12AM	3.54PM	9.10PM	
	Lv GRAND LEDGE	11.20AM	4.00PM	9.20PM	6.30AM
108	Lv MULLIKEN	11.33AM		* 9.32PM	7.00AM
113	Lv SUNFIELD	11.41AM		* 9.40PM	7.25AM
117	Lv WOODBURY	*11.48AM	4.23PM	* 9.46PM	7.58AM
121	Lv LAKE ODESSA	11.55AM	4.29PM	9.54PM	8.30AM
127	Lv CLARKSVILLE	12.06PM		*10.06PM	8.55AM
137	Ar LOWELL VIA L & H	2.30PM	6.20PM		
	Lv LOWELL VIA L & H	11.50AM	4.20PM		
131	Lv ELMDALE	12.13PM	4.43PM	*10.13PM	9.20AM
134	Lv ALTO	*12.19PM		*10.19PM	9.35AM
138	Lv McCORDS	*12.25PM		*10.25PM	9.50AM
145	Lv EAST PARIS	*			*
153	Ar GRAND RAPIDS	12.55PM	5.20PM	10.55PM	10.35AM

WESTERN DIVISION.

DETROIT TO HOWARD CITY.

Miles	STATIONS	No. 51 Week Days	Nos. 21 & 31 Week Days	No. 23 Week Days	No. 27 Week Days	No. 17 Week Days
0	Lv DETROIT		8.00AM	1.10PM	6.10PM	
100	Ar GRAND LEDGE		11.15AM	3.54PM	9.10PM	
	Lv GRAND LEDGE		11.20AM	4.00PM	9.20PM	
104	Lv EAGLE		*11.28AM	4.09PM	* 9.28PM	
112	Lv PORTLAND		11.40AM	4.22PM	9.42PM	
117	Lv COLLINS		*11.49AM	4.32PM	* 9.52PM	
120	Lv LYONS		11.54AM	4.38PM	9.58PM	
126	Ar IONIA		12.06PM	4.48PM	10.10PM	
	Lv IONIA	7.25AM	12.06PM	4.53PM		
130	Lv STANTON JUNCTION	7.37AM	12.14PM	* 5.02PM	No. 19	5.25PM
134	Lv ORLEANS	* 7.45AM	*12.22PM	* 5.12PM	Passenger	
137	Lv CHADWICK	* 7.50AM	*12.26PM	* 5.17PM		
140	Lv BELDING	8.02AM	*12.37PM	5.29PM	7.20PM	
145	Ar GREENVILLE	8.19AM	12.54PM	5.45PM	7.37PM	6 00PM
	Lv GREENVILLE		2.30PM			
146	Lv NORTH GREENVILLE	8.22AM	2.32PM	5.57PM	7.40PM	6.02PM
150	Lv GOWEN	8.35AM	2.42PM	* 6 07PM		
156	Lv TRUFANT	8.45AM	2.52PM	* 6.17PM		
160	Lv CORAL	8.52AM	3.00PM	* 6.25PM		
164	Ar HOWARD CITY	9.00AM	3.10PM	6.35PM		

No. 13 (passenger, week days) leaves Belding at 10.15 A. M, and arrives at North Greenville at 10.35 A. M.

* Flag Stations. Stop on signal or to leave passengers.

READ NOTES AND EXPLANATIONS.

Central Standard Time—In Effect June 19, 1898.

DETROIT GRAND RAPIDS WESTERN RAILROAD

MAIN LINE—GOING EAST.

GRAND RAPIDS AND LANSING TO DETROIT.

Miles	STATIONS	No. 2 Week Days	No. 4 Week Days	No. 8 Week Days	No. 48 Freight Week Days
0	Lv GRAND RAPIDS	7.00AM	1.35PM	5.25PM	11.35AM
3	Lv OAKDALE PARK				
8	Lv EAST PARIS			*	*
15	Lv McCORDS	* 7 24AM		* 5.50PM	12.50PM
18	Lv ALTO	* 7.29AM		* 5.56PM	1.10PM
22	Lv ELMDALE	7.35AM	2.09PM	6.02PM	1.30PM
28	Ar LOWELL VIA L & H	8.00AM	2.30PM	6.20PM	
	Lv LOWELL VIA L & H	7.00AM	11.50AM	4.20PM	
26	Lv CLARKSVILLE	7.42AM		6.08PM	1.50PM
32	Lv LAKE ODESSA	7.52AM	2.24PM	6.19PM	2.24PM
36	Lv WOODBURY	7.58AM	See Note	* 6.25PM	2.55PM
40	Lv SUNFIELD	8.05AM		6.32PM	3.20PM
45	Lv MULLIKEN	8.13AM		6.42PM	4.11PM
53	Ar GRAND LEDGE	8.25AM	2.53PM	6.55PM	4.40PM
	Lv GRAND LEDGE	8.30AM	2.58PM	7.00PM	
58	Lv DELTA	* 8.38AM		* 7.08PM	
64	Lv NORTH LANSING	8.47AM	3.13PM	7.17PM	
65	Lv LANSING	8.54AM	3.20PM	7.22PM	
67	Lv TROWBRIDGE	* 9.00AM		* 7.28PM	
71	Lv OKEMOS	* 9.06AM		* 7.33PM	
75	Lv MERIDIAN	See Note		* 7.38PM	
79	Lv WILLIAMSTON	9.18AM	3.40PM	7.45PM	
85	Lv WEBBERVILLE	9.28AM		7.54PM	
90	Lv FOWLERVILLE	9.37AM	3.57PM	8.04PM	
98	Lv HOWELL	9.52AM	4.12PM	8.20PM	
100	Lv HOWELL JUNC	9.55AM			
107	Lv BRIGHTON	10.10AM	4.28PM	8.35PM	
110	Lv ISLAND LAKE				
113	Lv GREEN OAK			* 8.43PM	
116	Lv SOUTH LYON	10.25AM	4.42PM	8.50PM	
121	Lv SALEM	10.35AM		* 9.00PM	
128	Lv PLYMOUTH	10.50AM	5.03PM	9.15PM	
132	Lv STARK	*10.57AM		* 9.21PM	
135	Lv ELM	*			
136	Ar BEECH	*11.06AM		* 9.29PM	
140	Lv OAK				
145	Lv MICHIGAN AVE				
148	Lv DELREY	*11.27AM	* 5.32PM	* 9.50PM	
153	Ar DETROIT	11.40AM	5.45PM	10.05PM	

No. 4 will stop at Woodbury for passengers to or from C. K. & S. R'y.

No. 2 will stop at Meridian to let off passengers from west of Trowbridge and to take on passengers for stations east of Fowlerville.

WESTERN DIVISION.

HOWARD CITY TO DETROIT.

Miles	STATIONS	No. 22 Week Days	No. 24 Week Days	Nos. 18 & 28 Week Days	No. 14 Week Days	No. 16 Week Days
0	Lv HOWARD CITY	6.00AM		4.00PM		
4	Lv CORAL	* 6.08AM		4.08PM		
8	Lv TRUFANT	* 6.15AM		4.15PM		
14	Lv GOWEN	* 6.24AM		4.25PM		
18	Lv NORTH GREENVILLE	6.34AM	1.08PM	4.35PM	8.35AM	10.50AM
19	Lv GREENVILLE	6.36AM	1.10PM	4.38PM	8.37AM	10.52AM
26	Lv BELDING	6.53AM	1.27PM	4.57PM	8.55AM	11.10AM
27	Lv CHADWICK	* 7.02AM	* 1.36PM	* 5.07PM		
30	Lv ORLEANS	* 7.06AM	* 1.41PM	* 5.12PM		
34	Lv STANTON JUNCTION	7.15AM	* 1.49PM	* 5.20PM		
38	Ar IONIA	7.25AM		5.30PM		
	Lv IONIA	7.30AM	2.01PM	6.00PM		
44	Lv LYONS	7.40AM	2.11PM	6.10PM		
47	Lv COLLINS	* 7.46AM	* 2.16PM	* 6.16PM		
52	Lv PORTLAND	7.56AM	2.26PM	* 6.26PM		
60	Lv EAGLE	* 8.10AM	* 2.40PM	* 6.40PM		
	Ar GRAND LEDGE	8.20AM	2.48PM	6.50PM		
64	Lv GRAND LEDGE	8.30AM	2.58PM	7.00PM		
164	Ar DETROIT	11.40AM	5.45PM	10.05PM		

No. 20 (passenger; week days) leaves North Greenville at 6.05 P. M., arrives Belding 6.25 P. M.

* Flag Stations. Stop on signal or to leave passengers.

READ NOTES AND EXPLANATIONS.

Detroit, Grand Rapids & Western 1898 Detroit-Lansing & Howard City service.

FROM AUTHOR'S COLLECTION.

CHAPTER 3

The Chicago & West Michigan

By 1840 Muskegon was developing into a sawmill center, using logs floated into Muskegon Lake from the surrounding area. By the early 1860s the sawmills that ringed Muskegon Lake cut about 100 million board feet of lumber; by 1867 the yearly cut was tripled to nearly 300 million board feet of lumber. The torrent of logs that came down the Muskegon River grew so much each year that by 1867 there were twenty-five sawmills around Muskegon Lake, with the number increasing each year. Muskegon Lake provided an ideal harbor on Lake Michigan, but ice closed shipping transport several months each year.[1]

Muskegon & Ferrysburg

Late in 1858 the Detroit & Milwaukee Railroad (D&M) completed its line across Michigan from Detroit to Grand Haven. The D&M was controlled by the Great Western Railway of Canada, a road with a line across southern Ontario from Windsor to the Niagara River. From there the New York Central line went to the major eastern lumber marketplace at Albany, New York. The Muskegon lumbermen saw the railroad as an opportunity for year-round shipping, not just to the Albany market, but to vital Ohio markets as well. Muskegon's first railroad, the Muskegon and Ferrysburg Rail Road Company (M&F), was formed on 6 May 1868. It proposed to build a 17-mile line from a connection with the D&M at Ferrysburg to Muskegon harbor. Historian John T. Percival stated that the road was completed in December 1869. Muskegon lumberman Chauncey Davis, a major stockholder, was named president. A specific impetus for building the M&F has not been found, but it did provide year-round access to railroad shipping. It may be

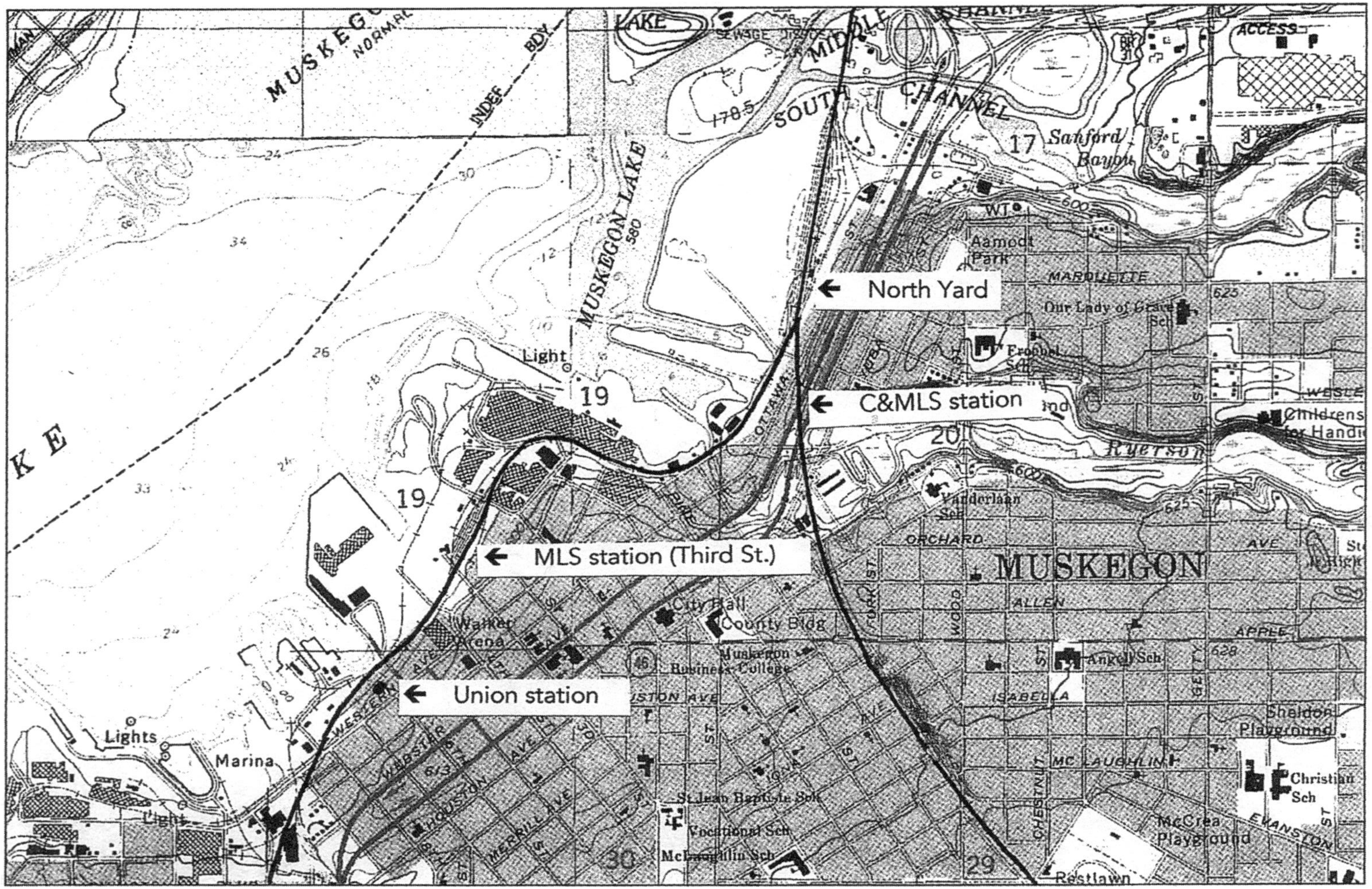
North Yard
C&MLS station
MLS station (Third St.)
Union station
MUSKEGON
MUSKEGON LAKE
SOUTH CHANNEL
Sanford Bayou
Aamodt Park
Our Lady of Grace Sch
Froebel Sch
Vanderlaan Sch
Ryerson
City Hall
County Bldg
Muskegon Business College
Walker Arena
Angell Sch
Sheldon Playground
Christian Sch
McCrea Playground
Restlawn
St Jean Baptiste Sch
Vocational Sch
McLaughlin Sch
Marina
Lights
Light
OTTAWA
MARQUETTE
ORCHARD
ALLEN
APPLE
ISABELLA
MC LAUGHLIN
CHESTNUT
EVANSTON
WESTERN AVE
HOUSTON AVE
MERRILL AVE
ACCESS
INDEF BDY

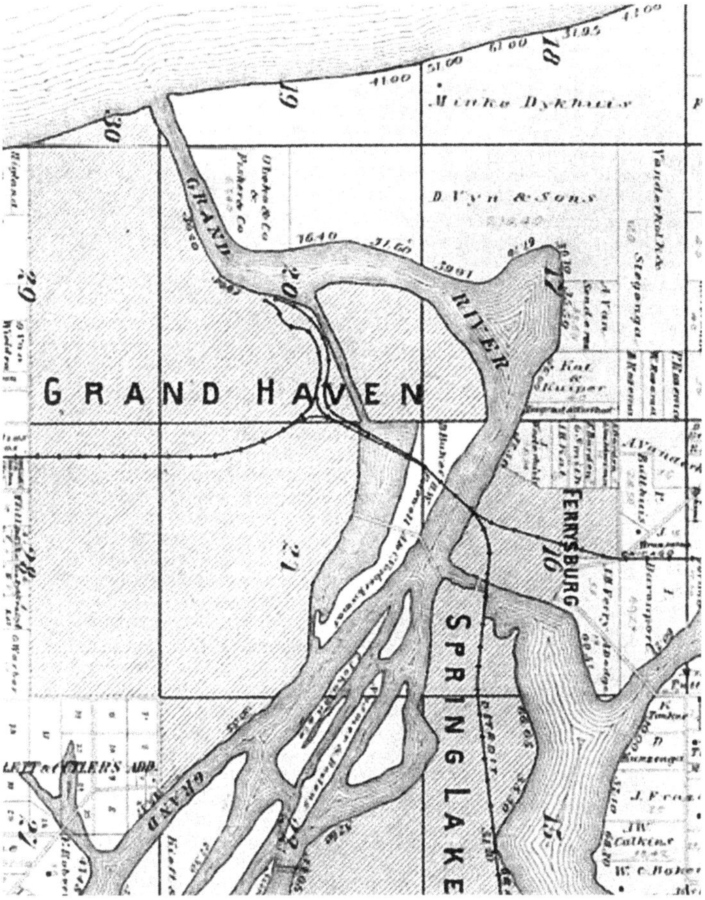

Ferrysburg–Grand Haven. The Muskegon & Ferrysburg line came down to a connection with the Detroit, Grand Haven & Milwaukee on the north side of the Grand River at Ferrysburg. The original DGH&M line ran almost to Lake Michigan along the north side of the Grand River. This was replaced in 1870 by a bridge over the Grand River to reach Muskegon, a bridge that was used by the Michigan Lake Shore when that line was built into Grand Haven.

FROM G. A. OGLE & CO., *STANDARD ATLAS OF OTTAWA COUNTY, MICHIGAN* (CHICAGO: GEORGE A. OGLE & CO., 1897).

that Spring Lake lumberman Hunter Savidge, a major operator, thought the logs floated down the Muskegon River could be moved to his sawmill at Spring Lake and the finished lumber then shipped out by rail.[2]

Various sources report the actual length of the M&F differently, and its length will be discussed later under the Michigan Lake Shore Railroad. The original corporate articles called for a line 17 miles long; in 1919 the Michigan Railroad Commission reported 15 miles were built. The original MLS depot in Muskegon was located on the north side of Third Street, a distance of 12 miles from Ferrysburg. The north end of the M&F appears to have been at its junction with the C&MLS, at the south end of what is now called North Yard, about a city block north of Hall Avenue, about 1.3 miles from Third Street. There is some evidence that M&F also had a short branch in Muskegon. An 1877 atlas shows a line that ran southwest from a connection

OPPOSITE: Muskegon. The original Muskegon & Ferrysburg line was built in 1868–1869 from the shore of Muskegon Lake near the mouth of Ryerson Creek, then snaked south along the shore line. The Chicago & Michigan Lake Shore built into Muskegon in 1870 from the southeast, and eventually built north from the city.

at Eighth Street, along the south shore of Muskegon Lake, ending in the vicinity of McCracken Street. The end-to-end distance is 2.25 miles. This branch is not reported in the MLS reports to the commissioner of railroads and is mentioned only incidentally by the Michigan Railroad Commission.[3]

By 1867, Kalamazoo railroad builder Ransom Gardner had bought and built a collection of lines that extended from White Pigeon, on the Michigan Southern & Northern Indiana line between Toledo and Chicago, north into Kalamazoo. In June 1867 Gardner decided to build north to Allegan and formed the Kalamazoo & Allegan (K&A) for that purpose. Sometime in early 1868, as he was building the line from Kalamazoo to Allegan, the citizens of Grand Rapids raised "a bonus of $10,000 on condition that the [Gardner's] road should reach Grand Rapids on or before March 1, 1869." The money incentive persuaded Gardner to alter his original project and extend his K&A line to Grand Rapids to take advantage of the Grand Rapids offer. He renamed his road the Kalamazoo, Allegan & Grand Rapids (KA&GR) and rolled an engine and a flat car into Grand Rapids on the deadline day.[4]

Allegan & Holland

The Allegan and Holland Rail Road Company (A&H) was incorporated on 18 July 1868 to build a 25-mile line between Allegan and Holland. The *Grand Rapids Eagle* reported:[5]

> The Hollanders . . . have already organized a company and subscribed for the stock to build a road from that place [Holland] to Allegan which will give them communication with southern Michigan, through the Gardner road. The people of Muskegon have also organized a company from that city to Ferrysburg, and the citizens of Grand Haven are being urged to take proper steps to build a road from Ferrysburg to Holland. This will give that large region on the lake . . . railroad facilities . . . that are very much needed. It will tend to open up that fruit region, and bring vast acres under cultivation that now lie waste.

The Allegan line would be the shortest route to provide Holland with a railroad connection to Ransom Gardner's Kalamazoo & Allegan road and to the outside world. Rather than wait longer, Hollanders put money into the Allegan road. The Holland city council was persuaded to authorize an issue of $16,000 in bonds to aid the new road, a move the voters approved enthusiastically, 234 to 1. Investors already had put in enough money to make a survey of the

OPPOSITE: Allegan detail. When built in 1870 the east-west Michigan Lake Shore line connected with the north–south Kalamazoo, Allegan & Grand Rapids on Allegan's northeast side. Of the streets shown, Sherman, Lee, May, and Charles no longer exist, and Elizabeth Street has been renamed North Main Street. The Michigan Lake Shore depot was on the east side of Main Street and Gardner's KA&GR is at Briggs Street. The tracks east from the MLS depot were the 1871 line of the Mansfield, Coldwater & Lake Michigan.

FROM D. J. LAKE, *ATLAS OF ALLEGAN COUNTY, MICHIGAN* (PHILADELPHIA: C. O. TITUS, 1873).

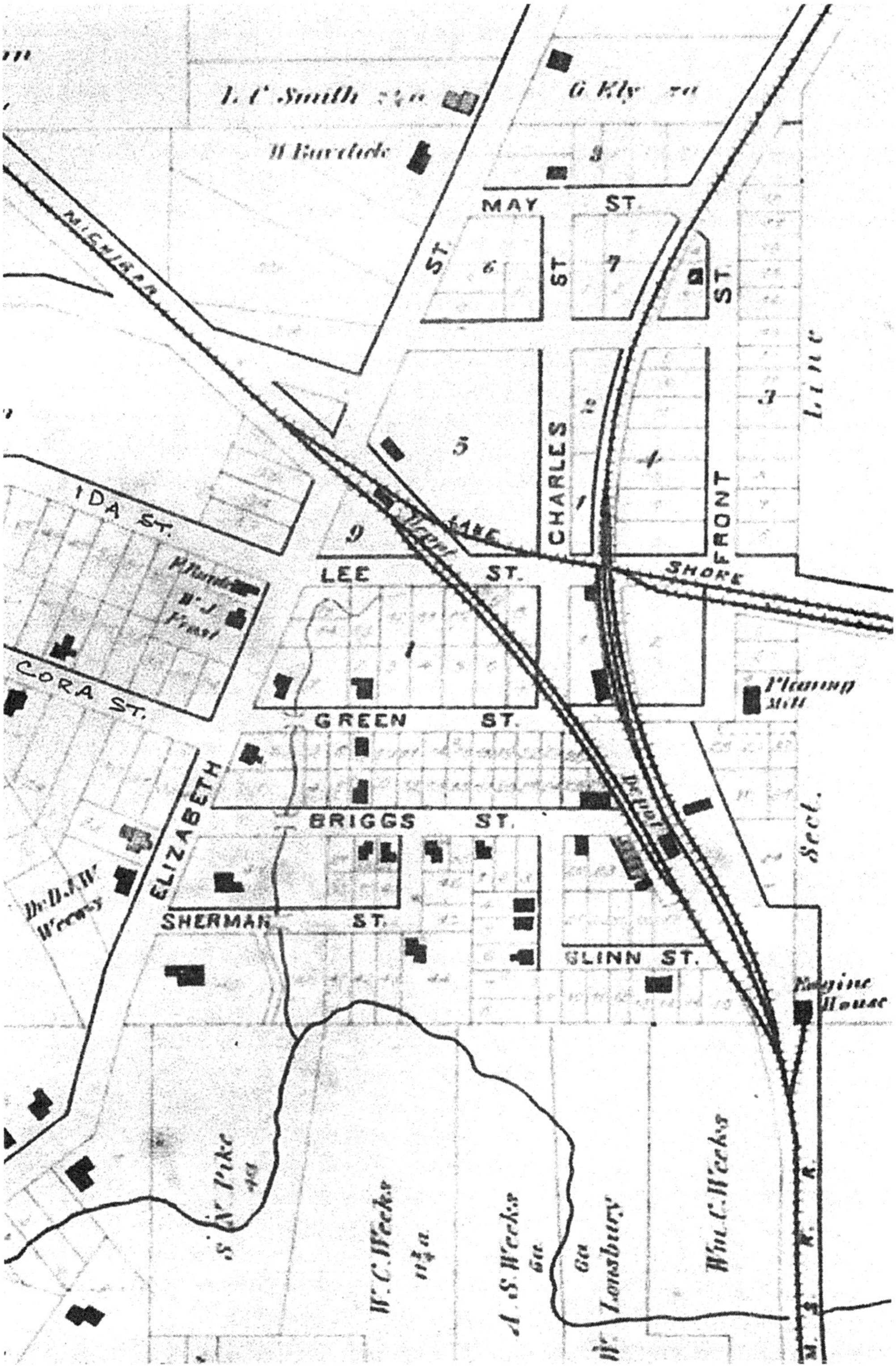
MAY ST.
ST.
ST.
ST.
CHARLES
FRONT
IDA ST.
LEE ST.
LAKE
SHORE
CORA ST.
GREEN ST.
ELIZABETH
BRIGGS ST.
SHERMAN ST.
GLINN ST.
Planing Mill
Engine House
Depot
Line
Sect.
W. C. Weeks
A. S. Weeks
Lonsbury
Wm. C. Weeks
G. Ely
H. Burdick
W. J. Frost
M. S. R. R.

road, and they named Allegan railroad contractor Joseph Fisk as president of the road. The survey was completed in August 1869, and soon after a construction contract was signed with Goss, Warner & Company, the company then building Ransom Gardner's line toward Grand Rapids. The contract called for the line to be completed by 1 June 1870. The Holland city bonds apparently were never issued, possibly as a result of the Michigan Supreme Court's decision in April 1870.[6]

The first train into Holland came from Allegan on Monday, 6 June 1870. The formal opening of the line was held the following Thursday, 9 June, when the locomotive *City of Holland* took dignitaries, the Holland City Band, and a few local citizens to Allegan and back. The Allegan station was built near the KA&GR station on the east side of Main Street and north of Green Street. Its Holland depot was located on the northeast corner of 7th Street and Columbia Avenue.[7]

Michigan Lake Shore

By 1869 Grand Haven businessmen saw a railroad already built between Muskegon and Ferrysburg and another line planned to run from Allegan to Holland. It was obvious to them that a railroad that ran through their city to close the gap between the two roads would be profitable. On 5 February 1869 they formed the Michigan Lake Shore Rail Road Company (MLS) to build a 22-mile line from Ferrysburg to Holland. Ransom Gardner saw this as a new opportunity, and in short order he was the president of the new company. On 29 September, before any of its line was put in service, Gardner amended the MLS corporate articles to allow the company to absorb both the Allegan & Holland and the Muskegon & Ferrysburg, and on that date the two roads were merged into MLS. On 29 October Gardner amended the MLS articles again, this time to change its northern terminus to Traverse City and increase its capitalization from $500,000 to $1.8 million. On 29 August 1870 building contractor Joseph Fisk completed the line into Grand Haven from the A&H station in Holland. To close the gap between Grand Haven and Ferrysburg the MLS arranged to use the new bridge over the Grand River that the Detroit & Milwaukee built in 1870 to give it a line into downtown Grand Haven. The MLS issued a total of $880,000 in first mortgage bonds, at an 8 percent interest rate, to finance construction. Gardner also persuaded Muskegon Township to issue $50,000 in bonds to aid the road, but the road never received any of that money.[8]

Reverend Albertus C. Van Raalte had preached in Muskegon on Sunday, 8 October 1871. The next day, riding an MLS train returning to Holland, it was brought to a stop just north of the Black River. The river bridge was burning. A trainman announced that the city had been destroyed by fire. Van Raalte's Dutch *kolonie*—the community that he had founded, nurtured, and supported—was in ashes. A fire that began Sunday afternoon had grown so furiously that, between one and three o'clock Monday morning, three-quarters of the city had been laid to waste. The destroyed river bridge kept MLS trains from bringing aid from Grand Haven and Muskegon. It was a comfort that only one life was lost in the city fire. Both the MLS depot and Morrison's Chicago & Michigan Lake Shore depot were saved. The great Chicago fire began

Joseph Fisk. He was an Allegan railroad builder.

FROM *AMERICAN BIOGRAPHICAL HISTORY OF EMINENT AND SELF-MADE MEN* (CINCINNATI: WESTERN BIOGRAPHICAL PUBL., 1878).

that same day, but burned two days longer. That same weekend the city of Manistee burned, as did the community of Grand Junction and, most horrific of all, Peshtigo, Wisconsin, with more than a thousand deaths.[9]

In 1872 the MLS reported its main line as 57.5 miles in length. The commissioner of railroads' annual report for 1872 shows that the Michigan Lake Shore did not build any bridges north of Muskegon, and that the farthest north was a short one in Muskegon, presumably over Ryerson Creek. Without more adequate documentation, it is reasonable to assume that the north end of the M&F was at its junction with the C&MLS, at the south end of North Yard, about a city block north of Hall Avenue in Muskegon. Alternatively, using the mileages given in *Michigan Railroad Lines*, the distance from the junction on the northeast side of Allegan to North Yard is 56.8 miles. Companies usually included the mileage of running rights used over other roads. By adding the 0.6 miles over the Grand River drawbridge at Grand Haven owned by the Detroit, Grand Haven & Milwaukee, the total distance becomes 57.4 miles, one-tenth of a mile less than reported by the commissioner of railroads and the Michigan Railroad Commission.[10]

The Pennsylvania Railroad and its holding company, the Pennsylvania Company, formed the Continental Improvement Company in 1868 to build the Grand Rapids & Indiana Railroad (GR&I) and by 1873 had the line completed between Fort Wayne, Indiana, and Petoskey, Michigan. In 1872 the Pennsylvania made another move into west Michigan. The holding company gained an interest in the Mansfield, Coldwater & Lake Michigan Railroad (MC&LM), which proposed to build a line from Mansfield, Ohio, to Allegan. It appears that the Pennsylvania saw value in connecting its Pittsburgh-Chicago main line with access to the Muskegon sawmills and a Lake Michigan port. One part of the MC&LM was a 12.5-mile stretch of its main line built between Allegan and the GR&I line at Monteith that gave it access to the MLS. The Pennsylvania was soon disillusioned with its MLS venture. The market for lumber began to drop in 1872, the Panic of 1873 soon followed, and then a business depression followed. This combination was devastating for the Michigan Lake Shore. The bonds it had issued had an annual interest charge of $70,400. As table 17 shows, at no time in its life did MLS have enough net income to pay all of this charge, although in some years it was able to pay some of it.[11]

The Michigan Lake Shore was forced into receivership on 5 December 1873. It could not

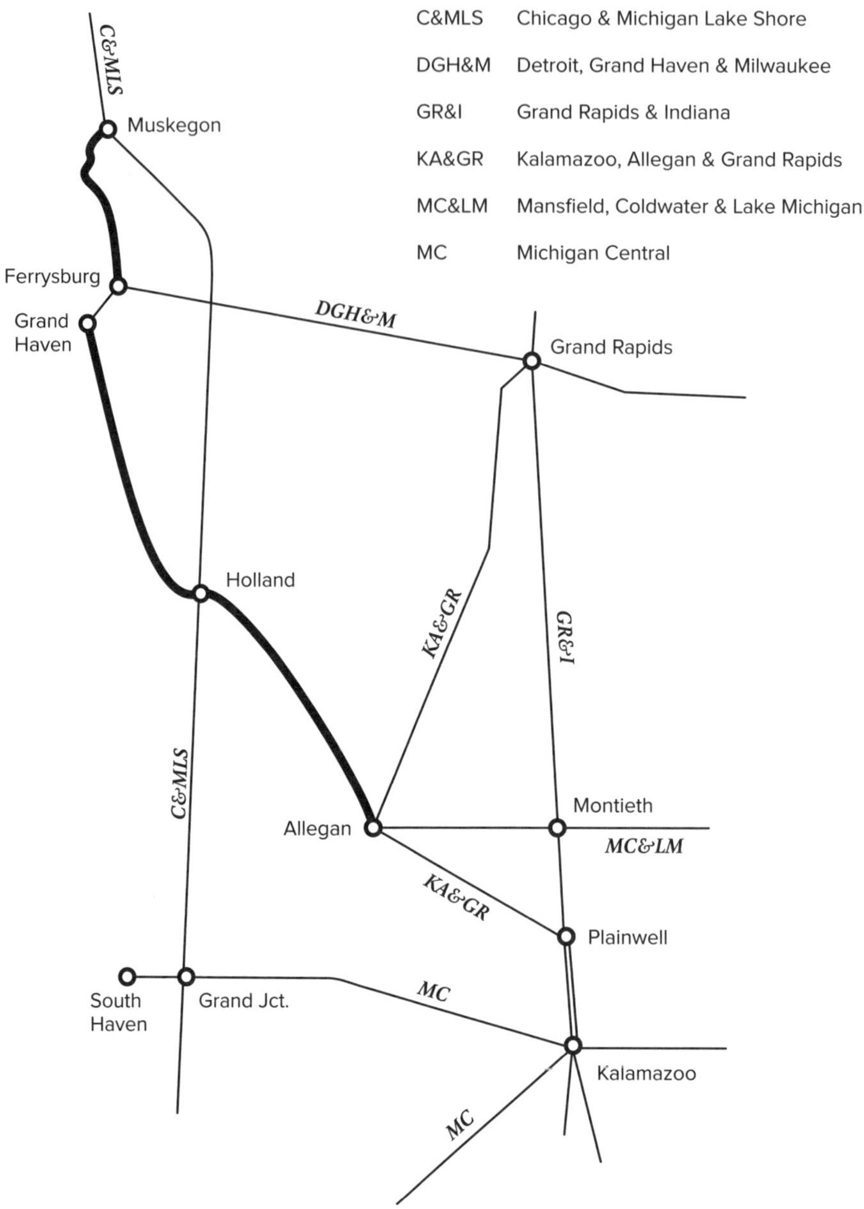

Michigan Lake Shore–Grand Haven line. The road as completed in 1870 was built in three sections. The Muskegon & Ferrysburg built between its namesake towns. The Allegan & Holland built between its namesake towns. The Michigan Lake Shore built between Holland and Grand Haven to connect the two ends of the road.

Table 17. Revenue and operating statistics for Michigan Lake Shore and Grand Haven, 1872–1880

YEAR	MILES OF ROAD	PASSENGER REVENUE	NUMBER OF PASSENGERS	PASSENGER MILES (THOUS.)	FREIGHT REVENUE	FREIGHT TONS	TON MILES (THOUS.)	OPERATING EXPENSE & TAXES	NET INCOME* (LOSS)
Michigan Lake Shore Railroad†									
1870			No report						
1871			No report						
1872	57.5	$54,357			$55,327	55,315		$165,605	($76,716)
1873	57.5	43,501			49,214			104,826	(7,095)
1874	57.5	33,087			47,097			59,138	25,687
1875	57.5	26,304	60,957	878	36,786			59,245	10,562
1876	57.5	27,996	60,577	933	31,893			52,517	13,588
1877	57.5	22,778	48,092	904	27,244	23,457	601	41,587	24,382
1–9/1878, MLS	57.5	16,737	34,886	555	20,115	19,030	513	57,152	(15,910)
10–12/1878, Grand Haven Railroad†	57.5	5,486	11,709	183	7,665	6,193	220	13,430	1,025
1878 full year, two companies combined	57.5	22,223	46,595	738	27,780	25,223	733	70,582	(14,885)
1879	57.5	27,355	58,233	926	29,101	28,801	1,281	69,236	(7,554)
1880	57.5	34,786	74,956	1,247	38,491	38,739	1,726	74,246	4,975
1–9/1881	57.5	31,248			48,960			60,336	23,695

Source: Data from Michigan Auditor General, *Annual Reports*, and Michigan Railroad Commission, *Annual Reports*.
Notes: There were no reports available for the years 1870 and 1871.
* Net income is passenger revenue, freight revenue, and miscellaneous revenue, less operating expense.
† The MLS reports to the commissioner of railroads are notable for being incomplete. So too is the final report of the Grand Haven.

continue to operate with a deficit that now totaled $466,816. David P. Clay, a Grand Rapids industrialist and founder of the Grand Rapids, Newaygo & Lake Shore Railroad, was appointed the receiver. The road remained under his control until it was sold at foreclosure on 19 June 1878.[12]

Grand Haven

The Grand Haven Railroad Company (GH) was formed on 21 September 1878 to buy and reorganize the Michigan Lake Shore road. Clay's reorganization plan was simple. He canceled all the outstanding common stock, then replaced all of the outstanding bonds with an issue $800,000 in new common stock. The reorganization ended the Pennsylvania Company's interest in the property, although that holding company was so powerful financially that it must have agreed to it. James W. Converse became president of the new company and Frederick H. May of Allegan was named general manager. Over its three-year life the GH was almost profitable. With only a small amount of unfunded debt, its interest expense was minimal. But the road did not carry the amount of lumber traffic that the competing Chicago & Michigan Lake Shore did. In its last year the Grand Haven had 31 percent of its tonnage

James W. Converse. This Grand Rapids businessman invested in several west Michigan railroad projects.
FROM GRAND RAPIDS PUBLIC LIBRARY.

in manufactures and merchandise. The GH's weakness was the amount of revenue it took in; its freight revenue per mile of road was barely half that of the C&MLS and reflected its relatively smaller market.[13]

Soon after Converse became president of the Grand Haven road he planned an extension. On 15 October 1879 he incorporated the Muskegon Lake Railroad Company to build a 5-mile line from his Grand Haven line along the south shore of Muskegon Lake to the mouth of the lake, a point also called Port Sheldon. In 1881 it built 4.7 miles of line from its connection at Eighth Street to Port Sherman; in 1882 it built an additional 1.3 miles that have not been identified. The original line later became known as the South Horn Branch.[14]

On 20 May 1881, in an attempt to strengthen itself, the GH amended its corporate articles to allow it to have a line that was to extend from Allegan to Battle Creek. This was a plan similar to that of the earlier Mansfield, Coldwater & Lake Michigan, but nothing came of it. On 16 July 1881, effective 30 September, the Grand Haven was merged into its side-by-side competitor, the Chicago & West Michigan. About that same time control of the Muskegon Lake passed to the Chicago & West Michigan.[15]

Chicago & Michigan Lake Shore

The people of St. Joseph had high hopes for a railroad. In 1832 the Detroit & St. Joseph Railroad had proposed to build a cross-state line to St. Joseph, but the company accomplished little except near Detroit. In 1837 the new State of Michigan created an ambitious internal improvement program that planned to build three cross-state rail lines. For its "central" line it adopted the D&SJ plans and by the end of 1837 began building west from Detroit. Rails reached Kalamazoo in 1846, 50 miles from St. Joseph, but the state was out of money and could not build farther. The state sold the Detroit-Kalamazoo line to the Michigan Central Railroad (MC) in September 1846 with the provision it must build "to a point on or near Lake Michigan accessible to

Alexander H. Morrison. He founded the Chicago & Michigan Lake Shore that first built from St. Joseph to New Buffalo. His road later extended farther north along the Lake Michigan shore as the Chicago & West Michigan.

FROM LEONARD A. MORRISON, *THE HISTORY OF THE MORISON OR MORRISON FAMILY* (BOSTON: A. WILLIAMS & CO., 1880).

steamboats," but did not specify St. Joseph. The next spring MC superintendent John Woods Brooks began grading west out of Kalamazoo. He made two surveys for lines from Mattawan to St. Joseph and a third from Mattawan to New Buffalo. In June 1847 MC president John Murray Forbes came to Michigan to decide the better port to use. He was unimpressed with the swamp lands around St. Joseph, and decided on New Buffalo at the terminus. By 1849 the MC had laid its rails into the tiny port of New Buffalo, well south of the somewhat larger St. Joseph. To get themselves a railroad local businessmen formed two companies, one in 1848 and another in 1850, to connect St. Joseph with some point on the MC. Unfortunately, nothing came of either of them, and events rested there until the end of the Civil War.[16]

Investors and speculators were flush with new money at the end of the war, and some of it was put into a surge of railroad building, nationally and in Michigan. A new project was floated in 1868, to connect Chicago with the Grand Trunk Railway of Canada at its St. Clair River crossing at Sarnia; the line was to run through Lansing and St. Joseph. It came to nothing. The impatient businessmen of St. Joseph finally acted on their own by forming the Chicago and Michigan Lake Shore Rail Road Company (C&MLS) on 23 April 1869. Their company had rights to build a 30-mile line from St. Joseph to the Indiana state line. The driving force behind the railroad was businessman Alexander H. Morrison; he had moved to St. Joseph in 1850, opened a general store, and involved himself in local and state politics and a variety of businesses. Morrison was named president of the railroad.

To finance construction Morrison sold stock and was able to persuade several townships along the line to issue bonds to assist the railroad. The bonds were authorized by a new 1869 state law that gave general permission to any Michigan city or township to issue bonds up to 10 percent of its assessed valuation to aid in building a railroad. The measure passed in part because Henry H. Crapo—who opposed such bonds—was no longer governor and because Henry P. Baldwin as the new governor favored them. St. Joseph Township donated $4,000 in cash to help the railroad; and Lincoln, Lake, Chickaming, and New Buffalo Townships along the route agreed to bonds for an added $16,100.[17]

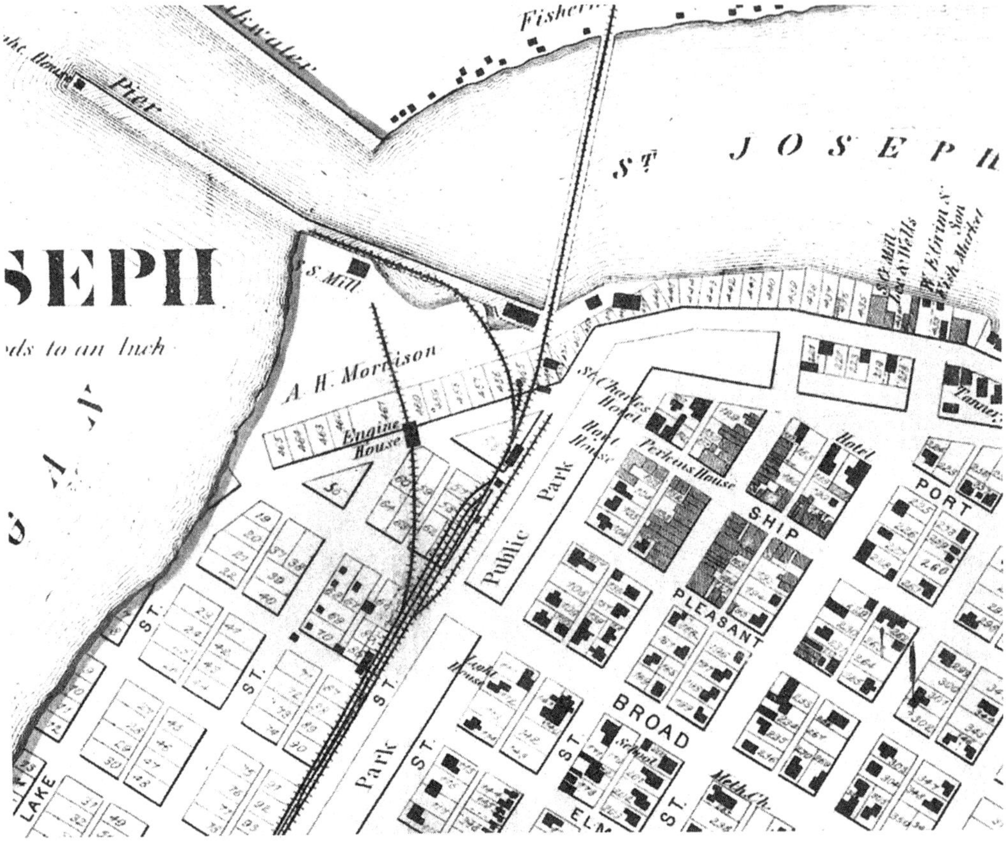

Detail map of St. Joseph. The original St. Joseph depot was located on the lake side of the tracks almost opposite the present station. Some of Morrison's land west of the station was later developed into the site for Silver Beach Amusement Park.

FROM *ATLAS OF BERRIEN COUNTY, MICHIGAN* (PHILADELPHIA: C. O. TITUS, 1873).

Robert A. Conolly, the road's chief engineer, started grading at St Joseph. Conolly had earlier experience as a civil engineer and as building contractor on an early section of the Chicago & North Western Railway. By October he had Morrison's roadbed ready. A ship brought the needed rails, two flatcars, and the locomotive *Swallow* for the track laying. Track work was finished 28 January 1870, and the road formally opened for business on 2 February.[18]

Their railroad now completed, the residents of St. Joseph demanded "a grand celebration." One group of celebrants rode Michigan Central trains to New Buffalo in a crowd that overflowed the cars. In New Buffalo they found no more cars for the ride to St. Joseph. A crowd of nearly a thousand commandeered boxcars and happily rode them to the festivities. One commentator reported that when the train arrived at St. Joseph it was met with "the ringing of bells, the roar of cannon, and the shouts of the multitude. It was estimated that some five or six thousand people were in St. Joseph." The railroad encouraged new communities as well. Stevensville was founded by Thomas Stevens in 1871. Lumberman George W. Bridgman, a C&MLS director, had moved to the lakeshore in 1856, and platted his namesake village in 1870.[19]

201 CHICAGO AND MICHIGAN LAKE SHORE ROAD.

A. H. Morrison, President. | H. W. Guernsey, Secretary.
S. R. Hughes, Superintendent. | Gen. Office, St. Joseph, Mich.

Trains Leave. May 9, 1870. **Trains Arrive.**

Mix	Mix	Mls	STATIONS.	Mls	Mix	Mix
P. M.	A. M.				A. M.	P. M.
7 10	11 45	0	lv. **New Buffalo**[1] ar	27	6 15	5 10
7 20	11 58	4	.....Town Line.....	23	6 06	4 55
7 25	12 03	6	....Wilkinson's....	21	6 02	4 51
7 32	12 09	7	....Chickaming....	20	5 58	4 46
7 42	12 19	10	........Troy........	17	5 52	4 38
7 50	12 24	11	......Brown's......	16	5 47	4 33
8 00	12 39	15	....Bridgeman's....	12	5 37	4 21
8 08	12 49	16	.......Morris.......	11	5 33	4 08
8 16	1 02	20	....Stevensville....	7	5 2:	3 53
8 24	1 12	22	......Lincoln.......	4	5 15	3 43
8 40	1 30	27	....**St. Joseph**[2]...	0	5 00	3 25
P. M.	P. M.		ARRIVE] [LEAVE		A. M.	P. M.

CONNECTIONS.

[1] At *New Buffalo* with trains on Michigan Central Railroad.
[2] At *St. Joseph* with stages for Royalton and Berrill daily, and tri-weekly for Millburg, Colonia, Watervliet and Hartford.

Chicago & Michigan Lake Shore 1870 schedule. This 1870 timetable was issued just months after the road was completed between New Buffalo and St. Joseph.

FROM AUTHOR'S COLLECTION.

Morrison planned to connect with the Michigan Central at New Buffalo and to use MC tracks to reach Chicago. Morrison's line made a track connection with the MC on the west side of its New Buffalo depot. Between Union Pier and New Buffalo the C&MLS line was to the west of the present line, coming near the Lake Michigan shore just north of New Buffalo. The MC allowed Morrison to use its New Buffalo station and to run some of its passenger trains through to Chicago. Other trains made close connections for riders to change trains.

As their railroad was being launched, Morrison and his partners dreamed of expansion. On 25 June 1869 they formed the Lake Shore Railroad Company of Western Michigan, an ambitious project to build a 90-mile road from St. Joseph north to the Muskegon River. Muskegon was already an important town for its many sawmills, and must have been desirable for its freight potential. The ink was barely dry on the corporate papers when, on 12 July, the Lake Shore was merged into the Chicago & Michigan Lake Shore. This gave Morrison's road expansive new rights, but put little money in the bank.

Morrison had promises of a total of $332,100 in municipal financial aid in Berrien, Van Buren, and Allegan Counties to build his line. Of this amount the railroad eventually received only $20,100; the remainder was declared unconstitutional by the state's supreme court and was never paid out. Morrison approached the city of Holland for assistance. The city voters had approved $16,000 in bonds in June 1869 to bring the Allegan & Holland to their community. But aid for Morrison's road was not forthcoming.[20]

Morrison then turned to a friend—James F. Joy. The two were Republicans from the early days of the party in Jackson in 1854 and had served together in Michigan's house of representatives in the 1861–1862 session. More importantly Joy had gained a substantial reputation as a railroad builder, and in 1867 he became president of the Michigan Central Railroad. As a further bonus Joy had friends in New England, some of them directors of the Michigan Central, and they had money that they were willing to invest at Joy's recommendation. To pay for the construction, with Joy's help, C&MLS was able to sell $4 million in mortgage bonds, probably at some discount, and gather in as well nearly $800,000 in stock subscriptions. Joy must have

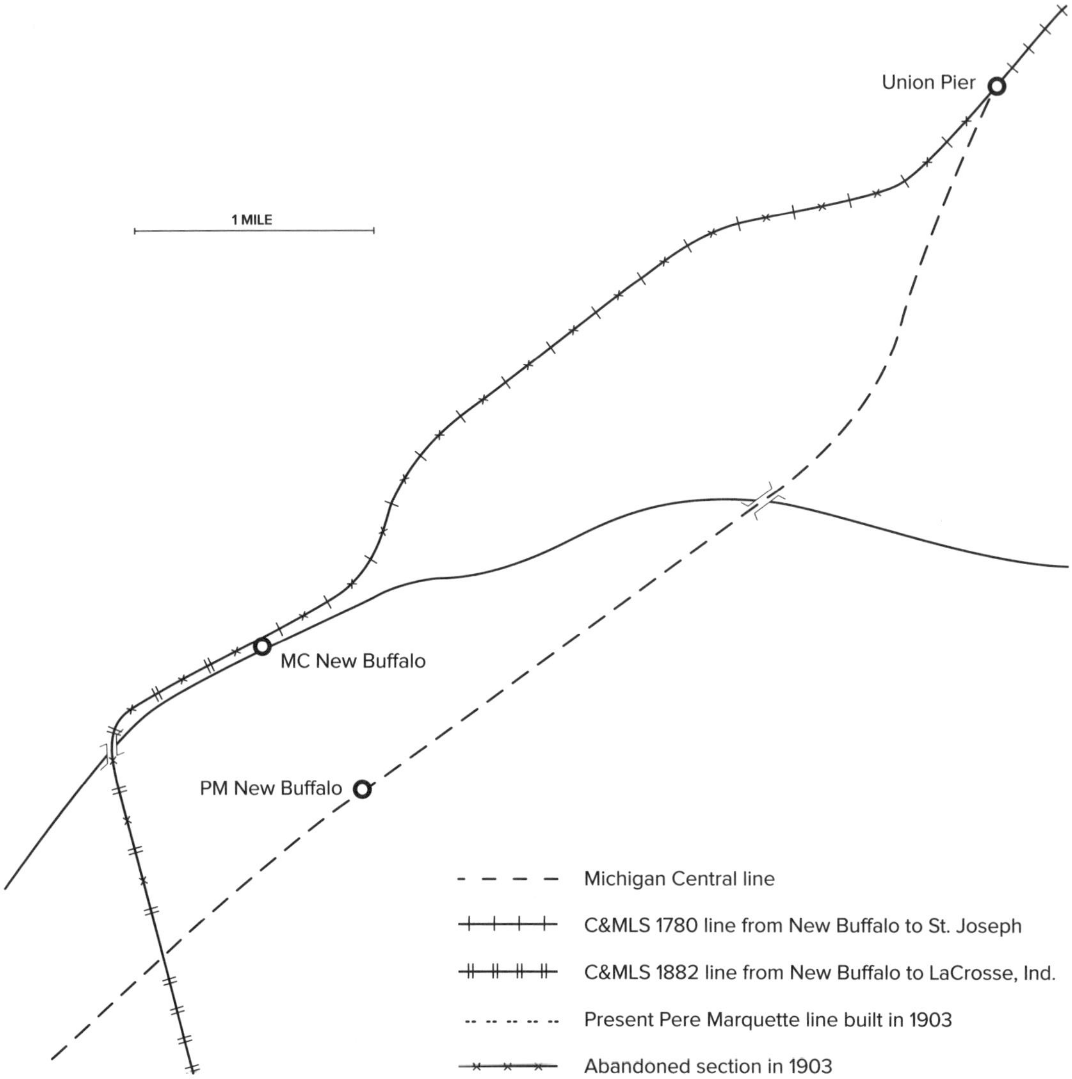

New Buffalo area. The original Chicago & Michigan Lake Shore line left the present tracks just north of Union Pier Road, used the grade of the present Red Arrow Highway as far as Community Hall Road, then turned southwest toward Lake Michigan and ran along the south side of Marquette Drive. The tracks ran on the bluff west of the Galien River, then curved to the south-southeast to cross Whittaker Street. The Michigan Central station was located just west (left) of Whittaker Street and was also used by the Chicago & Michigan Lake Shore.

wanted to be sure that his investment was well managed and took over as president of the road in 1870; Morrison stepped aside to become vice president and general manager.[21]

Joy and Morrison started building north. Once across the St. Joseph River and through Benton Harbor, the line headed inland, east to Hartford near the center of Van Buren County. There the road turned northeast and then north in almost a straight line to Holland. This inland route gave the C&MLS access to the pine forests of Van Buren and Allegan Counties. On 28 February 1871 the road was completed from St. Joseph into Grand Junction; Morrison put down his rails just before Joy's Michigan Central-controlled Kalamazoo & South Haven line was built through town. At the crossing of two railroads, Grand Junction was platted in 1871 to be a place of promise. In October of that year that bright future was lost when a fire destroyed every building in the community. Other better-known fires destroyed Chicago and Holland. A dozen tiny communities grew up along Morrison's line. Watervliet had had a sawmill for nearly fifty years before his rails came to town, but now fruit and grain were being shipped. Hartford and Watervliet were designated on the route of the Detroit & St. Joseph; building the C&MLS brought a burst of prosperity to the hamlet of Hartford. Bangor, another sawmill town until the rails came, had a blast furnace and a chemical works built in 1872, and the town's first bank opened that year. Fennville, not far from Elam Fenn's sawmill, was platted in 1871 and large amounts of fruit were shipped from its depot. It is not an official record, but it appears that the first C&MLS train into Holland ran on 24 May 1871.[22]

Getting into Holland required crossing the Kalamazoo River at New Richmond. The 3.3-mile section of road south of Holland, from the bridge at New Richmond to the station at East Saugatuck, was an operational challenge from the day it was built. To get out of the river valley northbound (technically eastbound) trains had to climb a very stiff grade averaging 1.23 percent. The grade severely limited the size of the freight trains that the small locomotives could pull up the hill. The grade was never removed and hindered movements as long as steam engines were run. In some cases a freight could pull only half of its train up the hill to East Saugatuck siding, then had to "double" back to bring up the remainder. For many years a helper engine was stationed at New Richmond with the sole purpose of pushing freight trains to East Saugatuck.[23]

Muskegon attracted another railroad on 3 February 1869 when the Grand Rapids & Lake Shore Railroad (GR&LS) was formed. Its promoter, Edward L. Craw, was the founder of the town of Crawville in 1868, which he renamed Fruitport in 1869. Craw will appear later with his involvement in the Chicago, Saginaw & Canada line. He proposed to build a line from Grand Rapids, along the Grand River, into Muskegon, then extend north to Whitehall. Early in 1870 the company twice changed its proposed northern terminus, first to Pentwater, then to Manistee. It appears that Craw may have started to build his line from Muskegon southeast toward Nunica, but whether Craw had the segment built or had Morrison and Joy build it is not clear. One source states that this 15.8-mile segment was built sometime during 1870, and the work is credited to the C&MLS. The road's Muskegon depot was located on the west side of and facing Ottawa Street, at the foot of Giddings Avenue, one block north of Hall Avenue. In any event, The C&MLS bought the GR&LS on 15 August 1870. With this purchase Joy and Morrison gained rights to build as far north as Manistee. A county history states that the first

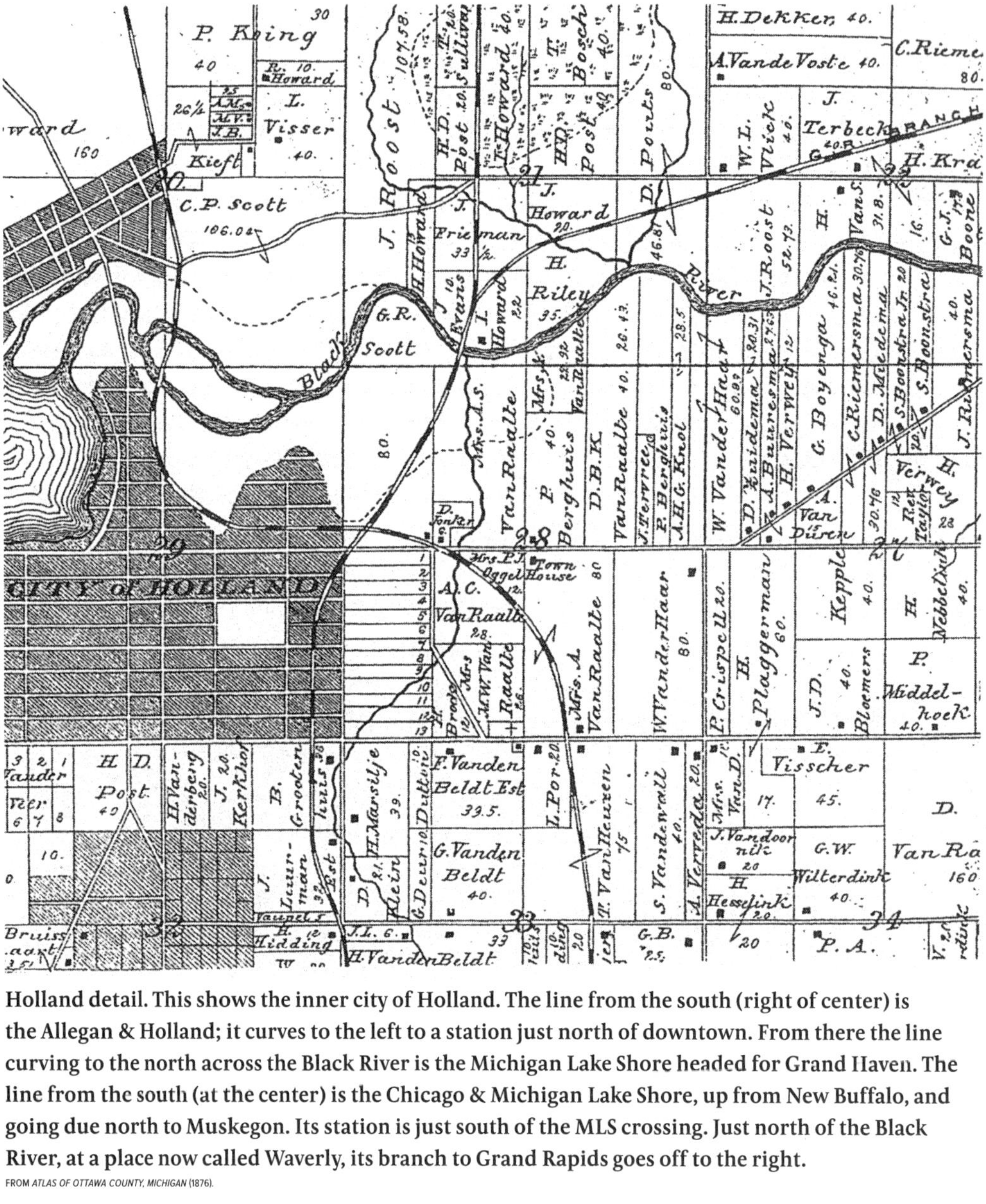

Holland detail. This shows the inner city of Holland. The line from the south (right of center) is the Allegan & Holland; it curves to the left to a station just north of downtown. From there the line curving to the north across the Black River is the Michigan Lake Shore headed for Grand Haven. The line from the south (at the center) is the Chicago & Michigan Lake Shore, up from New Buffalo, and going due north to Muskegon. Its station is just south of the MLS crossing. Just north of the Black River, at a place now called Waverly, its branch to Grand Rapids goes off to the right.

FROM *ATLAS OF OTTAWA COUNTY, MICHIGAN* (1876).

C&MLS train north of Muskegon came into Whitehall on a 13-mile line on 29 October 1870. Whitehall was incorporated as a village in 1867, and was then reported to have ten sawmills, six stores, three hotels, and a tannery.[24]

Before the Muskegon-Nunica segment was completed Craw turned his attention to another project, the Fruitport and Lake Shore Rail Road Company. This road was organized on 29 January 1870 to build a 22-mile line from Fruitport to Holland. This shadowy company, by one report, is said to have built some of the line between Nunica and Holland, but no official

Lyman G. Mason. He promoted building two PM predecessor lines out of Muskegon. Later he supported bringing the Grand Rapids & Indiana and Grand Trunk systems to Muskegon.
FROM WIKITREE.

record confirms this. Apparently Craw was able to persuade Fruitport Township to issue $13,300 in municipal aid to his railroad, but there is no record that the money was paid. The Fruitport-Holland route the company proposed to build was recorded as completed by the Chicago & Michigan Lake Shore on 30 June 1871, but no transfer of franchise or record of the corporation has been found.[25]

On 25 October 1871 Morrison & Joy bought the Grand Rapids and Holland Railroad Company (GR&H). It was formed on 20 February 1871 by a group of Grand Rapids men who, it appears, soon realized the advantage of affiliating with the C&MLS. The GR&H may have graded some part of its line, but it completed none of it until Joy became involved. Grading began about August 1871 at Grandville. The date the road was completed is unclear. The commissioner of railroads reports the Grand Rapids–Holland line was put in service on 1 January 1872. Baxter's *History of Grand Rapids* has the opening date as 6 January 1872. The *Grand Rapids Daily* Eagle reported Morrison's announcement that it would open on 8 January. The road's passenger station was on Ottawa Street, about a block south of Fulton Street, on the west side of Van Andel Arena. Its freight station was on Cherry Street. This branch gave the C&MLS access to the state's second largest city, which was developing into an important manufacturing center.[26] Also on 25 October Morrison and Joy bought a second road—the Montague, Pentwater and Manistee Railroad Company (MP&M). Organized on 7 July 1871 by a group of five Pentwater men, the road apparently laid no tracks but did have value for a franchise that extended from Montague to Manistee.[27]

Next Joy and Morrison bought the Muskegon and Big Rapids Railroad Company (M&BR) on 27 July 1872. The company was organized on 24 August 1871 and was promoted by Muskegon lumberman Lyman G. Mason, who served as the road's president. He contracted with Thompson, Smith & Company of Detroit to build the road under a contract with Morrison and Joy. To reach more of the forested area in Newaygo County, Mason kept the route inland, 10 miles and more north of the river. It appears that Mason intended his road to haul sawed lumber and other forest products, not logs, to Muskegon. The M&BR completed its 51.1-mile line to Big Rapids on 21 July 1873. The branch ran from a connection at Berry, about 5 miles north of Muskegon, passed through Fremont and White Cloud, and gave C&MLS access to a large expanse of uncut forest along the line. Fremont was then a community of but a few hundred

Big Rapids. The Chicago & Michigan Lake Shore extended its line from Muskegon into Big Rapids in 1873. The station stood on the southeast corner of State and Pine Streets. Eventually the Detroit, Lansing & Northern built across the Muskegon River to reach this station.
FROM AUTHOR'S COLLECTION.

souls and was still called Fremont Center. The eastern Newaygo County townships were heavily timbered; the C&MLS built several short spurs and branches to reach farther into the woods. In Big Rapids the line extended to the Muskegon River to reach industries on the west bank of the river. The C&MLS now owned 246 miles of road, with lumber and forest products making up more than half of its freight traffic.[28]

The town of Pentwater, on the Lake Michigan shore 40 miles north of Muskegon, believed it was to become an important economic center as well as the terminus of a railroad. Early in 1869 the Ionia & Lansing had made plans to build there. The Detroit, Lansing & Lake Michigan, which had absorbed the I&L in 1871, built as far as Howard City, but made little effort to complete a line into Pentwater. In February 1870 a delegation from Pentwater went to Grand Rapids to meet with the organizers of the Grand Rapids and Lake Shore Railroad Company (GR&LS). That road was organized on 3 February 1869 to connect Grand Rapids with Muskegon and Whitehall. It appears that the Pentwater men influenced the GR&LS to change its northern terminus to Pentwater in February 1870. But in May they changed its northern goal again, this time to Manistee, which remained its goal when Joy and Morrison bought the road.[29]

Two weeks later, on 17 February 1870, Ransom Gardner, the president of the Michigan Lake Shore Railroad, wrote to the Pentwater delegation that he would complete a line from

Pentwater.

FROM *OCEANA COUNTY, MICHIGAN* (BATTLE CREEK, MICH., STANDARD ATLAS CO., 1895).

Muskegon to Pentwater by 1 October 1871. To do this the communities along the line would have to provide financial aid and the residents would have to subscribe to enough stock. Apparently Gardner's offer was not sufficiently tempting. James F. Joy then came forward with a promise that his Chicago & Michigan Lake Shore would have a line built to Pentwater by

Nathaniel Thayer Jr. He was a financial investor in the Detroit, Lansing & Lake Michigan and the Chicago & Michigan Lake Shore.

FROM GEORGE E. ELLIS, *MEMOIR OF NATHANIEL THAYER, A.M.* (CAMBRIDGE, MASS.: JOHN WILSON & SON, 1885).

1 July 1871. The citizens of both Hart and Pentwater accepted his offer. Soon after, on 15 August 1870, the C&MLS bought the GR&LS.[30]

This northern extension, 27 miles from Montague to Pentwater, was built on the franchise rights of the very obscure Montague, Pentwater & Manistee Railroad (MP&M), a company that was organized on 7 July 1871 by Pentwater businessmen led by Samuel A. Browne. His Pentwater Lumber Company was the catalyst for the development of the community. By his own effort Browne raised $50,000 in pledges for the right-of-way and to build the railroad. The C&MLS bought the Pentwater road's rights on 25 October 1871. Apparently Morrison and Joy started building north from Montague even before they bought the MP&M.[31]

Oceana County, north of Montague, was heavily forested and could provide still more revenue for the C&MLS. Stretched along the 15 miles north of Montague were the towns of Rothbury, New Era, and Shelby. The railroad brought the village of Shelby to life in a convoluted manner. As the railroad was being built, two parts of the town were platted, one named Shelby and one named Barnett. The story is that a railroad brakeman named Barnett reportedly offered to pay for the platting if the promoters would name it for him. When the work was done and the plat recorded, the promoters asked the brakeman for the promised money; he claimed he was joking and refused to pay the promised fees. The railroad and the post office quickly picked Shelby, the township in which the community was located, as the town name, although Barnett lasted as the municipal name for a short time longer. North of Shelby, Morrison and Joy contracted with Thompson, Smith & Company of Detroit to build the road. Train service to Pentwater started on 1 January 1872. By building on a direct route to Pentwater, the C&MLS bypassed the Oceana County seat of Hart, an oversight that was not remedied until 1880. The junction with the branch to Hart was named Mears after lumberman Charles Mears. In 1874 Mears made it his headquarters; the town gained three sawmills and several other factories. When the lumber played out Mears moved on, died in 1895, and the community faded.[32]

Morrison left his railroad in 1873 to move to Chicago to repair his health and to pursue other ventures. The financial panic of 1873 brought such critical times that the Michigan

Table 18. Revenue and operating statistics for Chicago & Michigan Lake Shore, 1870–1878

YEAR	MILES OF ROAD OWNED	PASSENGER REVENUE	NUMBER OF PASSENGERS	PASSENGER MILES (THOUS.)	FREIGHT REVENUE	FREIGHT TONS	TON MILES (THOUS.)	OPERATING EXPENSE & TAXES	NET INCOME*
1870	27.5							$13,184	
1871	143	$68,468	101,945	2,345	$78,289	58,509		57,328	
1872	250	191,413			288,873	137,158		275,498	227,525
1873	246	248,769	285,077	8,292	343,857	187,254	11,700†	410,127	242,504
1874	246	261,248	289,790	8,708	371,859	213,811	12,367	536,843	146,602
1875	246	232,217	262,478	7,900†	354,574	249,377	15,664	567,295	55,160
1876	246	210,701	240,726	7,022	322,063	223,710	14,042	487,649	79,168
1877	246	171,124	205,294	5,650	287,636	197,636	12,869	407,877	80,908
1878	246	175,921	219,147	5,818	333,809	266,701	14,930	500,479	37,543

Source: Data from Michigan Auditor General, *Annual Reports*, and Michigan Railroad Commission, *Annual Reports*.
* Net income is passenger revenue, freight revenue, and miscellaneous revenue, less operating expense and taxes.
† Estimated.

Table 19. Costs, equipment, capitalization for Chicago & Michigan Lake Shore 1872–1878

YEAR	MILES OF ROAD OWNED	COST OF ROAD (THOUS.)	COST OF EQUIPMENT (THOUS.)	NUMBER ENGINES	NUMBER FREIGHT CARS	NUMBER PASSENGER CARS	NUMBER EMPLOYEES	COMMON STOCK (THOUS.)	TOTAL DEBT (THOUS.)
1872	250.0	$7,859	$799	25	612	19		$1,688	$6,975
1873	246.0	7,864	n.a.					1,688	6,975
1874	246.0	6,185	n.a.	25	602	18	900	1,511	7,723
1875	246.0	6,200	868	25	602	18	830	1,515	7,864
1876	246.0	6,205	870	25	596	21	700	1,515	8,357
1877	246.0	6,216	894	26	587	21	580	1,515	8,501
1878	246.0	6,225	899	26	490	22	650	1,515	8,988

Source: Data from Michigan Railroad Commission.
Note: No dividends were paid.

Table 20. Freight and lumber traffic statistics for Chicago & Michigan Lake Shore, 1872–1878

YEAR	REVENUE	YTY % CHANGE (THOUS.)	REVENUE TRAIN MILES	REVENUE TONS (THOUS.)	YTY % CHANGE	REVENUE PER TON (THOUS.)	REVENUE TON MILES (THOUS.)	TONS LUMBER	YTY % CHANGE	% OF ALL TONS
1872	$288,873		198.1	137.1		$0.47		76.1		55.5
1873	343,857	19.0	222.7	187.3	36.6	0.54		129.3	60.9	69.0
1874	371,859	8.1	239.8	213.8	14.1	0.57	12,367	137.5	6.3	64.3
1875	354,574	-4.6	203.2	249.4	16.7	0.72	15,664	159.5	16.0	64.0
1876	322,063	-10.2	161.6	223.7	-10.3	0.69	14,042	127.7	-19.9	57.1
1877	287,636	-10.7	170.7	197.6	-11.7	0.69	12,869	100.3	-21.5	50.8
1878	333,809	16.1	209.5	266.7	35.0	0.80	14,930	153.6	53.1	57.6

Source: Data from Michigan Railroad Commission.

Table 21. Freight traffic statistics for Chicago & Michigan Lake Shore, 1872–1878

YEAR	REVENUE TONS (THOUS.)	LUMBER TONS (THOUS.)	% OF ALL TONS	AGRICULTURAL PRODUCTS TONS (THOUS.)	% OF ALL TONS	MANUFACTURES TONS (THOUS.)	% OF ALL TONS	MERCHANDISE TONS (THOUS.)	% OF ALL TONS
1872	137.1	76.1	55.5	32.2	23.5	12.1	8.8	6.7	4.9
1873	187.3	129.3	69.0	16.6	8.9	6.8	3.6	23.3	12.4
1874	213.8	137.5	64.3	22.8	10.7	–	–	33.4	15.6
1875	249.4	159.5	64.0	23.5	9.4	–	–	37.5	15.0
1876	223.7	127.7	57.1	18.7	8.3	–	–	28.4	12.7
1877	197.6	100.3	50.8	19.7	10.0	–	–	42.6	21.5
1878	266.7	153.6	57.6	26.9	17.5	–	–	38.2	14.3

Source: Data from Michigan Railroad Commission.

Central—the flagship of James F. Joy's railroads—was forced to omit a dividend, and he gave up the C&MLS president's chair that same year. Joy had brought financing for the C&MLS from a number of New Englanders, among them Charles Francis Adams Jr., Alpheus Hardy, Horatio H. Hunnewell, Charles Merriam, and Nathaniel Thayer. Thayer, a wealthy Bostonian and a major benefactor of Harvard University, replaced Joy as president. Thayer persuaded George C. Kimball to become general manager of the C&MLS. Kimball had been with the Flint & Pere Marquette, had just returned to Springfield, Massachusetts, to enter his brother's business, but now returned to Michigan. Thayer and Kimball also hired Charles M. Lawler away from the Chicago & North Western to become the C&MLS division superintendent. Both Kimball and Lawler took up residence in St. Joseph.[33]

During 1875 Kimball moved the company's general offices from St. Joseph to Muskegon, to the second story of the Ottawa Street depot, a more central location for the sprawling railroad. As part of the move Kimball also built new locomotive and car repair shops in Muskegon, bringing possibly a hundred jobs to the city. The shops and a new roundhouse were located near the south end of North Yard, on the west side of Western Avenue south of Marquette Street.[34]

There were similarities between Chicago & Michigan Lake Shore and the competing the Michigan Lake Shore–Grand Haven combine, and one important difference. The basic purpose of both was to move forest products. The C&MLS was far more aggressive in its pursuit of traffic. It built into the north woods more rapidly and bought two important connecting branches to add traffic. The C&MLS had adequate financing to do all that it planned, thanks to the money that came from James F. Joy and his New England supporters. The MLS-GH road was slower in getting built. When the Pennsylvania Company gained control, it appears its interest was only to reach Muskegon Lake. It may have been that trans–Lake Michigan shipping was a more important goal than the traffic in lumber, but the motivations are not of record. The sawmills were concentrated along the north shore of Muskegon Lake and accessible to the MLS only by barges, a difficulty that further limited the company's profitability.

The future of the C&MLS was most affected by the considerable amount of borrowing it did to build its line and to buy other companies. By the end of 1870 the C&MLS had spent

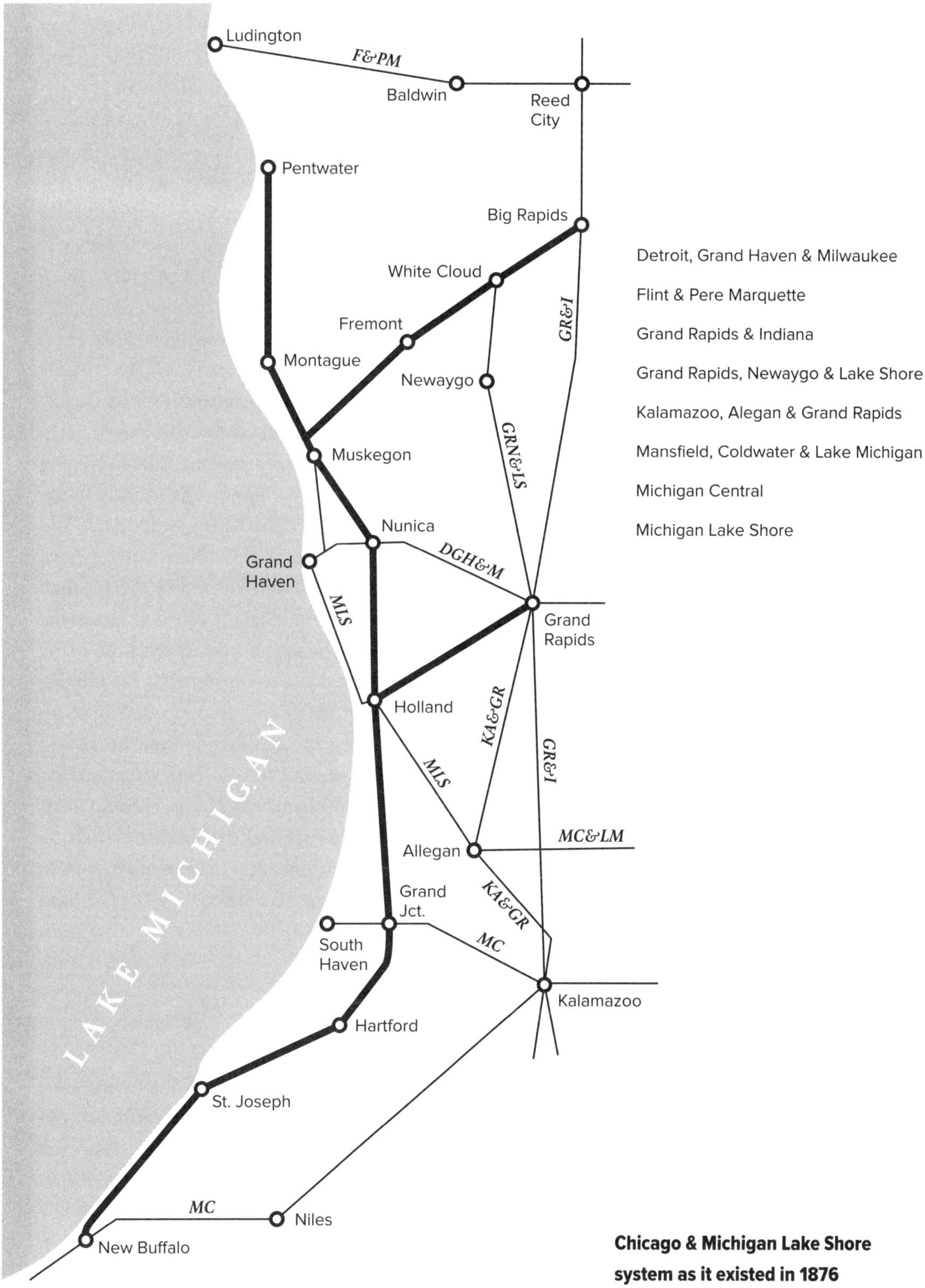

Chicago & Michigan Lake Shore system as it existed in 1876

$2,021,824 to build and in 1871 another $2,102,263. To raise the needed money for this Morrison and Joy issued $477,000 in mortgage bonds in 1869, $3,253,000 in 1870, $1,350,000 in 1871, and $1,280,000 in 1872. The debt then totaled $6,630,000, had to be sold at roughly a 20 percent discount, and carried an 8 percent interest rate—a cost of $530,400 per year. As table 18 shows, the financial panic of 1873 and the depression that followed for the next two years did not provide enough income for the company to pay its debt interest. By 1875 the unpaid interest had built up to over $1 million, with slim prospects that economic conditions would improve enough to allow its being paid. On 11 November 1876 the Chicago & Michigan Lake Shore went into receivership. General Manager Kimball, a friendly face, was appointed receiver. On 28 December 1878 the road was sold and reorganized as the Chicago & West Michigan Railroad.[35]

The story of the Chicago & Michigan Lake Shore is a representative Michigan experience. The road was conceived, financed, and built as a local project in the post–Civil War era. As such it was caught up in and benefited from a national bubble of enthusiasm for railroads. Two sources contributed to this: the Civil War soldier who for the first time experienced a trip on railroad, and the investor who wanted to put to work the profits he had made by supplying the military during the war. The investor and the railroad promoter joined one another in the late 1860s and early 1870s. The lure of building a railroad to reach Michigan's woodlands and forests was difficult to resist. The resulting railroad was built in a hurry without much regard to cost. The mortgage bonds issued to borrow money had to be discounted, often by as much as 20 percent, to make them salable. What was so promising might have succeeded except for the onset of the financial panic of 1873. Overnight, lenders shut their doors, and the panic was followed by a business depression that lasted for several years. The demand for lumber dropped dramatically and with it the revenue mainstay that the new roads depended on. Profits dropped so much that some roads could pay none of the interest due on their borrowed money. This would be followed by a receivership and this with some sort of reorganization that restructured the debt to more affordable levels. The reorganization usually was accompanied by ownership moving from the stockholders to the bondholders. For the C&MLS the situation was worse. At no time in its life did its net income from operations provide enough money to pay more than half of the interest on its debt. After 1873 the income dropped to the point no interest could be paid.[36]

Grand Rapids, Newaygo & Lake Shore

Grand Rapids businessman David P. Clay shared Alexander Morrison's vision of the future—a railroad that moved forest products from Michigan's north woods to city markets and would produce profits for its owners. On 8 September 1869 Clay formed the Grand Rapids, Newaygo and Lake Shore Rail Road Company (GRN&LS) to build such a line. He planned that his railroad would be 80 miles in length and extend from Grand Rapids, through Newaygo, to the Lake Michigan shore somewhere in Mason or Oceana County (south of Ludington and north of Whitehall).[37]

This venture fit neatly with an earlier speculation of his. Earlier in 1869, on 11 March, Clay had joined forces with Ransom Gardner in forming the Michigan Northern Rail Road Company. Gardner was then completing his Kalamazoo, Allegan & Grand Rapids line into Grand Rapids, and cast a covetous eye on the railroad land grant that the state had awarded to the Grand Rapids & Indiana (GR&I). The land grant would make the Michigan Northern both successful and very profitable for Gardner. Both Gardner and Michigan's attorney general, Dwight May, were convinced that the GR&I was an insolvent company and therefore should forfeit its land grant. To fend off Gardner and to hold on to its land grant, GR&I president Joseph K. Edgerton had put his company into a receivership. Gardner had his associate Joseph Fisk, of Allegan, file a nuisance suit against the GR&I under the guise of recovering some damages, but more importantly to have the GR&I declared insolvent. May filed a similar suit. In February 1869 circuit court Judge Flavius Littlejohn heard Fisk's and May's suits together. Littlejohn ruled that, since the GR&I had filed for receivership in federal court, this was a case of "concurrent jurisdiction"—a case filed in both state and federal court—and case had been filed in federal court before the state court. As a state judge Littlejohn would not hear the case and certainly could not decide in favor of Gardner. The decision stopped Gardner's try for the GR&I land grant.[38]

A citizens' meeting in Newaygo in August 1869 came out with firm support for Clay's rail line from Grand Rapids, and attendees may have subscribed to some stock. Clay finally started construction in July 1871, turning the first shovel on Grand Rapids west side, between 4th and 5th Streets, near St. Adalbert Church. On 9 May 1872 the Clay completed 14.7 miles of road from Grand Rapids to Sparta, in June another 7.7 miles to Casnovia, and on Wednesday, 11 September the 13.7 miles to Newaygo, for a total of 36.1 miles. The *Newaygo Republican* of 18 September reported that an excursion train had been expected on the preceding Wednesday (11 September), probably bringing only a handful of people. The train unloaded some three hundred people and the Valley City Brass Band. The reporter wrote that "when the train appeared, it seemed that every one was frantic for joy. Boys screamed, girls giggled, men cheered and women look on with hearts too full for utterance. It was the greatest day in the history of Newaygo." At the time Clay also was logging in the Newaygo area, which provided his railroad with sawed lumber to haul. Clay already owned a general store in the town and later added a planing mill, a pail factory, the Newaygo Furniture Company, and a second sawmill. In 1877 Clay bought the Newaygo Company, which operated a large sawmill.[39]

In 1872 James W. Converse, a wealthy Bostonian, became a director and invested in the Newaygo road. Converse had been involved in Grand Rapids lands and businesses since 1850, and was adding to his other business investments in Grand Rapids and Newaygo. The financial panic of 1873 put a two-year damper on railroad building, but on 24 September 1875 Clay was able to complete another 10.6 miles to extend his road to White Cloud. There he connected with the Muskegon–Big Rapids line of the Chicago & Michigan Lake Shore built in 1873. When White Cloud hosted an opening celebration, two locomotives were needed to pull the train of six hundred riders. No hotel in town was large enough to handle the crowd that spilled out into local restaurants. A welcoming salute was fired off to greet the travelers, but it also broke the glass in several railcar windows.[40]

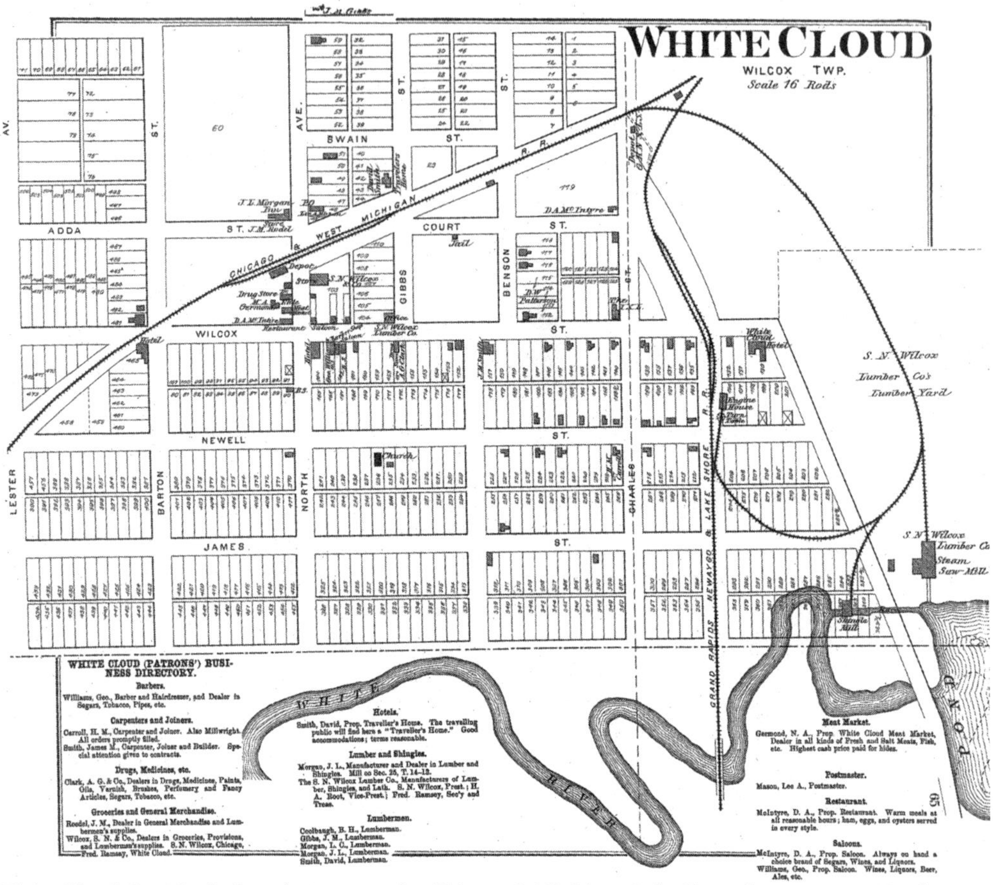

White Cloud. In 1880, before the merger, the Chicago & Michigan Lake Shore depot was on North Avenue just north of Wilcox, and the Grand Rapids, Newaygo & Lake Shore depot was on Evergreen Drive a block north of Court Street.

FROM *ATLAS OF NEWAYGO COUNTY* (PHILADELPHIA: C. O. TITUS, 1880).

Clay's railroad was quite profitable. It cost $1,294,000 to build—just over $28,000 per mile—and spent another $216,000 for cars and locomotives. To finance this Clay issued $576,000 in 8 percent first mortgage bonds in 1871 and followed with another $200,000 in 1875 to complete the extension to White Cloud. The books showed $532,000 in common stock paid in, but it is likely that some of this was used to encourage the bond sales. As table 22 shows, net income usually was enough to cover the $46,000 annual interest expense. The road did carry several hundred thousand dollars of unfunded debt, but the interest due on that amount is not of record. The second bond issue of $200,000 in 1875 added another $14,000 in annual interest charges, a cost that made the road only marginally profitable. Paul Wesley Ivey states that by 1881 the road had accumulated a deficit of $36,554.[41]

Table 22 shows that Clay's road was more profitable than the Chicago & Michigan Lake Shore, although it cost slightly more to build. In 1878, as an example, the C&MLS received $1,356 in freight revenues per mile of road, while for Clay's road freight brought in $1,863 per mile.

Table 22. Revenue and operating statistics for Grand Rapids, Newaygo & Lake Shore, 1872–1881

YEAR	MILES OF ROAD OWNED	PASSENGER REVENUE	NUMBER OF PASSENGERS	PASSENGER MILES (THOUS.)	FREIGHT REVENUE	FREIGHT TONS	TON MILES (THOUS.)	OPERATING EXPENSE & TAXES	NET INCOME*
1872	35.4	$20,099			$33,316			$44,388	$18,472
1873	35.4	38,242	67,905	1,149	80,068	58,265		69,524	63,248
1874	35.4	33,076			86,959			63,840	71,350
1875	46.0	33,843	62,672	1,128	69,933			57,529	54,318
1876	46.0	35,371	62,053	1,179	66,651			48,727	63,895
1877	46.0	31,827	53,846	1,077	61,226	64,314	1,728	45,780	54,452
1878	46.0	33,819	127,790	2,556	76,672	77,184	2,060	52,263	66,256
1879	46.0	35,402	51,340	1,181	85,740	94,122	2,534	64,790	78,839
1880	46.0	42,300	62,635	1,441	117,553	130,246	3,395	78,177	90,821
1–9/1881	46.0	31,428			68,894			77,597	25,987

Source: Data from Michigan Railroad Commission, *Annual Reports*. Company did not furnish all requested information.
* Net income is passenger revenue, freight revenue, and miscellaneous revenue, less operating expense.

Table 23. Costs, equipment, capitalization for Grand Rapids, Newaygo & Lake Shore, 1872–1881

YEAR	MILES OF ROAD OWNED	COST OF ROAD (THOUS.)	COST OF EQUIPMENT (THOUS.)	NUMBER ENGINES	NUMBER FREIGHT CARS	NUMBER PASSENGER CARS	NUMBER EMPLOYEES	COMMON STOCK (THOUS.)	TOTAL DEBT (THOUS.)
1872	35.4	$1,030	$215	5	225	5		$519	$726
1873	35.4	1,143	217	5	225	5		532	764
1874	35.4	1,150	217	5	225	5	75	533	800
1875	46.0	1,281	217	5	225	5	75	533	1,041
1876	46.0	1,294	217	5	225	5	75	533	1,041
1877	46.0	1,294	217	5	225	5	75	533	1,047
1878	46.0	1,295	217	5	225	5	90	533	1,046
1879	46.0	1,296	217	5	225	5	105	533	1,046
1880	46.0	1,297	217	5	225	5	98	550	779

Source: Data from Michigan Railroad Commission.

The C&MLS was more expensive to operate, with an operating cost of $2,034 per mile, while the Newaygo Road's cost was only $1,136 per mile. Part of this can be attributed to the larger amount of passenger traffic on the C&MLS. Another critical measurement is net income per mile of road; the Newaygo road took in $1,440 per mile, while the C&MLS produced a scant $152 per mile.

In 1877 the GRN&LS amended its corporate articles to allow it to build to Manistee, but nothing came from this attempt to expand the company. David Clay had built the road to haul lumber and forest products; in its first years these products made up 80 percent of the road's freight business. This traffic declined annually; in 1881 only 50 percent came from this source. After this time it showed no sign of future improvement. At its two termini, Grand Rapids and White Cloud, the Newaygo road connected with the Chicago & Michigan Lake Shore, making it a natural purchaser. On 16 July 1881 Clay agreed to let the C&MLS acquire his road, effective at the end of September. In 1889 James Converse bought most of Clay's other operations and businesses in Newaygo as well as a factory in Grand Rapids. After Converse's death in 1894, his son Costello took over their management.[42]

Chicago & West Michigan

When James F. Joy involved himself financially with the Chicago & Michigan Lake Shore (C&MLS) in 1870 he brought with him several New England investors. Bostonians Nathaniel Thayer and Horatio H. Hunnewell had earlier invested in the Michigan Central (MC) in 1858, with Hunnewell made a vice president in 1860 and Thayer becoming one in 1867. The two men joined the C&MLS board in 1872, and were accompanied by Charles Francis Adams Jr. and Charles Merriam as well as John Wood Brooks, who with Joy was one of the founders of the MC. A few years later they were joined on the C&MLS board by two more Boston financiers: George O. Shattuck in 1874 and Alpheus Hardy in 1875. Many of these same men accompanied Joy in his participation in the Detroit, Lansing & Lake Michigan, as recounted earlier.[43]

Two years of C&MLS receivership, which began in 1876, had to pass before the bondholders finally were able to agree on a reorganization plan. On 20 December 1878 the Chicago and West Michigan Railroad Company was incorporated to reorganize the Chicago & Michigan Lake Shore. The C&MLS ended its life with $1,514,700 in paid-in common stock, $6,630,000 in mortgage bonds, and $2,215,800 in unpaid interest. The C&WM began its life with $6,151,000 in common stock and just $480,000 in mortgage bonds. In short, the bondholders exchanged a thousand dollars of bonds with the unpaid coupons for a thousand dollars of common stock. The new company began business on 1 January 1879. Nathaniel Thayer continued as president, George C. Kimball continued as general manager and was made a vice president as well, Charles Merriam stayed as secretary and treasurer, Charles M. Lawler remained division superintendent, and Andrew M. Nichols was general freight agent and general passenger agent.[44]

Hart, the seat of Oceana County, had been bypassed when the C&MLS built to Pentwater. To get a railroad a group of twelve Hart citizens put up $12,000, paid for and then graded the right-of-way, and provided the Hart depot and the land it stood on. The short branch of 3.2 miles from Mears to Hart was completed on 1 July 1880. The C&WM also built a 13.1-mile branch out of Woodville, in northeastern Newaygo County, naming it the Muskegon River Branch. The purpose of this extension was to tap more forests, some of them owned by a subsidiary, the West Michigan Lumber Company, that was to operate in the vicinity of Woodville. During 1881 the company spent $134,237 on the extension. The lumber company profits would go to the railroad and, hopefully, add to its profitability. On 13 November 1879 it formed the White River Railroad Company, which is discussed subsequently.[45]

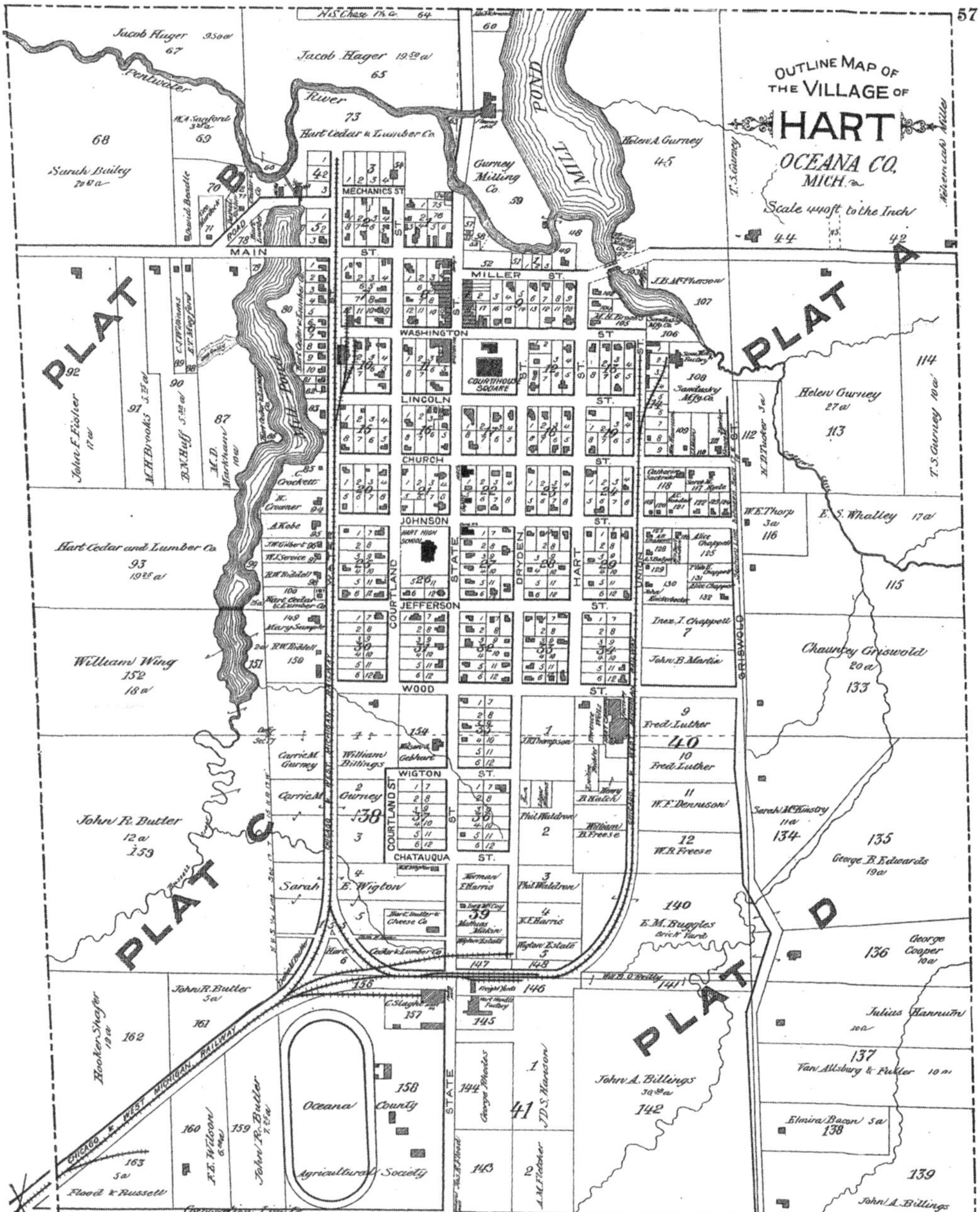

Hart.

FROM *OCEANA COUNTY ATLAS.*

Kimball also recommended an extension of the branch line from Allegan into Ohio; he believed the amount of lumber moving out of Muskegon would ensure its profitability. Manistee still seemed a desirable goal for the C&WM, and on 20 April 1881 it amended its corporate articles to make it its northern terminus. The predecessor Chicago & Michigan Lake Shore had gained rights to build to Manistee when it bought the Montague, Pentwater & Manistee, but apparently the C&WM wanted to be reassured that it had the necessary extension rights.[46]

In 1880 Nathaniel Thayer retired, he had served as the C&WM's president since 1874, and of the Chicago & Michigan Lake Shore before that. His health was beginning to fail and he found it difficult to manage his wide range of outside businesses. His son, Nathaniel Thayer Jr. then age twenty-nine, replaced him as the new president.[47]

On 16 July 1881 the C&WM renamed itself as the Chicago and West Michigan Railway Company when it consolidated the old C&WM Railroad, the Grand Haven, the Grand Rapids Newaygo & Lake Shore, and the then-building Indiana & Michigan. The merger was effective 1 October 1881 and resulted in a company that owned 366.6 miles of road, including the White River subsidiary. The merger gave the C&WM duplicate lines between Holland and Muskegon: the C&MLS line via Nunica and the MLS line via Grand Haven. During 1881 the line through Nunica was abandoned between Waverly, just north of Holland, and Pickand, a mile north of Fruitport. It appears that a spur track of about a mile in length was retained into Fruitport to reach some industry. The line north of Pickand, to North Yard in Muskegon, was retained since it provided an easier route to the Muskegon yard than that of the original MLS main line that snaked along the waterfront through downtown Muskegon. To reach Pickand a 3.8-mile connection was built between Kirk, 2 miles north of Ferrysburg on the line to Muskegon, and Pickand.[48]

The Grand Rapids, Newaygo & Lake Shore line from the north into Grand Rapids had no direct connection to the C&WM's Holland–Grand Rapids line. The 1881 merger made a direct connection between the two a necessity. The Newaygo road did run its passenger trains into the Grand Rapids union station on Ionia Street, using the Grand Rapids & Indiana tracks between the west side and that station. How the needed connection was built is not completely clear. One part of the connecting link may have been the Grand Rapids Transfer & Junction Railroad, which was formed in February 1882 to build a line between River Street and South Front Street. It appears that at some earlier time the GRN&LS line had been extended south some distance toward River Street. In 1882 the C&WM completed a connection to its Holland–Grand Rapids line south of Wealthy Street, an undertaking that included a drawbridge across the Grand River.[49]

In 1880 the C&WM began replacing wood with coal as locomotive fuel. General Manager Kimball remarked that the road could no longer get enough wood to fuel the fleet of the dozen new engines that were bought to handle the increase in business. The price of wood, which the road had bought locally, was now 30 percent more expensive. The road received its coal at New Buffalo from the Michigan Central and distributed it to coal docks over the line. To improve coal movements the C&WM directors approved an extension from New Buffalo into Indiana and on 9 June 1881 created the Indiana and Michigan Railroad Company in Indiana. Grading was completed between New Buffalo and La Porte, Indiana, by the end of the year. Trains began running on the Indiana extension, from New Buffalo to La Porte on 24 May 1882. The road was completed to La Crosse, Indiana, on 12 November 1882, adding 36.8 miles of line, to give the company a total of 409.7 miles owned. Manager Kimball reported the line "has given us many

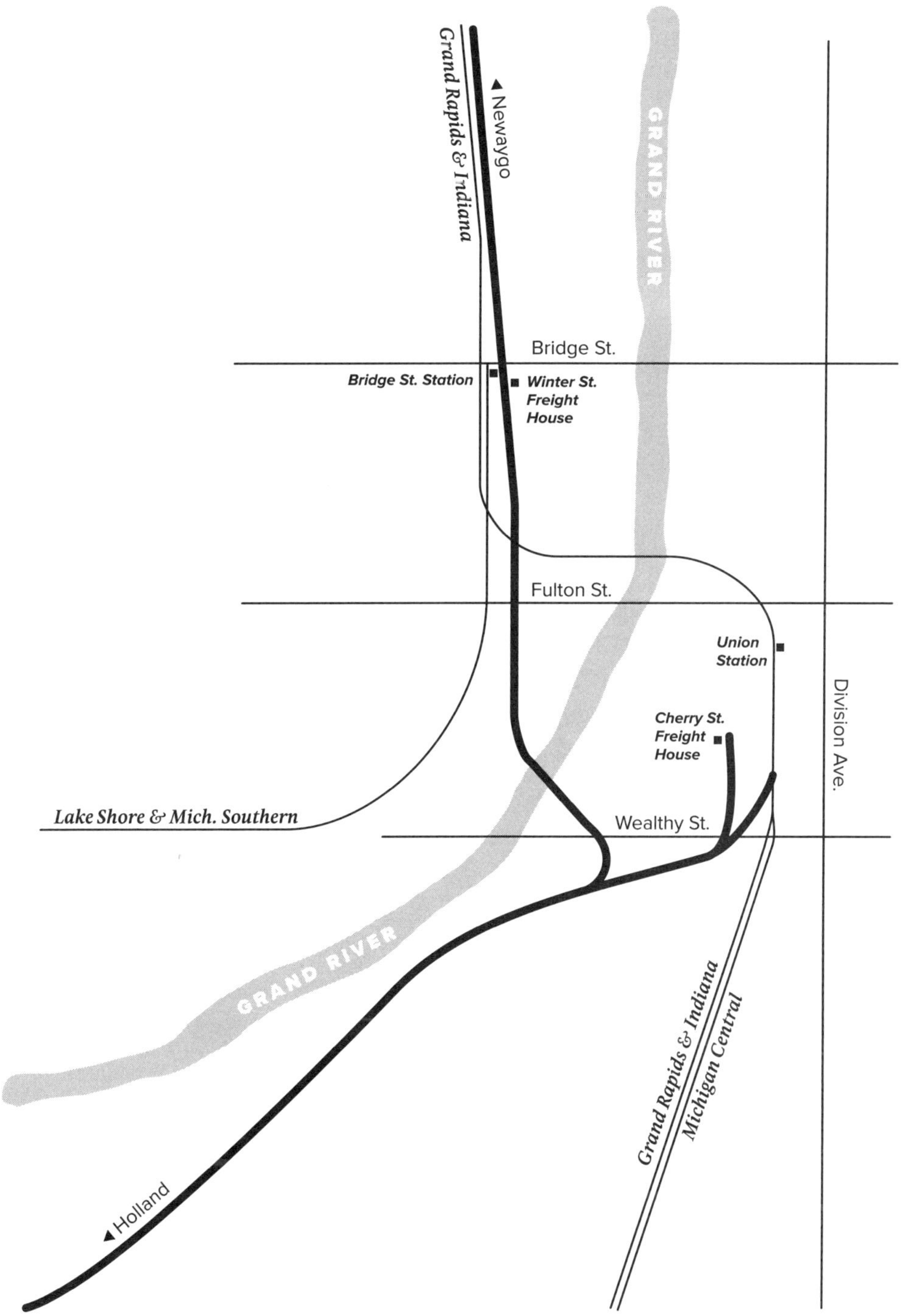

Grand Rapids map detail in 1884. All Chicago & West Michigan passenger trains operated into Union Station, and trains to the north also stopped at a Bridge Street station. C&WM also had two freight houses in Grand Rapids, at Cherry Street near Union Station and at Winter Street on the west side. The Grand Rapids & Indiana and Lake Shore & Michigan Southern had separate facilities on the west side of the river.

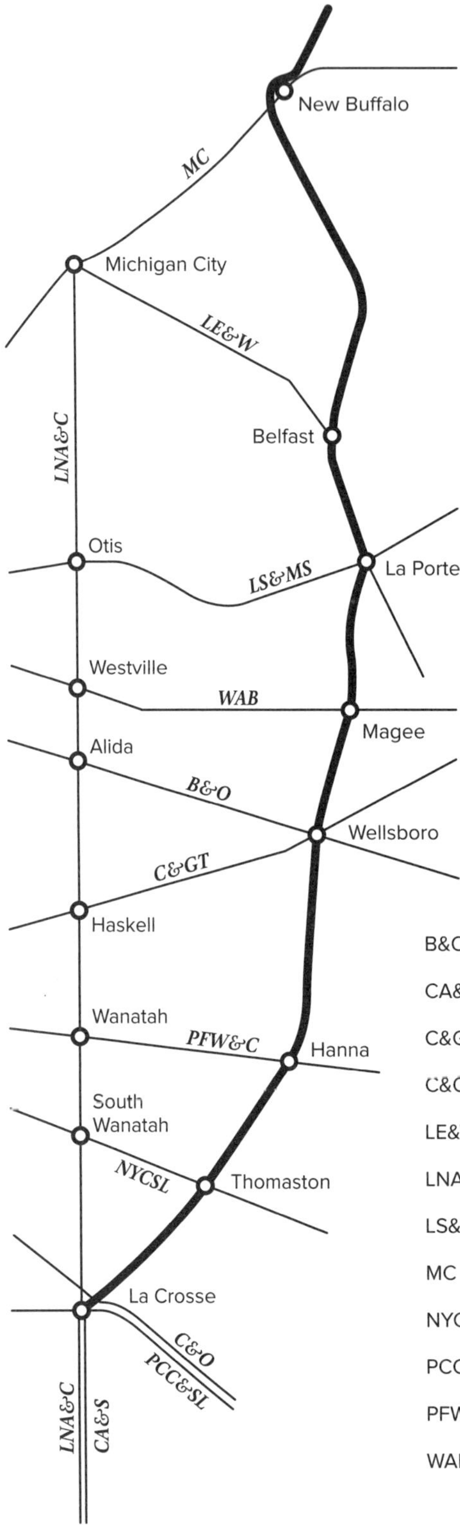

New Buffalo–La Crosse map. To improve moving coal from southern Indiana onto its lines, the Chicago & West Michigan built a branch from New Buffalo to La Crosse, Indiana. There it connected with four roads that could bring coal to it. The line crossed seven other roads and each of these required an interlocked crossing.

B&O	Baltimore & Ohio
CA&S	Chicago, Attica & Southern
C&GT	Chicago & Grand Trunk (GTW)
C&O	Chesapeake & Ohio
LE&W	Lake Erie & Western (NKP)
LNA&C	Louisville, New Albany & Chicago (Monon)
LS&MS	Lake Shore & Mich. Southern (NYC)
MC	Michigan Central (NYC)
NYCSL	New York, Chicago & St. Louis (NKP)
PCC&SL	Pittsburgh, Cincinnati, Chicago & St. Louis (PRR)
PFW&C	Pittsburgh, Forty Wayne & Chicago (PRR)
WAB	Wabash

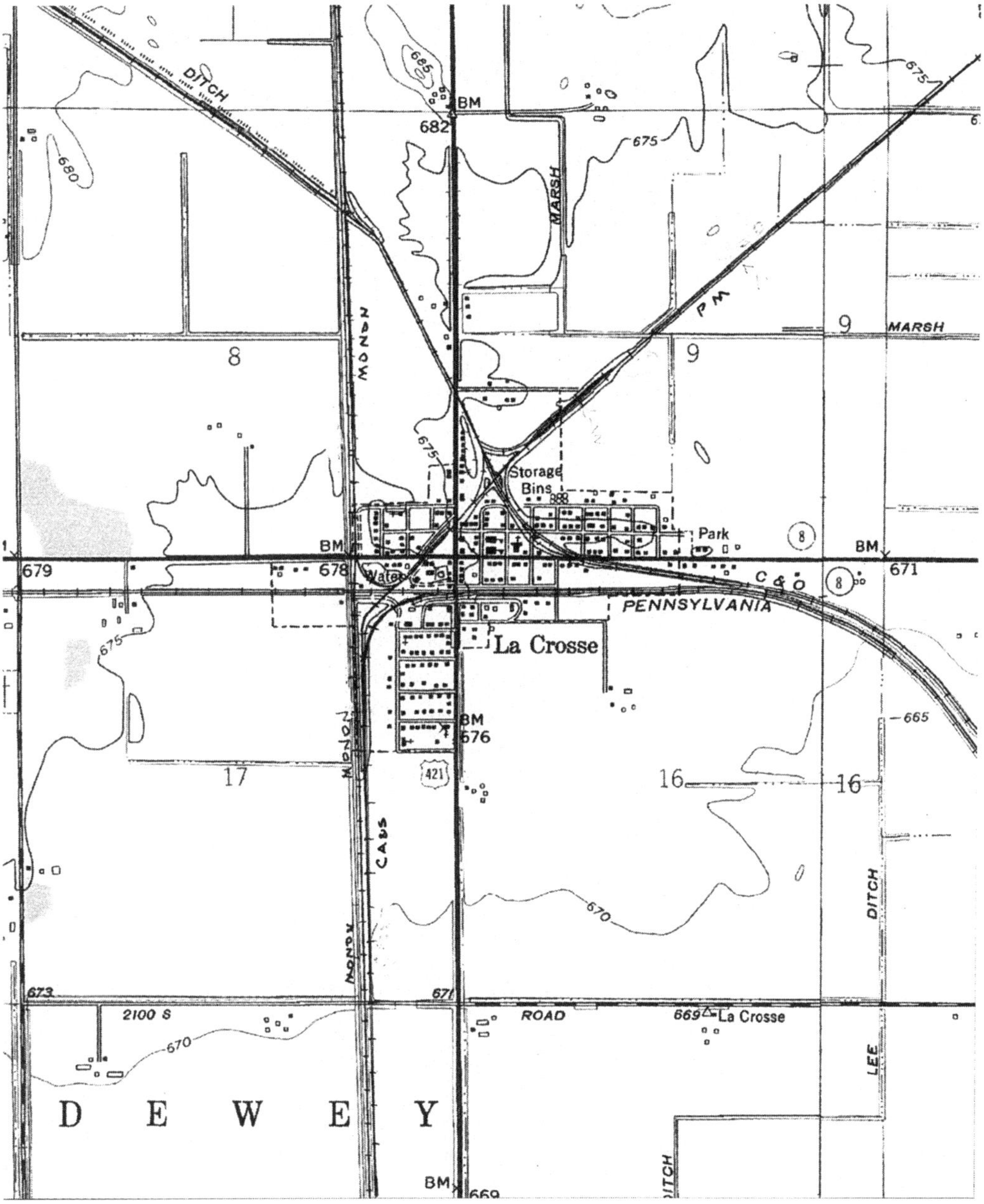

La Crosse map detail.

new connections, and is developing a good business, which will necessarily increase. Amicable arrangements have been made with the lines reaching Indianapolis, Cincinnati, Louisville, St. Louis, and Kansas City, as well as Pacific coast points and other Missouri River points." He reported that through coaches were running between Grand Rapids and Indianapolis, using the Louisville, New Albany & Chicago (later Monon) south of La Crosse.[50]

The C&WM gained an important new connection at La Crosse when the Chicago & Indiana

Baldwin. This station was on the Grand Rapids–Petoskey line and south of the crossing of the Saginaw–Ludington line. The view is a postcard of the north façade of the building. The near train on the line is headed for Ludington. The train behind the building is northbound on the Grand Rapids–Petoskey line.
FROM MICHIGAN RAILROAD HISTORY MUSEUM.

Coal Railway (C&IC) was built there from the south in January 1887. (The C&IC was renamed the Chicago, Attica & Southern in 1922.) The C&IC was a coal-hauling road that extended from the area around Brazil, Indiana, east of Terre Haute, north to a connection with the Chicago & Eastern Illinois that gave it access to Chicago. Former C&WM general manager George C. Kimball was then the manager of the C&IC. It appears that the C&IC wanted to add new connections at its north end, and chose La Crosse as a new terminus. At La Crosse it could connect with the Pennsylvania subsidiary Pittsburgh, Cincinnati, Chicago & St. Louis, with the Chesapeake & Ohio, and with the competing Louisville, New Albany & Chicago (later the Monon Road). The C&WM branch into La Crosse already connected with those three roads to reach the Ohio River. The C&IC now gave the C&WM direct access to the southern Indiana coalfields. It facilitated the C&WM converting its locomotive fuel from wood to coal; and coal was used increasingly for home heating and industrial power. By the 1890s coal developed into about 5 percent of the C&WM's freight tonnage.

By 1879 the final effects of the Panic of 1873 were fading; the demand for lumber began to pick up and money became more available. General Manager Kimball considered the prospects for lumber traffic, and the area north of White Cloud looked appealing. On 13 November 1879 Kimball and some associates incorporated the White River Railroad Company (WR); its corporate articles called for it to build a 13-mile line from White Cloud to Crooked Lake. WR stock was controlled by the C&WM, and the road was leased on 1 April 1880 to the C&WM. In April 1880 the WR built 5 miles from White Cloud to Mud Lake, now known as Diamond Loch, in the vicinity of Ramona. The next year it built another 8 miles to reach Crooked Lake, now in the area of Woodland Park. In 1882 it built another 4 miles to reach the Troy Lumber Company camp northwest of Bitely. The next year, on 9 December 1883, it completed 12 more miles to reach north to Baldwin, where it connected with the Flint & Pere Marquette line from Saginaw to Ludington. In the company's 1883 annual report Kimball wrote that C&WM was running a through coach between Muskegon and Manistee via White Cloud and Baldwin. Also he reported, "Contracts have been made for the drawing of logs from this new extension. New saw-mills have been built in the past year, the product of which will be shipped by our line." On 7 February 1884 the C&WM absorbed the WR.[51]

CHICAGO & WEST MICHIGAN R. R.

Nathaniel Thayer, President, Boston, Mass.
Chas. Merriam, Treasurer, Boston, Mass.
J. B. Mulliken, Gen. Manager, Muskegon, Mich.
A. M. Nichols, Gen. Supt., E. Grand Rapids
J. K. V. Agnew, Asst. Gen. Supt, Grand Rapids, Mich.
U. B. Rogers, Auditor, Muskegon, Mich.
J. H. Palmer, G. F. & P. A., E. Grand Rapids.
A. Bourne, Purchasing Agent, Detroit, Mich.
H. P. Dearing, Gen. Baggage Agent., Chicago.

6	8	1	Mls	Tk't fare	Aug. 10, 1884.	2	4	6
P. M.	P. M.	A. M.			Lve. Arr.	P. M.	P. M.	A. M.
9 45	5 45	8 30	0	.....	LA CROSSE....+	6 45	5 35	6 15
10 25	6 02	9 05	9	.....	Hanna.......185	6 02	5 15	5 35
10 55	6 15	9 30	15	.....	Wellsboro....101	5 30	5 03	5 10
11 35	6 35	10 05	23	.....	LAPORTE....6159	4 45	4 45	4 30
9 55	8 40	8 55	...	...	Chicago.........	6 50	6 50	7 30
12 45	7 13	11 30	38	.00	New Buffalo1000	3 00	4 10	3 30
1 20	.....	12 02	52	.45	Bridgeman..180	1 52	.....	2 23
1 50	7 55	12 30	65	.85	ST. JOSEPH..2700	1 15	3 10	1 50
1 55	8 00	12 40	67	.90	Benton Har.1500	1 05	3 00	1 25
18	.....	12 59	77	1.20	Coloma.......575	12 42	.....	1 00
50	8 43	1 30	84	1.45	Hartford....1000	12 25	2 30	12 35
10	8 55	1 45	92	1.65	Bangor......1210	11 50	2 17	11 55
30	9 07	2 05	99	1.90	GRAND JUNC...+	11 30	2 05	11 32
05	.....	2 30	113	2.25	Fennville....270	10 55	.....	10 55
18	.....	2 37	117	2.40	Richmond..1113	10 45	....	10 40
00	10 05	3 00	128	2.70	HOLLAND....2621	10 15	1 15	10 05
13	.....	3 12	133	2.85	Zeeland.......480	10 02	.....	9 40
45	.....	3 43	147	3.30	Grandville....605	9 32	...	8 55
00	10 45	4 00	153	3.45	G'D RAPIDS.32015	9 15	12 25	8 35
A. M.	P. M.	9 05	0	.00	ALLEGAN....3010	4 15	....	.....
P. M.	A. M.	9 42	13	.40	Hamilton....204	3 35	P. M.	P. M.
00	5 20	10 10	90	.....	Holland.....2621	3 00	1 10	9 40
00	6 35	11 00	110	.....	G'd Haven..4862	2 05	12 25	8 50
05	6 40	11 08	111	.....	Ferrysburgh.450	2 00	12 20	8 40
40	7 15	11 45	120	.....	MUSKEGON..11262	1 25	11 55	8 05
P. M.	A. M.	A. M.			Arr. Lve.	P. M.	A. M.	P. M.
A. M.		P. M.			Lve. Arr.		A. M.	P. M.
25	.....	4 40	120	.....	Muskegon.11262	.....	11 55	7 40
57	.....	5 07	135	.....	Twin Lake...611	.....	11 32	7 10
15	.....	5 22	143	.....	HOLTON......263	.....	11 17	6 57
10 20	.....	6 05	158	.....	Alleyton......405	.....	10 40	6 15
11 35	.....	7 10	180	.....	BIG RAPIDS..3750	.....	9 25	‡5 10
A. M.	A. M.	P. M.			Arr. Lve.	A. M.	A. M.	P. M.
.....	7 30	7 10	126	3.80	MUSKEGON.11262	11 40	8 00	.....
.....	8 07	7 55	142	4.30	Whitehall...1895	11 00	7 15	.....
.....	8 12	8 00	143	4.30	Montague...1297	10 55	7 10	.....
.....	8 52	8 40	157	4.75	Shelby.......335	10 20	6 30	.....
.....	9 10	9 00	163	4.90	Mears........335	10 00	6 10	.....
.....	9 25	.....	...	.....	Hart.........480	9 45	.....	.....
	A. M.	9 20	170	5.10	PENTWATER.1151	.....	5 50	.....
P. M.	A. M.	A. M.			Lve. Arr.	P. M.	P. M.	P. M.
00	10 10	5 20	128	2.70	HOLLAND....2621	1 10	3 00	9 40
07	11 10	6 42	151	3.30	Kirks Jc......+	12 18	1 54	8 35
17	11 20	6 52	155	3.50	Pickand's Jc..+	12 10	1 48	8 25
40	11 45	7 15	163	3.80	MUSKEGON.11262	11 55	1 25	8 05
P. M.	A. M.	A. M.			Arr. Lve.	A. M.	P. M.	P. M.

Additional trains leave New Buffalo †7.50 am., arr. Holland 5 40 pm. Lve. Holland 5.50 am., arr. New Buffalo 8 45 pm. Leave New Buffalo †12.45 am., arr Grand Rapids 10.05 am. Leave Grand Rapids 6 10 am., arr New Buffalo 5 35 pm. Train leaves Muskegon 8.15 am., arr Holland 10 00 am., ret. lvs. Holland 5.15 pm., arr. Muskegon 6.55 pm.

Grand Rapids & Newaygo Division.

		4†	2†	Mls	Aug. 10, 1884.	1	3	
	A. M.	P. M.	A. M.		Lve. Arr.	A. M.	P. M.	P. M.
....	4 00	4 00	8 30	0	G'D RAPIDS.32015	10 15	8 40	5 15
....	5 15	4 47	9 02	14	Sparta........550	9 40	7 55	3 55
....	8 47	5 45	10 05	36	NEWAYGO....1217	8 47	6 55	12 40
....	9 35	6 40	10 45	46	WHITECLOUD442	8 20	6 30	11 05
....	2 15	8 15	12 00	74	Baldwin.....200	6 40	5 10	5 30
	P. M.	P. M.	no'n		Arr. Lve.	A. M.	P. M.	A. M.

Chicago & West Michigan 1884 schedule.

FROM AUTHOR'S COLLECTION.

In 1884, after ten years with the company, George C. Kimball resigned his position as vice president and general manager. At the request of his friend Charles Francis Adams Jr., he took on a special assignment at the Union Pacific Railroad. John B. Mulliken succeeded Kimball as general manager. Mulliken had served as general superintendent and then general manager of the Detroit, Lansing & Northern since 1875. The Boston owners of the two roads felt Mulliken could handle the increased responsibility as general manager of both roads. He kept his office in Detroit, hired John K. V. Agnew away from the Chicago & Grand Trunk, and installed him as assistant general superintendent in Grand Rapids in October 1884. In January 1885 Agnew was promoted to general superintendent.[52]

In his 1885 annual report Mulliken recommended extending the C&WM line within the city of Big Rapids. The new track would reach new industries along the Muskegon River that had grown enough in recent years to demand service. Also, it would provide a connection to the lines of the Detroit, Lansing & Northern and the Grand Rapids & Indiana on the east side of the Muskegon River. In 1886 Mulliken built the extension at Big Rapids, and also reported he had begun making surveys for a line north of Baldwin. As Mulliken put it, "I am very favorably impressed with the promising outlook for traffic from the country already examined (about forty

High Bridge. Looking southwest this Grand Rapids–Traverse City line crossing over the Manistee River, four miles north of Peacock, was originally built in 1889 as a 1,200-foot-long timber trestle. At ninety-five feet, it was the tallest railroad bridge in Michigan.

FROM CLIFFORD VANDERYACHT COLLECTION

miles). . . . I am fully convinced that the building of such extension, with branches to Manistee and Frankfort Harbor, will add largely to the value of our present property." At that time the Flint & Pere Marquette had built its branch from Walhalla to Manistee and the Grand Rapids & Indiana had built from Cadillac to Petoskey and had a branch into Traverse City. Neither the Ann Arbor nor the Manistee & Northeastern had built any line in the area that Mulliken's surveyors were crossing.[53]

George Kimball, as the manager of the Chicago & Indiana Coal Railway, proposed that his road rent the New Buffalo–La Crosse branch. Mulliken wrote that a deal was struck and that C&IC trains would begin running on 1 May 1887. On other matters, by the end of 1887, he said, the company had put in steel rails on all of its main line and the Big Rapids branch, and had only 75 miles of iron rails remaining, and he had plans to replace them. Mulliken reported that a survey to Traverse City had been completed. This line would be 74 miles long; the agricultural products and hardwood timber along the line would "derive a good traffic for many years." The line also put the C&WM "in direct communication with nearly all the summer resorts located around Grand Traverse Bay, from which we would receive a very large passenger traffic during the season."[54]

Throughout 1889 John Mulliken's health began to decline, and resigned from the railroad in March 1890. President Thayer persuaded Charles M. Heald to replace Mulliken. To relieve Heald of some of the sort of pressure that had shortened Mulliken's career, President Thayer named his brother, Eugene Van Rensselaer Thayer, as a C&WM vice president. Although the

Eugene V. R. Thayer. Managing his father's extensive fortune was his life's work.
FROM FINDAGRAVE.

brother did not bring railroad experience to his duties, he was a skilled manager of the family's extensive financial interests and investments.[55]

Work on the extension from Baldwin to Traverse City began in July 1889, with all but the last 15 miles of track laying done by the end of the year. It was expected that the line could be finished into Traverse City by the 1 July 1890. The most difficult obstacle on the route was the crossing of the Little Manistee River, 3.5 miles north of Peacock. The rail line would have to drop more than fifty feet to the river crossing, then climb out through rough terrain. The alternative used was a 1,170-foot iron trestle, named High Bridge, that was built in 1889. It remained in use until the tracks were removed in 1956. The U.S. secretary of war ordered the railroad to replace the St. Joseph River drawbridge at St. Joseph. The original bridge was a jack-knife drawbridge sixty feet in length; the replacement was a swing bridge with one hundred feet of channel width on each side of the center pier. Mulliken used a half page of his report to detail the work done to keep the road operating: new stations, an engine house, hand car houses, water tanks, coaling stations, crossing gates, station repairs, bridge and culvert work, and several grade reductions.[56]

The 74-mile line to Traverse City was put in service 15 September 1890, and cost $1,506,571 to build. The road started passenger train service into Traverse City on 6 July although work was still being done on the tracks. The Traverse City station was located on the west side of the Boardman River, just southeast of the Union Street bridge and north of 7th Street. Also, a new branch from Waverly to Ottawa Beach, on the north side of Black Lake (now known as Lake Macatawa) at Holland, 7.1 miles long, was authorized the year before and completed on 1 July 1890 at a cost of $63,000. It saw heavy traffic each summer with riders to and from the resorts and cottages along the line. As part of this it appears that the bridge over the Black River, built by the Michigan Lake Shore in 1870, was abandoned and a connection made at Cronje to the line toward Grand Haven. A new yard was built at Waverly in Holland to move switching away from the city streets.[57]

The board of directors was so pleased at the success of reaching Traverse City that they authorized another 93-mile extension farther north, although the 1890 annual report does not

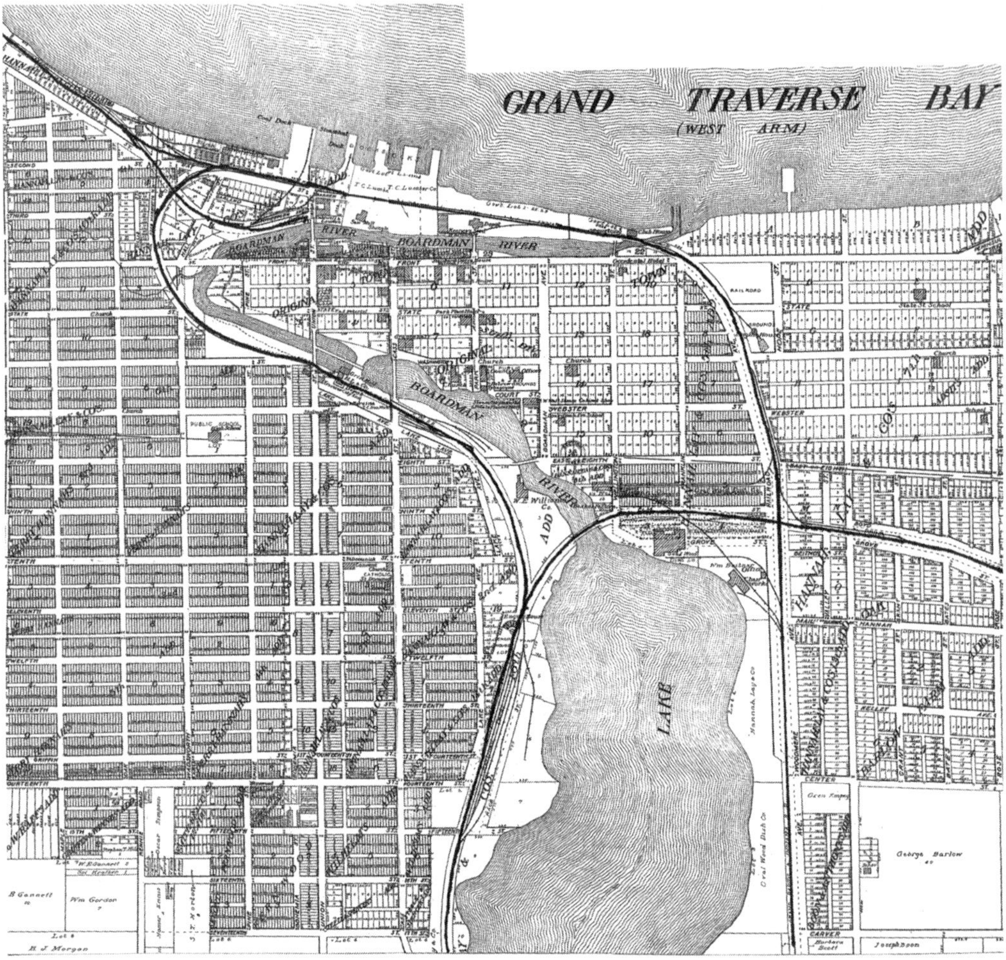

Traverse City detail. The Chicago & West Michigan entered town at the bottom center of the map and followed the Boardman River to its first depot at Union Street and Lake Drive. Farther north it connected with the Grand Rapids & Indiana and the Manistee & Northeastern near the shore of the bay. The C&WM line to Petoskey went around the north end of Boardman Lake and then east, crossing the Grand Rapids & Indiana east of the lake.

FROM *STANDARD ATLAS OF GRAND TRAVERSE COUNTY, MICHIGAN* (CHICAGO: GEORGE A. OGLE & CO., 1908).

specify any location. To build it the C&WM created a new company on 28 February 1891, the Chicago and North Michigan Railroad Company (C&NM). Its rights provided for a 135-mile line from Leland, on the west side of the Leelanau Peninsula, to the Straits of Mackinac, and a capitalization of $1.5 million. The C&WM owned all of the C&NM stock, and on 1 June 1891 leased the road while it was being built. The commissioner of railroads, in his 1890 annual report, stated that a map was filed in his office for the proposed line, 79 miles from Traverse City to the resort grounds at Bay View, and that the line was under construction.[58]

In his 1891 annual report, the commissioner of railroads wrote, "The line from Traverse

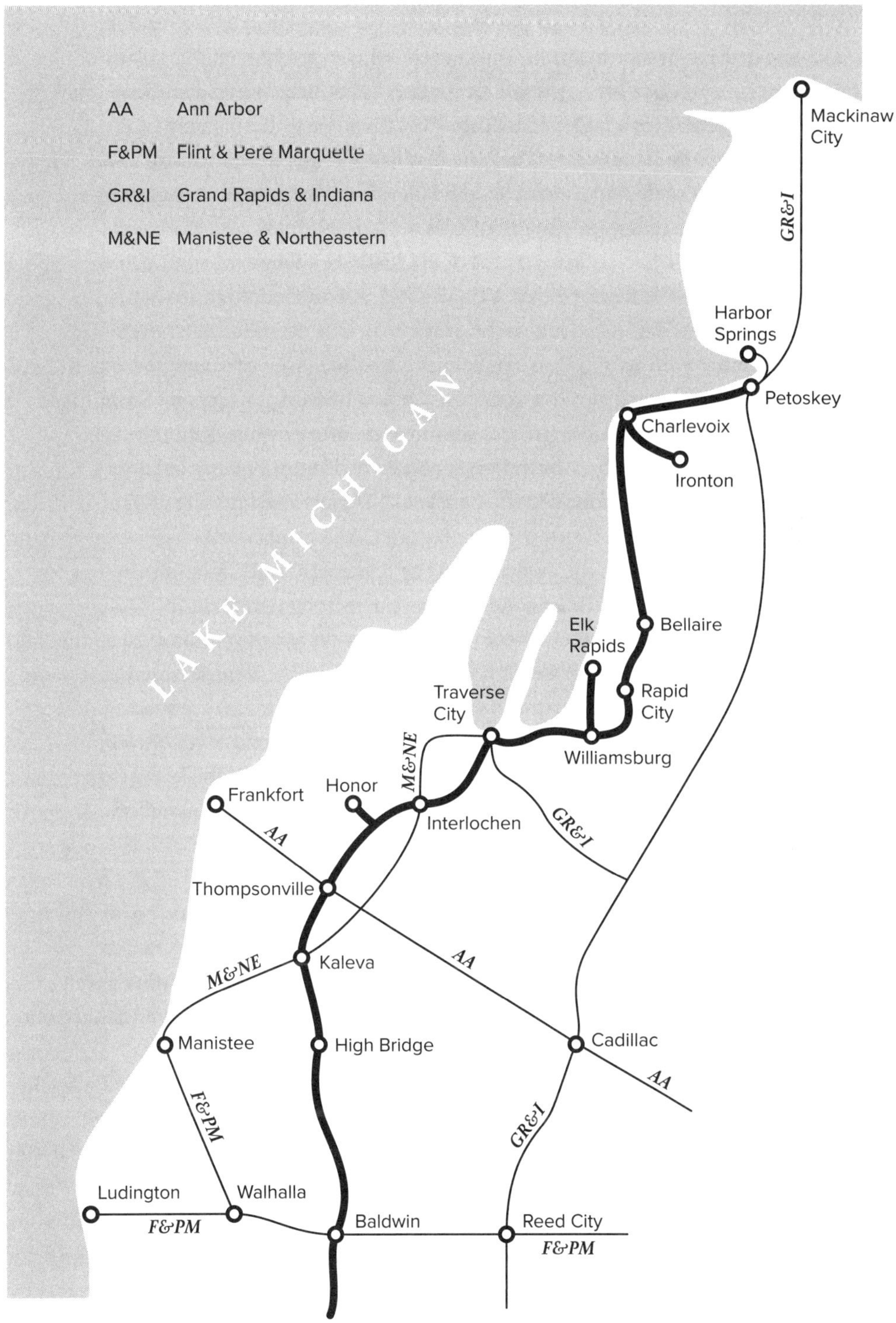

Chicago & North Michigan lines, 1896

City to Petoskey was completed and put into operation last spring. The track has been very well laid, the bridges are substantial, the station houses are handsome, commodious, and contain every convenience for the traveling public." The section between Boardman, where it connected with the Baldwin–Traverse City line, through Williamsburg to Elk Rapids on a spur line was completed 3 January 1892. The extension from Williamsburg to Bay View was completed on 17 July 1892, and a branch from Cherrie to Ironton on 26 September 1892. The main line was 79 miles in length, the Elk Rapids branch 9.5 miles, and the Ironton branch 4.1 miles. Two drawbridges had to be built, one at Elk Rapids and another at Charlevoix. The railroad first planned to build a pile bridge at Charlevoix, at cost estimated about $10,000, but the U.S. secretary of war ordered an iron drawbridge be built that added $25,000 to the cost. The Ironton branch was built to allow an extension to East Jordan, but it was never built beyond Ironton. To handle the increase of business the C&WM bought eleven new locomotives, eight new passenger coaches, two baggage cars, fifty boxcars, and one hundred flatcars.[59]

The new C&NM line reached both logging areas and summer resorts. In 1878 a group of Kalamazoo businessmen had founded the Charlevoix Resort, also known as Kalamazoo Resort and the Baptist Resort, on the south shore of Round Lake in Charlevoix. The resort expanded during following decades into the area around the Belvedere Hotel, and in 1923 was renamed Belvedere. Across the lake the Chicago Resort was started by members of the First Congregational Church of Chicago in 1880. One reporter wrote that "it has the patina of time, the solidity of permanence and tradition, the feel of home, unlike the ephemeral seasonableness and the hyper tempo of places where activity and social relationships both are always on the trigger." Steamships brought vacationers in the early years, but the railroad made travel much easier. The railroad built impressive stations at Charlevoix and Petoskey. At Charlevoix the station was close to the Chicago Resort, and the railroad felt obliged to provide a second station south of the drawbridge for the Charlevoix Resort. Petoskey was a ready-made market for tourists. The Grand Rapids & Indiana had built there almost twenty years earlier, and all of Little Traverse Bay had grown to be a popular resort area. Bay View, founded in 1876, was the inspiration for the Charlevoix and Chicago Resorts. General manager Heald reported that "the station grounds at Charlevoix and Petoskey were laid out, trees, shrubs and flowers planted, and walks made, in order to render them attractive to tourists and resorters who visit these and other points at the northern end of the line during the summer season."[60]

Near Holland the West Michigan Park Association developed another Lake Michigan resort. Among its developers were several officers of the Chicago & West Michigan, including Charles Heald. In 1886 they built the 36-room Hotel Ottawa and platted lots for individual cottages. With no roads to the resort, two excursion steamships provided the only access. In 1890 a 104-room annex was added to the renamed Ottawa Beach Hotel and the C&WM built a 7.1-mile branch to reach it. Although the railroad ran summers only, it is not clear if was operated between 1891 and 1895. In 1896 operations were resumed and through trains from Grand Rapids provided a popular service.[61]

In 1892 the C&WM ran a survey for a line between Sparta and Howard City that would connect the Detroit, Lansing & Northern to the C&WM. This would allow traffic to move off

Charlevoix. This photo of the station at this important resort city, taken about 1893, shows pride of ownership with the extensive landscaping. The station was later painted white and remains in use today by private owners.

FROM LIBRARY OF CONGRESS CALL LC-D4-12290.

Petoskey. The Chicago & North Michigan built its impressive Petoskey station in 1892. Passenger train service ended in October 1962, but the summers-only Resort Special last ran in 1957. The station now serves as the home of the Traverse Bay Historical Society.

FROM LIBRARY OF CONGRESS CALL LC-D4-12342.

Table 24. Chicago & North Michigan revenues

YEAR	PASSENGER REVENUE	FREIGHT REVENUE
1892	$52,807	$35,134
1893	63,488	65,300
1894	58,912	58,789
1895	75,398	70,398
1896	44,591	64,692
1897	48,131	78,983

Source: Data from Michigan Railroad Commission, *Annual Reports*.
Note: The Chicago & West Michigan, as owner of C&NM, did not separate other traffic statistics but included them in its own reports.

the Saginaw Valley & St. Louis line, pass through Grand Rapids, and move to the south and southwest. The surveyed line was never built. Also in 1892 the C&WM assisted in building the Lake Harbor Railroad Company. Formed on 1 July 1892, the road proposed to extend from some point on Lake Michigan to Muskegon Lake. Apparently it was built, about 5 miles in length, from Lake Michigan Park, now Pere Marquette Park in Muskegon, along the Lake Michigan shore to the Lake Harbor resort at the outlet of Mona Lake. Lake Harbor resort was located on the grounds of Hackley Park, now the site of the Maranatha Bible Conference. The C&WM 1892 annual report states that the line built was 4.7 miles long and that construction started in early July and was completed thirty days later. "This is a summer resort line strictly." It is possible that C&WM's general manager, Charles Heald, and its attorney, Frederick Nims, were investors in the resort and its railroad. The resort grounds appear to have run into financial trouble, it

Muskegon's Union Station was the second station built on this site in downtown Muskegon. Designed by Sidney J. Osgood, this unique Richardsonian Romanesque building was opened to the public in September 1895. Trains of the Chicago & West Michigan used this station and, for a time, the trains of the Grand Rapids & Indiana. The building now serves as a visitor's center with offices on the upper floor.
FROM MICHIGAN RAILROAD HISTORY MUSEUM.

Table 25. Revenue and operating statistics for Chicago & West Michigan, 1879–1899

YEAR	MILES OF ROAD OWNED	PASSENGER REVENUE	NUMBER OF PASSENGERS	PASSENGER MILES (THOUS.)	FREIGHT REVENUE	FREIGHT TONS	TON MILES (THOUS.)	OPERATING EXPENSE & TAXES	NET INCOME*
1879	245.6	$198,633	250,901	6,606	$426,061	345,467	23,776	$541,557	$113,867
1880	267.0†	255,366	310,792	8,502	552,227	433,400	29,187	500,438	244,497
1–9/1881		225,251	521,874			603,915	170,368		
10–12/1881	113,500			238,207			313,133	50,022	
1881 Year	366.6‡	338,751	541,980	13,970	760,081	774,279	43,455	917,048	220,390
1882	409.7‡	458,949	636,470	17,477	995,674	875,166	50,566	1,047,789	455,644
1883	429.7‡	466,052	659,301	16,779	1,026,983	1,102,300	61,318	1,185,224	372,434
1884	413.5	449,099	616,514	16,220	950,801	947,502	58,837	1,000,690	471,194
1885	413.5	418,384	571,722	16,355	818,325	855,068	54,494	948,513	352,860
1886	413.9	451,638	613,260	18,097	869,327	944,343	58,867	1,025,498	370,482
1887	413.9	450,014	585,211	17,385	889,116	916,063	62,256	1,064,629	349,393
1888	408.4	497,189	687,679	19,668	846,351	936,270	60,125	1,046,901	370,900
1889	408.4	495,433	679,070	22,850	818,565	883,892	58,441	1,018,466	356,368
1890	488.6	517,076	704,496	20,412	1,026,962	1,161,214	77,697	1,042,624	563,795
1891	481.5	585,963	848,889	25,140	1,104,368	1,271,458	85,568	1,231,800	525,753
1892†	574.1	885,188	956,829	29,340	1,262,142	1,492,710	103,080	1,595,385	527,155
1893†	574.6	764,338	952,579	n.a.	1,032,000	1,224,032	82,805	1,491,143	398,567
1894†	574.6	582,128	842,086	26,891	907,359	1,005,237	67,427	1,277,760	318,758
1895†	575.7	587,195	851,099	27,711	1,031,598	1,205,263	86,412	1,404,097	319,950
1896†	581.1	534,662	766,837	24,972	993,262	1,174,727	92,595	1,321,476	321,141
1897§	581.1	529,670	741,567	23,765	1,012,047	1,210,360	93,422	1,300,398	350,326
1898§	614.1	602,200	926,525	29,880	1,270,061	1,574,067	130,456	1,548,347	435,173
1899§	614.1	695,397	1,077,399	34,502	1,463,038	1,921,208	154,881	1,755,752	528,055

Source: Data from Michigan Railroad Commission.

* Net income is passenger revenue, freight revenue, and miscellaneous revenue, less operating expense.

† Includes data from Chicago & North Michigan.

‡ Includes mileage of White River Railroad; its revenue and operating statistics included in C&WM report (5.1 miles in 1880).

§ Includes data from Chicago & North Michigan and Grand Rapids, Kalkaska & Southeastern.

was not used after 1896, and the shadowy little railroad appears to have been abandoned by 1897.[62] In his 1893 report General Manager Heald repeated that there was a pressing need for a new and larger passenger station in Muskegon, and that new stations also were needed at St Joseph, Benton Harbor, and White Cloud.[63]

The financial panic of 1893 damaged the C&WM, as shown in tables 25 and 27. From 1892 to 1894 freight revenues dropped 28 percent and passenger revenues 34 percent. Aggravating the situation was the sharp decline in lumber traffic—46 percent in two years—and a railroad strike in July 1894. Heald attempted to control operating expenses, but could reduce them by only 20 percent over the two years. As a result net income fell by nearly 40 percent and no dividend was paid after 1893. Between 1890 and 1899 the C&WM added just over 200 miles of rail line to its system. Most of this was the line from Baldwin to Traverse City, the Chicago & North Michigan between Traverse City and Petoskey, and the Grand Rapids, Kalkaska &

Table 26. Costs, equipment, capitalization for Chicago & West Michigan, 1879–1899

YEAR	MILES OF ROAD OWNED	COST OF ROAD (THOUS.)	COST OF EQUIPMENT (THOUS.)	NUMBER ENGINES	NUMBER FREIGHT CARS	NUMBER PASSENGER CARS	NUMBER EMPLOYEES	COMMON STOCK (THOUS.)	TOTAL DEBT (THOUS.)	DIVIDEND PAID (THOUS.)
1879	245.6	$6,238	$430	29	524	26	700	$6,151	$480	0
1880	261.9	6,291	501	31	869	25	770	6,151	480	0
1881	353.6	8,037	763	43	1,331	34	1,505	6,797	3,087	$154
1882	409.7	8,131	818	43	1,386	38	1,317	6,797	3,239	154
1883	429.7	8,931	923	47	1,490	45	1,504	6,797	4,035	185
1884	413.5	9,094	951	46	1,555	45	1,251	6,797	4,003	246
1885	413.5	9,097	956	46	1,606	45	1,134	6,797	4,073	92
1886	413.9	9,130	1,000	48	1,589	52	1,258	6,797	4,104	185
1887	413.9	9,178	1,137	47	1,802	61	1,319	6,797	4,241	154
1888	408.4	9,227	1,137	48	1,805	61	1,279	6,797	4,307	123
1889	408.4	9,266	1,136	49	1,834	61	1,229	6,797	5,440	123
1890	488.6	10,844	1,391	55	2,020	65	1,410	6,797	5,594	194
1891	481.5	10,784	1,472	70	2,282	73	2,103	6,797	7,624	232
1892*	574.1	10,944	1,493	77	2,268	73	1,868	7,448	8,203	232
1893*	574.6	10,936	1,493	76	2,823	73	1,921	7,448	8,283	112
1894*	574.6	10,992	1,497	76	2,821	73	1,673	7,448	8,351	0
1895*	575.7	12,864	1,503	76	2,821	73	1,498	7,512	8,528	0
1896*	581.1	12,917	1,503	77	2,818	73	1,474	7,512	8,646	0
1897†	581.1	12,923	1,505	62	2,814	73	1,400	7,512	8,646	0
1898†	614.1	14,892	n.a.	63	2,614	72	1,586	7,512	8,878	0
1899†	614.1	14,910	n.a.	65	3,212	73	1,722	7,512	8,861	0

Source: Data from Michigan Railroad Commission.
* Includes data from Chicago & North Michigan.
† Includes data from Chicago & North Michigan and Grand Rapids, Kalkaska & Southeastern.

Southeastern, which will be discussed later. During this period the C&WM added $3.3 million in debt, as shown in table 26, most of it to finance construction, but also to add to its fleet of locomotives and freight cars. This increase raised its annual interest charges to be more than net income. In 1894 the company did have not enough cash on hand to pay all of the interest on its bonds. It announced it would pay one-half of the coupon amount in cash and issue scrip (a sort of promissory note) for the other half, payable in ten years with interest. Bondholders were requested to turn in the coupons due for payment to President Thayer or Director Alpheus Hardy, who acted as trustees to fulfill the promised payment. Not until 1898 did net income increase enough to cover interest expense.[64]

In 1893 General Manager Heald announced that a new station had to be built in Muskegon. The company would spend $15,000 for the new building; construction started in August 1894. The new station was opened in September 1895 and also used by Grand Rapids & Indiana trains. In the 1894 annual report C&WM secretary Charles Merriam wrote that lumber traffic had not revived, the fruit crop was lighter than the prior year, and the potato crop could not be sold and was therefore not shipped. Merriam wrote that "the pine timber from which the road formerly

Table 27. Freight and lumber traffic statistics for Chicago & West Michigan, 1879–1899

YEAR	REVENUE	YTY % CHANGE	REVENUE TRAIN MILES (THOUS.)	REVENUE TONS (THOUS.)	YTY % CHANGE	REVENUE PER TON	REVENUE TON MILES (THOUS.)	TONS LUMBER (THOUS.)	YTY % CHANGE	% OF ALL TONS
1879	$426,061	27.6*	272.5	345.5	29.5*	$1.23	23,776	190.0		55.0
1880	552,227	29.6	313.1	433.4	25.4	1.27	29,187	215.2	13.3	49.7
1881	760,081	37.6	442.4	774.3	76.3	1.13	43,455	494.7	129.9	63.8
1882	995,674	31.0	512.1	875.2	13.0	1.14	50,556	606.2	22.5	69.3
1883	1,026,983	3.1	582.6	1,102.3	25.9	1.07	61,318	797.3	31.5	72.3
1884	950,801	-7.4	595.5	947.5	-14.0	1.09	58,837	683.1	-14.3	72.1
1885	818,325	-13.9	561.3	855.1	-9.8	1.15	54,494	562.9	-17.6	65.8
1886	869,327	6.5	544.0	944.3	10.4	1.48	58,867	625.4	11.1	66.2
1887	889,116	2.2	581.2	916,1	-3.0	1.43	62,256	551.9	-11.8	60.3
1888	846,351	-4.8	546.5	936.3	2.2	1.41	60,125	579.2	4.9	61.9
1889	818,565	-3.3	500.9	883.9	-5.6	1.41	58,441	543.7	-6.1	61.5
1890	1,026,962	25.5	648.6	1,161.2	31.4	1.32	77,697	780.1	43.5	67.2
1891	1,104,368	7.5	696,4	1,271.5	9.5	1.29	85,568	774.0	-0.1	60.9
1892†	1,262,142	14.2	829.9	1,492.7	17.4	1.23	103,080	865.7	11.8	58.0
1893†	1,032,000	-18.2	784.2	1,224.0	-18.0	1.27	82,805	638.2	-26.3	52.1
1894†	907,359	-12.1	695.3	1,005.2	-17.9	1.35	67,427	462.5	-27.5	46.0
1895†	1,031,598	13.7	724.8	1,205.3	19.9	1.11	86,412	582.2	25.9	48.3
1896†	993,262	-3.7	751.5	1,174.7	-2.5	1.07	92,595	511.3	-12.2	47.1
1897‡	1,012,047	1.9	708.2	1,210.4	3.0	1.08	93,422	509.6	-0.3	42.1
1898‡	1,270,061	25.8	912.2	1,574.1	30.0	0.97	130,456	659.6	29.4	41.9
1899‡	1,463,038	15.2	1,006.4	1,921.2	22.1	0.95	154,881	847.6	28.5	44.1

Source: Data from Michigan Railroad Commission.
* 1879 YTY changes are comparisons with 1878 amounts of Chicago & Michigan Lake Shore.
† Includes data from Chicago & North Michigan.
‡ Includes data from Chicago & North Michigan and Grand Rapids, Kalkaska & Southeastern.

reaped its earnings, largely, has been cut off and shipped. There is still remaining a large quantity of hardwood timber which should afford revenue for many years to come." He reported that the road was considering establishing a car ferry service on Lake Michigan, "the advantages . . . more apparent every year." To tap a new timber area and an industry, in 1895 the company built the 9.6-mile Turtle Lake Branch from Clary, 3 miles north of Thompsonville, to Honor.[65]

Early in 1897 Nathaniel Thayer Jr. resigned the presidency of the Chicago & West Michigan after nearly twenty years in the chair. It is likely that Thayer spent little time in Michigan on the property while president, but rather left administration to General Manager Charles Heald and General Superintendent John Agnew. With Thayer's departure Heald was named the new president.[66] In the 1897 annual report Heald repeated his recommendation that the company build a new line from Hart to Pentwater and abandon the existing line between Mears and Pentwater. This extension would reach that community on the north side of Pentwater Lake and give direct access to the community's industries. Despite Heald's urging, the alternative line to Pentwater was never built. On 1 December 1897 the C&WM leased its Allegan-Holland line to the Detroit, Toledo & Milwaukee Railroad (DT&M). The commissioner of railroads reports

Table 28. Freight traffic statistics for Chicago & West Michigan, 1879–1899

YEAR	REVENUE TONS (THOUS.)	LUMBER TONS (THOUS.)	% OF ALL TONS	AGRICULTURAL PRODUCTS TONS (THOUS.)	% OF ALL	MANUFACTURES TONS (THOUS.)	% OF ALL	MERCHANDISE TONS (THOUS.)	% OF ALL TONS
1879	345.5	190.0	55.0	42.2	12.2	n.a.	n.a.	53.3	15.4
1880	433.4	215.2	49.7	57.2	13.2	n.a.	n.a.	61.7	14.2
1881	774.3	494.7	63.8	65.9	8.5	n.a.	n.a.	102.5	13.3
1882	875.2	606.2	69.3	49.3	5.6	n.a.	n.a.	156.9	17.9
1883	1,102.3	797.3	72.3	55.6	5.0	n.a.	n.a.	132.7	12.1
1884	947.5	683.1	72.1	54.6	5.8	n.a.	n.a.	133.9	14.1
1885	855.1	562.6	65.8	53.6	6.3	n.a.	n.a.	121.5	14.2
1886	944.3	625.4	66.2	62.6	6.6	n.a.	n.a.	120.2	12.7
1887	916.1	551.9	65.5	58.6	7.1	n.a.	n.a.	128.7	14.1
1888	936.3	579.2	61.9	66.4	7.1	n.a.	n.a.	116.2	12.4
1889	883.9	543.7	61.5	74.1	8.4	85.7	9.7	81.8	9.3
1890	1,161.2	780.1	67.2	97.2	8.3	103.1	8.9	77.9	6.7
1891	1,271.5	774.0	60.9	185.9	14.6	99.9	7.9	58.3	4/6
1892*	1,492.7	865.7	58.0	157.2	10.5	136.8	9.2	141.7	9.5
1893*	1,224.0	638.2	52.1	148.4	12.1	112.5	9.2	155.0	12.7
1894*	1,005.2	462.5	46.0	180.9	18.0	80.2	8.0	147.9	14.7
1895*	1,205.3	582.2	48.3	155.0	12.9	102.7	8.5	114.9	9.5
1896*	1,174.7	511.3	47.1	186.2	15.8	97.8	8.3	112.2	10.3
1897†	1,210.4	509.6	42.1	214.3	17.7	101.4	8.4	120.4	10.0
1898†	1,574.1	659.6	41.9	291.0	18.5	163.7	10.4	143.1	9.1
1899†	1,921.2	847.6	44.1	286.7	14.9	217.7	11.3	185.6	9.7

Source: Data from Michigan Railroad Commission.
* Includes data from Chicago & North Michigan.
† Includes data from Chicago & North Michigan and Grand Rapids, Kalkaska & Southeastern.

the DT&M also gained the use of C&WM tracks between Holland and Grand Haven, although what sort of arrangement it was never was made clear. It appears that the DT&M planned to operate a car-ferry service between Grand Haven and Milwaukee. The lease was short-lived and ended on 1 April 1898.[67] Also in 1898 the company built a 3.4-mile spur in Benzie County to serve the Gerber Lumber Company.

C&WM president Nathaniel Thayer ventured into Michigan lumbering in 1878 when he bought Lyman G. Mason's 1865 sawmill in Muskegon. Thayer installed new machinery that made the mill the largest lumber producer on Muskegon Lake. In 1881 Thayer formed the Thayer Lumber Company for his Michigan timber interests. As the son of a very wealthy Boston family, Thayer already served as a director of several large American companies. He was already president of the Boston, Clinton & Fitchburg Railroad, director of the New York, New Haven & Hartford, and in 1880 president of the Chicago & West Michigan. His father died in 1883, leaving an estate estimated at $17 million. Thayer expanded his lumber involvements by buying timberland in Newaygo and Missaukee Counties, and shipping the logs on his railroad to his mill in Muskegon.[68]

Central Standard Time—In Effect June 19, 1898.

Chicago & West Michigan Ry.

MAIN LINE—GOING NORTH.

CHICAGO TO GRAND RAPIDS AND PETOSKEY.

Miles	STATIONS	No. 1 Week Days	Nos. 3 and 9 Week Days	No. 5 Every Day to Gr'd Rapids	No. 7 Express Every Day	No. 11 Express Week Days	No. 31 Freight Week Days
0	Lv CHICAGO M C R R	7.20 AM	4.15 PM	8.45 PM			
1	Lv 22d STREET	7.23 AM	4.18 PM	8.48 PM			
3	Lv 39th STREET	7.29 AM	4.24 PM	8.54 PM			
5	Lv HYDE PARK	7.36 AM	4.30 PM	9.00 PM			
6	Lv 63d STREET	7.40 AM	4.33 PM	9.03 PM			
13	Lv KENSINGTON	8.00 AM	4.50 PM	9.20 PM			
56	Lv MICHIGAN CITY	9.05 AM	5.56 PM	10.28 PM			
66	Ar NEW BUFFALO	9.22 AM	6.15 PM	10.45 PM			
0	Lv LA CROSSE	7.40 AM	4.00 PM	No. 5 Runs			
6	Lv THOMASTON	7.55 AM	4.15 PM	North of			
9	Lv HANNA	8.04 AM	4.25 PM	G'd Rapids			
15	Lv WELLSBORO	8.20 AM	4.40 PM	every day			
28	Lv LA PORTE	8.45 AM	5.15 PM	Except			
38	Ar NEW BUFFALO	9.20 AM	6.00 PM	Monday			
66	Lv NEW BUFFALO	9.30 AM	6.20 PM	10.55 PM			6.00 AM
74	Lv HARBERT	*					
86	Lv STEVENSVILLE	10.06 AM	6.32 PM				7.15 AM
93	Lv ST. JOSEPH	10.20 AM	7.15 PM	11.35 PM	5.45 AM		7.45 AM
95	Lv BENTON HARBOR	10.30 AM	7.25 PM	11.42 PM	5.50 AM		8.15 AM
105	Lv COLOMA	10.46 AM	7.43 PM		6.08 AM		9.25 AM
107	Lv WATERVLIET	10.51 AM	7.49 PM		6.14 AM		10.22 AM
112	Lv HARTFORD	11.10 AM	8.10 PM		6.35 AM		11.01 AM
120	Lv BANGOR	11.24 AM	8.25 PM		6.50 AM		
127	Lv GRAND JCT	11.35 AM	* 8.43 PM		7.03 AM		
140	Lv FENNVILLE	11.58 AM	9.07 PM		7.32 AM		2.30 PM
145	Lv NEW RICHM'ND	12.05 PM	* 9.15 PM		7.40 AM		2.50 PM
156	Lv HOLLAND	12.25 PM	9.35 PM	1.15 AM	8.05 AM	4.15 PM	3.45 PM
164	Ar OTTAWA BEACH	12.55 PM			10.20 AM		
	Lv OTTAWA BEACH	12.15 PM	9.15 PM		7.05 AM	3.50 PM	
177	Ar GRAND HAVEN	1.16 PM	10.20 PM		9.06 AM		
190	Ar MUSKEGON	1.50 PM	10.50 PM		9.40 AM		
157	Lv WAVERLY	12.35 PM	9.45 PM		8.20 AM	4.25 PM	
160	Lv ZEELAND	12.42 PM			8.26 AM	4.31 PM	
169	Lv HUDSONVILLE	12.59 PM			8.43 AM	4.48 PM	
174	Lv JENISON	1.08 PM			8.52 AM	4.56 PM	
175	Lv GRANDVILLE	1.10 PM			8.55 AM	5.00 PM	Freights
181	Ar GRAND RAPIDS	1.25 PM	10.30 PM	2.00 AM	9.10 AM	5.15 PM	Week Days
181	Lv GRAND RAPIDS	2.10 PM	8.05 AM	2.15 AM		No. 9	
182	Lv BRIDGE ST	2.15 PM	8.12 AM			Passenger	5.55 AM
184	Lv D. & M. CROSS'G	2.22 PM	8.20 AM				6.05 AM
186	Lv MILL CREEK	2.27 PM	8.25 AM			Leaves Ot-	6.20 AM
196	Lv SPARTA	2.49 PM	8.43 AM			tawa Beach	7.10 AM
203	Lv CASNOVIA	3.05 PM	8.59 AM			at 7.05 a m.	7.55 AM
211	Lv GRANT	3.20 PM	9.13 AM			week days	8.45 AM
217	Lv NEWAYGO	3.33 PM	9.27 AM			and arrives	9.27 AM
228	Ar WHITE CLOUD	3.55 PM	9.50 AM	3.40 AM		at Grand	10.45 AM
228	Lv WHITE CLOUD	4.00 PM	9.55 AM	3.45 AM		Rapids at	6.55 AM
256	Lv BALDWIN	4.43 PM	10.55 AM			8.00 a. m.	9.30 AM
291	Lv MANISTEE CR'G	5.38 PM	12.07 PM				1.15 PM
302	Lv THOMPSONV'LE	5.55 PM	12.27 PM		No. 181	No. 173	2.10 PM
329	Ar TRAVERSE CITY	6.45 PM	1.20 PM	6.10 AM	Passenger	Mixed	4.20 PM
329	Lv TRAVERSE CITY	7.00 PM	1.40 PM	6.10 AM	8.50 AM	Week Days	6.50 AM
340	Ar WILLIAMSBURG	7.20 PM	2.05 PM		9.20 AM		7.50 AM
340	Lv WILLIAMSBURG	7.25 PM	2.18 PM		9.40 AM	3.50 PM	
348	Ar ELK RAPIDS	7.50 PM	2.35 PM		10.05 AM	4.20 PM	
350	Lv VAN BUREN	7.35 PM	2.24 PM				8.40 AM
353	Lv ALDEN		2.30 PM				9.03 AM
364	Lv BELLAIRE	7.59 PM	2.53 PM				10.15 AM
372	Lv CENTRAL LAKE	8.15 PM	3.09 PM				10.50 AM
379	Lv ELLSWORTH	8.29 PM	3.22 PM				11.25 AM
390	Lv BELVEDERE	8.47 PM	3.45 PM	7.43 AM			
391	Lv CHARLEVOIX	8.52 PM	3.50 PM	7.48 AM			1.00 PM
406	Ar PETOSKEY	9.20 PM	4.20 PM	8.15 AM			2.30 PM
407	Ar BAY VIEW	9.25 PM	4.25 PM	8.20 AM			
	Ar ROARING BRO'K	By Steamer from Petoskey					
	Ar WEQUETONSI'G						
	Ar HARBOR SP'GS.						
	Ar HARBOR POINT						

* Flag Stations. Stop on signal or to leave passengers.

No. 3 will stop at stations north of Waverly to let off passengers from south.

READ NOTES AND EXPLANATIONS.

Central Standard Time—In Effect June 19, 1898.

Chicago & West Michigan Ry.

MAIN LINE—GOING SOUTH.

PETOSKEY TO GRAND RAPIDS AND CHICAGO.

Miles	STATIONS	No. 170 Week Days	No. 4 Week Days	No. 8 Week Days	No. 6 Every Day Ex Sat. to Gd. Rapids	No. 56 Freight Week Days	Nos 44 & 48 Freight Week Days
	Lv HARBOR POINT	By Steamer to Petoskey					
	Lv HARBOR SP'GS.						
	Lv WEQUETONSI'G						
	Lv ROARING BRO'K						
0	Lv BAY VIEW		7.15 AM	1.25 PM	7.40 PM		
1	Lv PETOSKEY		7.20 AM	1.30 PM	7.45 PM	6.30 AM	
17	Lv CHARLEVOIX		7.50 AM	2.00 PM	8.10 PM	7.48 AM	
17	Lv BELVEDERE		7.53 AM	* 2.02 PM	* 8.13 PM		
28	Lv ELLSWORTH		8.12 AM	2.22 PM		8.55 AM	
35	Lv CENTRAL LAKE		8.25 AM	2.37 PM		9.30 AM	
43	Lv BELLAIRE		8.40 AM	2.53 PM		10.15 AM	
55	Lv ALDEN		9.03 AM	3.16 PM		11.00 AM	
58	Lv VAN BUREN		9.10 AM	3 22 PM		11.20 AM	
0	Lv ELK RAPIDS	7.40 AM		3.10 PM		1.25 PM	
9	Ar WILLIAMSBURG	8 00 AM		3.35 PM		1.55 PM	
68	Lv WILLIAMSBURG	8.00 AM	9.31 AM	3.44 PM		2.05 PM	
80	Ar TRAVERSE CITY	8.30 AM	10.00 AM	4.15 PM	9.50 PM	3.00 PM	
80	Lv TRAVERSE CITY		10.05 AM	4.20 PM	9.50 PM		6.00 AM
106	Lv THOMPSONV LE		11.02 AM	5.15 PM			9.35 AM
117	Lv MANISTEE CR'G		11.25 AM	5.38 PM			12.07 PM
153	Lv BALDWIN		12.29 PM	6.45 PM			3.00 PM
179	Ar WHITE CLOUD		1.25 PM	7.40 PM	12.25 AM		5.15 PM
179	Lv WHITE CLOUD		1.45 PM	8.00 PM	12.30 AM		11.45 AM
190	Lv NEWAYGO	No. 2	2.05 PM	8.20 PM			12.30 PM
197	Lv GRANT	Week Days	2.19 PM	8.34 PM			1.05 PM
204	Lv CASNOVIA		2.33 PM	8.53 PM			1.45 PM
212	Lv SPARTA		2.49 PM	9.12 PM			2.55 PM
221	Lv MILL CREEK		3.10 PM	9.35 PM	1.40 AM	No. 14	3.50 PM
224	Lv D. & M. CROSS'G		3.15 PM	9.40 PM		Passenger	4.05 PM
226	Lv BRIDGE ST		3.23 PM	9.48 PM		Week Days	4.15 PM
226	Ar GRAND RAPIDS		3.30 PM	9.55 PM	2.00 AM		
226	Lv GRAND RAPIDS	7.30 AM	3.40 PM	6.25 PM	2.15 AM	9.15 AM	No. 10
233	Lv GRANDVILLE	7.40 AM		6.39 PM		9.26 AM	Passenger
234	Lv JENISON	7.44 AM		6.43 PM		9.30 AM	
238	Lv HUDSONVILLE	7.53 AM		6.51 PM		9.39 AM	Leaves G'd
247	Lv ZEELAND	8.12 AM		7.08 PM		9.55 AM	Rapids at
251	Lv WAVERLY	8.25 AM	4.20 PM	7.20 PM		10.02 AM	5.20 p. m.
	Lv MUSKEGON	7.05 AM	2.55 PM	7.25 PM			week days
	Lv GRAND HAVEN	7.37 AM	3.27 PM	7.45 PM			and arrives
252	Lv HOLLAND	8.30 AM	4.25 PM	7.25 PM	2.55 AM		at Ottawa
258	Ar OTTAWA BEACH			7.40 PM		10.20 AM	Beach at
	Lv OTTAWA BEACH	7.05 AM		6.20 PM			6.10 p. m.
263	Lv NEW RICHM'ND	8.52 AM	* 4.43 PM	7.47 PM	No. 6 Runs	No. 32	
267	Lv FENNVILLE	9.01 AM	4.50 PM	7.56 PM	Every Day	Freight	
280	Lv GRAND JUNC	9.28 AM	* 5.09 PM	8.25 PM	South	9.05 AM	
287	Lv BANGOR	9.42 AM	5.21 PM	8 42 PM	of	11.24 AM	
295	Lv HARTFORD	10.10 AM	5.34 PM	9.00 PM	Grand	12.30 PM	
300	Lv WATERVLIET	10.22 AM	5.43 PM	9.11 PM	Rapids	12.50 PM	
303	Lv COLOMA	10.29 AM		9.17 PM		1.05 PM	
313	Lv BENTON HARBOR	10.53 AM	6.05 PM	9.40 PM	4.32 AM	2.20 PM	
314	Lv ST. JOSEPH	11.03 AM	6.14 PM	9.50 PM	4.42 AM	3.50 PM	
322	Lv STEVENSVILLE	11.16 AM	* 6 25 PM	No. 12		4.25 PM	No. 34
341	Ar NEW BUFFALO	11.55 AM	7.05 PM	Every D.y	5.25 AM	6.00 PM	Freight
341	Lv NEW BUFFALO	12.30 PM		South of	5.35 AM		7.30 AM
356	Lv LA PORTE	1.25 PM		Grand	6.15 AM		9.20 AM
364	Lv WELLSBORO	2.10 PM		Rapids	6.35 AM		10.30 AM
370	Lv HANNA	2.30 PM			6.48 AM		11.00 AM
373	Lv THOMASTON	2.40 PM			6.57 AM		11.25 AM
379	Ar LA CROSSE	3.00 PM			7.15 AM		12.00 NN
341	Lv NEW BUFFALO	12.05 PM	7.12 PM		5.30 AM		
351	Lv MICHIGAN CITY	12.22 PM	7 29 PM		5.47 AM		
394	Lv KENSINGTON	1.35 PM	8 30 PM		6 55 AM		
401	Lv 63d STREET	1 52 PM	8.47 PM		7.12 AM		
402	Lv HYDE PARK	1.55 PM	8.50 PM		7.15 AM		
404	Lv 39th STREET	2 01 PM	8.56 PM		7.21 AM		
406	Lv 22d STREET	2.07 PM	9.02 PM		7.27 AM		
407	Ar CHICAGO M C R R	2.10 PM	9.05 PM		7.30 AM		

* Flag Stations. Stop on signal or to leave passengers.

Trains between New Buffalo and LaCrosse run week days only.

READ NOTES AND EXPLANATIONS

Chicago & West Michigan 1898 Chicago-Petoskey service.

FROM AUTHOR'S COLLECTION.

In 1896 Thayer shut down his Muskegon operations and in January 1897 paid $1.25 million to buy a large tract of timberland in southern Kalkaska and northern Missaukee Counties. He incorporated the Grand Rapids, Kalkaska & Southeastern Railroad (GRK&SE) on 30 August 1897 to build a line from Van Buren to Lake City in Missaukee County. When built the 33-mile road extended from the C&NM line at Rapid City (originally named Van Buren), southeasterly through Kalkaska, to the logging community of Stratford. The C&WM's general attorney, William Alden Smith, acting on Thayer's instructions, took the contract to build the GRK&SE. On 4 October 1897 the company amended its corporate articles to provide for a 52-mile line

Central Standard Time—In Effect June 19, 1898.

Chicago & West Michigan Ry.

MUSKEGON DIVISION—GOING SOUTH.

PENTWATER TO MUSKEGON AND ALLEGAN.

Miles	STATIONS	Nos. 80-94 Week Days	No. 82 Week Days	Nos. 84 & 90 Week Days	No. 86 Week Days	No. 102 Freight Week Days
0	Lv PENTWATER	4.45AM		1.35PM		5.00AM
7	Ar MEARS	5.00AM		1.50PM		5.30AM
10	Lv HART	5.11AM		2.02PM		
7	Lv MEARS	5.25AM		2.15PM		5.30AM
10	Lv EAST GOLDEN					
13	Lv SHELBY	5.37AM		2.27PM		6.20AM
17	Lv NEW ERA	5.45AM		2.35PM		6.50AM
21	Lv ROTHBURY	*		*		7.10AM
27	Lv MONTAGUE	6.05AM		2.55PM		7.50AM
28	Lv WHITEHALL	6.10AM		3.00PM		8.45AM
34	Lv SWEETS	*		*		
40	Lv B. R. JUNCTION	6.35AM		3.25PM		9.35AM
44	Ar NORTH YARD					10.00AM
45	Ar MUSKEGON	7.00AM		3.55PM		
	Lv MUSKEGON	7.05AM	10.50AM	8.05PM	2.55PM	
48	Lv MUSKEGON HEIGHTS	*	*	*	*	
50	Lv LAKE HARBOR	* 7.16AM	*11.02AM	* 8.18PM	* 3.06PM	Nos. 96 & 92
56	Lv KIRKS JUNCTION	7.30AM	11.15AM	8.30PM	3.20PM	
58	Lv FERRYSBURG	7.34AM	11.19AM	8.34PM	3.24PM	Leave
59	Lv GRAND HAVEN	7.37AM	11.22AM	8.37PM	3.27PM	Muske'n
67	Lv AGNEW	* 7.50AM	*11.36AM		* 3.42PM	at 7.55
70	Lv WEST OLIVE	* 7.57AM	*11.44AM		* 3.49PM	a. m. and
75	Lv NORTH HOLLAND	* 8.06AM	*11.54AM		* 4.00PM	5.00 p. m.,
79	Lv WAVERLY	8.15AM	*12.05PM	9.15PM	4.10PM	arrive
80	Lv HOLLAND	8.35AM			4.30PM	at Lake
86	Lv FILMORE	8.52AM			4.45PM	Harbor
89	Lv HAMILTON	9.05AM			4.53PM	at 8.07
94	Lv DUNNING	* 9.20AM			* 5.05PM	a. m. and
99	Lv MILL GROVE	* 9.32AM			* 5.15PM	5 10 p. m.
103	Ar ALLEGAN	9.45AM			5.25PM	

BIG RAPIDS DIVISION.

Miles	STATIONS	No. 86 Week Days	Nos. 114, 110 Mixed Week Days
0	Lv BIG RAPIDS	6.50PM	7.30AM
7	Lv HUNGERFORD	* 7.05PM	* 7.55AM
9	Lv LUMBERTON	*	*
11	Lv WOODVILLE	7.15PM	8.30AM
15	Lv FIELD'S	*	*
20	Ar WHITE CLOUD	7.35PM	9.15AM
	Lv WHITE CLOUD	8.05PM	10.05AM
26	Lv WORCESTER HILL	*	*
31	Lv FREMONT	8.29PM	10.50AM
37	Lv REEMAN	*	*
36	Lv BRUNSWICK	*	*
39	Lv HOLTON	8.45PM	11.25AM
45	Lv TWIN LAKE	9.00PM	*11.45AM
51	Lv B. R. JUNCTION	9.15PM	12.15PM
56	Ar MUSKEGON	9.45PM	12.40PM

C. & W. M. CONNECTIONS.

Allegan—D. T. & M., L. S. & M. S. (U).
Bay View—G. R. & I. (U).
Baldwin—F. & P. M. (U).
Belfast—L. E. & W. R. R. (U).
Big Rapids—D., G. R. & W. (U), G. R. & I. (T).
Benton Harbor—C. C. C. & St. L. (U), M., B. H. & C. (T).
Ferrysburg—G. T. (D. & M. Div.) (U).
Grand Junction—M. C. (U).
Grand Rapids—D., G. R. & W. (U), M. C. (U), G. R. & I. (U), L. S. & M. S. (T), G. T. (D. & M. Div.) (T).
Hartford—S. H. & E. (U).
Hanna—P. F. W. & C. (T).
LaPorte—L. S. & M. S. (T), L. E. & W. (T).
LaCrosse—C. I. & L. (U), P. C. C. & St. L. (U), C. & I. C. (U), I. I. & I. (U)
Magee—Wabash R. R. (U).
Manistee Crossing—M. & N. E. (U).
Muskegon—G. R. & I. (U), G. T. (T. S. & M. Div.) (T).
New Buffalo—M. C. (U).
Petoskey—G. R. & I. (T).
Sparta—G. T. (T. S. & M. Div.) (T).
St. Joseph—Vandalia Line (U), G. & M. T. Co.'s Steamers (U).
Traverse City—G. R. & I. (T), M. & N. E. (T).
Thompsonville—Ann Arbor R. R. (U).
Thomaston—N. Y. C. & St. L. (U).
Wellsboro—B. & O. (U), C. & G. T. (U).

U Union Station. T Transfer

Trains arrive at and depart from Michigan Central Station, foot of 12th Street, Chicago, and Union Station, Grand Rapids.

READ NOTES AND EXPLANATIONS.

Central Standard Time—In Effect June 19, 1898.

Chicago & West Michigan Ry.

MUSKEGON DIVISION—GOING NORTH.

ALLEGAN TO MUSKEGON AND PENTWATER.

Miles	STATIONS	Nos. 83-85 Week Days	No. 93 Week Days	No. 87 Week Days	Nos. 91-89 Week Days	Nos. 105-101 Freight Week Days
0	Lv ALLEGAN	7.15AM			5.50PM	11.15AM
4	Lv MILL GROVE	* 7.24AM			*	
8	Lv DUNNING	* 7.34AM			* 6.11PM	*11.35AM
13	Lv HAMILTON	7.45AM			6.25PM	11.55AM
17	Lv FILMORE	7.55AM			6.37PM	12.15PM
23	Lv HOLLAND	8.10AM			7.00PM	12.35PM
24	Lv WAVERLY	8.25AM	9.45PM	12.35PM	7.20PM	
28	Lv NORTH HOLLAND	* 8.34AM			* 7.28PM	
33	Lv WEST OLIVE	* 8.45AM		*12.54PM	* 7.37PM	
36	Lv AGNEW	* 8.50AM		* 1.02PM	* 7.44PM	
44	Lv GRAND HAVEN	9.06AM	10.20PM	1.16PM	7.58PM	
45	Lv FERRYSBURG	9.09AM	10.23PM	1.20PM	8.01PM	
46	Lv KIRKS JUNCTION	9.14AM	10.26PM	1.24PM	8.05PM	
53	Lv LAKE HARBOR	* 9.27AM	*10.39PM	* 1.37PM	8.18PM	
55	Lv MUSKEGON HEIGHTS	9.30AM	*	* 1.40PM	*	
57	Ar MUSKEGON	9.40AM	10.50PM	1.50PM	8.30PM	
	Lv MUSKEGON	9.05AM			8.45PM	
59	Lv NORTH YARD			Nos. 95 & 97		9.00AM
63	Lv B. R. JUNCTION	9.35AM			9.15PM	9.35AM
69	Lv SWEETS	* 9.45AM		Leave	*	
75	Lv WHITEHALL	9.55AM		Lake	9.35PM	10.45AM
76	Lv MONTAGUE	10 00AM		Harb'r at	9.40PM	11.10AM
82	Lv ROTHBURY	*		8.20 a. m.	*	11.30AM
86	Lv NEW ERA	10.17AM		and 5.20	9.57PM	11.50AM
90	Lv SHELBY	10.25AM		p. m. and	10 05PM	12.30PM
93	Lv EAST GOLDEN			arrive at		
96	Ar MEARS	10.40AM		Musk'gn	10.20PM	12.55PM
98	Ar HART	10.51AM		at 8.35	10.35PM	2.02PM
96	Lv MEARS	11.05AM		a. m. and	10.50PM	2.45PM
103	Ar PENTWATER	11.20AM		5 35 p. m.	11.05PM	3.15PM

BIG RAPIDS DIVISION.

Miles	STATIONS	No. 81 Week Days	No. 109 Mixed Week Days	No. 113 Freight Week Days
0	Lv MUSKEGON	8.00AM		
5	Lv B. R. JUNCTION	8.30AM	4.20PM	
12	Lv TWIN LAKE	8.44AM	* 4.40PM	
18	Lv HOLTON	8.59AM	5.05PM	
20	Lv BRUNSWICK	*	*	
22	Lv REEMAN	*	*	
25	Lv FREMONT	9.16AM	6.00PM	
30	Lv WORCESTER HILL	*	*	
36	Ar WHITE CLOUD	9.45AM	6.50PM	
	Lv WHITE CLOUD	10.00AM		11.30AM
41	Lv FIELD'S	*		*
46	Lv WOODVILLE	10.22AM		1.45PM
48	Lv LUMBERTON	*		*
49	Lv HUNGERFORD	*10.32AM		* 2.00PM
56	Ar BIG RAPIDS	10.50AM		2.30PM

D., G. R. & W. CONNECTIONS.

Alma—Ann Arbor R. R. (U).
Big Rapids—C. & W. M. (U), G. R. & I. (T).
Delrey—M. C. (U), Wabash (U), F. & P. M. (U), L. S. & M. S. (U)
Detroit—M. C. (T), G. T. (T), L. S. & M. S. (T), Wabash (U), C. P. (U), D. & C. S. N. Co. (T), F. & P. M. (U), D. & L. N. (U).
Elmdale—L. & H. (U)
Grand Rapids—C. & W. M. (U), M. C. (U), G. R. & I. (U), L. S. & M. S. (T), G. T. (D. & M. Div.) (T).
Greenville—G. T. (T. S. & M. Div.) (U).
Howell Junction—Ann Arbor R. R. (U).
Howard City—G. R. & I. (U).
Ionia—G. T. (D. & M. Div.) (T).
Lansing—M. C. (U), L. S. & M. S. (T), G. T. (C. & G. T. Div.) (T).
Plymouth—F. & P. M. (U).
South Lyon—G. T. (Air Line Div.) (U).
Sheridan—G. T. (T. S. & M. Div.) (T).
Saginaw—M. C. (U), F. & P. M. (U), S. T. & H. (U), G. T. (C. S. & M. Div.) (T).
Trowbridge—G. T. (C. & G. T. Div.) (U).
Woodbury—C. K. & S. (U).

U Union Station. T Transfer.

Trains arrive and depart from FORT STREET UNION STATION, Cor. Fort and Third Sts., Detroit, and Union Station, Grand Rapids.

READ NOTES AND EXPLANATIONS.

Chicago & West Michigan 1898 Allegan-Pentwater service and Big Rapids branch.

FROM AUTHOR'S COLLECTION.

from Elk Rapids to Grayling, a branch that was never built. GRK&SE completed its 32.9-mile line from Rapid City to Stratford on 10 January 1898. To capture its lumber traffic, the C&WM leased the GRK&SE on 20 January 1898 for ten years. General Manager Heald reported that "the operation of this road for the year has proved remunerative," and leased one hundred log cars to move the new traffic. In addition to its main line, the GRK&SE built two short branches: one from Mahan in Kalkaska Township 4.8 miles west into Wilson Township, and the other from Naples in Garfield Township southwest 2.7 miles. It appears both branches may have been built about 1898. It is likely that GRK&SE built other short logging branches, but these have

Central Standard Time—In Effect June 19, 1898.

Chicago & West Michigan Ry.

KALKASKA BRANCH.

GOING EAST						GOING WEST		
No. 227 Week Days	No. 225 Week Days	No. 223 Week Days	Miles	STATIONS	Miles	No. 222 Week Days	No. 224 Week Days	No. 226 Week Days
PM	PM	AM				AM	PM	PM
7.42	3.30	9.15	0	Lv...... VAN BUREN...... Ar	33	8.50	2.15	7.25
* 7.50	* 3.42	* 9.25	3	.... RICKER	29	* 8.35	* 2.00	* 7.10
*	*	*	6	.... RUGG	27	*	*	* ......
*	*	*	7	.... LEIPHART	26	*	*	* ......
8.20	4.20	10.05	11	.... KALKASKA	22	8.00	1.30	6.40
PM	PM	* 10.20	16	.... SAUNDERS	17	......	* 1.00	......
......	......	*	18	.... SPENCER	14	......	*	......
......	......	* 10.50	22	.... SANDS	11	......	*	......
......	......	* 10.55	23	.... SHARON	10	......	*	......
......	......	*	30	.... DEMPSEY	3	......	*	......
......	......	11.30	33	Ar...... STRATFORD Lv	0	......	12.00	......
		AM				AM	NOON	PM

How to Reach some Popular Summer Resorts.

ROARING BROOK. WEQUETONSING. HARBOR SPRINGS. HARBOR POINT.

Are located on Little Traverse Bay, and reached by ferry steamers from Petoskey. Steamers connect with all trains, and through tickets and baggage checks are issued

OTTAWA BEACH.

30 miles from Grand Rapids on Lake Michigan. 6 miles from Waverly, where connection is made with main line. See main line table for trains to Waverly.

OTTAWA BEACH TRAINS—WEEK DAYS ONLY.

Lv WAVERLY	6.35AM	10.05AM	12.40PM	5.55PM	7.25PM
Ar OTTAWA BEACH	6.55AM	10.20AM	12.55PM	6.10PM	7.40PM
Lv OTTAWA BEACH	7.05AM	12.15PM	3.50PM	6.20PM	9.15PM
Ar WAVERLY	7.17AM	12.30PM	4.05PM	6.40PM	9.35PM

MACATAWA PARK.

Opposite Ottawa Beach, across the channel connecting Macatawa Bay and Lake Michigan. Reached by ferry steamer from Ottawa Beach, or by steamer from Holland (6 miles).

PAW PAW LAKE.

One mile from Coloma by branch railroad, or about same distance by stage from Watervliet. Through trains are run between St Joseph and Paw Paw Lake.

TO THE LAKE.

Lv ST. JOSEPH	* 5.45AM	‡ 9.00AM	† 10.20AM	* 2.15PM	§ 6.15PM
Lv BENTON HARBOR	5.50AM	9.10AM	10.30AM	2.20PM	6.20PM
Lv COLOMA	6.13AM	9.35AM	10.46AM	2.45PM	6.45PM
Ar PAW PAW LAKE	6.20AM	9.45AM	11.00AM	3.00PM	7.00PM

FROM THE LAKE.

Lv PAW PAW LAKE	‡ 8.00AM	* 1.15PM	§ 4.00PM	* 9.05PM	† 10.15AM
Ar COLOMA	8.10AM	1.25PM	4.10PM	9.17PM	10.29AM
Ar BENTON HARBOR	8.35AM	1.50PM	4.35PM	9.40PM	10.53AM
Ar ST JOSEPH	8.40AM	2.00PM	4.45PM	9.50PM	11.03AM

* Every day. † Week days. ‡ Sunday only. § Saturday and Sunday.

On Mondays a train leaves Paw Paw Lake at 6 50 a. m; Coloma 7,00; Benton Harbor 7.25; St. Joseph 7.35, and arrives at New Buffalo at 8.30, connecting with M. C. R. R. train, arriving at Chicago at 11.10 a. m.

LAKE HARBOR.

About 6 miles from Muskegon. Reached by train to Lake Harbor Station, thence by small steamer to the hotel. Steamer connects with all trains.

See Muskegon Division time card on other pages.

READ NOTES AND EXPLANATIONS.

Chicago & West Michigan 1898 short branch lines.

FROM AUTHOR'S COLLECTION.

not been documented. It is impossible to determine how much benefit the GRK&SE provided the C&WM, since the latter did not report GRK&SE operations separately. In his study Ivey states that the northern area of the C&WM and the GRK&SE was heavily timbered when the lines were built, but that the timber was cut quickly and left the roads with no other traffic.[69]

Conceived in optimism, the early predecessors of the Chicago & West Michigan first proposed building quite local rail lines. When James F. Joy and his New England financiers joined the road, the promise of lumber traffic from Michigan's north woods became a reality. In his study of the Pere Marquette system, Paul Wesley Ivey wrote that "for most of its lifetime

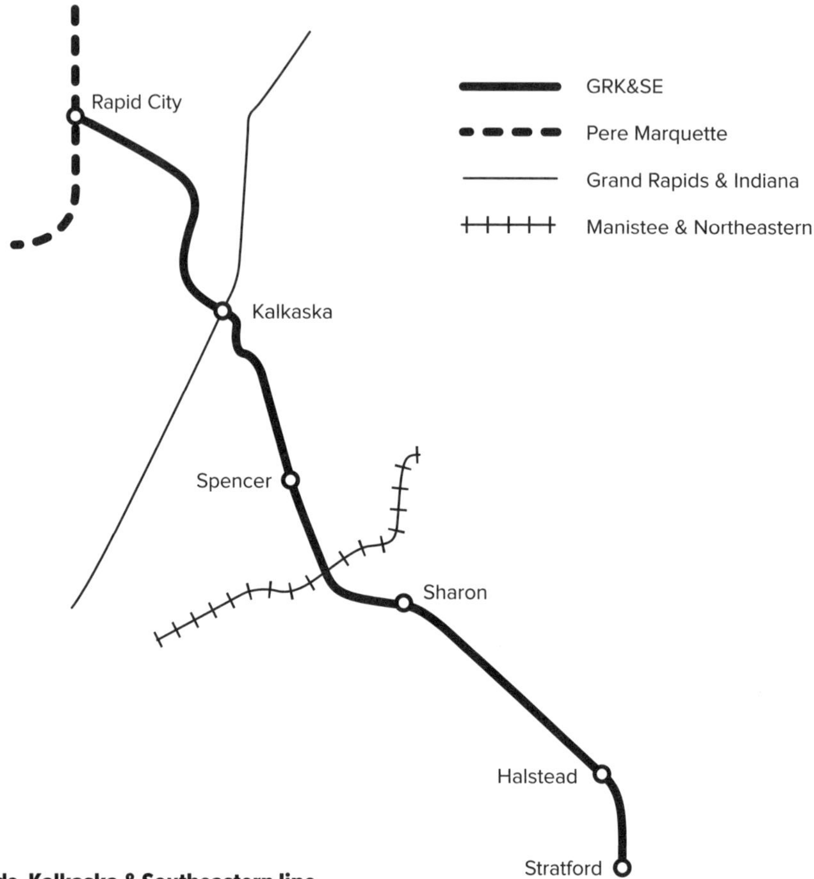

Grand Rapids, Kalkaska & Southeastern line

the Chicago and West Michigan Railway was essentially a lumber road." Ivey studied the Pere Marquette constituents from a financial point of view, but equally important was its economic impact. In the twenty years of its life, the company more than doubled its track miles, from 245.6 to 614.1. Likewise, its workforce rose from 700 to 1,722. On its passenger business it had 2.5 times the revenue in 1899 that it had in 1879, and increased the revenue per mile of road from $803 in 1879 to $1,132 in 1899. It moved four times more passengers in 1899 than twenty years earlier.

For freight traffic, considering the growth in track miles, freight revenue more than doubled between 1879 and 1899, and the $1,734 in revenue per track mile in 1879 increased to $2,382 in 1899. Tons of freight moved more than quadrupled in twenty years, and tons per track mile also grew, from 1,406 to 3,128 in 1899. The result is that as the track miles grew, both passenger and freight traffic and the revenue from them grew faster. The important negative factor in all of the freight business was that of forest products traffic. When the C&WM first penetrated the more heavily forested areas, lumber tonnage made up 72 percent of all freight moved. Both the depletion of the amount of lumber to be moved and the vagaries of the lumber market nationally steadily reduced lumber tonnage to 42 percent by 1898. The amount of lumber moved fluctuated between 500,000 and 800,000 tons per year. Fortuitously other types of freight traffic developed in this period; had they not, the C&WM would have been bankrupt many years earlier.

The C&WM was fortunate in several respects. It had good access to Chicago, to its markets, and to rail connections there. Except for the Grand Rapids & Indiana and a Grand Trunk Western subsidiary that reached Muskegon, it had few rail competitors in its service area. Its access to a number of Lake Michigan ports allowed the road to move some bulk commodities during the season lake shipping was closed. Reaching North Michigan resorts gave a welcome boost to passenger ridership.

All of this provided only guarded optimism for the C&WM's future. As the road grew in size it became more expensive to operate. Bridges and structures demanded constant renewal and replacement, locomotives and cars had to have regular maintenance, and every supply became increasingly more expensive to buy. Operating expenses plus taxes were $2,205 per mile of road in 1879, and increased to $2,859 per mile in 1899. Heald and Agnew could control the operating expenses only so much. Another expense weighed more heavily. The road added 200 miles of line during the 1890s and financed by borrowing more than $3 million and increasing total debt to nearly $9 million by 1899. Interest on this debt was nearly $450,000—an amount that exceeded net income after 1892. Issuing scrip in place of interest payments, as seen earlier, kept the road out of the bankruptcy courts, but added a new burden on future earnings. Paul Wesley Ivey's study lays one more fault on C&WM financial management. It was the custom with each acquisition that any deficit that should have been carried forward was, instead, written off. This practice, as common as it was in the railroad industry, gave the acquiring company an undeserved illusion of profitability. Ivey calculated that by writing off deficits the C&WM, instead of a surplus at the end of 1899 of $48,528, should have shown a net deficit of $3,226,008.[70]

Early in 1899 Nathaniel Thayer Jr. and William Crapo began serious discussions about a merger of their three railroads: Chicago & West Michigan, Detroit, Grand Rapids & Western, and Flint & Pere Marquette. A merger plan was put forward on 20 May 1899 and a final agreement was signed in December 1899. The new Pere Marquette Railroad Company was incorporated on 1 November 1899, combining the three roads, and began operations effective 1 January 1900.

CHAPTER 4

The 1899 Merger and the Formation of the Pere Marquette

The Pere Marquette Railroad Company was formed on 1 November 1899 to consolidate three companies: the Flint & Pere Marquette, the Detroit, Grand Rapids & Western, and the Chicago & West Michigan. The PM's first board of directors was divided between six men involved with the F&PM (William W. Crapo of New Bedford, Massachusetts, the president of the F&PM; his son Stanford T. Crapo of Detroit; John M. Graham, Oliver W. Mink, and Frederick H. Prince, all of Boston; and Thomas F. Ryan of New York City) and five from the DGR&W and C&WM (past president Nathaniel Thayer, Charles Merriam, and Horatio H. Hunnewell, all of Boston; Mark T. Cox of New York City; and President Charles M. Heald of Detroit). William Crapo was named chairman of the board, Heald the president, Cox the vice president, and Merriam as secretary and treasurer. Stanford T. Crapo, William Crapo's son, was named general manager of the new railroad that began operations on 1 January 1900.[1]

A record of the negotiations that led to the consolidation of the three roads is not available. It is reasonable to think that Presidents Crapo and Heald saw the economic forces that were at work. By 1893 a business depression was starting that lasted until 1897. Several major railroads were forced into bankruptcy in those years. Crapo and Heald could see the start of a decline in lumbering in northern Michigan. The sawmills in Saginaw were cutting less lumber and the railroads were moving less as well, and general demand was affected by the developing depression. The first road affected was the Detroit, Lansing & Northern, which lost 12 percent of its lumber traffic in 1891, had smaller losses the next two years, and in 1894 lost 15 percent of that tonnage. The Flint & Pere Marquette had a 24 percent drop in lumber tonnage moved in 1893, followed by another 26 percent loss the next year. The Chicago & West

Stanford T. Crapo. He followed his grandfather Henry and father William into railroad management.
FROM ANCESTRY.COM.

Michigan experienced a 26 percent drop in 1893, followed by a 24 percent reduction the next year. The loss of forest products revenue was made up in part by gains in other types of traffic, but sagging revenues accompanied by steadily rising operating costs made it more and more difficult to pay interest on company's debt.

Heald and Crapo appear to have had a free hand in designing their solution to their financial problem. The need for profitability, or rather reducing the uncertainty of future profitability, led the three railroads to consider, then agree, to a merger to improve their financial prospects. At this time the Interstate Commerce Commission had no authority over mergers, reorganizations, sales, or financial matters generally. Congress did not give it that authority until the Transportation Act of 1920. The Commission did publish *Statistics of Railways of the United States* each June, but these contain only tables of data without commentary. Also, the reports of Michigan's commissioner of railroads mentioned but did not comment on mergers and consolidations. He was concerned with tax collections, safety concerns, and data about the physical plant and some financial matters, but he had no authority over mergers.

The deed transferring the C&WM to the new company included the short branch to La Crosse, Indiana. Attorneys discovered a problem in Michigan law that made the transfer of the Indiana section invalid. The C&WM had to be continued as a corporation, its sole asset being the Indiana section, and it was operated by the new Pere Marquette by an agreement. If a transfer of ownership was finally made it must have occurred well after 1920, for it was still in effect when the Interstate Commerce Commission valuation made in 1927.[2]

When the Commission reviewed the merger as part of its investigation into the financial manipulations that took place between 1902 and 1917, its emphasis was on the financial structure of the company and its methods of financing. The Commission had no particular interest in the operating conditions or even the profitability of the company. Its charge, by 1917, was to regulate securities and finance arrangements, not to consider the profits of the railroad or from its efficient operations.

On 31 December 1899 the three roads that made up the new Pere Marquette had the following track mileage:

Flint & Pere Marquette	680.71
Detroit, Grand Rapids & Western	380.00
Chicago & West Michigan	581.11
Total	*1,650.82*

Nearly all of this mileage was in the state of Michigan, with only 33 miles of the La Crosse branch in the state of Indiana. Also, the F&PM had an extensive trans–Lake Michigan car ferry service out of Ludington, and the DGR&W had one from Muskegon to Milwaukee.

On 31 December 1899 the three roads had issued both common and preferred stock:

	COMMON	PER MILE	PREFERRED	PER MILE
Flint & Pere Marquette	$3,298,200	$4,845	$6,342,000	$9,317
Detroit, Grand Rapids & Western	2,510,000	6,605	3,183,500	8,378
Chicago & West Michigan	7,512,800	12,929	none	0
Total	*13,321,000*	*8,069*	*9,525,500*	*5,7703*

The result is that the F&PM issued $14,162 in common and preferred stock per mile of road; the DGR&W $14,983 per mile, the C&WM $12,929 per mile, for an average of the three of $13,840 per mile of road. It should be remembered that some of the common stock on the books was given out as an incentive to encourage purchases by bond buyers and the company received no cash from such gifts.

On 31 December 1899 the three roads had issued both funded and unfunded debt:

	FUNDED DEBT	TOTAL FUNDED & UNFUNDED DEBT	ALL DEBT PER MILE	ANNUAL INTEREST
Flint & Pere Marquette	$5,440,622	$8,861,058	$15,248	$425,523
Detroit, Grand Rapids & Western	5,384,168	5,755,644	15,146	215,417
Chicago & West Michigan	11,750,000	12,546,736	18,158	635,428
Total	*22,574,750*	*27,163,438*	*16,455*	*1,2763,3684*

Of the three constituent roads it appears that the Chicago & West Michigan had the heaviest debt load, the highest annual interest cost, and the largest stock issue.[5]

Several responsible bodies conducted studies of the Pere Marquette in the years following the 1900 consolidation. There is ample evidence that a considerable amount of financial skullduggery occurred that began in early 1903 under the machinations of a syndicate formed by Frederick H. Prince. This evidence includes the following documents:

- On 24 April 1913, a report of the Michigan Senate and House of Representatives special committee was printed in the *Journal of the House of Representatives*, covering the period from 1900 through 1913.[6]

- On 21 April 1914 the U.S. House of Representatives released its response to House Resolution number 409: an investigation into the Pere Marquette's affairs. The document reports on the U.S. Department of Labor investigation and deals solely with negotiations by the Department of Labor with a federal judge and the several brotherhoods that were on strike at Grand Rapids and Saginaw.[7]
- A Plan and Agreement for the Reorganization of the Pere Marquette Railroad Company was prepared by railroad's reorganization committee, dated 30 October 1916.[8]
- The Interstate Commerce Commission issued its Document No. 137, dated 13 March 1917, of its investigation into the financial affairs of the Prince syndicate, the Pere Marquette, and of the Cincinnati, Hamilton & Dayton Railway. This is the final report that followed an investigation and hearings that began in 1914. These hearings were the basis for Paul Wesley Ivey's book, *The Pere Marquette Railroad Company*, published in 1919 by the Michigan Historical Commission. In the document's 263 pages the ICC chronicled more than a dozen years of financial maneuvers for the substantial profit of the owners but of limited benefit to the railroad.[9]
- The ICC released Valuation Docket No. 260 on 8 July 1927. The Valuation Act of 1913 required the ICC to establish a value for each U.S. railroad that could be used to set reasonable rates that would allow the company a fair profit. On pages 497–519 the ICC justifies the costs it uses in determining value; pages 520–34 have the valuation and a financial history of the company; pages 535–37 deal with the valuation of the Grand Rapids, Kalkaska & Southeastern; pages 537–39 with the Huron & Western; pages 539–44 with trackage in Indiana; pages 544–62 hold appendix 1, which presents the general characteristics of the road and has tables of the cost of reproduction; pages 563–96 hold appendix 2, which identifies all predecessor companies with a table of lines built (showing mileage and dates) and a history of corporate financing.[10]

Acquired Roads and Additional Construction

During the first four years of its life the Pere Marquette (PM) acquired several independent roads that were built in the nineteenth century and also built some new lines. In 1900 the Pere Marquette bought control of the Grand Rapids, Belding & Saginaw Railroad (GRB&S). This company was formed 26 September 1898 to own a 44-mile road from Greenville, through Belding, Lowell, and Freeport, to Hastings. Its first president apparently was Thomas Hefferan, a Grand Rapids banker who had made his wealth in lumbering. On 1 May 1899 the GRB&S bought the Lowell and Hastings Railroad Company (L&H). The L&H had been formed on 2 May 1887 to own a line between its named termini. It bought some of the rights of the Hastings, Lowell & Northern Michigan and completed its 12.5-mile line between Lowell and Freeport in December 1887. Its line crossed the Grand Rapids, Lansing & Detroit main line at Elmdale when that road was built in 1887 and 1888. The GRB&S may have been leased initially, but the record is not clear. Ivey's study states that "it also took over [referring to 'early in 1900'] under lease the

LEFT: Thomas Hefferan. With money made in lumbering, he went into banking in Grand Rapids. He was the first president of the Grand Rapids, Belding & Saginaw road and an investor in the Grand Rapids, Kalkaska & Southeastern.
FROM GRAND RAPIDS PUBLIC LIBRARY.

RIGHT: Frederick H. Prince. A Pere Marquette investor after the 1900 merger, he expanded the road from a Michigan line into a Midwestern carrier.
FROM FINDAGRAVE.

Grand Rapids Belding and Saginaw Railroad . . . which, at the time of the reorganization of the Pere Marquette Railroad, was under lease to the Detroit, Grand Rapids and Western Railroad."[11]

On 1 January 1900 the GRB&S extended its line 16.4 miles from Lowell to Belding to connect with the PM's Ionia-Greenville-Howard City line, but it never extended south of Freeport into Hastings. The Pere Marquette saw a way to use the GRB&S to improve its route between Grand Rapids and Saginaw. In 1901 it built a 12.2-mile line between Greenville and Stanton to improve operations. This construction was the last done by the William Crapo-Charles Heald management that had organized the Pere Marquette.[12]

In the Thumb a group of local businessmen founded the Sanilac Railroad Company on 11 October 1901. The 7.1-mile line, from a connection at Poland with the Port Huron–Bad Axe line, into Sandusky, apparently was built about 1902. The Pere Marquette bought the branch effective 1 June 1902, the last purchase made by the Crapo-Heald team.[13]

In September 1902 control of the PM passed to a syndicate headed by Frederick H. Prince, a director of the PM since its organization. William Crapo and Charles Heald left the company abruptly at the end of 1902. By purchase and by construction Price also added some extensions in Michigan to gain added business. In January 1903 he bought the Lake Erie & Detroit River Railway (LE&D) from the Hiram Walker family. The LE&D extended from Walkerville, near Detroit, to St. Thomas, Ontario, and also had a line from Sarnia, opposite Port Huron, that intersected the line from Walkerville. Prince then approached the Vanderbilt family for running rights over their Canada Southern line from St. Thomas to the Niagara River. By 1904 Price was able to run trains into Niagara Falls and Buffalo.[14]

Newman Erb, a PM executive with Prince, testified at a Michigan House hearing about the plans of Prince and Erb to expand the PM. "They contemplated a railroad system the mileage

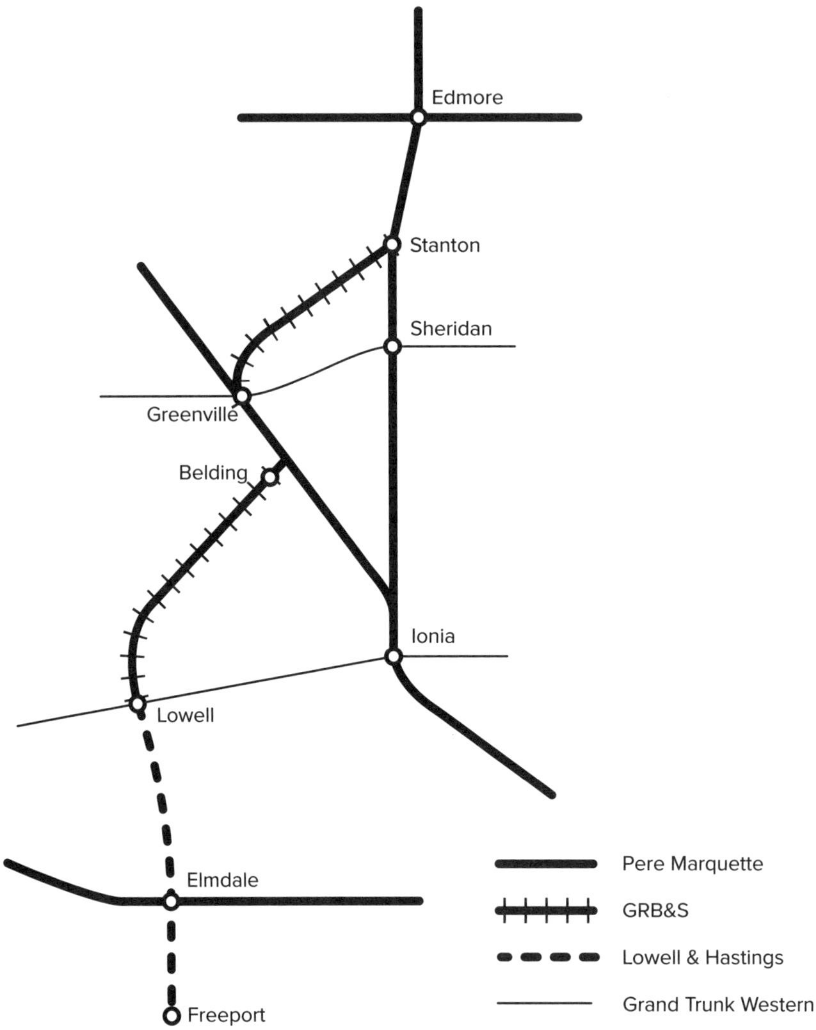

Grand Rapids, Belding & Saginaw line

of which would be second to none in the country. Their plan was . . . to acquire lines running south to New Orleans and several lines west of Chicago, and a line south-east to the Atlantic board over the Chesapeake & Ohio."[15]

To complete one of his plans for the PM Prince formed the Pere Marquette Railroad Company of Indiana on 23 February 1903. This 46-mile road was to operate from New Buffalo to the Indiana-Illinois state line near Hammond, Indiana. Construction started promptly at Union Pier to build the extension around the east side of New Buffalo, through Michigan City, for a 26-mile line from Union Pier to Porter, Indiana. On 15 December 1903 this project was completed at a cost of $713,000. West of Porter he added a collection of running rights over the Lake Shore & Michigan Southern and other roads that allowed him to run trains from

New Buffalo. This served as the New Buffalo station when the extension to Chicago was built in 1903. The building remains in use as a museum.

FROM MICHIGAN RAILROAD HISTORY MUSEUM.

Porter into Chicago. Within two years' time Prince had remade the PM from a local carrier in Michigan into a Chicago–Niagara River through freight line.[16]

In April and May 1903 Prince bought three rail lines from Frederick M. Steele, paying $726,000 for them. The three had their origins in the nineteenth century—one of them was the second oldest, after the Flint & Pere Marquette, of the companies that went into the Pere Marquette. The first of the Steele roads was incorporated on 25 April 1857, as the Paw Paw Railroad Company. It proposed to build a 4.28-mile line from Paw Paw to some point on the Michigan Central main line. The Civil War brought delays in raising money to build, even with a state representative and a former state senator on the board. It was not until September 1867 that the line was built from Lawton to a station on St. Joseph Street in Paw Paw.[17]

Soon after the Paw Paw's completion the phenomenon known as "narrow-gauge fever" gained acceptance as a less expensive and more desirable alternative method of building very local railroads. The Flint & Pere Marquette built one narrow-gauge branch, and the Port Huron & North Western and the Saginaw, Tuscola & Huron, as seen earlier, were built as narrow-gauge lines.[18] In southwest Michigan, in 1876 three lines were proposed as sections of the Toledo & South Haven Railroad (T&SH). On 29 January 1876 the Bangor & South Haven Division of the T&SH was formed, but it lapsed. On 2 February the Van Buren Division of the T&SH was organized to own 22 miles of line from Lawton to the Black River in Bangor. It began building soon after and was completed from Paw Paw to Lawrence on 1 October 1877. A county historian records that the T&SH took control of the Paw Paw line in January 1878. The Paw Paw

Franklin B. Adams. His success in lumbering and as a merchant took him into banking and railroading.
FROM FINDAGRAVE.

was first built as a standard-gauge line, but in January 1878 was changed to the same narrow gauge as the T&SH, and the two roads were operated as a unit until 1886. Franklin B. Adams became president of both roads and hired John Ihling as general superintendent to operate them. Ihling was Adams's business partner in Lawton and had worked for seventeen years in the Michigan Central depot at Lawton. Ihling stayed with the T&SH to its end, serving as its receiver from 1891 to 1893.[19]

On 26 June 1882 Adams filed corporate papers to change the T&SH western terminus to Hartford, where it could connect with the Chicago & West Michigan Railroad, and completed the segment from Lawrence to Hartford on 8 March 1883. The next year, on 8 November 1884, a

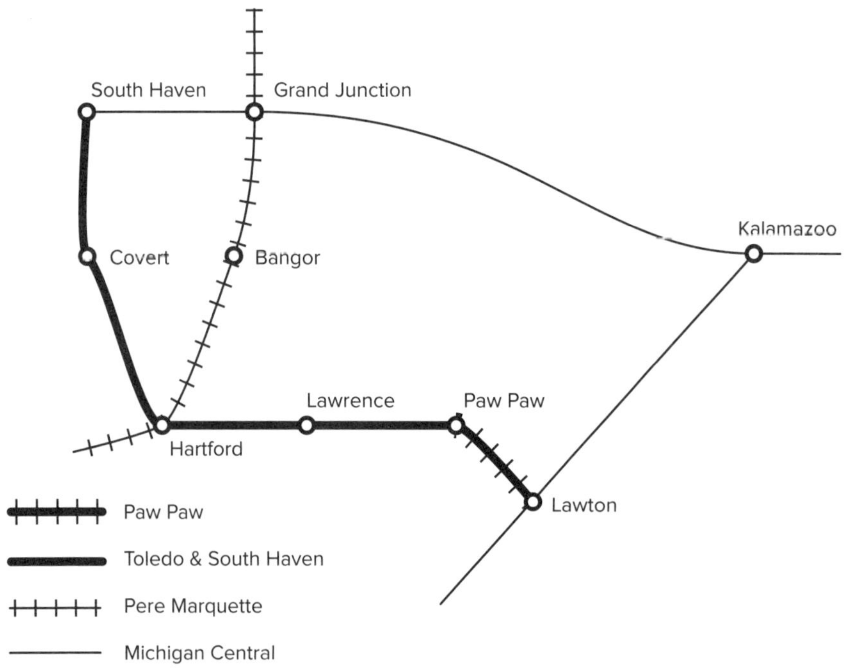

Paw Paw–Toledo & South Haven line

Table 29. Revenue and operating statistics for Paw Paw Railroad, 1868–1886

YEAR	MILES OF ROAD OWNED	PASSENGER REVENUE	NUMBER OF PASSENGERS	PASSENGER MILES (THOUS.)	FREIGHT REVENUE	FREIGHT TONS	TON MILES (THOUS.)	OPERATING EXPENSE & TAXES	NET INCOME*
1868	4.0	$6,240			$5,138	6,422			
1869	4.0								
1870	4.0	4,068			3,366	4,841			
1871	4.0	5,252			5,752	7,281			
1872†	4.0					2,445			
1873	4.0	4,516	18,061	–	3,385	2,011	–	$3,444	$6,408
1874	4.0	4,320	17,280	69	3,575	4,007	16	9,343	645
1875	4.0	4,027	17,104	68	4,274	4,272	18	8,211	1,518
1876	4.0	3,526	14,104	56	4,373	4,868	19	7,923	1,495
1877	4.0	3,392	13,570	54	4,359	4,952	20	4,311	4,932
1878	4.0	3,454	13,760	57	4,099	4,756	19	3,949	5,272
1879	4.0	3,489	14,150	57	4,282	4,870	19	5,513	3,174
1880	4.0	4,009	17,136	69	4,698	5,344	21	6,451	3,148
1881	4.0	4,267	17,066	68	5,934	7,031	28	7,592	3,923
1882	4.0	4,777	19,108	68	6,254	7,456	30	9,668	2,329
1883	4.0	5,043	20,170	81	6,053	7,239	29	6,285	6,172
1884	4.0	4,245	17,480	69	4,331	4,680	19	3,876	5,394
1885	4.0	4,196	16,784	67	4,446	4,790	19	10,713	1,285
1886	4.0	4,295	19,176	77	4,840	5,374	21	10,422	-324
Revenue and operating statistics for Toledo & South Haven 1877–5/1894 and South Haven & Eastern, 5/1894–1902									
1877‡	9.0	783	2,187	18	599	380	3	263	1,119
1878	9.0	2,812	10,372	83	1,872	1,146	9	2,864	2,090
1879	9.0	2,520	9,372	75	1,528	1,030	9	3,733	551
1880	9.0	2,946	10,911	87	2,647	1,786	16	3,203	2,589
1881	9.0	2,902	9,674	87	3,569	2,683	23	5,373	1,298
1882	15.6	3,508	12,098	97	4,281	2,905	26	5,423	2,567
1883	15.6	6,208	20,693	166	4,614	3,910	63	4,847	6,421
1884	15.6	5,725	19,742	158	3,413	2,783	31	3,870	7,518
1885	15.6	6,507	22,450	200	4,146	2,917	23	3,130	8,331
1886	15.6	6,172	20,310	173	3,763	2,911	20	3,972	6,757
1887	36.6	12,048	25,099	377	8,566	8,112	–	8,519	13,908
1888	36.6	13,201	36,703	503	9,358	10,522	210	12,947	11,519
1889	36.6	12,267	37,410	409	9,598	11,673	212	14,243	9,940
1890	36.6	12,728	42,409	509	11,374	10,772	226	19,507	7,135
1891	36.6	13,837	41,932	461	10,353	10,134	223	19,940	7,098
1892	36.6	14,431	43,906	482§	8,685	10,190	221	21,086	4,843
1893	36.6	12,270	40,802	449§	7,277	9,172	202	19,091	4,158
1894	36.6	11,560	38,532	424§	6,481	8,211	172	19,690	1,577
1895	36.6	9,703	32,871	389	5,705	7,876	168	15,906	3,736
1896	36.6	13,624	33,062	463	10,572	8,275	182	32,748	-4,962
1897	36.6	13,079	44,900	655	10,052	10,384	164	23,958	2,270
1898	36.6	15,620	49,858	813	16,654	16,829	198	26,719	8,351
1899	36.6	20,069	61,287	903	21,930	30,000	333	28,730	16,551
1900	36.6	24,740	63,416	945	39,778	36,100	600	51,395	17,203
1901	36.6	27,842	71,305	1,098	35,172	41,173	584	60,762	6,262
1902	36.6	32,117	71,370	1,071	51,588	46,060	756	60,381	29,906

Source: Data from Michigan Auditor General, *Annual Reports*, and Michigan Railroad Commission, *Annual Reports*.

* Net income is revenue of all types less operating expense and taxes.

† President reported "books and papers are lost or stolen" and could not prepare a proper report.

‡ Three months, 1 October–31 December 1877.

§ Estimated.

group of South Haven men organized the Lake Michigan Division of the Toledo & South Haven Railroad. This little road was to be a 16-mile line extension from Hartford to South Haven. On 9 September 1886 the T&SH absorbed both the Lake Michigan Division and the Paw Paw road. During 1887 Franklin Adams left the T&SH presidency, and it appears that the road was sold to a group headed by Lucius Clark, a South Bend, Indiana, paper mill owner. On 27 July 1887 the line was completed into South Haven, but to do it Clark had to increase his borrowings from $35,000 to $216,000. This raised the road's interest cost to nearly $13,000 a year.[20]

What developed financially is not clear, but on 11 June 1890 the company went into receivership; the court appointed John Ihling, the road's general manager, as a receiver. Ihling reduced maintenance to the extent that in 1893 the railroad commissioner slapped a 12 miles per hour speed restriction on all trains. At some time in 1890 the company was taken over by a group headed by Robert B. Dodson, a New York City stockbroker, who held the presidency until the company was reorganized and renamed the South Haven & Eastern Railroad (SH&E) on 23 May 1894. Dodson remained as president of the SH&E until 1897, when the company, apparently, was sold to Alexander A. Patterson Jr. and his brother David H. Patterson, who had bought the St. Joseph Valley road, discussed later, in 1890. In 1899 the new owners changed the three-foot narrow gauge over to standard gauge. In 1902 the Pattersons sold the SH&E, still losing money, to a new investor, Frederick M. Steele.[21]

Steele's plans for the South Haven–Lawton line are not known. It appears that Prince wanted the road for an expansion and had to buy all three to get the one he wanted. In an effort to shorten the PM route between Chicago and Buffalo, Prince began negotiating with the Chicago, Kalamazoo & Saginaw (CK&S)—a short line carrier between Kalamazoo and a PM connection at Woodbury. By building a 15-mile connection between Paw Paw and Kalamazoo, a PM route via Kalamazoo and the CK&S was 30 miles shorter than its current line via Grand Rapids. During the negotiations with the Vanderbilts for the CK&S, Prince raised the possibility that he would build his own line east of Kalamazoo if the sale did not go through. Prince claimed he might build from Paw Paw to Kalamazoo, then another hundred miles from Kalamazoo, through Charlotte and Mason, to his main line at Howell—a move that would shorten the Chicago-Detroit by about 70 miles. The Vanderbilts, the owners of the Michigan Central, saw no advantage in helping the PM improve its competitive position, and they bought the CK&S in 1906 and kept Prince out of Kalamazoo.[22]

The second Steele railroad that Prince bought was the Milwaukee, Benton Harbor and Columbus Railway Company (MBH&C). The oldest part of this road was the St. Joseph Valley Railroad Company (SJV), which was incorporated on 27 January 1880 to build a 14-mile line from Berrien Springs to the Indiana state line in Bertrand Township. On 1 September 1881 it completed a 10-mile, three-foot narrow-gauge line between Berrien Springs and a connection with the Michigan Central Railroad at Buchanan. The road's first president was William R. Rough, a Buchanan wagonmaker. On 2 June 1884 the SJV bought the rights of the South Bend & St. Joseph Railroad that would have provided an extension to South Bend, Indiana, but it never built it. The company had exceedingly hard times in its first five years, so much so that late in 1885 the commissioner of railroads found the road's bridges and track so unsafe that

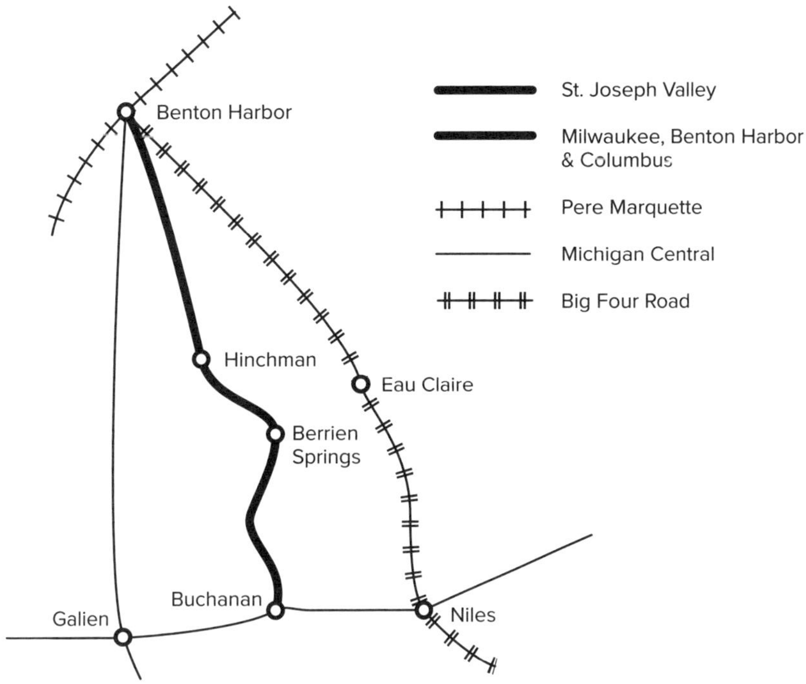

Milwaukee, Benton Harbor & Columbus line

he ordered the company to stop operations until repairs were made. It was not until 1889 that trains ran again, but the company filed no report with the commissioner for that year to identify what work had been done except to change the line from narrow gauge to standard gauge. On 29 July 1889 the company was reorganized as the St. Joseph Valley Railway Company, and it bought the predecessor company at a foreclosure sale. Most of the new owners were men from Goshen, Indiana, headed by businessman Jonas J. Burns. He brought in enough money to allow the road to change over from narrow gauge to standard gauge, but the next year Burns sold the road to Alexander A. Patterson Jr. and his brother David H. Patterson. In 1890 the company reported it had graded another 6 miles of an extension, but did not identify its location. But good fortune did not smile on the Patterson brothers. They were unable to operate their road for eight months of 1892 "for the lack of a locomotive." The financial panic of 1893 halted service for the last six months of that year, and no trains ran for the next three years.[23]

When the financial panic ebbed away the Pattersons put new life into their railroad. They renamed it the Milwaukee, Benton Harbor & Columbus Railway (MBH&C), incorporating it on 6 April 1897. As part of the revitalized venture, they obtained an Indiana subsidiary, the Benton Harbor and South Eastern Railway, that they had bought from South Bend businessman John M. Caulfield. A better promoter than railroad builder, Caulfield announced he would build a branch line from the Baltimore & Ohio Railroad at Nappanee, Indiana, into South Bend and then connect to the MBH&C, but nothing came of his promises. The Pattersons did

Table 30. Revenue and operating statistics for Saint Joseph Valley, 1881–1896, and Milwaukee, Benton Harbor & Columbus, 1897–1902

YEAR	MILES OF ROAD OWNED	PASSENGER REVENUE	NUMBER OF PASSENGERS (THOUS.)	PASSENGER MILES	FREIGHT REVENUE	FREIGHT TONS	TON MILES (THOUS.)	OPERATING EXPENSE & TAXES	NET INCOME*
1881	10.0	$733	–	–	$533	–	–	$4,026	-$2,760
1882	10.0	3,950	9,192	83	2,072	2,076	17	2,700	3,321
1883	10.0	3,208	7,408	69	1,913	2,243	15	2,294	2,827
1884	10.0	3,012	4,819	45	1,430	1,494	15	5,989	-1,547
1885	10.0	1,855	4,580	46	1,692	2,150	22	4,366	16
1886	Did not operate								
1887	Did not operate								
1888	Did not operate								
1889	Did not operate								
1890	10.0	2,711	6,786	–	2,291	–	–	7,500	-2,499
1891	10.0	1,003	–	–	2,704	–	–	5,052	-424
1892†	10.0	259	–	–	600	–	–	2,107	-512
1893‡	10.0	347	–	–	835	–	–	2,522	-713
1894		Did not operate							
1895	Did not operate								
1896	Did not operate								
1897	26.9	2,026	–	–	1,597	–	–	5,262	-1,533
1898	26.9	11,072	–	–	10,863	–	–	25,072	-1,562
1899	26.9	10,956	–	–	12,323	–	–	26,584	-1,896
1900	26.9	12,360	–	–	13,867	–	–	26,258	1,642
1901	26.9	12,238	–	–	16,505	–	–	29,177	1,157
1902	26.9	15,309	–	–	17,393	–	–	42,024	-7,573

Source: Data from Michigan Railroad Commission, *Annual Reports*.
* Net income is revenue of all types less operating expense and taxes.
† Road was not operated for eight months of 1892.
‡ Road not operated 15 July to 31 December 1893.

extend their road from Berrien Springs north to Benton Harbor and finished this project on 9 August 1897. To fund all of this the road issued $405,000 in 5 percent bonds. The $20,000 annual interest charge guaranteed that the road would lose money every year. In 1902 the Patterson brothers sold the MBH&C to Frederick M. Steele. On 1 April 1903 Steele sold the road to Frederick H. Prince.[24]

The third Steele railroad that Prince bought was the Benton Harbor, Coloma and Paw Paw Lake Train Railway Company. It was incorporated on 3 September 1895 by five Coloma businessmen who intended to build an 11-mile line from Benton Harbor to the popular resort area at Paw Paw Lake. In 1896 the owners were able to build a 2.7-mile line from the Chicago & West Michigan station in Coloma to the resort. The Pere Marquette bought the little road on 6 May 1903 and did so very likely because it was part of a package deal with Steele. The line eventually was sold, about 1910, to the Benton Harbor–St. Joe Railway & Light Company, and it became part of its electric interurban route from Benton Harbor to Watervliet.[25]

One Michigan House hearing witness claimed that Prince bought the three Steele roads to increase PM track miles. A 1901 bond issue restricted borrowing to miles owned, and the 63 miles of Steele lines could permit additional bonds to be issued to finance Prince's projects. The same reasoning was brought forward later to explain Prince's purchase of the Grand Rapids, Kalkaska & South Eastern.[26]

In the mid-1890s Thomas L. Handy, a Bay City entrepreneur, located a field of high-quality bituminous coal west of Bay City and developed it by digging three mines in Williams and Monitor Townships. Handy needed a railroad to move the coal, so he formed the Huron & Western Railroad Company (H&W) on 26 May 1902 to build an 11-mile line. The Grand Trunk Western Railway built the line for Handy in 1903. The H&W line extended west from a connection with the Detroit & Mackinac at its yards at North Bay City. In August 1903 the PM bought the H&W and a half interest in the Wolverine Coal Company, paying $325,000 in cash and assuming $106,000 of its bonds. The purchase included an agreement that the coal company would provide locomotive coal to the PM at cost of production plus ten cents per ton—a very profitable arrangement for the railroad.[27]

In February 1900 the PM formally leased the Saginaw, Tuscola & Huron, and on 6 May 1903 its ownership was transferred to the PM. The Pere Marquette, and before it the Flint & Pere Marquette, had controlled the line from its inception.[28]

Another short extension was built in 1903 from Harbor Beach to Port Hope in Michigan's Thumb. The 7.8-mile line was built by the Harbor Beach and Port Hope Railroad Company. The company was organized on 25 March 1903 and apparently was controlled by the Pere Marquette from its origin. Built by the PM at a cost of $77,000 and completed in October 1903, it was conveyed to the PM on 21 December 1903.[29]

This is not the place to discuss the effects of Frederick H. Prince, his syndicate, and the devastation inflicted on the Pere Marquette. Prince did transform the PM from a local Michigan road, something unlikely to be done by the conservative Crapo-Heald administration. Other studies, as well as investigations by both the U.S. House of Representatives and the Interstate Commerce Commission, have not been kind to the Prince syndicate. Often they have concluded that every move that Prince and his syndicate made had the sole aim of enriching themselves at the expense of the Pere Marquette.

Biographies

Each of the men in this appendix appears in the two volumes of Graydon M. Meints, *Biographical Directory of Michigan Railway Officials, 1830–1917* (East Lansing: Michigan State University Libraries, 2013).

ADAMS, Franklin B. (1828–1910)

Franklin Bildad Adams was born in Ohio on 11 January 1828. Early in 1837 his parents, Horace Hale Adams (1805–1847) and Lorania Gates Kinney (1803–1860), moved their family to Porter Township, Van Buren County, Michigan, just south of the present community of Lawton.

Adams went into lumbering and then became a hardware merchant. Success in that endeavor took him into banking.

Adams married twice. He married his first wife, Lucinda Fletcher, in 1850; she was born in 1830 and died in 1879. In 1881 he married his second wife, Sarah Anna Fletcher; she was born in 1856 and died in 1946. Each marriage resulted in two children. Adams died 4 June 1910 on his Porter Township farm. He and both wives are interred at Kern Cemetery, Porter Township.

AGNEW, John K. V. (1851–1919)

John Kirkman V. Agnew was born 16 May 1851 in Ghent, Belgium. He began railroading in 1868 on the Detroit & Milwaukee as a telegraph operator. He was promoted to chief train dispatcher on the D&M and several other roads. In September 1881 he became assistant superintendent on the Atchison, Topeka & Santa Fe, then a year later moved to the Chicago & Grand Trunk.

In October 1884 he was named assistant general superintendent on the Chicago & West Michigan, moved to Grand Rapids, and was promoted the next year to its general superintendent. In April 1889 the position of general superintendent of the Detroit, Lansing & Northern was added to his responsibilities.

He remained with the two roads, and after January 1900 with the Pere Marquette as division superintendent of the PM's Grand Rapids division. In June 1904 he left the PM to become assistant general manager of the Boyne City, Gaylord & Alpena, and remained with that road until February 1906.

In 1876 he married Mary Stewart in Detroit. After Mary's death he married Lillian M. Quigley. Agnew died 17 December 1919 in Grand Rapids and is interred in Oakhill Cemetery, Grand Rapids.[1]

BIRNEY, James G. (1817–1888)

James Gillespie Birney was born 7 June 1817 in Dansville, Mercer County, Kentucky, and was the son of the Liberal Party presidential candidate (1840, 1844) and Bay City pioneer James G. Birney and Elizabeth Potts Fitzhugh. He graduated Miami University (of Ohio) in 1836. He taught at the university for two years, studied law at Yale University, and started his legal practice at Cincinnati, Ohio, about 1840.

Birney moved to Bay City, then called Lower Saginaw, in 1856, shortly before his father's death. His only railroad involvement was to serve for a time as the second president of the Bay City & East Saginaw road beginning about 1866.

He served as a Michigan state senator in 1859–1860. In 1860 he was elected lieutenant governor and served for four months in 1861. He resigned to accept an appointment as circuit court judge. In 1870 he established the *Bay City Chronicle*. From 1872 until 1882 was a minister to the Netherlands.

He married Amanda S. Moulton; she was born about 1822 and died in 1883. The couple had four children. Birney died 8 May 1888 in Bay City. Amanda and James are interred in Pine Ridge Cemetery, Bay City.[2]

CLAY, David P. (1833–1911)

David P. Clay was born 8 November 1833 in Piermont, Grafton County, New Hampshire. He was the son of John Clay and Phoebe Reesbury.

In the late 1860s he became involved in railroad construction. Most important was his 1869 formation of the Grand Rapids, Newaygo & Lake Shore Railroad. It appears one motive for building was to use his lumbering interests in Newaygo County to supply a factory in Grand

Rapids he founded in the 1860s. Soon after, he formed a working relationship with Ransom Gardner (which see) in several other projects.

In 1889 Clay sold most of his businesses to James W. Converse of Boston, who was a financier of his railroad. The sale included the Newaygo Furniture Company, the Newaygo Manufacturing Company, and two sawmills, a gristmill, a tub and pail factory, a planing mill, a furniture factory, and a general store in Newaygo, as well as a factory in Grand Rapids.

Clay married Laura A. Colby in 1855; she was born in 1836 and died in 1926. Clay died 5 April 1911 in East Grand Rapids, Kent County, Michigan. The couple is interred at Fulton Street Cemetery, Grand Rapids. Their daughter Charlotte married Louis J. DeLamarter, the general manager of the Grand Rapids street railway system.[3]

CONVERSE, James W. (1808–1894)

James Wheaton Converse was the son of Elisha Converse (1786–1854) and Betsey Wheaton (1783–1873). He was born 11 January 1808 in Thompson, Windham County, Connecticut. At age thirteen he went to Boston to work for his uncles Joseph and Benjamin Converse in their leather and boot and shoe business. He was so successful that he was a founder of and in 1847 made president of the Mechanics Bank of Boston, an office he held for the next forty years.

Beginning about 1870 Converse involved himself in manufacturing and railroad building. In Grand Rapids he was president of the Grand Rapids Plaster Company, the Phoenix Furniture Company, and in Newaygo of the Converse Manufacturing Company.

His Michigan railroad interests began in 1871 with the Chicago & Canada Southern Railway, followed in 1872 by his investment in the Grand Rapids, Newaygo & Lake Shore road. From 1878 to 1881 he was president of the Grand Haven Railroad.

Converse married Emeline Goddard Collidge. She was born in 1810 and died in 1891. The couple had three children, James W. Jr., Costello, and Maria. Costello followed his father in his interest in railroad investments. Converse was an ardent and faithful Baptist, so much so he was known as "Deacon Converse." Converse died 26 August 1894 in Boston. The couple is interred in Mount Auburn Cemetery, Cambridge, Massachusetts.[4]

CRAPO, Henry H. (1804–1869)

The fourteenth governor of Michigan, Henry Howland Crapo was born 24 May 1804 in Dartmouth, Bristol County, Massachusetts. He was the son of Jesse Crapo and Phoebe Howland. His mother was a direct descendant of an arrival who came on the *Mayflower*.

In 1832 Crapo moved to New Bedford, Massachusetts, became a surveyor and went heavily in local politics and became so interested in horticulture that he established a nursery. He became president of the Bristol County Fire Insurance Company.

In the 1850s he began investing heavily in Michigan timberlands. To better manage his new investments and business Crapo moved to Flint in 1856. He preferred personal involvement to hiring managers. After five years of such involvement, his logging and sawmilling began to turn substantial profits. In 1863 he formed the Flint & Holly Railroad to move his lumber to market more efficiently; he was the road's president until its merger with the Flint & Pere Marquette in 1868.

Crapo was elected a state senator in 1862 and served one term. In 1864 he was elected governor of Michigan and reelected two years later. In religion was he was a member of the Disciples of Christ and in politics was a Whig until 1854 and the formation of the Republican Party.

On 22 May 1825 Crapo married Mary Ann Slocum. She was born in 1805 in Dartmouth and died 21 February 1875 in Flint. The couple had nine daughters and one son, William W. Crapo, who followed his father into lumbering and railroading. Crapo died 22 July 1869 in Flint. The couple is buried in Glenwood Cemetery, Flint.[5]

CRAPO, Stanford T. (1865–1939)

Stanford Tappan Crapo was born 13 June 1865 in New Bedford, Bristol County, Massachusetts. He was the son of William W. Crapo and Sarah Ann Davis Tappan, and the grandson of Henry H. Crapo and Mary Ann Slocum.

In 1886 he graduated from Yale University and came to Michigan to work on his father's railroads. He started as a clerk on the Flint & Pere Marquette in 1888 and was promoted rapidly. By 1894 he became general manager of the F&PM. It was his leadership that started F&PM Lake Michigan car ferry service in 1897.

When the F&PM was consolidated as part of the new Pere Marquette Railroad, Crapo continued as general manager. With a change in PM ownership in 1902, Crapo, his father, and PM president Charles Heald resigned and left the company. Except for a few directorships, Crapo left Michigan railroading in age thirty-seven. He invested extensively in banking, coal mining, and Portland cement manufacturing.

In 1894 he married Emma Caroline Morley. She was born in 1872 and died in 1937. Her uncle, George Morley, became a major Saginaw retailer. The couple had three children. Crapo died 26 January 1939 in Tryon, Polk County, North Carolina, of a cerebral hemorrhage. The couple is buried in Rural Cemetery, New Bedford.[6]

CRAPO, William W. (1830–1926)

William Wallace Crapo was born 16 May 1830 in Dartmouth, Bristol County, Massachusetts. He was the son of Michigan governor and lumberman Henry H. Crapo and Mary Ann Slocum. He graduated from Yale University in 1852, then studied at Harvard Law School and became an attorney in 1855. That year he moved to New Bedford, Massachusetts, and set up his practice.

He also handled his father's business interests after 1856. In 1856 he spoke frequently on behalf of the Republican presidential candidate John C. Fremont. Crapo was elected to the Massachusetts House of Representatives and served one term. He served in the U.S. House of Representatives from 1875 to 1883.

He joined the board of the Flint & Pere Marquette in 1859, after it acquired his father's Flint & Holly Railroad, and remained a director until 1902. In 1876 he became an F&PM vice president and in 1882 its president. He was made president of the merged Pere Marquette Railroad in 1900 and served until he resigned in 1902. Despite his railroad involvements Crapo rarely visited Michigan.

William Crapo married Sarah Ann Davis Tappan on 22 January 1857 in New Bedford. She was born in 1831 and died in 1893. The couple had six children. One son, Stanford T. Crapo, followed his father into railroad work. William Crapo died 28 February 1926 in New Bedford. The couple is buried in Rural Cemetery, New Bedford.[7]

CRAW, Edward L. (1832–1912)

Edward Livingston Craw, the founder of the Chicago, Saginaw & Canada Railroad, was born 7 June 1832 in South Butler, Wayne County, New York. He was the son of Morris Craw (1792–1872) and Silence Clapp (1793–1844).

He served in Company E, Sixth Michigan Cavalry and rose to the rank of captain. After being discharged he lived in Spring Lake and in 1868 platted the town of Crawville, which later was renamed Fruitport. In 1872 he formed the Chicago, Saginaw & Canada Railroad and was its president in its early years.

At some time Craw moved to Grand Rapids. Craw married Julia Annah Soule in 1858; she was born in 1835 and died in 1912. Her father was a very successful patent medicine manufacturer and salesman. Craw died 18 June 1912 in Grand Rapids. The couple is interred in Oakhill Cemetery, Grand Rapids.[8]

DAVIS, Chauncey (1812–1888)

Chauncey Davis was born in Jefferson County, New York, on 15 March 1812. After teaching school for a few years, he moved to Kenosha, Wisconsin, in 1835 and built homes. In 1848 he moved to Muskegon and opened a general store. Within a year or so he became involved in buying and selling lumber. In 1850 he formed a partnership to manufacture lumber to be sold in Chicago and Kenosha. In 1853 he opened his own sawmill and ran it until he retired in 1880.

In 1858 he was one of the organizers, a major investor, and president of the Muskegon & Ferrysburg Railroad, the first rail line into Muskegon. He served as director of several successor rail companies in the Muskegon area. He is named as a liberal contributor to building schools and supported a variety of benevolent causes. He worked for state funding to improve the Muskegon River. He took part in the formation of several lumbermen's associations, and was president of the Muskegon Booming Company in 1864. He was president of the Lumberman's National Bank of 1873.

In 1859 he worked for recognition of Muskegon County as a political unit. He served in the Michigan House of Representatives from 1861 through 1864. In 1870 he was elected the first mayor of Muskegon and served a second term in 1872. He was a Democrat until the formation of the Republican Party in 1854.

Davis married his first wife, Martha Gurrue, in 1850; she was born in 1829 and died in 1851. He married his second wife, Ursa A. V. Hyde, in 1853; she was born in 1824 and died in 1854. He married his third wife, Julia Wheeler, in 1859; she was born about 1833 and died in 1861. His only child died at age ten. Davis died 9 February 1888 in Muskegon and is interred with his three wives in Evergreen Cemetery, Muskegon.[9]

DEWEY, George M. (1817–1891)

George Meeker Dewey, the first president of the Flint & Pere Marquette Railway, was born 1 January 1817 in Canandaigua, Ontario County, New York. He was the son of Ebenezer Bingham Dewey and Harriet Meeker. His father was a farmer, innkeeper, and stagecoach line owner who followed his son to Michigan in 1848.

In 1836 Dewey decided to move to Missouri, but during a stop in Detroit, he was persuaded to stay in Michigan. By stagecoach and on foot he journeyed to Flint, and in 1838 became one of Flint's first merchants. About 1841 he began buying and selling land and became a major landowner in Genesee County. He was the receiver at the general land office in Flint from 1848 to 1852.

He served as president of the Flint & Pere Marquette from its founding in 1857 until 1860 and was a major supporter of the road in its earliest years. He worshiped as an Episcopalian and was a member of the Odd Fellows.

Dewey married Ellen Cummings in 1848. His date of death is uncertain: he died 21 December 1891 in Mount Morris or 24 December 1891 in Flint, Michigan. The couple is buried in Glenwood Cemetery, Flint.[10]

EASTMAN, Loton H. (1815–1879)

The first president of the Saginaw Valley & St. Louis Railroad was Loton Hosford Eastman. He was born 24 August 1815 in Corinth Center, Orange County, Vermont, the son of Oramus Ward Bailey Eastman (1783–1862) and Lydia Annis (1788–1863).

His family moved to Michigan in 1836 and to Saginaw in 1854. He founded a foundry and machinery firm and in 1859 built a sawmill and later began to manufacture salt.

He married Elizabeth T. Taplin (1820–1896) in 1843 in Vermont. Eastman died 26 September 1879 in Saginaw. He and his wife are interred in Brady Hill Cemetery, Saginaw.[11]

ELWELL, John A. (1832–1910)

John A. Elwell was born 13 December 1832 in Goteborg, Sweden. At fourteen he graduated high school and began working in an office. At fifteen he emigrated to New York City to work for his uncle in his shipping business. In 1855 he joined Company G, Thirteenth Regiment, National Guard of the State of New York, remained with the unit through the start of the Civil War, and gained the rank of colonel. In 1863 the unit was sent to Harrisburg, Pennsylvania, to assist in stopping Robert E. Lee's invasion of the state. With his health beginning to fail, he resigned from the service in 1863.

In 1874 Edward L. Craw invited Elwell to come to St. Louis, Michigan. Elwell came with his personal friend Benjamin Richardson, the two of them looking for investments. Craw's railroad, the Chicago, Saginaw & Canada, was in financial trouble and needed help in building its line. In 1875 Elwell joined the board of the CS&C and became its treasurer. When the road went into receivership Elwell petitioned the court to allow him to lease the line. He was the road's lessee and general manager from 1876 until 1883, when the road again went into receivership.

In 1857 Elwell married Catharine M. Jenkins in New York City; she was born in 1836 and died in 1898. He died 28 June 1910 in St. Louis, Michigan. The couple is interred in Oak Grove Cemetery, St. Louis. Elwell's St. Louis home, built in 1884 at the northwest corner of Washington and Delaware Streets, still stands.[12]

FARWELL, Samuel B. (1795–1875)

Samuel B. Farwell was born 19 May 1795 in Paris, Oneida County, New York, the son of Isaac Moors Farwell and Thankful Brigham.

A resident of Utica, New York, he was an established contractor of public works. In 1825 he worked on the Erie Canal, and built the Croton Aqueduct and parts of the Boston waterworks. After these projects he became a railroad builder with his first work on the New York & Erie in the 1840s, then on the Utica & Black River from 1854 to 1856. About 1859 he contracted to build a part of the Flint & Pere Marquette. He became a vice president of the F&PM and served until his death.

In 1820 Farwell married Philomela Trowbridge; she was born in 1798 and died in 1880. Farwell died 11 November 1875 in Utica, New York. The couple's daughter, Sarah, married Henry C. Potter. The couple is buried in Forest Hill Cemetery, Utica.[13]

FISK, Joseph (1810–1884)

Joseph Fisk was born 22 May 1810 in Charlemont, Franklin County, Massachusetts, the son of Jasper Fisk and Hannah Christie.

In 1834 he and his wife moved to Marengo Township, Calhoun County, Michigan, stayed there only a few months, then moved to Allegan the next year to be the second settlers in that town. He made his log home into the first hotel in the town. He built the first gristmill in the county, and served as county register of deeds and county sheriff, then as president of the village. In 1852 he moved to Chicago to become a public works and railroad contractor. His first project was the breakwater on the Lake Michigan shore in Chicago used by the Illinois Central Railroad. In 1853 he became a construction contractor and built nearly two thousand miles of railroad in Midwestern states.

In 1867, wealthy from his railroad building, he returned to Allegan. He was a contractor for Ransom Gardner in building the Kalamazoo, Allegan & Grand Rapids in 1867–1869 and later worked with Gardner on other contracts. Fisk was a principal force in the formation of the Allegan & Holland Railroad and served as its first president and also of the Michigan Lake Shore until 1871.

In 1832 he married Betsey Davis; she was born in 1811 and died in 1892. Fisk died 19 May 1884 in Allegan. The couple is interred in Oakwood Cemetery, Allegan.[14]

GARDNER, Ransom (1813–1876)

Born in 1813 in Fort Ann, New York, Ransom Gardner grew up in Elbridge, Cayuga County, New York, where his father was a hotelkeeper.

In March 1837 he moved to Jonesville, Hillsdale County, Michigan, and became a partner in a store. About 1850 he built the line from Hillsdale to Jonesville and the first Michigan Southern railroad station in Jonesville. From that time on he was involved in railroad contracting. He graded part of the line of the Michigan Southern & Northern Indiana between Jonesville and Chicago. In 1855 and 1856 he built a line between Detroit and Toledo that became part of the Lake Shore & Michigan Southern. He completed the LS&MS line into Jackson from Adrian.

In 1853–1854 Gardner served a term as state senator from the Fifteenth District (Hillsdale County).

He lived for a short time in Detroit and Three Rivers, and in 1866 moved to Kalamazoo. Between 1866 and 1869 he completed a line from White Pigeon to Kalamazoo, then built a road to Allegan and extended it to Grand Rapids by 1869. He became president of the Michigan Lake Shore that built between Allegan and Grand Haven. He led a group that made a failed attempt to gain the land grant of the Grand Rapids & Indiana. In 1870 and 1871 Gardner was involved in building a part of the Canada Southern line between the Detroit River and Chicago through northern Indiana. Apparently his last major project was on a part of the Cincinnati, Wabash & Michigan line in Indiana about 1872.

In 1839 Gardner married Olivia A. Smith. She died in 1899. Ransom died 9 June 1876 in Kalamazoo. The couple is buried in Mountain Home Cemetery, Kalamazoo.[15]

HARDY, Alpheus (1815–1887)

Alpheus Hardy was born 1 November 1815 in Chatham, Barnstable County, Massachusetts, the son of Isaac Hardy (1782–1846) and Betsey Eldredge (1786–1856). He studied at Phillips Academy and was later, from 1857 to 1885, a trustee of the school. He served one term in the Massachusetts State Senate in 1861.

Hardy went into business about 1840 and made his fortune in foreign trading using his own ships. He then put his money to use by making investments in the Midwest, many of them in railroads. He served as president of the Detroit, Lansing & Northern from 1878 until his death in 1887.

He married Susan Warren Holmes, who was born in 1818 and died in 1904. He died 7 August 1887 in Boston. When he was clipping coupons, he dropped the scissors on his leg; which the injury developed into an infection of blood poisoning. The couple is interred at Mount Auburn Cemetery, Cambridge, Massachusetts. Hardy's summer home "Ullikana" at Bar Harbor, Maine, built about 1885, is still standing.[16]

HARRINGTON, Daniel B. (1807–1878)

Daniel Brown Harrington was born 23 April 1807, in Sodus, Ontario County, New York, the son of Jeremiah Harrington (1774–1853) and Mercy Baker. In 1811 Jeremiah moved his family to a wilderness area at Fremont, Ohio. After the death of his mother and his stepmother, at the age of twelve, Daniel went on an expedition to Saginaw, Michigan, then returned to Fremont. In 1822 Daniel moved back to Michigan, this time to near Port Huron, and went into the lumber business. After the Black Hawk War in 1832 he began investing and dealing in timberlands.

Harrington started Port Huron's first newspaper, served as postmaster in Port Huron, built the city's opera house, served in the Michigan House of Representatives for one term in 1847, and then as state senator in 1853–1854. He also was president of two different banks. A biographer wrote he was "a pushing, enterprising, public spirited citizen."

He owned a sawmill in Sanilac County, north of Port Huron, and saw a future in the timber and agriculture of the area. He was one of the founding directors of the Port Huron & Northwestern in 1878, was named the road's first president in March 1878, and died three months later. His biographer, again, writes that "to his energy, push and public spirit is due most of its success."

In 1840 he married Sarah Luce; she was born in Pittsfield, Massachusetts, in 1814 and died in Port Huron in 1881. He and Sarah had one son, Charles F., and four daughters. Daniel Harrington died 7 July 1878 in Port Huron. The couple is interred in Lakeside Cemetery, Port Huron.[17]

HEALD, Charles M. (1849–1939)

Charles Mercer Heald was born 5 July 1849 in Baltimore, Maryland. He was not able to complete his education at Yale University when economic circumstances forced him to leave in 1868. In 1890 he received a master of arts degree from the university and was restored to full standing.

Heald began railroad work in 1872 with the Baltimore & Ohio, and also worked with the Long Island Rail Road, and the Philadelphia & Reading. From January 1889 until 1890 he served as president of the New York, Susquehanna & Western Railroad.

In March 1890 Heald was made general manager of the Detroit, Lansing & Northern and the Chicago & West Michigan Railroads. These two were separate companies with identical managements and ownerships. After his two roads were consolidated with the Flint & Pere Marquette to form the new Pere Marquette Railroad in January 1900, Heald became president of the company. In December 1902 he resigned his office, very likely following a disagreement with the road's new owner, Frederick H. Prince.

About 1903 Heald moved to Buffalo, New York, to manage a Great Lakes shipping company. He was elected one of Buffalo's city commissioners and served until 1920. He then returned to Grand Rapids.

In 1871 Heald married Elizabeth Clark, a Marylander born in 1850 who died in 1920. A second marriage was with Florence Smiley née Fitts in 1921; she died in 1941. Heald died 1 January 1939 in South Pasadena, California. He is interred in Forest Lawn Memorial Park in Glendale, California. Heald's Grand Rapids home, built in 1893 at 455 College Avenue SE, is still standing.[18]

HEFFERAN, Thomas (1831–1915)

Thomas Hefferan was born 28 July 1831 in Granville, Washington County, New York, the son of Patrick Hefferan and Mary Grogan. In 1840 his family moved to Barry County, Michigan, then to Ottawa County, then to Eastmanville. He worked in Chicago in a lumberyard from 1852 until 1858. When he returned to Eastmanville, he went into the lumber business for himself.

In thirty years he was an important factor in west Michigan lumbering. In the words of one biographer, he "never lost sight of the lumber interests of Michigan . . . and [had] seen the rise and decay of that industry in the State." In 1889 he ended his lumber interests and moved to Grand Rapids. In 1891 he founded the People's Savings Bank and remained its president until his death. With Nathaniel Thayer he was founder of the Grand Rapids, Kalkaska & Southeastern Railroad. He was a founder and president of the Grand Rapids, Belding & Saginaw.

He married Amelia Kent Eastman on 1 January 1865. She was born 19 March 1831 and died 28 October 1910. Their son, George Hefferan (1866–1916), was his partner in lumbering and banking. Thomas Hefferan died 31 January 1915 in Grand Rapids. Husband and wife are interred in Fulton Street Cemetery, Grand Rapids.[19]

HOWARD, Henry (1833–1894)

Henry Howard was born 8 March 1833 in Detroit. He was the son of John Howard and Nancy Hubbard. At the age of twenty he began a partnership with his father as a lumber merchant. He also was in the grocery business and was president of a bank, the Port Huron Gas Company, the *Port Huron Times* newspaper, and the Star Line of ships sailing between Port Huron and Detroit. Howard was an incorporator of the Port Huron & Northwestern Railway in 1878 and served as the road's president until 1881 following the death of President Daniel B. Harrington, and then ended his ties to the railroad.

As a Republican Howard served in the Michigan House of Representatives from 1873 to 1875, and as mayor of Port Huron in 1882. He was a regent of the University of Michigan from 1892 until his death.

Howard married Elizabeth Experience Spaulding in 1856. She was born in 1835 and died in 1897. Howard died 25 May 1894 in Port Huron. The couple is buried in Port Huron's Lakeside Cemetery.[20]

HOYT, Jesse (1815–1882)

Jesse Hoyt was born 12 March 1815 in New York City. He was the son of James Moody Hoyt and Mary Nesbitt. His father was a wealthy New York City merchant who became an investor in Michigan land. He sent his younger son Alfred M. Hoyt to manage his interests. Jesse came to East Saginaw a few years later and took over management. When the father died in 1854, Jesse formed Jesse Hoyt & Company. This business built a hotel and other buildings in East Saginaw. One historian wrote that "his great success in accumulating wealth proved that he had the capacity to foresee the result of the enterprises in which he was engaged, and that he had the courage to act upon his convictions."

Hoyt was an early investor in the Flint & Pere Marquette, probably sensing its importance as a tool to promote his interest in Saginaw's economy. He became a director in the 1860s and remained one for the rest of his life. He served as F&PM president from 1875, after the death of President Eber Brock Ward, until his own death in 1882.

Although Hoyt never moved from New York City to East Saginaw, his visits and fondness for the town brought substantial legacies for East Saginaw, and later the city of Saginaw. He built the Bancroft House hotel (now the Bancroft Building) that still stands. Hoyt Park was his gift, and Hoyt Library, opened in 1890, was funded by Hoyt's estate. That part of his estate located in Michigan was administered by his attorney William L. Webber, a close friend and confidant.

He married Helena Maria Demaray in 1836. The Hoyts had one daughter, Mary Irene. Hoyt died 14 August 1882 in New York City. His burial site is unknown.[21]

IHLING, John (1832–1905)

John Ihling was born 30 May 1832 in Tiefenort, Wartburgkreis, Thuringen, Germany. He was the son of William Ihling and Charlotte Seseman.

At eighteen Ihling went to work for the Michigan Central Railroad in Lawton, first as a freight handler, then clerk, and finally as station agent. In 1868 Ihling became superintendent of the Paw Paw Railroad. As the company expanded, it was renamed the Toledo & South Haven Railroad, and Ihling remained with the successor. In 1890 he was named general manager.

Ihling married twice. With his first wife Kate (1833–1894) he had a daughter and two sons, Otto and Reinhold Ihling, who founded Ihling Brothers Everard Company of Kalamazoo, a major manufacturer of military and secret society uniforms and regalia. His second wife, Eunice Harper, was born in 1831 and died in 1922. Ihling died 8 January 1905. He is buried at Oak Grove Cemetery, Lawton. Eunice is buried in Arlington Hill Cemetery, Bangor, Van Buren County.[22]

JEROME, David H. (1829–1896)

David Howell Jerome was born 17 November 1829 in Detroit, the son of Horace J. Jerome (1780–1831) and Elizabeth Rose Hart (1787–1860). His brother Timothy (1820–1891) also was a Saginaw lumberman; another brother George (1822–1897) was a Detroit attorney and politician. In 1834 his mother moved to St. Clair County, Michigan, after living three years in New York state. In 1853 he went to California and entered the Live Yankee Mine claim. In 1854 he moved to Saginaw and became a merchant.

In 1862 he raised the Twenty-Third Michigan Infantry, but did not go into the field with the unit. From 1863 to 1868 he served in the Michigan State Senate. In 1865 and 1866 he was military aide to Governor Crapo, and he was named to the state military board. He was governor of Michigan from January 1881 to January 1883. He was a Republican and an Episcopalian. He supported building the Saginaw Valley & St. Louis Railroad and served as its president from 1874 until 1879. He also was president of the Saginaw Street Railroad.

In 1859 he married Lucy Amelia Peck; she was born in 1834 and died in 1897. David died 23 April 1896 in Watkins Glen, New York. He and Lucy are interred in Oakwood Cemetery, Saginaw.[23]

JOY, James F. (1810–1896)

History has not been kind to James F. Joy. There is no full-length study of the man—only short sketches, the best of which is in *Encyclopedia of American Business History and Biography: Railroads in the Nineteenth Century.* Yet no man stands taller in the history of railroads in Michigan.

James Frederick Joy was born 20 December 1810 in Durham, New Hampshire, the son of James Joy (1778–1857) and Sarah Gee Pickering (1781–1858). His father was a maker of edge tools, his mother the daughter of a New Hampshire judge. Joy attended Dartmouth College, graduated in 1835, then attended the law school at Cambridge. He moved to Detroit in 1836, studied law, and was admitted to the bar.

In 1846 he had a part in persuading the state legislature to sell one of its state-built railroads to a company he helped form—the Michigan Central Railroad. He developed legal and political skills working on behalf of the MC. Within a few years he became involved in building the Burlington & Missouri River—an early component of the Chicago, Burlington & Quincy road.

In 1867 he became president of the Michigan Central. He expanded that road by loaning connecting lines money to for their construction, then leasing them and integrating them into the MC. In a half dozen years he quadrupled the MC's track miles and established a system that lasted for a hundred years, until it was weakened by Penn Central and taken apart by Conrail.

In 1870 he became president of the Chicago & Michigan Lake Shore after arranging financing to get that road built. He also played the same role with the Detroit, Lansing & Northern and eventually was president of that road. The successful Michigan Central was his main focus, but when it was unable to pay its dividend in 1874 the Vanderbilt family saw an opportunity. Within two years Joy was forced out and William Henry Vanderbilt had a chance to keep a competitor from falling into unfriendly hands.

About 1879 Joy began working with Jay Gould and helped him build the Wabash, St. Louis & Pacific into Detroit and establish a direct line to St. Louis. When Joy left the presidency of the WSL&P in 1887 he ended his direct management in railroading.

Joy always kept up his political involvements, first as a Whig and then as a Republican. He was present at the formation of the party in Jackson, Michigan, in 1854.

In 1841 he married Martha Alger Reed; she was born in 1819 and died in 1850. He married Mary Bourne in 1860; she was born in 1831 and died in 1890. Joy died 24 September 1896 in Detroit and is interred with both wives at Elmwood Cemetery, Detroit.[24]

KEELER, Sanford (1837–1924)

Sanford Keeler was born 21 December 1837 in the town of Union, near Binghamton, New York. He was the son of Lewis Sanford Keeler and Sarah Warner.

Keeler moved to Saginaw in 1855, then became apprenticed to become a machinist. In 1859, when he successfully drilled the first salt well in Saginaw, he came to the attention of Henry C. Potter. His first work on the Flint & Pere Marquette was locomotive fireman in 1860. He became the F&PM's first master mechanic in 1864. In 1874 he was named assistant superintendent and in 1875 as superintendent. From September 1891 to September 1894 he was the general superintendent of the Iron Range & Huron Bay Railroad. From 1894 to 1896 he was the general manager of the Saginaw, Tuscola & Huron, an F&PM subsidiary. After that date he worked for several other railroads, then eventually moved back to Saginaw in 1911.

Keeler married Lucy Nelson in 1859. She was born about 1840 and died in 1917. The couple had two daughters. Keeler died 18 March 1924 in Saginaw. The couple is buried in Brady Hill Cemetery, Saginaw.[25]

KIMBALL, George C. (1829–1901)

George Caleb Kimball was born 10 February 1829 in Dover, New Hampshire. He was the son of Abel Kimball and Dolly Spofford. After a basic education he began training as a machinist. Next he worked for his brother at the Springfield Locomotive Company, delivering engines to their purchasers.

After 1857 he went to work at Cocheco Railroad and come to the notice of Henry H. Crapo, who wanted a manager for his just-built Flint & Holly Railroad. In September 1865 he took the job as superintendent. After the F&H was merged in 1868 he moved to the Flint & Pere Marquette. In 1874 Kimball decided to move back to Springfield, Massachusetts, to resume business there. But soon after his return to New England Nathaniel Thayer contacted him about becoming manager of the Chicago & Michigan Lake Shore. Kimball took the job in 1874, remained as the road's receiver when it was reorganized, and became vice president and general manager of its successor, the Chicago & West Michigan.

In 1884, at the request of Charles Francis Adams Jr., he went to the Union Pacific Railroad. His assignment was to evaluate the state of its physical plant, and also of several of the road's operating departments. He stayed two years at the UP, then became manager of the Chicago & Indiana Coal Railway. In 1890 Kimball returned to Grand Rapids as an occasional railroad consultant. He spent most of his time managing his investments and companies that he owned.

Kimball married Azubah Fairbrother née Sargent in 1855 in his hometown of Dover. She was born in 1828 and died in 1926. The couple had six children. Kimball died 21 December 1901 in Grand Rapids. The couple is interred at Pine Hill Cemetery, Dover.[26]

LAWLER, Charles M. (1840–1909)

Charles M. Lawler was born 17 March 1840 in Jersey City, New Jersey. He began railroad work on the New York & Erie when he was thirteen years old. In the next ten years he worked for the Niagara Falls Railroad, the Pennsylvania, and the Missouri Pacific. In 1862 he moved to the Chicago & North Western and rose through the ranks from station agent to trainmaster and then general agent.

He came to the Chicago & Michigan Lake in 1874 as division superintendent with headquarters at St. Joseph, and remained the same with the Chicago & West Michigan until 1881.

He transferred to the Wabash Railroad in 1881, stayed there one year, then became general superintendent of the Sioux City & Pacific and the Fremont, Elkhorn & Missouri Valley. In June 1887 he joined the Philadelphia & Reading as division superintendent and from 1893 to 1896 was the road's general manager.

In 1870 Lawler married Frances Hulse. Lawler died 13 May 1909 in Columbus, Indiana, and is buried in the Columbus City Cemetery.[27]

LYON, Theodatus T. (1817–1900)

Theodatus Timothy Lyon was born 13 January 1813 in Lima, Livingston County, New York, the son of Timothy Lyon (1788–1861) and Mary Davis (1791–1872). In the spring of 1828 his family moved to Wayne County to what became the village of Plymouth. He tried and worked at a number of trades until 1844, when he started a nursery, growing trees for his own use and then for others. In 1864 he was a force behind and became president of the Detroit & Howell Railroad, and in 1867 of the Howell & Lansing Railroad. He left railroading in 1871 when the Detroit, Howell & Lansing was acquired by the Detroit, Lansing & Lake Michigan.

In 1874 Lyon moved to South Haven to become president of the Michigan Lake Shore Nursery Association, and two years later was elected president of the Michigan State Pomological Society. He closed his nursery in 1889 and began work at the state agricultural experiment station. He was the first vice president of the American Pomological Society, serving four years.

He married Marilla Gregory in 1838; she was born in 1823 and died in 1891. Lyon died 3 February 1900 in South Haven and is interred at Lakeview Cemetery, South Haven.[28]

MASON, Lyman G. (1829–1898)

Lyman Gates Mason was born 22 June 1829 in Belchertown, Hampshire County, Massachusetts. He was the son of Lemuel Saunders Mason (1800–1846) and Margaret Dwight Gates. He ended his schooling at age fourteen (1843) and began clerking in a store at Worcester, Massachusetts. In 1850 he sailed to San Francisco; over the next five years he entered a variety of profitable businesses. In 1855 he returned to New England, and late in the year he traveled to Muskegon. The next year he built the first of several sawmills that he owned and operated.

In 1869 he promoted the Muskegon & Ferrysburg Railroad and was the road's first president. In 1871 he promoted the idea of a railroad from Muskegon to Big Rapids and was the president of the Muskegon & Big Rapids Railroad from its organization until its merger with the Chicago & Michigan Lake Shore in 1872. In 1884 he supported the concept of the rail line between Grand Rapids and Muskegon and supported construction of the Muskegon branch of the Grand Rapids & Indiana. He also supported the Toledo, Saginaw & Milwaukee, which built a line from Ashley to Muskegon that became part of the Grand Trunk Western system.

Mason served as Muskegon's first village president in 1861 and its mayor in 1886–1887. A lifelong Democrat, he was twice a candidate for the U.S. House of Representatives and once for the state senate. He served on the 1873 constitutional commission that produced a revised state constitution that was rejected by the voters. He erected a number of substantial buildings in downtown Muskegon.

In 1873 he married Ella Louise Mason. She was born in 1851 and died in 1932. Lyman died 14 December 1898 in Muskegon. The couple is interred in Evergreen Cemetery, Muskegon.[29]

McVEAN, John J. (1850–1910)

John Jay McVean was born 13 June 1850 in Darien, Genesee County, New York. He was the son of John and Isabella McVean. He attended Cornell University for three years. He worked as an engineer with the Rochester & State Line, the Erie Railway, and the Rochester, Hornellsville & Pine Creek. In March 1876 he became city engineer at Lansing, Michigan.

He was named assistant engineer of the Detroit, Lansing & Northern in March 1878, with offices at Ionia. In January 1881 he became division engineer and in 1883 chief engineer. In January 1888 he also became chief engineer of the Chicago & West Michigan, with his office moved to Grand Rapids. In January 1900 he became chief engineer of the Pere Marquette Railroad, and in April 1900 a consulting engineer but retired from active work. In 1909 the city of Grand Rapids chose him to prepare a grade separation plan for the city, but he passed away before the effort was completed.

McVean married Rachel K. Shankland in 1870. She was born in 1851 and died in 1947. McVean died 21 August 1910 in Grand Rapids, afflicted by intense arthritis. The couple is interred in Oakhill Cemetery, Grand Rapids.[30]

MORRISON, Alexander H. (1822–1890)

Alexander Hamilton Morrison was born in Berthier, Quebec, Canada, on 22 February 1822. His father was a fur trader and merchant with the Northwestern Fur Company. At age sixteen Morrison moved to Chicago to work as a clerk for contractor on the Illinois & Michigan Canal. After three years Morrison went into construction contracting on his own account.

In 1850 Morrison and his new wife moved to St. Joseph, where he opened a general merchandise store. He went into local politics as a member of the Michigan State Senate in 1857 and 1858, and in the Michigan House of Representatives in 1861 and 1862. St. Joseph also wanted a railroad, and since the Michigan Central was built in 1849, had had no success. Morrison was one of the organizers of the Chicago & Michigan Lake Shore, and became the road's first president. He remained with the road as its vice president and general manager, expanding the road, until he was forced out in 1873.

That year Morrison moved back to Chicago and tried his hand at several ventures. His health was not the best. He kept ownership of some businesses in St. Joseph. Morrison married Julia Ann Reynolds in 1848, when she was not quite sixteen years old. She died in 1914. Morrison died 4 September 1890. The couple are interred at Oak Woods Cemetery in Chicago.[31]

MULLIKEN, John B. (1837–1892)

John Burritt Mulliken was born in the town of Campbell, Steuben County, New York on 30 May 1837. He was the son of Henry Mulliken (1809–1888) and Ermina Burritt. Between 1855 and 1875 he worked for the Illinois Central and Chicago & Northwestern Railroads. His last position with the C&NW was division superintendent at Escanaba.

In 1875 he moved to Detroit to work on the Detroit, Lansing & Northern. Between May 1875 and July 1877 he was general superintendent of that road, after July 1877 its general manager, and after June 1879 the managing director of the Saginaw Valley & St. Louis. In 1884 he was given responsibility of the Chicago & West Michigan and was made vice president and general manager of that road. During 1889 his health began to deteriorate, in part from the stresses he placed on himself. In March 1890 he resigned his railroad positions.

Mulliken married Emma Annette Batchelder in 1858. She was born about 1838 and died in 1914. The couple had seven children. Mulliken died 23 November 1892. The couple is buried in Woodmere Cemetery, Detroit.[32]

NOBLE, David A. (1802–1876)

David Addison Noble was born 9 November 1802 in Williamstown, Berkshire County, Massachusetts. He was the son of Deodatus Noble (1766–1853) and Betsey Bulkley. Noble graduated from Williams College in 1825 as a member of Phi Beta Kappa. Began to study law. He was a brother of Charles Noble of Detroit and Monroe, who pressed for the state to sell the Michigan Southern Railroad in 1846.

In 1831 Noble moved to Monroe, put out his shingle, and was soon into local politics. He served in the Michigan House of Representatives from 1846 to 1847, then as judge of the probate court, mayor of the city in 1852, and in the U.S. House of Representatives from 1853 to 1855. By 1858 he became president of the Holly, Wayne & Monroe Railroad and worked with George C. Kimball to get the road built. He served as president of the New Albany & Salem Railroad from 1859 to 1865, probably as a result of his investments.

Noble married Sarah A. Shaw in 1832. She was born about 1810 and died in 1885. Noble died 13 October 1876 in Monroe. They had two sons and a daughter. The couple is buried in Woodland Cemetery, Monroe.[33]

PATTERSON, Alexander A., Jr. (1852–1926)

Alexander A. Patterson Jr. was born 18 December 1852 at Saratoga, Saratoga County, New York. His father was born in Ireland and was an architect and builder by profession.

Alexander and his brother David H. Patterson became involved with Michigan railroads in 1889 when they bought the Saint Joseph Valley road after reorganization.

In 1889 Patterson married Jessie Kilpatrick. She was born in 1863 and died in 1945. The couple had a daughter and a son. Patterson died 1 October 1926 in Chicago. The couple is interred at Oak Woods Cemetery, Chicago.

PETHERAM, James W. (1842–1913)

James Wilson Petheram was born 22 October 1842 in Largo, Scotland. He was the son of Henry Petheram and Janet Gibson. He studied civil engineering at Madras College, St. Andrews University, Scotland.

From 1873 until 1881 he did engineering work on railroads in Argentina and Canada. In 1881 he came to the United States to begin working for the Wabash Railroad. In March 1882 he joined the Chicago & West Michigan as an assistant engineer working on building the line between La Porte and La Crosse, Indiana. He was promoted to chief engineer of the C&WM in January 1884. In January 1888 he resigned and began work with the Missouri, Kansas & Texas Railway of Texas. In October 1893 he became its chief engineer, first in Denison, Texas, and then in 1895 in Dallas.

In 1909 a stroke caused paralysis. James married Elizabeth Allison in 1874. She was born in 1847 and died in 1918. The couple had two children. James died 26 March 1913 in Dallas. He and his wife are buried in Oak Cliff Cemetery, Dallas.[34]

POTTER, Henry C. (1823–1909)

Henry Camp Potter was born 14 January 1823 in Utica, New York. He graduated from Union College in 1844 with literary and medical degrees. He practiced medicine in Utica for several years.

In 1852, after his marriage, Potter joined his father-in-law, Samuel B. Farwell, as a public works contractor. In 1859 he moved to Saginaw to work with Farwell building the F&PM. In 1862 he was named superintendent of the railroad, and in 1868 he was made secretary and treasurer of the road. In 1873 the position of general manager was added to his duties. In 1880 he was made vice president and a few years later relieved of being secretary and treasurer. When Jesse Hoyt became the road's president in 1875, Potter became the most important officer of the company located in Saginaw. He retired from active management in 1892. Despite a full railroad career Potter also served as president of two different Saginaw banks.

He married Sarah A. Farwell on 23 November 1847. The daughter of Samuel Farwell was born 6 August 1822 and died 11 May 1906. The couple had four children: Helen, James F., William F., and Henry C. Jr. William F. was an F&PM officer and later president of the Long Island Rail Road. Henry Jr. served as F&PM secretary and treasurer from 1881 until 1899. Potter died 3 April 1909 near Santa Barbara, California. By the time of his death, his wife and his four children already had passed away. Potter and his wife are interred in Forest Hill Cemetery, Utica, New York.

A memorialist wrote that "he was a brave and tender man, whose heart was filled with love and sympathy for his fellow-kind, and whose greatest happiness was found in doing good. His personal traits were towards deep study and he was a most discriminating student of literature, the arts, nature and music. In these he found the life and color which illumined his day and brought him to a period of life allowed to but a comparative few. His sense of humor was most keen and deep. His greatest sorrows have been the deaths of his family."[35]

PRINCE, Frederick H. (1859–1953)

Frederick Henry Prince was born 30 November 1858 in Winchester, Middlesex County, Massachusetts. His parents were Frederick O. Prince (1818–1899) and Helen Susan Henry (1824–1885). He attended Harvard University but left in his sophomore year to go into business. At age twenty-three he had a seat on the Boston Stock Exchange and at twenty-seven his own seat on the New York Stock Exchange.

Prince started out buying small stockyards in Chicago, and in 1890 Prince assembled a deal in which he formed the Union Stock Yards in Chicago and bought the Chicago Junction Railway. Among his partners were Nathaniel Thayer Jr. (1851–1911) and some members of the Vanderbilt family. With the profits from this venture, Prince bought into the Pere Marquette Railroad. His various railroad involvements continued nearly to his death. In the early 1920s Prince bought Armour and Company, the meatpacking firm.

Although a Republican he worked to aid President Roosevelt's efforts to end the depression of the 1930s. In 1933 he put forward the Prince Plan to consolidate the nation's railroads into seven national systems and to improve their profitability. Although much of the plan was drawn up by John W. Barriger III, Prince's reputation in railroading was greatly enhanced. The plan made such substantial changes that it garnered more enemies than supporters. The railroad industry, generally, the railroad brotherhoods in particular, and many shippers and community organizations opposed it. The federal government feared the massive cash outlay required. Prince's plan was never implemented.

By the end of his life he owned two homes in France; "Princemere," his home in Boston; a home in Aiken, South Carolina; and Marble House in Newport, Rhode Island, bought in 1932 from Henry K. Vanderbilt's widow.

In 1884 Prince married Abigail Kingsley Norman. She was born in 1860 and died in 1949. The couple had two sons, one of whom died in the Lafayette Escadrille in World War I. Prince died 3 February 1953 in Poitou-Charentes, France. The couple is interred at Washington National Cathedral in Washington, D.C.[36]

RICH, Hampton (1815–1900)

The son of Samuel Rich (1785–1828) and Mary Bailey (1781–1856), Hampton Rich was born 1 December 1815 at Shoreham, Addison County, Vermont. When he was young his family moved to St. Lawrence County, New York, and in 1819 to Prescott, Ontario. Upon his father's death he left school and became a clerk in a dry goods store. In 1837 walked to Ionia to begin work in a store—an occupation that he continued until 1875. He held a variety of local political offices, and from 1867 to 1870 he served in the Michigan State Senate. He promoted the Ionia & Lansing Railroad and served as its president from 1865 to 1871.

Rich was largely responsible for a state prison being located in Ionia in 1885. He was an active Methodist and a strong supporter of the local school system, and after 1854 he joined the Republican Party. In 1840 he married Jessie Stevenson, who was born in 1821 and died in 1860. In 1862 he married Charlotte Dygert. Rich died 1 November 1900 in Ionia and is interred at Oak Hill Cemetery.[37]

SANBORN, John P. (1833–1915)

John Pitts Sanborn was born 12 July 1833 in Belgrade, Kennebec County, Maine, the son of Dr. Benjamin Sanborn and Emily J. Pitts. In 1847 he moved to Port Huron and eventually became a merchant and then went into lumbering. From 1867 to 1883 Sanborn was collector of customs duties at Port Huron.

Not long after it was organized, Sanford was named vice president of the Port Huron & Northwestern. In 1883 Sanborn became president of the PH&NW, replacing the late Henry Howard, and remained in office until the road was sold in 1889.

In 1855 he married Mary A. Wastell, who died in 1920. Sanborn died in December 1915. The couple is buried in San Gabriel Cemetery, Los Angeles County, California.[38]

SEARS, William B. (1831–1922)

The Flint & Pere Marquette's chief engineer, William Barnard Sears, was born 26 November 1831 in Fairfax County, Virginia. He was the son of Presley W. Sears and Harriet Ann Caton or Katton. He began railway service in 1853 as surveyor and engineer on the Central Ohio Railroad. Between 1855 and 1857 he worked on the Marietta & Cincinnati and the Keokuk, Mountain Pleasant & Muscatine.

Sears joined the F&PM in May 1857 and until December 1859 worked on the survey of the road for its land grant route. Between 1860 and 1866 he completed some railroad surveys, returned to farming in Iowa, but soon returned to Saginaw as city engineer. He was named the F&PM's chief engineer in 1867 and held that office until May 1898, when he became a consulting engineer for it. In 1915 the University of Michigan awarded Sears with as master's degree in engineering.

Sears married Caroline Parrish in either 1864 or 1865; she was born in 1840 and died in 1919. The couple had three daughters and two sons. Sears died 2 May 1922 in Saginaw after a bout with pneumonia. The couple is buried in Forest Lawn Cemetery, Saginaw.[39]

SICKLES, Daniel E. (1819–1914)

Daniel Edgar Sickles is rarely acknowledged to be a Michigan railroadman. He was born 20 October 1819, not 1825, as he later claimed, in New York City, the son of George Garrett Sickles (1800–1887) and Susan Marsh (1799–1878). He studied at the University of the City of New York and later studied law with Benjamin Butler. He was admitted to the bar in 1846.

He began his political career by his election to the New York State Assembly in 1847. He married Teresa DaPonte Bagioili in 1852; she was born about 1835 and died in 1867. Sickles shot Philip Barton Key II in 1859 after learning Key and wife Teresa were having an affair. He pleaded temporary insanity as his defense, and ultimately he was acquitted. He served as a member of the New York State Senate in 1857, and in the U.S. House of Representatives from 1857 to 1861.

Sickles served as an officer in the Twelfth New York National Guard regiment. His participation throughout the Civil War was controversial, but in 1863 President Lincoln nominated him to be a major general. At Gettysburg he disobeyed orders and exposed his troops in a move that the commanding general, George G. Meade, strongly criticized. During the battle Sickles lost his right leg. His actions were so controversial that it took thirty-four years of lobbying to receive the Congressional Medal of Honor.

From 1869 to 1874 Sickles served as U.S. minister to Spain. In 1871 he married his second wife, Caroline Creagh, a member of an important Spanish family; she was born in 1840 and died in 1919. He served again in the U.S. House of Representatives from 1893 to 1895. He did important work in preserving the battlefield and cemetery at Gettysburg.

Sickles died 3 May 1914 in New York City. He is interred at Arlington National Cemetery.[40]

SMITH, Hiram H. (1809–1898)

Hiram Horton Smith was born 9 December 1809 in Malone, Franklin County, New York, the son of Oliver M. Smith and Anna Horton. At age sixteen he began clerking for several different merchants until 1836, when he moved to Ingham County, Michigan. He held two county offices, then was elected a state representative for the 1843 session. He spent a few years as merchant in Mason, then moved to Lansing in 1847 to build a flour mill. In 1859 he was elected the first mayor of Lansing.

In 1863 he became a director of the Lansing & Jackson Railroad and managed the construction of that road. In 1864 he moved to Jackson and in 1868, with several others from Jackson, began promoting a railroad between Jackson and Fort Wayne, Indiana. Smith was named president of the Fort Wayne, Jackson & Saginaw Railroad in 1869. Between 1871 and 1873 James F. Joy made him president of the Detroit, Lansing & Lake Michigan. Later in life he and his son Dwight S. Smith were involved with street railways in Jackson.

Smith married twice: first in 1842 to Mary Jane Waldo, who died in 1859, and then in 1865 to Harriett Gorham nee Bates, who died in 1893. Smith died 15 May 1898 in Jackson and is interred at Mount Evergreen Cemetery.[41]

STEELE, Frederick M. (1851–1932)

Frederick Morgan Steele was born 27 November 1851 in Albany, Albany County, New York. He was the son of John F. Steele, a hardware merchant, and Frances Mary Steele.

Steele moved to Chicago in 1879 and became connected to railway manufacturing companies, particularly the American Bridge Works and the Chicago Forge & Bolt Company. In 1904 a successor company, Standard Forgings Company, opened a new plant at Indiana Harbor, Indiana as a major producer of railroad car axles.

Steele studied genealogy avidly and was a member of the Society of the Mayflower Descendants and the Sons of the American Revolution. His wife was active in the Daughters of the American Revolution. Steele was considered a writer of some merit, publishing a book of poetry, *After Hour Idyls*, in 1909. He is credited with authorship of the lyrics of the Illinois state song.

In 1883 Steele married Ella A. Pratt. The death dates and interment of the Steeles could not be found.[42]

THAYER Family

- Nathaniel Thayer (1769–1840), a Congregational/Unitarian minister.
- John Elliott Thayer (1803–1857), the patriarch, son of Nathaniel Thayer (1769–1840). He made his fortune in banking. He was an initial investor and founder of the Michigan Central Railroad in 1846.
- Christopher Toppan Thayer (1805–1880), son of Nathaniel Thayer (1769–1840) and a minister.
- Nathaniel Thayer Jr. (1808–1883), son of Nathaniel Thayer (1769–1840) and a brother of John Elliott Thayer. He used "Junior" until after his father's death.
- Nathaniel Thayer III (1851–1911), the son of Nathaniel Thayer (1808–1883). He used "III" until his grandfather's death, then "Junior" until his father's death.
- Eugene Van Rensselaer Thayer (1855–1907), son of Nathaniel Thayer Jr. (1808–1883).
- Stephen Van Rensselaer Thayer (1847–1871), son of Nathaniel Thayer Jr. (1808–1883).
- Eugene Van Rensselaer Thayer Jr. (1881–1937), son of Eugene V. R. Thayer (1855–1907).

THAYER, Eugene V. R. (1855–1907)

Eugene Van Rensselaer Thayer was born 27 December 1855 in Boston, Massachusetts. He was the son of Nathaniel Thayer (1808–1883) and Cornelia Patterson Van Rensselaer.

He spent his life managing the Thayers' family fortune and its extensive business and financial interests. His obituary described him as a capitalist, philanthropist, horseman, and clubman.

In 1880 Thayer married Susan Spring; she was born in 1854 and died in 1911. The couple had three children. Thayer died 20 December 1907 in Boston. The couple is buried in North Village Cemetery, Lancaster, Massachusetts.[43]

THAYER, Nathaniel, Jr. (1808–1883)

Nathaniel Thayer Jr. was born 11 September 1808 in Lancaster, Massachusetts. He was the son of Nathaniel Thayer (1769–1840) and Sarah Parker Toppan. He was a brother of John Elliott Thayer (1803–1857), who was one of the founders of the Michigan Central Railroad in 1846. Two of his sons, Nathaniel Thayer (1851–1911) and Eugene Van Rensselaer Thayer (1855–1907), were heavily involved in railroad ownership.

In 1839 he joined his older brother John Elliott Thayer in his banking firm, John E. Thayer and Brother—a firm that provided a range of banking services and was the largest dealer in foreign exchange in Boston. He became senior director of the company in 1857. His exceptionally large fortune came from loaning and investing New Englanders' money in ventures in the Midwest.

He was as fellow of Harvard from 1868 to 1875 and a considerable benefactor to that university. Thayer joined the board of directors of the Detroit, Lansing & Lake Michigan in 1870, and remained a director until his death. He joined the Chicago & Michigan Lake Shore board in 1874 and served as that road's president from 1876 until 1880.

In 1846 he married Cornelia Patterson Van Rensselaer; she was born in 1823 and died in 1897. He died 7 March 1883 in Boston. The couple is interred at Mt. Auburn Cemetery, Cambridge, Massachusetts. His home, built in 1846 at 438 South Main Street, Lancaster, is still standing.[44]

THAYER, Nathaniel, III (1851–1911)

Nathaniel Thayer III was born in Boston 13 June 1851. He was the son of Nathaniel Thayer Jr. (1808–1883) and Cornelia Patterson Van Rensselaer. His father was heavily involved in railroad finance, and his uncle John Elliott Thayer (1803–1857) was one of the founders of the Michigan Central Railroad in 1846. His brother, Eugene Van Rensselaer Thayer (1855–1907), also was involved in railroad ownership.

Thayer graduated from Harvard in 1871. In 1876 he became president of the Boston, Clinton & Fitchburg Railroad. For the rest of his life he was actively involved in railroads as a director, officer, and investor. At the death of his father in 1883 he inherited $2 million, a fortune that his personal management increased. He served as director of a considerable number of nonrailroad companies.

In 1880 he was named president of the Chicago & West Michigan Railroad, and in 1887 of the Detroit, Lansing & Northern. His relationship with Pere Marquette properties ended in 1902 at the takeover by the Prince syndicate.

In 1881 he married Cornelia Street Barroll. She was born in 1856 and died in 1885. The couple had three children. In 1887 he remarried, to Pauline Revere. She was born in 1862 and died in 1934. The couple had no children. Thayer died 21 March 1911 in Boston and interred with Pauline in the Old Settlers Burial Yard in Lancaster, Worcester County, Massachusetts.

WADSWORTH, Isaac R. (1843–1911)

Isaac Roland Wadsworth was born in Derry Township, Westmoreland County, Pennsylvania, on 13 February 1843, the son of Thomas Wadsworth (1770–1861) and Jane Best.

In November 1859 he started work with the Pennsylvania Railroad as a track worker. Over the next five years he advanced to become a brakeman, then conductor, and eventually became an assistant dispatcher, then a train dispatcher. In 1874 he was made a general freight agent and in 1878 a master of transportation.

In June 1880 he moved to Port Huron to became general superintendent of the Port Huron & Northwestern—in charge of operations. In 1884 the position of general passenger and freight agent was added to his duties. Wadsworth left railroading when the Flint & Pere Marquette acquired the Port Huron road.

In 1866 Wadsworth married Mary Jane Fowler in Pittsburgh, Pennsylvania. She was born in 1851 and died in 1916. The couple had seven children. Isaac died 12 January 1911 in Webberville, Ingham County, Michigan, and is buried in Rowley Cemetery, Webberville. His death certificate shows him as a "mail carrier."[45]

WARD, Eber Brock (1811–1875)

Eber Brock Ward was born 25 December 1811 in Applegaths Mills, Ontario, Canada, not far from Toronto. With American parents, he was a U.S. citizen at birth. He was the son of Eber Ward and Sally Potter. Ward's father moved to Detroit in 1821, and Eber moved to Marine City about 1830. His uncle, Samuel Ward, was a shipbuilder at the town then called Newport, so Ward began working for him.

In 1835 Ward became master of a ship of his own, and eventually he went into partnership with his uncle in shipping. In 1850 he moved to Detroit and continued shipbuilding, and the two soon became the major ship owners on the Great Lakes. About 1852 Ward bought timberland near Ludington and over the years continued to enlarge his holdings, then built sawmills to make the logs into lumber.

About 1859 he invested in the fledgling Flint & Pere Marquette and became its president, a position he held until his death. In 1863 he founded the Eureka Iron and Steel Works in Wyandotte, the first company to successfully make steel by the Bessemer process. In 1865 he began producing rails, and some were used on his Flint & Pere Marquette.

In 1837 Ward married Mary McQueen; she was born in 1816 and died in 1869. About 1867 McQueen divorced Ward on the grounds of adultery. Two months later he married Catherine M. Lyons, a niece of Ohio senator Benjamin Wade; she was born in 1841 and died in 1915.

Ward dropped dead of a heart attack on 2 January 1875 in Detroit. He and Mary are interred in Elmwood Cemetery, Detroit.

At his death he was considered the wealthiest man in Michigan. In addition to his timber holdings and shipping interests, and owning extensive mining and mineral lands, he owned the Wyandotte works as well as the Chicago Rolling Mill and the Milwaukee Rolling Mill.[46]

WEBBER, William L. (1825–1901)

William Lewis Webber was born 19 July 1825 in Ogden, Monroe County, New York. He was the son of James S. Webber and Phebe Smith. In 1836 his family moved to Hartland, Livingston County, Michigan. After his mother's death in 1845, Webber went out on his own; he taught school, studied medicine, and then became an attorney. He moved to East Saginaw in 1853 to practice law.

Webber became attorney for the Flint & Pere Marquette in 1857. In 1870 he was named land commissioner to handle the sale of the road's land grant, and managed that until 1885. He continued as the railroad's legal counsel until 1 January 1892. Throughout his railroad career he also maintained a political life. He served as mayor of East Saginaw in 1873 and 1874 and as state senator in 1875 and 1876. In 1876 he was Democratic Party candidate for governor. When F&PM Jesse Hoyt died in 1882, Webber was made executor for Hoyt's Michigan properties.

Webber developed the stone quarries at Bay Port, helped found the first company to extract salt in the Saginaw area, encouraged developing coal mines, and was important in the commercial development of sugar beets.

He married Nancy Monk Withington on 7 October 1849 in Springwater, Livingston County, New York. She was born 24 December 1822 and died 21 May 1901. The couple had two daughters. Webber died 15 October 1901 in Saginaw. The couple is buried in Forest Lawn Cemetery, Saginaw.[47]

WRIGHT, Ammi W. (1822–1912)

Ammi Willard Wright was born 5 July 1822 in Grafton, Windham County, Vermont. He was the son of Nathan Franklin Wright and Mary Lamson. He came to Detroit in 1850, but soon after decided to move to Saginaw and go into the lumber business. By 1859 he had made enough money to buy out his partners. In the 1880s he bought timberland in Minnesota's Mesabi Range, land that proved to have iron. He continued to invest in land with timber and in a wide variety of other businesses, including banking, livestock raising, farming, cement manufacturing, and manufacturing companies.

He served as a director of the Saginaw Valley & St. Louis from its founding until 1885. Until his death he continued to be a director of a number of railroad companies. He was a Republican, an Episcopalian, and a longtime trustee of Alma College.

In 1848 Wright married Harriet Barton, who died in 1884. He then married Anna Case in 1885. Wright died on 5 May 1912 in Alma and is interred at Burgess Cemetery, Grafton, Vermont. Wright's home in Alma, built in 1888 at 503 North State Street, still stands. Wright's home in Saginaw, at 207 Garden Lane, still stands. The Wright Opera House, built in 1879–1880 at 101–107 East Superior Street, Alma, also remains.[48]

APPENDIX 2

Family Trees

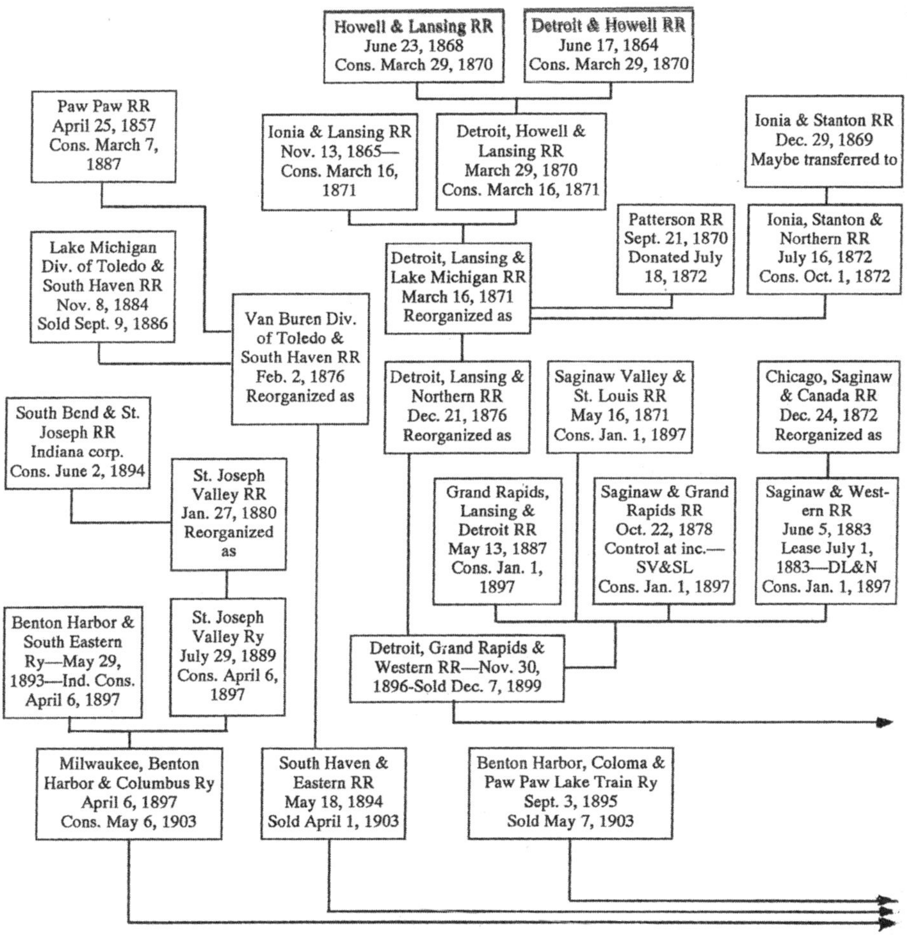

REPRINTED, BY PERMISSION, FROM GRAYDON M. MEINTS, *MICHIGAN RAILROADS AND RAILROAD COMPANIES* (EAST LANSING: MICHIGAN STATE UNIVERSITY PRESS, 1992), 184–86.

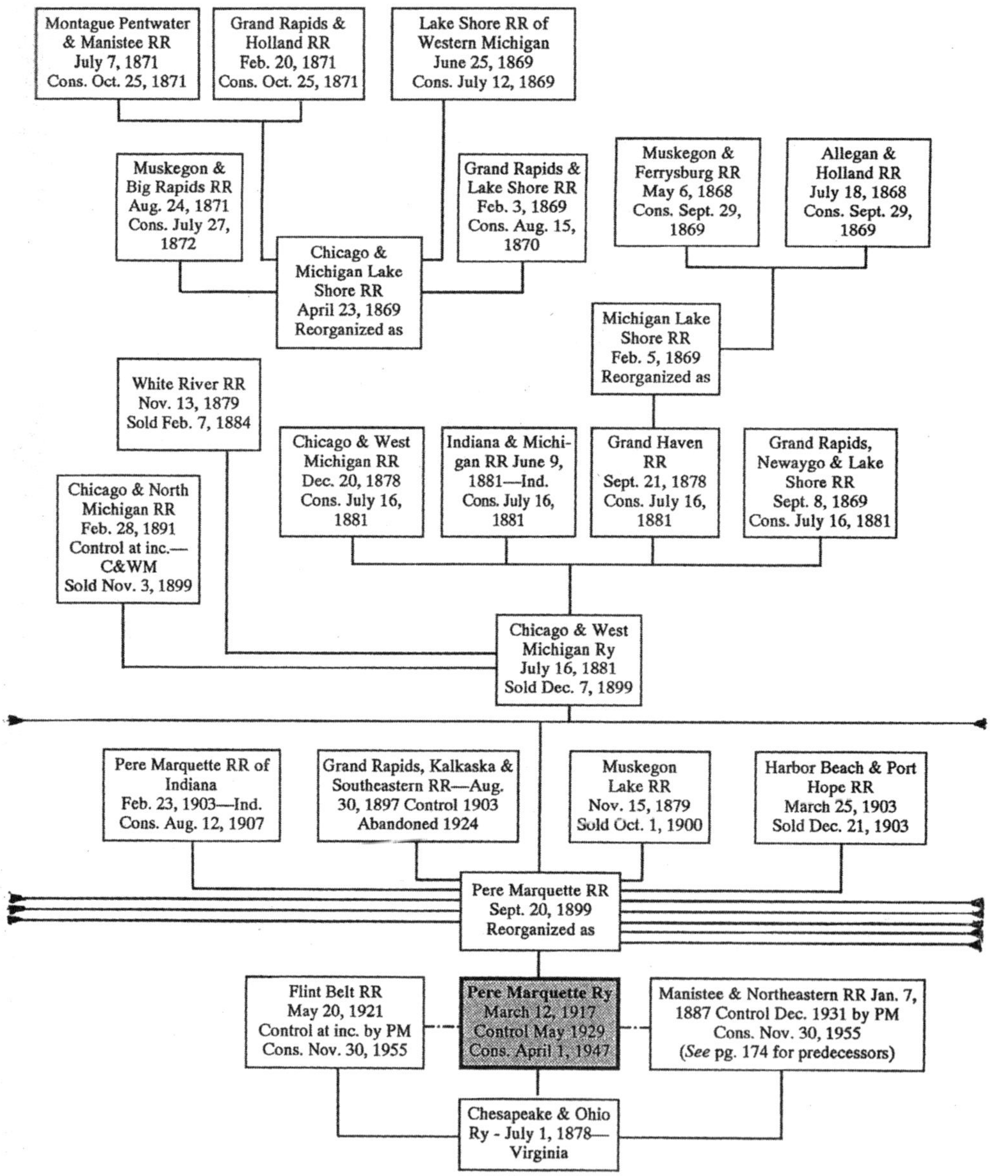
Montague Pentwater & Manistee RR July 7, 1871 Cons. Oct. 25, 1871
Grand Rapids & Holland RR Feb. 20, 1871 Cons. Oct. 25, 1871
Lake Shore RR of Western Michigan June 25, 1869 Cons. July 12, 1869
Muskegon & Big Rapids RR Aug. 24, 1871 Cons. July 27, 1872
Grand Rapids & Lake Shore RR Feb. 3, 1869 Cons. Aug. 15, 1870
Muskegon & Ferrysburg RR May 6, 1868 Cons. Sept. 29, 1869
Allegan & Holland RR July 18, 1868 Cons. Sept. 29, 1869
Chicago & Michigan Lake Shore RR April 23, 1869 Reorganized as
Michigan Lake Shore RR Feb. 5, 1869 Reorganized as
White River RR Nov. 13, 1879 Sold Feb. 7, 1884
Chicago & West Michigan RR Dec. 20, 1878 Cons. July 16, 1881
Indiana & Michigan RR June 9, 1881—Ind. Cons. July 16, 1881
Grand Haven RR Sept. 21, 1878 Cons. July 16, 1881
Grand Rapids, Newaygo & Lake Shore RR Sept. 8, 1869 Cons. July 16, 1881
Chicago & North Michigan RR Feb. 28, 1891 Control at inc.—C&WM Sold Nov. 3, 1899
Chicago & West Michigan Ry July 16, 1881 Sold Dec. 7, 1899
Pere Marquette RR of Indiana Feb. 23, 1903—Ind. Cons. Aug. 12, 1907
Grand Rapids, Kalkaska & Southeastern RR—Aug. 30, 1897 Control 1903 Abandoned 1924
Muskegon Lake RR Nov. 15, 1879 Sold Oct. 1, 1900
Harbor Beach & Port Hope RR March 25, 1903 Sold Dec. 21, 1903
Pere Marquette RR Sept. 20, 1899 Reorganized as
Flint Belt RR May 20, 1921 Control at inc. by PM Cons. Nov. 30, 1955
Pere Marquette Ry March 12, 1917 Control May 1929 Cons. April 1, 1947
Manistee & Northeastern RR Jan. 7, 1887 Control Dec. 1931 by PM Cons. Nov. 30, 1955 (See pg. 174 for predecessors)
Chesapeake & Ohio Ry - July 1, 1878—Virginia

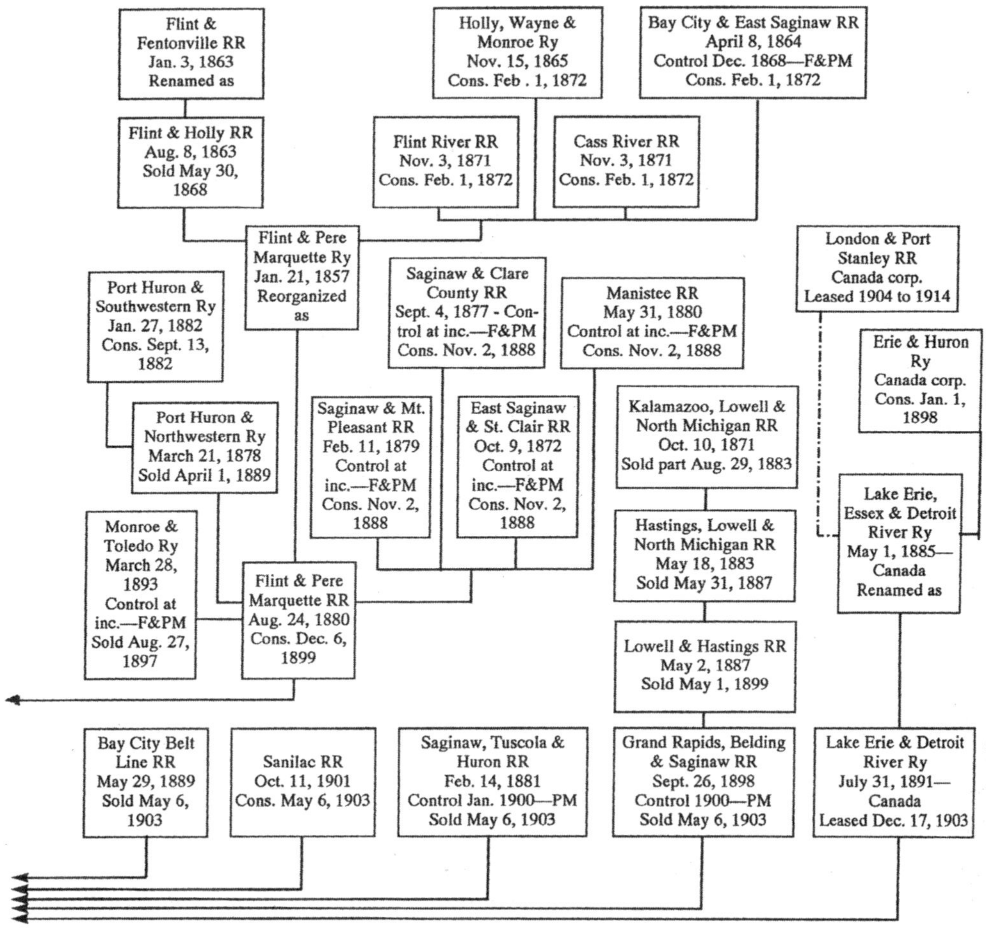
Flint & Fentonville RR Jan. 3, 1863 Renamed as
Holly, Wayne & Monroe Ry Nov. 15, 1865 Cons. Feb . 1, 1872
Bay City & East Saginaw RR April 8, 1864 Control Dec. 1868—F&PM Cons. Feb. 1, 1872
Flint & Holly RR Aug. 8, 1863 Sold May 30, 1868
Flint River RR Nov. 3, 1871 Cons. Feb. 1, 1872
Cass River RR Nov. 3, 1871 Cons. Feb. 1, 1872
Flint & Pere Marquette Ry Jan. 21, 1857 Reorganized as
London & Port Stanley RR Canada corp. Leased 1904 to 1914
Port Huron & Southwestern Ry Jan. 27, 1882 Cons. Sept. 13, 1882
Saginaw & Clare County RR Sept. 4, 1877 - Control at inc.—F&PM Cons. Nov. 2, 1888
Manistee RR May 31, 1880 Control at inc.—F&PM Cons. Nov. 2, 1888
Erie & Huron Ry Canada corp. Cons. Jan. 1, 1898
Port Huron & Northwestern Ry March 21, 1878 Sold April 1, 1889
Saginaw & Mt. Pleasant RR Feb. 11, 1879 Control at inc.—F&PM Cons. Nov. 2, 1888
East Saginaw & St. Clair RR Oct. 9, 1872 Control at inc.—F&PM Cons. Nov. 2, 1888
Kalamazoo, Lowell & North Michigan RR Oct. 10, 1871 Sold part Aug. 29, 1883
Lake Erie, Essex & Detroit River Ry May 1, 1885— Canada Renamed as
Monroe & Toledo Ry March 28, 1893 Control at inc.—F&PM Sold Aug. 27, 1897
Hastings, Lowell & North Michigan RR May 18, 1883 Sold May 31, 1887
Flint & Pere Marquette RR Aug. 24, 1880 Cons. Dec. 6, 1899
Lowell & Hastings RR May 2, 1887 Sold May 1, 1899
Bay City Belt Line RR May 29, 1889 Sold May 6, 1903
Sanilac RR Oct. 11, 1901 Cons. May 6, 1903
Saginaw, Tuscola & Huron RR Feb. 14, 1881 Control Jan. 1900—PM Sold May 6, 1903
Grand Rapids, Belding & Saginaw RR Sept. 26, 1898 Control 1900—PM Sold May 6, 1903
Lake Erie & Detroit River Ry July 31, 1891— Canada Leased Dec. 17, 1903

Notes

Preface

1. U.S. Interstate Commerce Commission, *Reports*, vol. 130, *Valuation Docket No. 260, Pere Marquette Railroad Company et al.* (Washington, D.C.: G.P.O., 1927).
2. Michigan Railroad Commission, *Aids, Gifts, Grants, and Donations to Railroads, including Outlines of Development and Successions in Titles to Railroads in Michigan* (Lansing, Mich.: Wynkoop, Hallenbeck, Crawford, 1919).
3. U.S. Interstate Commerce Commission, Document 137, in *Pere Marquette Railroad Company and Cincinnati, Hamilton & Dayton Railway Company* (Washington, D.C.: G.P.O., 1917).
4. Paul Wesley Ivey, *The Pere Marquette Railroad Company* (Lansing: Michigan Historical Commission, 1919).

Chapter 1. The Flint & Pere Marquette

1. George N. Fuller, *Historic Michigan* (Lansing, Mich.: National Historical Association, 1924), 285.
2. Graydon M. Meints, *Michigan Railroads and Railroad Companies* (East Lansing: Michigan State University Press, 1992), 74–75; Michigan Railroad Commission, *Aids, Gifts, Grants, and Donations to Railroads, Including Outlines of Development and Successions in Titles to Railroads in Michigan* (Lansing, Mich.: Wynkoop, Hallenbeck, Crawford, 1919), 40–41. The first directors of the Flint & Pere Marquette were Alvin T. Crossman, George M. Dewey, Henry M. Henderson, Robert D. Lamond, William Paterson, Benjamin Pierson, Josiah Pratt, Cornelius Roosevelt, and Artemas

Thayer, all of Flint. For more about Dewey, see appendix 1.

3. Charles T. Harvey, *Michigan Pioneer and Historical Collections* 35 (1907): 170–75.
4. Albert N. Bliss, "Federal Land Grants for Internal Improvements in the State of Michigan," *Pioneer Collections* (of Pioneer Society of the State of Michigan) (Lansing, Mich.: Thorp & Godfrey, 1886), 66–68; Michigan, *Documents Accompanying the Journal of the Senate of the State of Michigan, at the Biennial Session of 1857*, Document No. 1 (Lansing, Mich.: Hosmer & Fitch, 1857), 1–12; Charles T. Harvey, "Great Railway Connections between Lake Superior and the Gulf of Mexico," *Michigan Pioneer and Historical Collections* (1907), 35:170–75.
5. Willis F. Dunbar, *All Aboard!* (Grand Rapids, Mich.: Williams B. Eerdmans, 1969), 113; Paul Wesley Ivey, *The Pere Marquette Railroad Company* (Lansing: Michigan Historical Commission, 1919), 217, 221.
6. Jeremy W. Kilar, *Michigan's Lumbertowns* (Detroit: Wayne State University Press, 1990), 28–32.
7. Truman B. Fox, *History of the Saginaw Valley, Its Resources, Progress and Business Interests* (East Saginaw, Mich.: Daily Courier Steam Job Print, 1868), 14–15; Franklin Ellis, *History of Genesee County, Michigan* (Philadelphia: Everts & Abbott, 1879), 118.
8. Michael A Leeson, *History of Saginaw County, Michigan* (Chicago: Charles C. Chapman & Co., 1881), 447; James Cooke Mills, *History of Saginaw County, Michigan, Historical, Commercial, Biographical* (Saginaw, Mich.: Seeman & Peters, 1918), 721–22; W. R. Bates, *A History of the Saginaws* (East Saginaw, Mich.: E. W. Lyon, 1874), 55. For more on Keeler, see appendix 1. Million and Dixon's *Pere Marquette Power* (Alderson, W.Va.: Chesapeake & Ohio Historical Society, 1984) has no record of *Pioneer*.
9. Mills, *History of Saginaw County*, 722–23; Ellis, *History of Genesee County*, 47; Martin D. Lewis, *Lumberman from Flint* (Detroit: Wayne State University Press, 1958), 122; Bates, *History of the Saginaws*, 55. For more about Crapo, see appendix 1. In a rare error Michigan Railroad Commission, *Aids, Gifts*, gives the opening as 8 December 1863.
10. Lewis, *Lumberman from Flint*, 64–65, 128–29.
11. Ibid., 129; Meints, *Michigan Railroads*, 74. The original directors of the Flint & Fentonville were Henry H. Crapo, James B. Walker, and Levi Walker of Flint; David Smith of Fentonville; and Edward D. Mandell, Oliver Prescott, and John R. Thornton of New Bedford, Mass. Prescott was a major financial partner of Crapo in Michigan lumbering. When the F&F board was organized in June the directors were Crapo and James B. Walker from Flint, and Thomas Knowles, Pardon Tillinghast, J. G. Delano, and Humphrey W. Seabury, all of New Bedford.
12. Michigan Railroad Commission, *Aids, Gifts*, 40–41. The organizing directors of the Flint & Holly were the same men who formed the Flint & Fentonville. For more about George C. Kimball, see appendix 1.
13. Meints, *Michigan Railroads*, 74; Lewis, *Lumberman from Flint*, 135, 141–60; Michigan Railroad Commission, *Aids, Gifts*, 40–41. The organizing directors of the Flint & Holly were the same men as formed the Flint & Fentonville.
14. Lewis, *Lumberman from Flint*, 187–88, 211, 235–37; Michigan Railroad Commission, *Aids, Gifts*, 40–41; F&PM, *Annual Report for 1868* (Detroit: Daily Post Book and Job Printers, 1869), 11–12. Michigan Railroad Commission, *Aids, Gifts* has 30 May 1868 as the consolidation date.

15. George B. Catlin, *The Story of Detroit* (Detroit: Detroit News, 1923), 496–99; *History of Manistee, Mason and Oceana Counties, Michigan* (Chicago: H. R. Page & Co., 1882), 50–51.
16. Michigan Railroad Commission, *Aids, Gifts*, 40–41.
17. Ibid.; Ivey, *Pere Marquette Railroad Company*, 220; Graydon M. Meints, *Michigan Railroad Lines* (East Lansing: Michigan State University Press, 2005); "An Appreciation, William Bernard Sears," *Michigan Engineer* 33 (1915): 53–56. The mileages reported are those from Meints and have slight discrepancies from those in *Aid, Gifts*.
18. Michigan Railroad Commission, *Aids, Gifts*, 40–41; Meints, *Michigan Railroad Lines*; *History of Manistee, Mason and Oceana Counties*, 50–52.
19. Michigan Railroad Commission *Aids, Gifts*, 40–41; Meints, *Michigan Railroads*, 40; Fuller, *Historic Michigan* (Chicago: Lewis Publishing Co., 1939), 3:61. The organizing board of directors of the Bay City & East Saginaw was James G. Birney Jr., Nathan B. Bradley, W. M. Fitzhugh, James Frazer, and Algernon S. Munger, all of Bay City; Henry D. Braddock, Albert Miller, and Appleton Stevens of Portsmouth; and Henry C. Moore of Bangor Township. For more on Birney, see appendix 1.
20. Michigan Railroad Commission, *Aids, Gifts*, 40–41; *History of Bay County, Michigan* (Chicago: H. R. Page & Co., 1883), 218; Fuller, *Historic Michigan*, 3:61.
21. Meints, *Michigan Railroads*, 87; Michigan Railroad Commission, *Aids, Gifts*, 40–41; Talcott Enoch Wing, ed., *History of Monroe County, Michigan* (New York: Munsell & Company, 1890), 234–36; *Acts of the Legislature of the State of Michigan Passed at the Regular Session of 1865* (Lansing, Mich.: John A. Kerr & Co., 1865), 531–32; *Joint Documents of the State of Michigan for the Year 1869* (Lansing: W. S. George & Co., 1869), 60; Silas Farmer, *History of Detroit and Wayne County and Early Michigan* (New York: Munsell & Co., 1890), 1:905; Samuel W. Durant, *History of Oakland County, Michigan* (Philadelphia: D. W. Ensign & Co., 1880), 230. The organizing directors of the Holly, Wayne & Monroe were John L. Andrews, B. Campbell, and Caleb Ives of Monroe; John J. Palmer of Wayne; Jared S. Lapham of Northville; Austin N. Kimmis of West Novi; Daniel B. Chatfield of Spring Mills, Oakland County; Job Burnap of Southville; and John L. Andrews of Milford. The early officers of the company are not well recorded.
22. Michigan Railroad Commission, *Aids, Gifts*, 40–41; Farmer, *History of Detroit*, 497; Wing, *History of Monroe County*, 146–47; *Railroad Gazette* 3: 93 (20 May).
23. Farmer, *History of Detroit*, 905; Wing, *History of Monroe County*, 235–37; *Railroad Gazette* 3: 378 (9 December).
24. Michigan Railroad Commission, *Aids, Gifts*, 40–41; Meints, *Michigan Railroads*, 46. The organizing board of directors was Henry C. Potter and William L. Webber of East Saginaw, lumberman Edward F. Weeks of Flint, F&PM president Eber Brock Ward of Detroit, Jesse Hoyt of New York City, William W. Crapo of New Bedford, Massachusetts, and Samuel Farwell of Utica, New York.
25. Michigan Railroad Commission, *Aids, Gifts*, 40–41; Meints, *Michigan Railroads*, 75. The organizing board of directors of the Cass River was Thomas Edsall, Henry C. Potter, and William L. Webber, all of East Saginaw; lumberman William A. Heartt of Wahjamega; F&PM president Eber Brock Ward of Detroit; Jesse Hoyt of New York City; and Samuel Farwell of Utica, New York.
26. Michigan Railroad Commission, *Aids, Gifts*, 40–41; Meints, *Michigan Railroads*, 71. The organizing directors of the East Saginaw & St. Clair were Jesse Hoyt of New York City; William W. Crapo

of New Bedford, Mass.; and James T. Brown, Edwin Eddy, Charles L. Ortman, Henry C. Potter, Franklin P. Sears, William H. Warner, and William L. Webber, all of East Saginaw.

27. George W. Hilton, *The Great Lakes Car Ferries* (Berkeley, Calif.: Howell-North, 1962), 112; George W. Hilton, *Lake Michigan Passenger Steamers* (Stanford, Calif.: Stanford University Press, 2002), 297–98; Arthur C. and Lucy F. Frederickson, *Pictorial History of the C&O Train and Auto Ferries and Pere Marquette Line Steamers*, rev. ed. (Frankfort, Mich.: Lakeside Printing, 1965), 4–5.
28. Ivey, *Pere Marquette Railroad Company*, 221; Dunbar, *All Aboard!*, 113–15.
29. Catlin, *The Story of Detroit*, 493–99.
30. George N. Fuller, *Michigan: A Centennial History of the State and Its People* (Chicago: Lewis Publishing Co., 1939), 1:539.
31. Michigan Railroad Commission, *Aids, Gifts*, 40–43; Meints, *Michigan Railroad Lines*, 1:394–96; Mills, *History of Saginaw County*, 2:244–47; Meints, *Michigan Railroads*, 133; Michigan Railroad Commission, *Eighth Annual Report* (for 1879) (Lansing: W. S. George & Co., 1880), 196; Michigan Railroad Commission, *Ninth Annual Report* (for 1880) (Lansing: W. S. George & Co., 1881), 160. The founding directors of the Saginaw & Clare County were Jesse Hoyt, New York City; William W. Crapo, New Bedford, Mass; and Sanford Keeler, Henry C. Potter, and William L. Webber, all of East Saginaw. All of them were officers of the Flint & Pere Marquette.
32. Michigan Railroad Commission, *Aids, Gifts*, 40–41; Meints, *Michigan Railroads*, 133; Isaac A. Fancher, *Past and Present of Isabella County, Michigan* (Indianapolis: B. F. Bowen & Co., 1911), 139–40; Michigan Railroad Commission, *Eighth Annual Report*, 198; *Report of the Flint & Pere Marquette Railroad Company* (for the year 1884), (Detroit: F&PM Ry, 1885), 21. The founding directors of the Saginaw & Mt. Pleasant were Jesse Hoyt, New York City; Sanford Keeler, Henry C. Potter, and William L. Webber, all of East Saginaw; and Isaac A. Fancher and George L. Granger of Mount Pleasant.
33. Fancher, *Past and Present*, 139–40; Michigan Railroad Commission, *Aids, Gifts*, 30–31.
34. Michigan Railroad Commission, *Aids, Gifts*, 40–43; Meints, *Michigan Railroad Lines*, 1:394–96.
35. Meints, *Michigan Railroads*, 74–75; Ivey, *Pere Marquette Railroad Company*, 222–23.
36. Michigan Railroad Commission, *Aids, Gifts*, 40–41. The founding directors of the Manistee were Jesse Hoyt and Henry A. V. Post of New York City; and Henry C. Potter, Henry C. Potter Jr., and William L. Webber of East Saginaw. The senior Potter was named president.
37. Michigan Railroad Commission, *Aids, Gifts*, 40–41; Meints, *Michigan Railroads*, 102; Michigan Railroad Commission, *Ninth Annual Report*, 138; Michigan Railroad Commission, *Tenth Annual Report* (for 1881) (Lansing: W. S. George & Co., 1881), 160. A description of the line is given in the *History of Manistee, Mason and Oceana Counties*, 49.
38. Michigan Railroad Commission, *Aids, Gifts*, 40–41; Michigan Railroad Commission, *Eleventh Annual Report* (for 1882) (Lansing: W. S. George & Co., 1881), 195.
39. Michigan Railroad Commission, *Aids, Gifts*, 40–41.
40. For more biographical background of Crapo, see appendix 1.
41. The writer must give extensive credit to the research of Dr. James S. Hannum in his two books on Michigan logging lines, *Cut and Run* and *In The Pines*. Extensive maps in both works are of considerable help in locating obscure branches.

42. The dates and mileages of the branches in the earlier paragraphs were obtained from the Michigan Railroad Commission's *Annual Reports* and Flint & Pere Marquette *Annual Reports.*
43. Hilton, *Great Lakes Car Ferries*, 112–14; Michigan Railroad Commission, *Eleventh Annual Report*, 182; Michigan Railroad Commission, *Fifteenth Annual Report of the Commissioner of Railroads* (for 1886) (Lansing: W. S. George & Co., 1887), 401; Michigan Railroad Commission, *Sixteenth Annual Report of the Commissioner of Railroads* (for 1887) (Lansing: W. S. George & Co., 1888), 368; Michigan Railroad Commission, *Nineteenth Annual Report of the Commissioner of Railroads* (for 1890) (Lansing: W. S. George & Co., 1891), 237; Frederickson and Frederickson, *Pictorial History*, 10–14, 20–21.
44. *Report of the Flint & Pere Marquette Railroad Company* (Year 1885), 21–22.
45. Michigan Railroad Commission, *Aids, Gifts*, 40–41.
46. *Report of the Flint & Pere Marquette Railroad Company* (Year 1890), 16; Michigan Railroad Commission, *Aids, Gifts*, 42–43, has 1891 as the construction date.
47. *Portrait and Biographical Album of Sanilac County* (Chicago: Chapman Brothers, 1884), 519–27.
48. Michigan Railroad Commission, *Aids, Gifts*, 40–41; Meints, *Michigan Railroads*, 129. The organizing directors of the Port Huron & North Western all were Port Huron businessmen: Silas L. Ballentine, James Bear, Charles R. Brown, Daniel B. Harrington, William Hartsuff, Henry Howard, Henry McMorran, John P. Sanborn, Peter B. Sanborn, Charles A. Ward, and Fred L. Wells. For more on Harrington and Howard, see appendix 1.
49. Michigan Railroad Commission, *Aids, Gifts*, 42–43; Meints, *Michigan Railroads*, 129, 202–3; *History of St. Clair County, Michigan* (Chicago: A. T. Andreas & Co., 1883), 481.
50. Michigan Railroad Commission, *Ninth Annual Report*, 354–55.
51. Michigan Railroad Commission, *Aids, Gifts*, 42–43; Meints, *Michigan Railroads*, 130. The founding directors of the Port Huron & Southwestern were Charles F. Harrington, Edmund B. Harrington, Henry McMorran, John P. Sanborn, Peter B. Sanborn, Fred L. Wells, and James H. White, all of Port Huron. White was the newcomer to the group; possibly his position as a member of the Michigan House of Representatives played a part.
52. Michigan Railroad Commission, *Aids, Gifts*, 42–43; Michigan Railroad Commission, *Eleventh Annual Report*, 446–52.
53. *Portrait Album Sanilac*, 527–37; F. Clever Bald, *Michigan in Four Centuries* (New York: Harper & Row, 1954), 290.
54. *Public Acts . . . of the Legislature, 1889*, No. 10 (Lansing, Mich.: Darius D. Thorp, 1889), 11.
55. *Report of the Flint & Pere Marquette Railroad Company . . . for the Year 1889* (Saginaw, Mich.: Evening News Printers, 1890), 19–21.
56. *Report of the Flint & Pere Marquette Railroad Company . . . for the Year 1892* (Saginaw, Mich.: Seeman & Peters, 1893), 24.
57. Michigan Railroad Commission, *Aids, Gifts*, 52–53; Meints, *Michigan Railroads*, 135; John W. Leonard, *Industries of the Saginaws* (East Saginaw, Mich.: J. M. Elstner & Co., c. 1887); Michigan Railroad Commission, *25th Annual Report* (for 1896) (Lansing, Mich.: Robert Smith Printing Co., 1897), 461. The founding directors of the Saginaw, Huron & Tuscola were Jesse Hoyt of New York City and John S. Estabrook, John W. Howry, Erastus T. Judd, George W. Morley, Henry C. Potter, and

William L. Webber, all of East Saginaw. Webber was named president, Morley vice president, and Judd secretary and treasurer.

58. Michigan Railroad Commission, *Aids, Gifts*, 52–53.
59. Graydon M. Meints, *Biographical Directory of Michigan Railway Officials, 1830–1917* (East Lansing: Michigan State University Libraries, 2013), 126, 276.
60. Meints, *Michigan Railroads*, 59, 62; Michigan Railroad Commission, *Aids, Gifts*, 112–13.
61. *Report of the Flint & Pere Marquette Railroad Company . . . for the Year 1895* (Saginaw, Mich.: Seeman & Peters, 1896), 21; *Report of the Flint & Pere Marquette Railroad Company . . . for the Year 1896* (Saginaw, Mich.: Seeman & Peters, 1897), 22; Michigan, *Gifts, Grants*, 42–43; Meints, *Michigan Railroads*, 114.
62. Hilton, *Great Lakes Car Ferries*, 114–18; *Flint & Pere Marquette, 1895*, 21–22.
63. Michigan Railroad Commission, *Aids, Gifts*, 44–45; Flint & Pere Marquette Railroad, *Report of the Flint & Pere Marquette* for 1897 (Saginaw, Mich.: Seeman & Peters, 1898), 23; Thomas L. Underwood Jr. "A Survey of the C&O and Predecessor Lines in Michigan," *C&O Historical Newsletter*, November 1975, 7.

■ Chapter 2. Detroit, Lansing & Northern and Its Predecessors

1. Michigan Railroad Commission, *Aids, Gifts, Grants, and Donations to Railroads, Including Outlines of Development and Successions in Titles to Railroads in Michigan* (Lansing: Wynkoop, Hallenbeck, Crawford, 1919), 34–35, 46–47; v, 89; Detroit, Lansing & Lake Michigan Railroad, *Annual Report for 1874* (Boston: Alfred Mudge & Son, 1875), 15; Paul Wesley Ivey, *The Pere Marquette Railroad Company* (Lansing: Michigan Historical Commission, 1919), 49. The original incorporators of the Ionia & Lansing were John C. Blanchard, Winslow P. Burnham, George S. Cooper, Frederick Hall, Hampton Rich, Lewis D. Smith, and Osmond Tower of Ionia; Harvey Bartow, Charles H. Maynard, James Newman, and Robert B. Smith of Portland; and Charles M. Derbyshire and William F. Jennison of Eagle. For more about Rich, see appendix 1.
2. Samuel W. Durant, *History of Ingham and Eaton Counties, Michigan* (Philadelphia: D. W. Ensign & Co., 1880), 97; Frank N. Turner, *An Account of Ingham County from Its Organization*, vol. 3 of *Historic Michigan* (Dayton, Ohio: National Historical Association, 1924), 69; Michigan Historical Commission, *Michigan Biographies* (Lansing: Michigan Historical Commission, 1924), 2:373.
3. M. Dash, *A History of the City of Lansing . . .* (Lansing: W. S. George & Co., 1870), 31; Graydon M. Meints, *Michigan Railroad Lines* (East Lansing: Michigan State University Press, 2005), 1:311, 441; Michigan Railroad Commission, *Aids, Gifts*, 46–47, 88–89. The joint use of the track between Michigan Avenue and North Lansing and joint use of the station at Lansing continued until the days of Conrail.
4. Franklin Ellis, *History of Livingston County, Michigan* (Philadelphia: Everts & Abbott, 1880), 51–52, 55–56; Henry M. Utley and Byron M. Cutcheon, *Michigan as a Province, Territory and State, the Twenty-Sixth Member of the Federal Union* (New York: Publishing Society of Michigan, 1906), 3:315; Philip P. Mason, "The Plank Road Craze" at http://seekingmichigan.org/wp-content/

uploads/2013/08/The-Plank-Road-Craze.pdf.

5. Michigan Railroad Commission, *Aids, Gifts*, 46–47; Graydon M. Meints, *Michigan Railroads and Railroad Companies* (East Lansing: Michigan State University Press, 1992), 58. The organizers of the company were Theodatus T. Lyon, George A. Starkweather, and Samuel Hardenburgh of Plymouth; Oliver C. Abell of Dearborn; Egbert F. Albridge and Lyman Judson of Brighton; E. F. Burt, John H. Galloway, William McPherson, Royal C. Rumsey, and Joseph Y. Wilcox of Howell; Ely Barnard of Genoa Township; and J. M. Swift Jr. and William Tafts, residence not known. For more about Lyon, see appendix 1. About McPherson see *American Biographical History of Eminent and Self-Made Men* (Cincinnati: Western Biographical Publishing Co., 1878), 2.6:54–55.
6. Dash, *City of Lansing*, 82–83; Ellis, *History of Livingston County*, 58–59; *Acts of the Legislature of the State of Michigan Passed at the Extra Session of 1864* (Lansing, Mich.: John A. Kerr & Co., 1864), 96–98.
7. Meints, *Michigan Railroads*, 88; Michigan Railroad Commission, *Aids, Gifts*, 46–47; Ellis, *History of Livingston County*, 59. The organizing directors were Theodatus T. Lyon of Plymouth; Alexander H. Benedict and George W. Palmerton of Fowlerville; Joseph Dennis Jr. of Wheatfield Township; Joseph H. Wilcox of Howell; Joshua K. Kirtland of Locke Township; Egbert Grattan, James W. Waldo, and James M. Williams of Williamston; George N. Walker and James F. Smiley of Okemos; Alvin N. Hart of Lansing; and James Sullivan of place undetermined.
8. Meints, *Michigan Railroads*, 64; Michigan Railroad Commission, *Aids, Gifts*, 46–47; Ellis, *History of Livingston County*, 59. For more about Alvin N. Hart see *History of Lapeer County, Michigan* (Chicago: H. R. Page & Co., 1884), 59–60. About William Howard see *American Biographical History*, 2.5:61 and *Michigan Pioneer and Historical Collections* (Lansing: various publ., 1876–1917), 4:125–32; about Mills see *American Biographical History*, 1.3:100; about Harvey King see Friend Palmer, *Early Days in Detroit* (Detroit: Hunt & June, 1906), 808–9; about Wesson see Michigan Historical Commission, *Michigan Biographies*, 2:426.
9. Michigan Railroad Commission, *Aids, Gifts*, 46–47; Meints, *Michigan Railroads*, 65; John S. Schenck, *History of Ionia and Montcalm Counties, Michigan* (Philadelphia: D. W. Ensign & Co., 1881), 41. The organizing directors of the DL&LM were James F. Joy, William H. Tefft, and William B. Wesson of Detroit; Hampton Rich of Ionia; Hiram H. Smith of Jackson; Robert B. Smith of Portland; and John W. Brooks, John W. Burnham, George O. Shattuck, Nathaniel Thayer, and William F. Weld of Boston.
10. Meints, *Michigan Railroad Lines*, 1:441; Michigan Railroad Commission, *Aids, Gifts*, 46–47; Ellis, *History of Livingston County*, 59–60; Elam E. Branch, ed., *History of Ionia County, Michigan* (Indianapolis: B. F. Bowen & Co., 1916), 1:246.
11. Michigan Railroad Commission, *Aids, Gifts*, 46–47.
12. Detroit, Lansing & Lake Michigan Railroad, *Annual Report* (for 1874) (Boston: Alfred Mudge & Son, 1875), 7, 10, 12.
13. Meints, *Michigan Railroads*, 89. The organizing directors were Alexander F. Bell, John C. Blanchard, Frederick Hall, Benjamin Harter, Ethan S. Johnson, Wellington C. Page, Vernon H. Smith, William A. Stearns, and Osmond Tower, all of Ionia; Erastus P. Brown and Erastus H. Stanton of Sheridan; George Pray of Ronald Township; and Joseph P. Shoemaker of Amsden Township.

14. Michigan Railroad Commission, *Aids, Gifts*, 46–47; Meints, *Michigan Railroads*, 124. In addition to Joy and Smith, who was made president, the organizing directors were Wellington C. Page, Erastus H. Stanton, William B. Stone, Nelson W. Turner, and Edwin K. Wood.
15. Michigan Railroad Commission, *Aids, Gifts*, 46–47; Meints, *Michigan Railroads*, 124. See also Belding Brothers & Company at www.belding.michlibrary.org/our-history-1.
16. John W. Dasef, *History of Montcalm County, Michigan* (Indianapolis: B. F. Bowen & Co., 1916), 1:279–80. Of the New England directors Adams was the grandson of President John Quincy Adams and a well-respected railroad authority and regulator; Hunnewell was a railroad financier and a partner in a private banking firm; Merriam served as secretary and treasurer of many of Nathaniel Thayer's properties.
17. Meints, *Michigan Railroads*, 65; Michigan Railroad Commission, *Aids, Gifts*, 46–47; Michigan Railroad Commission, *First Annual Report* (for 1872) (Lansing: W. S. George & Co., 1874), 226; Ivey, *Pere Marquette Railroad Company*, 252.
18. Ivey, *Pere Marquette Railroad Company*, 50; Meints, *Michigan Railroads*, 65; Michigan Railroad Commission, *Aids, Gifts*, 46–47; Detroit, Lansing & Lake Michigan *Report to the Bondholders and Stockholders of the Detroit, Lansing and Lake Michigan Railroad Company* (Boston: Alfred Mudge & Son, 1876), 14.
19. Ivey, *Pere Marquette Railroad Company*, 54–55.
20. Michigan Railroad Commission, *Aids, Gifts*, 46–47; Meints, *Michigan Railroads*, 65; Detroit, Lansing & Northern Railroad Co., *Second Annual Report* (for 1878) (Boston: Alfred Mudge & Con, 1879), 17; Detroit, Lansing & Northern Railroad Co., *Third Annual Report* (for 1879) (Boston: Alfred Mudge & Son, 1880), 21; Detroit, Lansing & Northern Railroad Co., *Fourth Annual Report* (for 1880) (Boston: Alfred Mudge & Son, 1881), 20,
21. Nicholas A. Marsh, *Michigan Central Railroad: History of the Main Line, 1846–1901* (n.p., 2007), 165–69.
22. Detroit, Lansing & Northern Railroad Co., *Seventh Annual Report* (for 1883) (Boston: Alfred Mudge & Son, 1884), 15, 18–19.
23. Willard D. Tucker, *Gratiot County, Michigan* (Saginaw, Mich.: Seeman & Peters, 1913), 54.
24. Michigan Railroad Commission, *Aids, Gifts*, 46–47; Meints, *Michigan Railroads*, 135. The founding directors of the company were John P. Allison, Addison P. Brewer, Loton H. Eastman, and John G. Owen of East Saginaw; Newell Barnard, David H. Jerome, George F. Williams, and Ammi W. Wright of Saginaw; John L. Evans, Charles B. Kress, James McHenry, James F. Newton, and Luther Smith of St. Louis.
25. Michigan Railroad Commission, *Aids, Gifts*, 46–47; Michael A. Leeson, *History of Saginaw County, Michigan* (Chicago: C. C. Chapman & Co., 1881), 450; Michigan, Railroad Commission, *Second Annual Report* (for 1873) (Lansing, Mich.: W. S. George & Co., 1874), 195; U.S. Interstate Commerce Commission, *Reports*, vol. 130, *Valuation Docket No. 260, Pere Marquette Railroad Company et Al.* (Washington, D.C.: G.P.O., 1928). 513; Ivey, *Pere Marquette Railroad Company*, 51.
26. Michigan Railroad Commission, *Aids, Gifts*, 46–47; Meints, *Michigan Railroads*, 133; Dasef, *History of Montcalm County*, 1:280. The organizing directors of the S&GR were James Hay, David H. Jerome, Amasa Rust, Ezra Rust, Charles W. Wells, George F. Williams, and Ammi W. Wright, of

Saginaw; Orlando M. Barnes of Lansing; George Jerome of Detroit; and Jeptha H. Wade, Henry B. Payne, and Henry Chisholm of Cleveland.

27. Dasef, *History of Montcalm County*, 1:280. The new faces from Boston were John A. Burnham, Alpheus Hardy, Horatio H. Hunnewell, Charles Merriam, George O. Shattuck, Nathaniel Thayer, Nathaniel Thayer Jr., and Charles L. Young. Ammi W. Wright remained, as did David H. Jerome and Henry L. Holcomb. Another new name was John B. Mulliken, who was the new general manager of the road as well as a director.
28. Ivey, *Pere Marquette Railroad Company*, 50; Meints, *Michigan Railroads*, 65; Michigan Railroad Commission, *Aids, Gifts*, 46–47; *Portrait and Biographical Album of Gratiot County, Michigan* (Chicago: Chapman Brothers, 1884), 776–77. The founding directors of the road were Edward L. Craw of East Saginaw; Amos C. Barstow, William H. Bradford, William Corliss, and Earl P. Mason of Providence, Rhode Island; Rowland Hazard of Peace Dale, Rhode Island; William S. Slager of North Smithfield, Rhode Island; John F. Slater of Norwich, Connecticut; and Joseph H. McChesney of Chicago.
29. *Portrait Album Gratiot*, 777.
30. Tucker, *Gratiot County, Michigan*, 598.
31. Michigan Railroad Commission, *Aids, Gifts*, 48–49; Michigan, Commissioner of Railroads. *Annual Reports* (for 1876) (Lansing: various publishers, 1872–1905); *Biographical Memoirs of Gratiot County, Michigan* (Chicago: J. B. Beers & Co., 1906), 33–34.
32. Michigan Railroad Commission, *Aids, Gifts*, 48–49.
33. Ibid.
34. Richardson's Executor v. Green, 133 U.S. 30 (1890). (At https://supreme.justia.com/cases/ federal/us/133/30//case.html.) The court's summary sheds light on the murky financial dealings of Craw, Richardson, and Sickles with the railroad. The court ruled that Richardson had no special priority to the proceeds of the foreclosure sale.
35. *Wall Street Journal*, 25 Feb. 1999. The book is Jeff Kleiman, *The Rise and Fall of the CSCRR: A Short History of a Short-Lived Railroad* (Grand Rapids, Mich.: Friends of Public Museum, 1992).
36. Michigan Railroad Commission, *Aids, Gifts*, 48–49; Ivey, *Pere Marquette Railroad Company*, 56. The first directors of the road were Charles F. Adams, Jr., James H. Blake, John A. Burnham, Alpheus Hardy, Charles Merriam, George O. Shattuck, Eugene V. R. Thayer, Nathaniel Thayer, and Charles L. Young, all of Boston. For more on Hardy, and both Thayers, see appendix 1. Michigan, Commissioner of Railroads, *Thirteenth Annual Report . . . for the Year 1884* (Lansing: W. S. George & Co., 1885), 45; Michigan Railroad Commission, *Aids, Gifts*, 46–47; Detroit, Lansing & Northern Railroad Co., *Seventh Annual Report*, 18–21.
37. Meints, *Michigan Railroads*, 90, 211; Michigan Railroad Commission, *Aids, Gifts*, 48–49; *Portrait Album Gratiot*, 779–80; Tucker, *Gratiot County, Michigan*, 793. The organizing directors of the Ithaca & Alma were Ammi W. Wright, D. R. Sullivan, and William S. Turck of Alma; Nathan Church, Wilbur Nelson, Joseph H. Seaver, and Robert Smith, all of Ithaca. Church was the first president of the company.
38. Michigan Railroad Commission, *Aids, Gifts*, 48–49.
39. Meints, *Michigan Railroads*, 81; Ivey, *Pere Marquette Railroad Company*, 56; Graydon M. Meints,

Biographical Directory of Michigan Railway Officials, 1830–1917 (East Lansing: Michigan State University Libraries, 2013), 2:233; Detroit, Lansing & Northern Railroad Co., *Tenth Annual Report* (for 1886) (Boston: Alfred Mudge & Son, 1887), 14, 18; Detroit, Lansing & Northern Railroad Co., *Eleventh Annual Report* (for 1887) (Boston: T. W. Ripley, 1888), 6, 19–20.

40. Detroit, Lansing & Northern, *Eleventh Annual Report*, 19.
41. *Michigan Reports*, vol. 63 (Mich. Supreme Court, 1886) (Chicago: Callaghan & Co., 1888), 645–52.
42. Detroit, Lansing & Northern, *Eleventh Annual Report*, 20; Detroit, Lansing & Northern Railroad Co., *Twelfth Annual Report* (for 1888) (Boston: T. W. Ripley, 1889), 20.
43. *Railway Age*, 33:442; Detroit, Lansing & Northern Railroad Co., *Sixteenth Annual Report* (for 1892) (Boston: T. W. Ripley, 1893), 6. For more on Agnew and Heald, see appendix 1.
44. Detroit, Lansing & Northern Railroad Co., *Seventeenth Annual Report* (for 1893) (Boston: T. W. Ripley, 1894), 7.
45. Samuel Eliot Morrison, *The Oxford History of the American People* (New York: Oxford University Press, 1965), 795–96; Willis F. Dunbar, *Michigan: A History of the Wolverine State* (Grand Rapids, Mich.: Eerdmans, 1965), 532.
46. Detroit, Lansing & Northern Railroad Co., *Sixteenth Annual Report*, 6; Detroit, Lansing & Northern Railroad Co., *Seventeenth Annual Report* , 7; Meints, *Michigan Railroads*, 65; Michigan Railroad Commission, *Aids, Gifts*, 48–49; Ivey, *Pere Marquette Railroad Company*, 57–58.
47. Ivey, *Pere Marquette Railroad Company*, 260; Detroit, Grand Rapids & Western Railroad Co., *First Annual Report* (for 1897) (Boston: T. W. Ripley, 1898), 7; George W. Hilton, *The Great Lakes Car Ferries* (Berkeley, Calif.: Howell-North, 1962), 118–20.
48. Detroit, Grand Rapids & Western Railroad Co., *Second Annual Report* (for 1898) (Boston: T. W. Ripley, 1899), 6–7, 18.

■ Chapter 3. The Chicago & West Michigan

1. *History of Muskegon County, Michigan* (Chicago: H. R. Page & Co., 1882), 55–56.
2. The organizing directors were Henry Beidler, Samuel A. Brown, Chauncey Davis, Charles H. Hackley, Lyman G. Mason, Elias W. Merrill, and Samuel R. Sanford, all of Muskegon; William M. Ferry of Spring Lake; Thomas Merrill of Ferrysburg; Samuel W. Odell and Fletcher Fowler of Norton Township; Ezra Stevens of Laketon Township; and Hunter Savidge of Grand Haven. John T. Percival, "Railroads in Ottawa County," *Report of the Pioneer Society of the State of Michigan*, 2nd ed. (Lansing, Mich.: Wynkoop Hallenbeck Crawford Co., 1908), 9:277; Henry H. Holt, *History of the Settlement of Muskegon* (Muskegon, Mich.: Muskegon Chronicle Binding & Printing, c. 1887), 20; *Romance of Muskegon, Michigan* (Muskegon: Muskegon Chronicle, 1937), lxxi. The MLS annual report in the Michigan Railroad Commission's *First Annual Report* (for 1872) (Lansing: W. S. George & Co., 1874) dates all bridge construction north of Ferrysburg as built in 1869.
3. Michigan Railroad Commission, *Aids, Gifts, Grants, and Donations to Railroads, including Outlines of Development and Successions in Titles to Railroads in Michigan* (Lansing: Wynkoop, Hallenbeck, Crawford, 1919), 50–51; F. W. Beers, *County Atlas of Muskegon, Michigan* (New York

City: F. W. Beers, 1877), 58–59, 66–67.

4. For more on Gardner, see appendix 1.
5. *Grand Rapids Eagle*, 7 July 1868; Dwight Goss, *History of Grand Rapids and Its Industries* (Chicago: C. F. Cooper & Co., 1906), 1:619. The organizing directors were Joseph Fisk of Allegan; Manly D. Howard, Bernardus Ledeboer, Kummer Schaderlee, and Rev. Albertus C. VanRaalte of Holland; George Goss, Theodore P. Sheldon, and Allen G. Wells of Kalamazoo; and Chester Warner of Chicago. For more on Fisk, see appendix 1.
6. Albert Baxter, *History of the City of Grand Rapids, Michigan* (New York: Munsell & Co., 1891), 529–30; Donald L. van Reken, *The Railroads of Holland, Michigan*, vol. 1, *The Nineteenth Century* (Holland, Mich.: Published by the author, 1997), 8; Michigan Railroad Commission, *Aids, Gifts*, 20–21. By a report by state treasurer Ebenezer Grosvenor in *Journal of the Senate of the State of Michigan, Extra Session, 1870* (Lansing: W. S. George & Co., 1870), 56, a total of $31,000 was issued for the Allegan & Holland in municipal bonds as follows:

Allegan Co.	Heath Twp.	$7,000
Ottawa Co.	City of Holland	$15,000
	Holland Twp.	$8,000

And a total of $92,000 for the Michigan Lake Shore as follows:

Ottawa Co.	Olive Twp.	$8,000
	Grand Haven Twp.	$4,000
Muskegon Co.	Muskegon Twp.	$50,000
	Oceana Twp.	$30,000

Of the $123,000 in bonds deposited with the state treasurer for disbursement, none was paid out.

7. Van Reken, *Railroads of Holland*, vol. 1, 19–20, reporting *De Hope* of 8 June 1870.
8. Graydon M. Meints, *Michigan Railroads and Railroad Companies* (East Lansing: Michigan State University Press, 1992), 110; Michigan Railroad Commission, *Aids, Gifts*, 20–21, 50–51. The organizing directors were Healy C. Acker, George Banks, James C. Brayton, Henry Browner, Henry S. Clubb, Dwight Cutler, Edmund B. Ferry, Israel V. Harris, John W. Hopkins, Heber Squier, Sumner VanDrezer, and Charles E. Weyman, all of Grand Haven. The Grand River bridge at Grand Haven was built in late 1869 and put in service 1 January 1870 (see Percival, "Railroads in Ottawa County"). The MLS annual report in the Michigan Railroad Commission's *First Annual Report* for 1872 dates all bridges between Allegan and Grand Haven as built in 1870. Crisfield Johnson, *History of Allegan and Barry Counties, Michigan* (Philadelphia: D. W. Ensign & Co., 1880), 78, gives the opening date between Allegan and Grand Haven as 1 July 1870.
9. Gerrit Van Schelven, "The Burning of Holland, October 9, 1871," *Report of the Pioneer Society of the State of Michigan* (Lansing: Wynkoop Hallenbeck Crawford, 1886), 9:337–38; Robert P. Swierenga, *Holland Michigan, from Dutch Colony to Dynamic City* (Grand Rapids, Mich.: William B. Eerdmans Publishing Co., 2014), 1:119–27.
10. Meints, *Michigan Railroads*, 116; Michigan Railroad Commission, *Aids, Gifts*, 50–51; Graydon M. Meints, *Michigan Railroad Lines* (East Lansing: Michigan State University Press, 2005), 1:424–25.

11. Samuel H. Church, compiler, *Corporate History of the Pennsylvania Lines West of Pittsburgh . . .* (Baltimore: Friedenwald Co., 1899), 2:26–28.
12. Ibid.; Paul Wesley Ivey, *The Pere Marquette Railroad Company* (Lansing: Michigan Historical Commission, 1919), 33–34.
13. Meints, *Michigan Railroads*, 78; Ivey, *Pere Marquette Railroad Company*, 34–35; Church, *Corporate History*, 2:28. The organizing directors of the Grand Haven were Costello C. Converse and James W. Converse of Boston; Jeptha H. Wade and Jeptha H. Wade Jr. of Cleveland; Charles E. Price and Chester Warner of Grand Rapids; and Fred H. May of Allegan.
14. Michigan Railroad Commission, *Aids, Gifts*, 50–51; Meints, *Michigan Railroads*, 116. The founding directors of the Muskegon Lake were James W. Converse of Grand Rapids; Frederick H. May, Charles D. Nelson, and James E. Vane of Allegan; and Loftus N. Keating, Alexander V. Mann, and Newcomb McGrath of Muskegon.
15. Michigan Railroad Commission, *Aids, Gifts*, 50–51; Meints, *Michigan Railroads*, 78; Johnson, *Allegan and Barry Counties*, 78; *Railway World*, 4 June 1881, 537.
16. *History of Berrien and Van Buren Counties, Michigan* (Philadelphia: D. W. Ensign & Co., 1880), 54–55; Graydon M. Meints, "Race to Chicago," *Railroad History 183* (2000), 10–11.
17. *Acts of the Legislature of the State of Michigan . . . Regular Session of 1869 (Act 45)* (Lansing: W. S. George & Co., 1869), 1:89–95; Michigan Railroad Commission, *Aids, Gifts*, 20–21; Willis F. Dunbar, *All Aboard! A History of Railroads in Michigan* (Grand Rapids, Mich.: Eerdmans, 1969), 131–35.
18. Michigan Railroad Commission, *Aids, Gifts*, 48–49; *History of Berrien*, 54–55.
19. *History of Berrien*, 54–55; Meints, *Michigan Railroads*, 48; Michigan Railroad Commission, *Aids, Gifts*, 48–49; Orville W. Coolidge, *A Twentieth Century History of Berrien County, Michigan* (Chicago: Lewis Publishing Co., 1906), 256–57; "Visit to Saint Joseph, Mich.," *Michigan Freemason* 1 (1870): 374–75. The organizing directors of the C&MLS were Curtis Boughton, Warren Chapman, Horace W. Guernsey, Benjamin C. Hoyt, and Alexander H. Morrison, all of St. Joseph; George Bridgman of Bridgman; David Ballentine of Waukegan, Ill.; and Robert A. Conolly of Chicago. Bridgman and the St. Joseph men had been involved with the earlier Chicago & Michigan Grand Trunk project in 1868. For more on Morrison, see appendix 1.
20. Michigan Railroad Commission, *Aids, Gifts*, 20–21. By a report by state treasurer Ebenezer Grosvenor in *Journal of the Senate of the State of Michigan, Extra Session, 1870*, 56, the total of $332,100 in municipal bonds was made up of the following:

Berrien Co.	New Buffalo Twp.	$13,000
	Three Oaks Twp.	$16,000
	Lake Twp.	$13,500
	Chickaming Twp.	$11,500
	Lincoln Twp.	$13,500
	St. Joseph Twp.	$46,000
	Hagar Twp.	$6,840
	Watervliet Twp.	$13,800
Van Buren Co.	Hartford Twp.	$36,000

	Bangor Twp.	$30,000
	Deerfield (now Covert)	$6,960
	Deerfield (now Covert)	$22,000
	South Haven Twp.	$40,000
Allegan Co.	Ganges Twp.	$15,000
	Saugatuck Twp.	$48,000

Of the $332,000 in bonds deposited with the state treasurer for disbursement, only $16,100 was paid out.

21. Meints, *Michigan Railroads*, 96; Michigan Railroad Commission, *Aids, Gifts*, 48–49. The organizing directors were Alexander H. Morris, Benjamin C. Hoyt, Horace W. Guernsey, Robert B. Duncan, Warren Chapman, and Asa E. Perkins, all of St. Joseph, and David Ballentine of Waukegan, Ill.
22. *Grand Rapids Eagle*, 25 May 1871.
23. Michigan Railroad Commission, *Aids, Gifts*, 48–49; Pere Marquette Railway Co., *The Pere Marquette in 1945* (reprint, Alderson, W.Va.: Chesapeake & Ohio Historical Society, 1991), 21.
24. Michigan Railroad Commission, *Aids, Gifts*, 48–49; John T. Percival "Railroads in Ottawa County," *Report of the Pioneer Society of the State of Michigan* (Lansing, Mich.: Wynkoop, Hallenbeck, Crawford, 1886), 9:277.
25. Meints, *Michigan Railroads*, 76; van Reken, *Railroads of Holland*, 24; Michigan Railroad Commission, *Aids, Gifts*, 48–49; Michigan, *General Acts and Joint and Concurrent Resolutions of the Legislature of the State of Michigan . . . Regular Session of 1871* (Lansing: W. S. George & Co., 1871), 451; Walter Romig, *Michigan Place Names* (Grosse Pointe, Mich.: Published by the author, n.d.), 214; *History of Berrien*, 342–43, 459, 413–14; Johnson, *Allegan and Barry Counties*, 197; The founding directors of the Fruitport & Lake Shore were Edward L. Craw, Samuel W. Graves, Thomas W. Nelson, N. W. Peake, A. A. Stearns, and William H. Stevenson of Fruitport; Robert Little of Fruitport Township; and Worden B. Mason and William M. Robinson of Spring Lake. A short biography of Craw is in appendix 1.
26. Meints, *Michigan Railroads*, 78; Michigan Railroad Commission, *Aids, Gifts*, 48–49; van Reken, *Railroads of Holland*, 32–33; Baxter, *History of Grand Rapids*, 536; *Grand Rapids Daily Eagle*, 2 January 1872; James J. Smith, ed., *Historic Michigan*, vol. 3., *Muskegon County* (Dayton, Ohio: National Historical Association, 1924), 44–45. The organizing directors of the GR&H were Thomas D. Gilbert, Freeman Godfrey, John McConnell, Leonard H. Randall, Martin L. Sweet, all of Grand Rapids; Luman Jenison and Horace O. Weston of Grandville; and Manly D. Howard and Henry D. Post of Holland.
27. Meints, *Michigan Railroads*, 115; Michigan Railroad Commission, *Aids, Gifts*, 48–49. The organizing directors of the MP&M were Samuel A. Brown, James G. Gray, Sewell Moulton, Andrew J. Underhill, and Orvill J. Vincent, all of Pentwater.
28. Meints, *Michigan Railroads*, 96; Michigan Railroad Commission, *Aids, Gifts*, 48–49; Jonathan Eyler, *Muskegon County, Harbor of Promise* (Northridge, Calif.: Windsor Publications, 1986), 68. The founding directors of the M&BR were Samuel A. Brown, Chauncey Davis, Lyman G. Mason,

and Alexander Rodgers of Muskegon; Stewart Ives and Jacob O. Rose of Big Rapids; Morton B. Hull of Chicago; Thomas C. Platt of Oswego, New York; and Stephen Brown. For more on Lyman G. Mason and Chauncey Davis, see appendix 1.

29. Meints, *Michigan Railroads*, 79; Michigan Railroad Commission, *Aids, Gifts*, 48–49; *History of Manistee, Mason and Oceana Counties, Michigan* (Chicago: H. R. Page & Co., 1882), 114–15. The organizing directors of the GR&LS wee Dennis W. Bryant, Lowell Hall, Thomas Hefferan, and Harvey J. Hollister of Grand Rapids; Edward L. Craw of Crawville (later renamed Fruitport); George Luther of Lamont; and Uriah Culbert, Samuel B. Peck, and Wesley F. Wood of Muskegon.
30. Michigan Railroad Commission, *Aids, Gifts*, 48–49; L. M. Hartwick and W. H. Tuller, *Oceana County Pioneers and Business Men of Today* (Pentwater, Mich.: Pentwater News Steam Print, 1890), 69–72; Michigan Auditor General, *Compilation of the Annual Reports of the Railroad Corporation in the State . . . 1871* (Lansing: n.p., 1872), 16; *History of Muskegon County*, 125. In a number of the Michigan Railroad Commission's *Annual Reports*, the company reports that the entire line between Grand Junction and Montague was completed 1 July 1871.
31. Meints, *Michigan Railroads*, 115; Michigan Railroad Commission, *Aids, Gifts*, 48–49; *Manistee, Mason and Oceana Counties*, 114–15; Hartwick and Tuller, *Oceana County Pioneers*, 72. The organizing directors of the Montague road were Samuel A. Browne, James G. Gray, Sewell Moulton, Andrew J. Underhill, and Orvill J. Vincent, all of Pentwater.
32. Hartwick and Tuller, *Oceana County Pioneers*, 134–36; Michigan Railroad Commission, *Aids, Gifts*, 48–49; Roy L. Dodge, *Michigan Ghost Towns* (Troy, Mich.: Glendon Publishing, 1971), 2:119–20.
33. For more on the elder Thayer, Kimball, and Lawler, see appendix 1. Lawler left in 1880 to continue a successful career with the Philadelphia & Reading Railroad.
34. Michigan Railroad Commission, *Fourth Annual Report . . .* (Lansing, Mich.: W. S. George & Co., 1876), 26; *Romance of Muskegon, Michigan*, cxxxii.
35. Meints, *Michigan Railroads*, 48; Michigan Railroad Commission, *Aids, Gifts*, 48–49; Michigan Auditor General, *Annual Report for 1870* (Lansing, Mich.: n.p., 1871), xviii; Michigan Auditor General, *Annual Report for 1871*, 14–20; Ivey, *Pere Marquette Railroad Company*, 36–38.
36. Ivey, *Pere Marquette Railroad Company*, 37–39.
37. Meints, *Michigan Railroads*, 81; Michigan Railroad Commission, *Aids, Gifts*, 50–51. The organizing directors of the Newaygo road were Moses V. Aldrich, David P. Clay, Edward P. Fuller, Leonard H. Randall, and William A. Richmond, all of Grand Rapids; Edward L. Gray and Augustus Paddock of Newaygo; Ransom Gardner of Kalamazoo; and Chester Warner of Chicago. For more on David P. Clay, see appendix 1.
38. Meints, *Michigan Railroads*, 110; *Grand Rapids Daily Eagle*, 11 March 1869. The Michigan Northern's proposed line extended from Sturgis Township, at the Indiana state line, through Grand Rapids to Traverse Bay, and then to the Straits of Mackinac. The organizing directors of the Michigan Northern were David P. Clay, Leonard H. Randall, and Chester Warner of Grand Rapids; Ransom Gardner, George Goss, Theodore P. Sheldon, and Allen G. Wells of Kalamazoo; Evert B. Dyckman of Schoolcraft; Joseph B. Millard of Three Rivers, Samuel Medbury of Detroit; and F. B. Gardner of Chicago. Of this group Gardner, Goss, and Warner were among the founders of the Canada Southern Railway's Michigan subsidiary in 1871, the Chicago & Canada Southern.

39. Harry L. Spooner, *Lumbering in Newaygo County* (Fremont, Mich.: Hi-Lites Graphics, c. 1987), 7–8, 19.
40. Michigan Railroad Commission, *Aids, Gifts*, 50–51; *Portrait and Biographical Album of Newaygo County, Michigan* (Chicago: Chapman Brothers, 1884), 527–28. For more on James W. Converse, see appendix 1.
41. Ivey, *Pere Marquette Railroad Company*, 40–41.
42. Michigan Railroad Commission, *Aids, Gifts*, 50–51; Meints, *Michigan Railroads*, 110; Ivey, *Pere Marquette Railroad Company*, 49; Spooner, *Lumbering in Newaygo*, 8–9.
43. From the annual reports of the two companies as reported in Michigan commissioner of railroads in his *Annual Reports* and the annual reports of the Michigan Central Railroad.
44. Michigan Railroad Commission, *Aids, Gifts*, 48–49; Meints, *Michigan Railroads*, 49; Michigan Railroad Commission, *Seventh Annual Report* (for 1878) (Lansing: W. S. George & Co., 1879), 46–47; Michigan Railroad Commission, *Eighth Annual Report* (for 1879) (Lansing, Mich.: W. S. George & Co., 1880), 86–87. The organizing directors of the Chicago & West Michigan were Charles Francis Adams Jr., Alpheus Hardy, George O. Shattuck, Frank Shaw, and Nathaniel Thayer, all of Boston. For more on Hardy and Thayer, see appendix 1.
45. *Manistee, Mason and Oceana Counties*, 100; Michigan Railroad Commission, *Aids, Gifts*, 48–49.
46. Meints, *Michigan Railroads*, 89, 49; Chicago & West Michigan Railroad Co. *Second Annual Report for . . . the Year 1880* (Boston: Alfred Mudge & Son, 1881), 11; Chicago & West Michigan Railway Co. *First Annual Report for . . . the Year 1881* (Boston: Alfred Mudge & Son, 1882), 6, 9, 13.
47. George E. Ellis, *Memoir of Nathaniel Thayer, A.M.* (Cambridge, Mass.: John Wilson and Son, 1885), 50. For more on Nathaniel Thayer Jr., see appendix 1. To confuse the issue the senior Thayer (1808–1883) bore the name of his father (1769–1840) and was correctly reported with "Junior" for some years after his father's death. By the 1860s he no longer added the "Junior." His son, also named Nathaniel (1851–1911), used "Junior" until a few years after his father's death in 1883.
48. Michigan Railroad Commission, *Aids, Gifts*, 50–51.
49. Meints, *Michigan Railroads*, 82; Michigan Railroad Commission, *Aids, Gifts*, 50–51; Baxter, *History of Grand Rapids*, 536; Michigan Railroad Commission, *Eleventh Annual Report* (for 1882) (Lansing, Mich.: W. S. George & Co., 1883), 110, reports the construction of this bridge.
50. Michigan Railroad Commission, *Aids, Gifts*, 50–51; Chicago & West Michigan Railway Co., *Third Annual Report for . . . the Year 1883* (Boston: T. W. Ripley, 1884), 11–12.
51. Meints, *Michigan Railroads*, 152; Michigan Railroad Commission, *Aids, Gifts*, 50–51. The officers that formed the company were George C. Kimball, Walter B. Bowe, Charles L. Green, Hiram J. Hoyt, Frederick A. Nims, Hugh Park, and Francis Smith, all of Muskegon, and Charles Merriam of Boston.
52. William Richard Cutter, *Genealogical and Personal Memoirs Relating to the Families of the State of Massachusetts* (New York: Lewis Historical Publishing Co., 1910), 4:2615. For more on John B. Mulliken and John K. V. Agnew, see appendix 1.
53. Chicago & West Michigan, *Fifth Annual Report for the Year Ending December 31, 1885* (Boston: T. W. Ripley, 1886), 17; Chicago & West Michigan, *Sixth Annual Report for the Year Ending December 31, 1886* (Boston: T. W. Ripley, 1887), 10, 16, 18.

54. Chicago & West Michigan, *Sixth Annual Report*, 18; Chicago & West Michigan, *Seventh Annual Report for the Year Ending December 31, 1887* (Boston: T. W. Ripley, 1888), 18.
55. T. Addison Busbey, ed., *The Biographical Directory of the Railway Officials of America, 1901 Edition* (New York: Railway Age and Northwestern Railroader, 1901), 249; Chicago & West Michigan, *Ninth Annual Report for the Year Ending December 31, 1889* (Boston: T. W. Ripley, 1890). For more on Heald and Eugene Thayer, see appendix 1.
56. Chicago & West Michigan, *Ninth Annual Report*, 6, 14; Michigan Railroad Commission, *Nineteenth Annual Report of the Commissioner of Railroads, State of Michigan, for the Year 1890* (Lansing, Mich.: Robert Smith & Co., 1891), 357.
57. Chicago & West Michigan, *Tenth Annual Report for the Year Ending December 31, 1890* (Boston: T. W. Ripley, 1891), 6, 13, 17–18, 37.
58. Meints, *Michigan Railroads*, 49; Michigan Railroad Commission, *Aids, Gifts*, 50–51; Michigan Railroad Commission, *Nineteenth Annual Report*, iv.
59. Michigan Railroad Commission, *Twentieth Annual Report of the Commissioner of Railroads, State of Michigan, for the Year 1891* (Lansing, Mich.: Robert Smith & Co., 1892), iii; Michigan Railroad Commission, *Aids, Gifts*, 50–51; Chicago & West Michigan Railway, *Twelfth Annual Report for the Year Ending December 31, 1892* (Boston: T. W. Ripley, 1893), 18–19.
60. Chicago & West Michigan Railway, *Thirteenth Annual Report for the Year Ending December 31, 1893* (Boston: T. W. Ripley, 1894), 17; Perry F. Powers, *A History of Northern Michigan and Its People* (Chicago: Lewis Publishing Co., 1912), 1:283–84.
61. Donald L. Van Reken, *Ottawa Beach and Waukazoo: A History* (Holland, Mich.: Published by the author, 1988) is the source for much of the information about the hotel and the rail operations to the beach. Train service to the beach ended in 1914; the hotel burned in 1923, and the railroad sold the land in 1925 to the state of Michigan for a state park.
62. Chicago & West Michigan Railway, *Twelfth Annual Report*, 18–19; Meints, *Michigan Railroads*, 95; *Romance of Muskegon, Michigan*, cxix, cxxxix. The Lake Harbor's organizing officers were Charles M. Heald and Frederick A. Nims, both C&WM officers from Grand Rapids; and David D. Erwin, Louis Kanitz, William B. McLaughlin, John W. Moon, and Thomas Munroe, all lumbermen of Muskegon.
63. Chicago & West Michigan Railway, *Thirteenth Annual Report*, 17–18.
64. Chicago & West Michigan Railway, *Fourteenth Annual Report for the Year Ending December 31, 1894* (Boston: T. W. Ripley, 1895), 6.
65. Chicago & West Michigan Railway, *Fifteenth Annual Report for the Year Ending December 31, 1895* (Boston: T. W. Ripley, 1896), 6, 17–18; *Romance of Muskegon, Michigan*, cxix.
66. Chicago & West Michigan Railway, *Seventeenth Annual Report for the Year Ending December 31, 1897* (Boston: T. W. Ripley, 1898), 19; Chicago & West Michigan Railway, *Eighteenth Annual Report for the Year Ending December 31, 1898)* (Boston: T. W. Ripley, 1899), 7; Michigan Railroad Commission, *Twenty-Sixth Annual Report . . . for the Year 1898* (Lansing: Robert Smith Printing Co., 1899), 192.
67. Chicago & West Michigan Railway, *Seventeenth Annual Report for the Year Ending December 31, 1897* (Boston: T. W. Ripley, 1898), 19; Chicago & West Michigan Railway, *Eighteenth Annual Report*

for the Year Ending December 31, 1898 (Boston: T. W. Ripley, 1899), 7.

68. *American Lumbermen*, 3rd series (Chicago: American Lumberman, 1906), 385–87; *New York Times*, 30 March 1883.
69. *American Lumberman*, 385–87; Meints, *Michigan Railroads*, 81; Michigan Railroad Commission, *Aids, Gifts*, 50–51; Ivey, *Pere Marquette Railroad Company*, 44; Charles Moore, *History of Michigan* (Chicago: Lewis Publishing Co., 1915), 2:862–65; Chicago & West Michigan Railway, *Eighteenth Annual Report*, 8. The organizers of the Kalkaska road were Uriah S. Hayes, Thomas Hefferan, Charles B. Kelsey, and William Alden Smith of Grand Rapids, and Samuel McCall of Boston.
70. Ivey, *Pere Marquette Railroad Company*, 44–46.

Chapter 4. The 1899 Merger and the Formation of the Pere Marquette

1. U.S. Interstate Commerce Commission, *Reports*, vol. 44, No. 6833 (Washington, D.C.: G.P.O., 1917), 21.
2. U.S. Interstate Commerce Commission, *Reports*, vol. 130, *Valuation Docket No. 260, Pere Marquette Railroad Company et Al.* (Washington, D.C.: G.P.O., 1927), 540.
3. *Twenty-Eighth Annual Report of the Commissioner of Railroads of the State of Michigan for the Year 1900* (Lansing, Mich.: Wynkoop Hallenbeck Crawford, 1901), 216–217, 220–221.
4. Ibid.
5. U.S. Interstate Commerce Commission, Report No. 6833, 20, 21; Graydon M. Meints, *Indiana Railroad Lines* (Bloomington: Indiana University Press, 2011), 294.
6. Michigan, *Journal of the House of Representatives*, committee report of 24 April 1913, 1982–2006 (no publishing data given).
7. U.S. House of Representatives, *Hearing to Investigate the Pere Marquette Railroad* (Washington, D.C.: G.P.O., 1914).
8. Pere Marquette Railroad Company, *Plan and Agreement for Reorganization . . .* (no publishing data given).
9. U.S. Interstate Commerce Commission, Document 137, *Report on Pere Marquette Railroad Company and Cincinnati, Hamilton & Dayton Railway Company* (Washington, D.C.: G.P.O., 1917).
10. U.S. Interstate Commerce Commission, *Pere Marquette Railroad Company et Al.*
11. Graydon M. Meints, *Michigan Railroads and Railroad Companies* (East Lansing: Michigan State University Press, 1992), 80, 100; Michigan Railroad Commission; *Aids, Gifts, Grants, and Donations to Railroads, Including Outlines of Development and Successions in Titles to Railroads in Michigan* (Lansing, Mich.: Wynkoop, Hallenbeck, Crawford, 1919), 52–53; Paul Wesley Ivey, *The Pere Marquette Railroad Company* (Lansing: Michigan Historical Commission, 1919), 67. The founding directors of the Grand Rapids, Belding & Saginaw were Andrew Fyfe, Uriah S. Hayes, George Hefferan, Thomas Hefferan, and George Richardson Smith, all of Grand Rapids. For more on Thomas Hefferan, see appendix 1.
12. Michigan Railroad Commission, *Aids, Gifts*, 52–55.
13. Meints, *Michigan Railroads*, 137; Ivey, *Pere Marquette Railroad Company*, 88; Michigan Railroad

Commission, *Aids, Gifts*, 54–55. The founding directors of the Sanilac were J. H. Berry, George W. Heath, Alexander Mann, Charles McPherson, and W. G. Smith, apparently all from the Sandusky area.

14. U.S. Interstate Commerce Commission, *Pere Marquette Railroad Company et Al.*, 2; Ivey, *Pere Marquette Railroad Company*, 275–79; Michigan, *Journal of the House*, 1986–87.
15. Michigan, *Journal of the House*, 1987.
16. U.S. Interstate Commerce Commission, *Pere Marquette Railroad Company et Al.*, 2; Ivey, *Pere Marquette Railroad Company*, 80–81, 275–79; Meints, *Michigan Railroads*, 126.
17. Meints, *Michigan Railroads*, 124; Michigan Railroad Commission, *Aids, Gifts*, 52–53. The founding directors of the Paw Paw were Loyal Crane, Elisha J. House, Henry Ismon, Franklin M. Manning, John K. Pugsley, and Fitz H. Stevens, all of Paw Paw; and Charles M. Morrell of Lawton.
18. "Narrow-gauge fever" is discussed in full in George W. Hilton, *American Narrow Gauge Railroads* (Stanford, Calif.: Stanford University Press, 1990).
19. Meints, *Michigan Railroads*, 144; Michigan Railroad Commission, *Aids, Gifts*, 52–53; *History of Berrien and Van Buren Counties, Michigan* (Philadelphia: D. W. Ensign & Co., 1880), 56; T. Addison Busbey, *The Biographical Directory of the Railway Officials of America* (Chicago: Railway Age and Northwestern Railroader, 1893), 191. The first directors of the Van Buren Division were Franklin B. Adams of Lawton; John W. Free and George W. Longwell of Paw Paw; Horace Sebring of Bangor; and George A. Cross, James B. Johnson, Sylvanus Rowe, Lavoiry Stebbins, and Rufus Tillow, all of Lawrence. It appears that Adams, a banker, was named president of the road. For more on Adams, see appendix 1.
20. Meints, *Michigan Railroads*, 144; Michigan Railroad Commission, *Aids, Gifts*, 52–55. The founding directors of the Lake Michigan Division of the Toledo & South Haven were David B. Allen, Aaron S. Dyckman, George Hannahs, Charles J. Monroe, and Daniel G. Wright, all of South Haven; and Alfred S. Packard and William O. Packard of Covert.
21. Meints, *Michigan Railroads*, 140; Michigan Railroad Commission, *Aids, Gifts*, 52–53; Michigan Railroad Commission, *Twenty-Second Annual Report of the Commissioner of Railroads* (for 1893) (Lansing, Mich.: Robert Smith, 1894), v; Hilton, *American Narrow Gauge Railroads*, 427. For more on Patterson and Steele, see appendix 1.
22. Meints, *Michigan Railroads*, 50; Michigan Railroad Commission, *Aids, Gifts*, 96–97; *Kalamazoo Telegraph*, 6 February 1904, 8.
23. Meints, *Michigan Railroads*, 137; Michigan Railroad Commission, *Aids, Gifts*, 52–53; Michigan, *Fifteenth Annual Report of the Commissioner of Railroads* (for 1886) (Lansing, Mich.: Thorp & Godfrey, 1887), iii; Robert C. Myers, *Locomotives along the Lakeshore: Railroads of Berrien County, Michigan* (Berrien Springs, Mich.: Berrien County Historical Association, 2010), 127–30. The founding directors of the road were Leander Perry Fox, William Pears, George H. Richards, and William R. Rough, all of Buchanan; and J. H. Matthews, George H. Murdoch, and Roscoe D. Rix of Berrien Springs.
24. Meints, *Michigan Railroads*, 113; Michigan Railroad Commission, *Aids, Gifts*, 52–55; *Railway World* 41 (1897): 638–39; Hilton, *American Narrow Gauge Railroads*, 427. The founding directors of the Milwaukee, Benton Harbor & Columbus were F. B. Berton, Alexander A. Patterson Jr., David H.

Patterson, John A. Patterson, and Frederick M. Steele of Chicago; J. M. Caulfield of South Bend, Indiana; and Fred McComber of Berrien Springs.

25. Meints, *Michigan Railroads*, 42; Michigan Railroad Commission, *Aids, Gifts*, 54–55; Maximillian A. Zink et al., *Electric Railways of Michigan* (Chicago: Central Electric Railfans' Association, 1959), iv–13. The founding directors were William A. Baker, Frank W. Bryant, George W. Grant, Simon Hosbine, and Israel Kremer, all of Coloma.
26. Michigan, *Journal of the House*, 1987–89; Ivey, *Pere Marquette Railroad Company*, 84–85.
27. Meints, *Michigan Railroads*, 88; Michigan Railroad Commission, *Aids, Gifts*, 54–55; Ivey, *Pere Marquette Railroad Company*, 87–88. The founding officers of the Huron & Western were Thomas L. Handy, his brothers Charles W. Handy and George W. Handy, his wife Harriet G. Handy, and his son Frank S. Handy, all of Bay City.
28. Michigan Railroad Commission, *Aids, Gifts*, 52–53.
29. Meints, *Michigan Railroads*, 85; Michigan Railroad Commission, *Aids, Gifts*, 54–55; Ivey, *Pere Marquette Railroad Company*, 88.

■ Appendix 1. Biographies

1. See Harold F. Lane, compiler, *The Biographical Directory of the Railway Officials of America, 1913 Edition* (New York: Simmons-Boardman, 1913), 4; Michigan death certificate.
2. See "James Birney," *Michigan Pioneer and Historical Collections* (Lansing: Michigan Pioneer and Historical Society, 1894), 22:227–30.
3. See Albert Baxter, *History of the City of Grand Rapids* (New York: Munsell & Company, 1891), 471, 499.
4. See Chaim M. Rosenberg, *The Great Workshop: Boston's Victorian Age* (Charleston, S.C.: Arcadia Publishing, 2004), 142–43; Baxter, *History of Grand Rapids*, 421–22; William Gilbert Hill, *Family Record of Deacons James W. Converse and Elisha S. Converse, 1887* (Boston: Alfred Mudge & Son, 1887).
5. See Michigan Historic Commission, *Michigan Biographies* (Lansing: Michigan Historical Commission, 1924), 1:207–8; Martin D. Lewis, *Lumberman from Flint* (Detroit: Wayne State University Press, 1958).
6. See Graydon M. Meints, "The Men Who Made the Pere Marquette: Stanford T. Crapo," *PM Tracks* 20, no. 3 (May–June 2015): 4–5.
7. See Henry H. Crapo, *The Story of William Wallace Crapo* (Boston: Thomas Todd Co., 1933).
8. See *Portrait and Biographical Album of Gratiot County, Michigan* (Chicago: Chapman Brothers, 1884), 776–77.
9. See Michigan Historic Commission, *Michigan Biographies*, 1:226–27; Henry H. Holt, *History of the Settlement of Muskegon* (Muskegon, Mich.: Muskegon Chronicle Binding & Printing, c. 1887), 17–21.
10. See *Portrait and Biographical Record of Genesee, Lapeer and Tuscola Counties, Michigan* (Chicago: Chapman Brothers, 1892), 733–34; Franklin Ellis, *History of Genesee County, Michigan*

(Philadelphia: Everts & Abbott, 1879), 178.

11. See James Cooke Mills, *History of Saginaw County, Michigan, Historical, Commercial, Biographical* (Saginaw, Mich.: Seeman & Peters, 1918), 2:262; and George Woodward Hotchkiss, *History of the Lumber and Forest Industry of the Northwest* (Chicago: George W. Hotchkiss & Co., 1898), 122.
12. See *Biographical Memoirs of Gratiot County, Michigan* (Chicago: J. H. Beers & Co., 1906), 30–36.
13. See Henry J. Cookinham, *History of Oneida County, New York* (Chicago: S. J. Clarke Publishing Co., 1912), 1:550.
14. See *Michigan Pioneer and Historical Collections*, 40 vols. (Lansing, Mich.: various publ., 1876–1917), 7:305–7; *American Biographical History of Eminent and Self-Made Men* (Cincinnati: Western Biographical Publishing Co., 1878), 2.5:37; *History of Allegan and Barry Counties, Michigan* (Philadelphia: D. W. Ensign & Co., 1880), facing 156.
15. See Michigan Historic Commission, *Michigan Biographies*, 1:319; *American Biographical History*, 2.4:29–30.
16. See State Street Trust Co., *Some Merchants and Sea Captains of Old Boston* (Boston: State Street Trust Co., 1918), 24–26.
17. See *Michigan Pioneer and Historical Collections*, 5:138, 28:386–91; *American Biographical History*, 2.7:11–13; Michigan Historical Commission, *Michigan Biographies*, 1:374.
18. See T. Addison Busbey, ed., *The Biographical Directory of the Railway Officials of America, 1901 Edition* (New York: Railway Age and Northwestern Railroader, 1901), 249.
19. See Charles Moore, *History of Michigan* (Chicago: Lewis Publishing Co., 1915), 3:1647–48.
20. See *Cyclopedia of Michigan: Historical and Biographical* (New York: Western Publishing & Engraving, 1890), 66; Michigan Historical Commission, *Michigan Biographies*, 1:418.
21. See Mills, *History of Saginaw County*, 2:244–47.
22. See T. Addison Busbey, ed., *Biographical Directory of the Railway Officials of America* (Chicago: Railway Age and Northwestern Railroader, 1893), 191.
23. See *American Biographical History*, 2.8:24–25; Michigan Historical Commission, *Michigan Biographies*, 1:443; Findagrave website.
24. See *American Biographical History*, 1.1:86.
25. See Busbey, *Biographical Directory* (1901), 295; Mills, *History of Saginaw County*, 2:168–71.
26. See William Richard Cutter, *Genealogical and Personal Memoirs Relating to the Families of the State of Massachusetts* (New York: Lewis Historical Publishing Co., 1910), 4:2614–15.
27. See T. Addison Busbey, *The Biographical Directory of the Railway Officials of America* (Chicago: Railway Age and Northwestern Railroader, 1896), 277.
28. See *Portrait and Biographical Record of Kalamazoo, Allegan and Van Buren Counties, Michigan* (Chicago: Chapman Brothers, 1892), 273–75.
29. See *Cyclopedia of Michigan*, 100–102; also Wikitree and Findagrave entries.
30. See Busbey, *Biographical Directory* (1901), 350; *Transactions of the American Society of Civil Engineers*, vol. 71 (1911), 430.
31. See *American Biographical History*, 2.4:48.
32. See Silas Farmer, *History of Detroit and Wayne County and Early Michigan*, 3rd ed. (New York: Munsell & Co., 1890), 2:1221–22.

33. See Michigan Historical Commission, *Michigan Biographies*, 2:146–47; *American Biographical History*, 1: Michigan 2nd Dist. of U.S. House of Representatives: 54.
34. See obituary in *Dallas News*, 27 March 1913; *Engineering News* 69: 758.
35. See Mills, *History of Saginaw County*, 2:193–97; *Albany Medical Annals*, vol. 30 (1909) (Albany, N.Y.: Brandow Printing Co., 1909), 483–86.
36. See *Commercial and Financial New England* (Boston: Boston Herald, 1906), 46.
37. See *American Biographical History*, 2.5:103–4; *Portrait and Biographic Album of Ionia and Montcalm Counties, Mich.* (Chicago: Chapman Bros., 1891), 245–46; Michigan Historical Commission, *Michigan Biographies*, 2:230.
38. See *American Biographical History*, 2.7:22–23.
39. See "An Appreciation, William Bernard Sears," *Michigan Engineer* 33 (1915): 53–56; Busbey, *Biographical Directory* (1901); H. C. A. Maisonville, "William Barnard Sears, M. E.," *Pere Marquette Magazine* (July 1922), 22–23.
40. See *Biographical Directory of the United States Congress*. About his nonrailroad career see W. A. Swanberg, *Sickles the Incredible* (New York: Scribner, 1956).
41. See *American Biographical History*, 1.3:85–86; Charles V. DeLand, *History of Jackson County* (Indianapolis: B. F. Bowen & Co., 1903), 268.
42. See J. Seymour Currey, *Chicago: Its History and Its Builders*, vol. 5 (Chicago: S. J. Clarke Publishing Co., 1912), 66–70.
43. See *Proceedings of the Most Worshipful Grand Lodge of Ancient Free and Accepted Masons of the Commonwealth of Massachusetts* (Boston: Rockwell and Churchill Press, 1905), 28–31.
44. See George E. Ellis, *Memoir of Nathaniel Thayer, A.M.* (Cambridge, Mass.: John Wilson and Son, 1885).
45. See *History of St. Clair County, Michigan* (Chicago: A. T. Andreas & Co., 1883), 599–600; *The Biographical Directory of the Railway Officials of America for 1887* (Chicago: Railway Age Publishing Co., 1887), 342.
46. See *History of Manistee, Mason and Oceana Counties, Michigan* (Chicago: H. R. Page & Co., 1882), 50–52, 62; George N. Fuller, *Michigan: A Centennial History of the State and Its People* (Chicago: Lewis Publishing Co., 1939), 1:539.
47. See *Portrait and Biographical Record of Saginaw and Bay Counties, Michigan* (Chicago: Biographical Publishing Co., 1892), 191–94.
48. See *American Biographical History*, 2.6:62; Albert Nelson Marquis, *The Book of Detroiters* (Chicago: A. N. Marquis & Co., 1908), 494–95; Meints, *Biographical Directory*, 2:306–7.

Bibliography

American Biographical History of Eminent and Self-Made Men. 2 vols. Cincinnati: Western Biographical Publishing Co., 1878.

American Lumbermen. 3rd Series. Chicago: American Lumberman, 1906.

"An Appreciation, William Bernard Sears." *Michigan Engineer* 33 (1915): 53–56.

Bald, F. Clever. *Michigan in Four Centuries.* New York: Harper & Row, 1954.

Bates, W. R. *History of the Saginaws.* East Saginaw, Mich.: E. W. Lyon, 1874.

Baxter, Albert. *History of the City of Grand Rapids.* New York: Munsell & Company, 1891.

The Biographical Directory of the Railway Officials of America. Chicago: Railway Age, 1887.

Biographical Memoirs of Gratiot County, Michigan. Chicago: J. B. Beers & Co., 1906.

Bliss, Albert N. "Federal Land Grants for Internal Improvements in the State of Michigan." In *Pioneer Collections* (of Pioneer Society of the State of Michigan). Lansing, Mich.: Thorp & Godfrey, 1886.

Branch, Elam E., ed. *History of Ionia County, Michigan.* 2 vols. Indianapolis: B. F. Bowen & Co., 1916.

Brock, Thomas D. "Paw Paw Versus the Railroads." *Michigan History* 39, no. 2 (June 1955): 129–82.

Busbey, T. Addison. *The Biographical Directory of the Railway Officials of America.* Chicago: Railway Age and Northwestern Railroader, 1893.

———. *The Biographical Directory of the Railway Officials of America.* Chicago: Railway Age and Northwestern Railroader, 1896.

———. *The Biographical Directory of the Railway Officials of America.* Chicago: Railway Age and Northwestern Railroader, 1901.

Catlin, George B. *The Story of Detroit.* Detroit: Detroit News, 1923.

Catton, Bruce. *Michigan: A History.* New York: W. W. Norton & Co., 1976.

Chesapeake & Ohio Historical Society. *The Pere Marquette in 1945.* Alderson, W.Va.: Chesapeake & Ohio

Historical Society, 1990.

Church, Samuel H., compiler. *Corporate History of the Pennsylvania Lines West of Pittsburgh. . . .* Vol. 2. Baltimore: Friedenwald Co., 1899.

Coolidge, Orville W. *A Twentieth Century History of Berrien County, Michigan.* Chicago: Lewis Publishing Co., 1906.

Crittenden, A. Riley. *A History of the Township and Village of Howell, Michigan.* Howell, Mich.: Livingston Tidings Print, 1911.

Cutter, William Richard. *Genealogical and Personal Memoirs Relating to the Families of the State of Massachusetts.* New York: Lewis Historical Publishing Co., 1910.

Cyclopedia of Michigan: Historical and Biographical. New York: Western Publishing and Engraving, 1890.

Dasef, John W. *History of Montcalm County, Michigan.* 2 vols. Indianapolis: B. F. Bowen & Co., 1916.

Dash, M. *A History of the City of Lansing. . . .* Lansing, Mich.: W. S. George & Co., 1870.

DeLand, Charles V. *History of Jackson County.* Indianapolis: B. F. Bowen & Co., 1903.

Dixon, Thomas W., Jr., and Art Million. *Pere Marquette Power.* Alderson, W.Va.: C&O Historical Society, 1984.

Dunbar, Willis F. *All Aboard! A History of Railroads in Michigan.* Grand Rapids, Mich.: Eerdmans, 1969.

———. *Michigan: A History of the Wolverine State.* Grand Rapids, Mich.: Eerdmans, 1965.

Durant, Samuel W. *History of Ingham and Eaton Counties, Michigan.* Philadelphia: D. W. Ensign & Co., 1880.

———. *History of Oakland County, Michigan.* Philadelphia: L. H. Everts & Co., 1877.

East Saginaw, Historical, Biographical and Commercial. East Saginaw, Mich.: W. J. Raymond & S. W. Roberts, publishers, 1880.

Elliott, Frank N. *When the Railroad Was King: The Nineteenth-Century Railroad Era in Michigan.* Lansing: Michigan Historical Commission, 1966.

Ellis, Franklin. *History of Genesee County, Michigan.* Philadelphia: Everts & Abbott, 1879.

———. *History of Livingston County, Michigan.* Philadelphia: Everts & Abbott, 1880.

———. *History of Shiawassee and Clinton Counties, Michigan.* Philadelphia: D. W. Ensign & Co., 1880.

Ellis, George E. *Memoir of Nathaniel Thayer, A.M.* Cambridge, Mass.: John Wilson & Son, 1885.

Eyler, Jonathan. *Muskegon County, Harbor of Promise.* Northridge, Calif.: Windsor Publications, 1986.

Farmer, Silas. *History of Detroit and Wayne County and Early Michigan.* 3rd ed. New York: Munsell & Co., 1890.

Fecht, Michelle M. *Northville.* Charleston, S.C.: Arcadia Publishing, 2010.

Fox, Truman B. *History of the Saginaw Valley, Its Resources, Progress and Business Interests.* East Saginaw, Mich.: Daily Courier Steam Job Print, 1868.

Frederickson, Arthur C., and Lucy F. Frederickson. *Pictorial History of the C&O Train and Auto Ferries and Pere Marquette Line Steamers.* Rev. ed. Frankfort, Mich.: Lakeside Printing, 1965.

Fuller, George N. *Historic Michigan.* 3 vols. Chicago: Lewis Publishing Co., 1939.

———. *Michigan: A Centennial History of the State and Its People.* 5 vols. Chicago: Lewis Publishing Co., 1939.

Gaffney, T. J. *Rails around the Thumb.* Charleston, S.C.: Arcadia Publishing, 2012.

Gansser, Augustus H. *History of Bay County, Michigan.* Chicago: Richmond & Arnold, 1905.

Goss, Dwight. *History of Grand Rapids and Its Industries.* Chicago: C. F. Cooper & Co., 1906.

Green, James J. *Railroads Come and Go in Allegan County.* Allegan, Mich.: Allegan County Historical Society, 1976.

Hardy, Arthur S. *Life and Letters of Joseph Hardy Neesima.* Boston: Houghton Mifflin & Co., 1892.

Hannum, James S. *Cut and Run! Railroad Logging in Clare County, Michigan.* Olympia, Wash.: Hannum House Publications, 2014.

———. *In the Pines: An Atlas of Michigan Logging Railroads.* Olympia, Wash.: Hannum House Publications, 2017.

Hartwick, L[ouis] M., and W[illiam] H. Tuller. *Oceana County Pioneers and Business Men of Today.* Pentwater, Mich.: Pentwater News Steam Print, 1890.

Hilton, George W. *American Narrow Gauge Railroads.* Stanford, Calif.: Stanford University Press, 1990.

———. *The Great Lakes Car Ferries.* Berkeley, Calif.: Howell-North, 1962.

———. *Lake Michigan Passenger Steamers.* Stanford, Calif.: Stanford University Press, 2002.

———. "Pere Marquette." *Trains,* August 1945, 9–19.

Hilton, George W., and Joseph F. Due. *The Electric Interurban Railway in America.* Stanford, Calif.: Stanford University Press, 1960.

History of Allegan and Barry Counties, Michigan. Philadelphia: D. W. Ensign & Co., 1880.

History of Bay County, Michigan. Chicago: H. R. Page & Co., 1883.

History of Berrien and Van Buren Counties, Michigan. Philadelphia: D. W. Ensign & Co., 1880.

History of Lapeer County, Michigan. Chicago: H. R. Page & Co., 1884.

History of Manistee, Mason and Oceana Counties, Michigan. Chicago: H. R. Page & Co., 1882.

History of Muskegon County, Michigan. Chicago: H. R. Page & Co., 1882.

History of St. Clair County, Michigan. Chicago: A. T. Andreas & Co., 1883.

History of Tuscola and Bay Counties, Michigan. Chicago: H. R. Page & Co., 1883.

Holt, Henry H. *History of the Settlement of Muskegon.* Muskegon, Mich.: Muskegon Chronicle Binding & Printing, c. 1887.

Huron County Historical Society. *Huron County, Michigan.* Charleston, S.C.: Arcadia Publishing, 2001.

Hyde, Charles K. *The Lower Peninsula of Michigan: An Inventory of Historic Engineering and Industrial Sites.* Washington, D.C.: U.S. Department of the Interior, National Park Service, 1976.

Ivey, Paul Wesley. *The Pere Marquette Railroad Company.* Lansing: Michigan Historical Commission, 1919.

Johnson, Crisfield. *History of Allegan and Barry Counties, Michigan.* Philadelphia: D. W. Ensign & Co., 1880.

Kilar, Jeremy W. *Michigan's Lumbertowns.* Detroit: Wayne State University Press, 1990.

———. *Saginaw's Changeable Past.* St. Louis, Mo.: G. Bradley Publishing, 1994.

Kirkpatrick, Frank A. "The Saginaw, Tuscola and Huron: An Early Railroad of the Michigan Thumb." *Michigan History* 52, no. 3 (September 1968): 196–217.

Kleiman, Jeff. *The Rise and Fall of the CSCRR: A Short History of a Short-Lived Railroad.* Grand Rapids, Mich.: Friends of Public Museum, 1992.

Latham, Earl. *The Politics of Railroad Coordination, 1933–1936.* Cambridge, Mass.: Harvard University Press, 1959.

Leeson, Michael A. *History of Saginaw County, Michigan.* Chicago: Charles C. Chapman & Co., 1881.

Leonard, John W. *Industries of the Saginaws.* East Saginaw, Mich.: J. M. Elstner & Co., c. 1887.

Lewis, Martin D. *Lumberman from Flint.* Detroit: Wayne State University Press, 1958.

Marquis, Albert Nelson. *The Book of Detroiters.* Chicago: A. N. Marquis & Co., 1908.

Marsh, Nicholas A. *Michigan Central Railroad: History of the Main Line, 1846–1901.* N.p., 2007.

Massie, Larry B. *Haven, Harbor and Heritage: The Holland, Michigan, Story.* Allegan, Mich.: Priscilla Press, 1996.

Maybee, Rolland H. *Michigan's White Pine Era.* Lansing: Michigan Department of State, 1976.

McMacken, David. *Built on Pine: The Story of Ammi Willard Wright.* Alma, Mich.: Alma Public Library, 2004.

———. *Images of America, Alma.* Charleston, S.C.: Arcadia Publishing Co., 2009.

Meints, Graydon M. *Biographical Directory of Michigan Railway Officials, 1830–1917.* 2 vols. East Lansing: Michigan State University Libraries, 2013.

———. *Indiana Railroad Lines.* Bloomington, Ind.: Indiana University Press, 2011.

———. *Michigan Railroad Lines.* 2 vols. East Lansing: Michigan State University Press, 2005.

———. *Michigan Railroads and Railroad Companies.* East Lansing: Michigan State University Press, 1992.

———. *Railroads for Michigan.* East Lansing: Michigan State University Press, 2013.

———. "A Short History of Railroads in Van Buren County." *Historical Van Buren County,* May 1987.

Michigan. *Joint Documents of the State of Michigan for the Year 1869.* Lansing, Mich.: W. S. George & Co., 1869.

Michigan. *Journal of the House of Representatives,* 24 April 1913. 1982–2006.

Michigan Auditor General. *Annual Reports.* Lansing, Mich.: various publishers, 1869–1871.

Michigan Historical Commission. *Michigan Biographies.* 2 vols. Lansing: Michigan Historical Commission, 1924.

Michigan Legislature. *General Acts and Joint and Concurrent Resolutions of the Legislature of the State of Michigan Passed at the Regular Session of 1871.* Lansing, Mich.: W. S. George & Co., 1871.

Michigan Legislature. *Acts of the Legislature of the State of Michigan Passed at the Extra Session of 1864.* Lansing, Mich.: John A. Kerr & Co., 1864.

Michigan Legislature. *Acts of the Legislature of the State of Michigan Passed at the Regular Session of 1865.* Lansing, Mich.: John A. Kerr & Co., 1865.

Michigan Legislature. *Acts of the Legislature of the State of Michigan Passed at the Regular Session of 1867.* Lansing, Mich.: John A. Kerr & Co., 1867.

Michigan Pioneer and Historical Collections. 40 vols. Lansing, Mich.: various publ., 1876–1917.

Michigan Railroad Commission. *Aids, Gifts, Grants, and Donations to Railroads, Including Outlines of Development and Successions in Titles to Railroads in Michigan.* Lansing, Mich.: Wynkoop, Hallenbeck, Crawford, 1919.

———. *Annual Reports.* Lansing, Mich.: various publishers, 1872–1905.

Michigan Senate. *Journal of the Senate of the State of Michigan, Extra Session 1870.* Lansing, Mich.: W. S. George & Co., 1870.

Million, Arthur B. *Pere Marquette Passenger Car Pictorial.* Grand Haven, Mich.: Pere Marquette

Historical Society, 2002.

Million, Arthur B., and Thomas W. Dixon Jr. *Pere Marquette Power.* Alderson, W.Va.: Chesapeake and Ohio Historical Society, 1984.

Million, Arthur B., and John Paton. *Revenue Freight Cars of the Pere Marquette.* Edmonds, Wash.: Hundman Publishing, 2001.

Mills, James Cooke. *History of Saginaw County, Michigan, Historical, Commercial, Biographical.* 2 vols. Saginaw, Mich.: Seeman & Peters, 1918.

Moore, Charles. *History of Michigan.* 3 vols. Chicago: Lewis Publishing Co., 1915.

Morrison, Samuel Eliot. *The Oxford History of the American People.* New York: Oxford University Press, 1965.

Myers, Robert C. *Locomotives along the Lakeshore: Railroads of Berrien County, Michigan.* Berrien Springs, Mich.: Berrien County Historical Association, 2010.

Myers, Robert C. "The St. Joseph Valley Railroad." *Michigan History* 72, no. 1 (January 1988): 24–30.

Neithercut, Mark Edward. "The White Pine Industry and the Transformation of Nineteenth-Century Michigan." Ph.D. diss., University of British Columbia, 1984.

Olds, Fred C. "Michigan's Iron Cobweb." *Railroad History* 129 (Autumn 1973): 18–34.

Palmer, Friend. *Early Days in Detroit.* Detroit: Hunt & June, 1906.

Percival, John T. "Railroads in Ottawa County." *Report of the Pioneer Society of the State of Michigan.* Vol. 9. Lansing, Mich.: Wynkoop, Hallenbeck, Crawford, 1886.

Pere Marquette Railroad Company. *Purchase of Flint & Pere Marquette R. R., Chicago & West Michigan Ry., Detroit, Grand Rapids & Western R. R. et Al.* Saginaw, Mich.: Seemann & Peters, 1900.

Pere Marquette Railway Company. *The Pere Marquette in 1945.* Reprint, Alderson, W.Va.: Chesapeake & Ohio Historical Society, 1991.

Portrait and Biographical Album of Gratiot County, Michigan. Chicago: Chapman Brothers, 1884.

Portrait and Biographical Album of Ionia and Montcalm Counties, Michigan. Chicago: Chapman Bros., 1891.

Portrait and Biographical Album of Newaygo County, Michigan. Chicago: Chapman Brothers, 1884.

Portrait and Biographical Record of Berrien and Cass Counties, Michigan. Chicago: Biographical Publishing Co., 1893.

Portrait and Biographical Record of Genesee, Lapeer and Tuscola Counties, Michigan. Chicago: Chapman Brothers, 1892.

Portrait and Biographical Record of Kalamazoo, Allegan and Van Buren Counties, Michigan. Chicago: Chapman Brothers, 1892.

Portrait and Biographical Record of Saginaw and Bay Counties, Michigan. Chicago: Biographical Publishing Co., 1892.

Powers, Perry F. *A History of Northern Michigan and Its People.* 3 vols. Chicago: Lewis Publishing Co., 1912.

Romance of Muskegon, Michigan. Muskegon: Muskegon Chronicle, 1937.

Romig, Walter. *Michigan Place Names.* Grosse Pointe MI: Published by the author, n.d.; reprint, Detroit: Wayne State University Press, 1986.

Rosentreter, Roger L. *Michigan: A History of Explorers, Entrepreneurs, and Everyday People.* Detroit:

Wayne State University Press, 2014.

Saginaw, Michigan, U.S.A., 1857–1907: Semi-centennial Souvenir. Saginaw, Mich.: Board of Trade, 1907.

Sanborn, John Bell. "Congressional Grants of Land in Aid of Railways." Ph.D. diss., University of Wisconsin, 1899.

Schenck, John S. *History of Ionia and Montcalm Counties, Michigan*. Philadelphia: D. W. Ensign & Co., 1881.

Smith, James L., ed. *Historic Michigan*. Vol. 3, *Muskegon County*. Dayton, Ohio: National Historical Association, Inc., 1924.

Spooner, Harry. *Lumbering in Newaygo County*. Fremont, Mich.: Hi-Lites Graphics, c. 1987.

———. *Newaygo County History*. Fremont, Mich.: Fremont Times Indicator, 1954–1955.

State Street Trust Co. *Some Merchants and Sea Captains of Old Boston*. Boston: State Street Trust Co., 1918.

Stimson, Glen K. "Rail Growth of Michigan's Capital City." *Michigan History* 5 (1921): 461–92.

Swierenga, Robert P. *Holland Michigan: From Dutch Colony to Dynamic City*. Grand Rapids, Mich.: William B. Eerdmans Publishing Co., 2014.

Thomas, Henry F. *A Twentieth Century History of Allegan County, Michigan*. Chicago: Lewis Publishing Co., 1907.

Thompson, Robert I. *Newaygo White Pine Heritage*. Newaygo, Mich.: Newaygo City Bicentennial Committee, 1976.

Tocqueville, Alexis de. *Democracy in America*. 2 vols. Cambridge: Sever & Francis, 1863.

Tucker, Willard D. *Gratiot County, Michigan*. Saginaw, Mich.: Seeman & Peters, 1913.

Turner, Frank N. *An Account of Ingham County from Its Organization*. Vol. 3 of *Historic Michigan*. Dayton, Ohio: National Historical Association, 1924.

Underwood, Thomas L., Jr. "A Survey of the C&O and Predecessor Lines in Michigan." *C&O Historical Newsletter*, November 1975.

U.S. House of Representatives. *Hearing to Investigate the Pere Marquette Railroad*. Washington, D.C.: G.P.O., 1914.

U.S. Interstate Commerce Commission. *Report on Pere Marquette Railroad Company and Cincinnati, Hamilton & Dayton Railway Company*. Document 137. Washington, D.C.: G.P.O., 1917.

———. *Reports*, vol. 130. *Valuation Docket No. 260, Pere Marquette Railroad Company et Al.* Washington, D.C.: G.P.O., 1927.

Utley, Henry M., and Byron M. Cutcheon. *Michigan as a Province, Territory and State, the Twenty-Sixth Member of the Federal Union*. 4 vols. New York: Publishing Society of Michigan, 1906.

Van Reken, Donald L. *Ottawa Beach and Waukazoo: A History*. Holland, Mich.: Published by the author, 1988.

———. *The Railroads of Holland, Michigan*. Vol. 1: *The Nineteenth Century*. Holland, Mich.: Published by the author, 1997.

———. *The Railroads of Holland, Michigan*. Vol. 2: *The Twentieth Century*. Holland, Mich.: Published by the author, 1998.

Waggoner, Clark. *History of the City of Toledo and Lucas County, Ohio*. New York: Munsell & Co., 1888.

Wakefield, Lawrence, and Lucille Wakefield. *Sail and Rail: A Narrative History of Transportation in*

Western Michigan. Holt, Mich.: Thunder Bay Press, 1996.

Wing, Talcott Enoch, ed. *History of Monroe County, Michigan*. New York: Munsell & Company, 1890.

Zimmerman, Karl. *Lake Michigan's Railroad Car Ferries*. Andover, N.J.: Andover Junction Publications, 1993.

Zink, Maximillian A., et al. *Electric Railways of Michigan*. Chicago: Central Electric Railfans' Association, 1959.

Index

U

V

W

Y